Doctrine & Covenants

of the Church of Jesus Christ
Journal & Study Edition

CFI
An imprint of Cedar Fort, Inc.
Springville, Utah

This journal and study edition of the Doctrine & Covenants was created to help and support us as we come closer to Christ in our studies of the Come Follow Me program. It has extra space around the edges of the pages as well as between verses and at the end of sections to enable you to record your inspiration and personal revelation.

This edition is designed to be used alongside your regular Scriptures, study guides, Come Follow Me manuals and other resources. There are no footnotes, enabling you to mark up the scriptures as you feel prompted to as you seek personal revelation and a further testimony of the truths of the Restoration of the Gospel of Jesus Christ.

ISBN 13: 978-1-4621-3699-5

Published by CFI, an imprint of Cedar Fort, Inc.

2373 W. 700 S., Springville, UT 84663

Distributed by Cedar Fort, Inc., www.cedarfort.com

Cover Art: © "This is my Beloved Son" by Darryl Quinn, Sunday Sketchbook.

Printed in the United States of America

10 9 8 7 6 5 4 3 2 1

Printed on acid-free paper

Journal & Study Edition

Of the Doctrine & Covenants of The Church of Jesus Christ of Latter-day Saints.

There is a great Church history behind us. There is an even greater Church history ahead of us for every member, every unit of the Church.

("The Future History of the Church", General Conference, April 1982, G. Homer Durham)

I encourage each of you to study the Articles of Faith and the doctrines they teach. They are "one of the most important statements of inspiration, history, and doctrine for the Church. . . . Each article is a positive statement [explaining] the differences between Mormonism and the [beliefs of other peoples of the world]" (*Church History in the Fulness of Times*, 257). If you will use them as a guide to direct your studies of the Savior's doctrine, you will find yourselves prepared to declare your witness of the restored, true church of the Lord. You will be able to declare with conviction: "We believe these things."

("The Articles of Faith", General Conference, April 1998, L. Tom Perry Of the Quorum of the Twelve Apostles)

The Book of Mormon and the Doctrine and Covenants are bound together as revelations from Israel's God to gather and prepare His people for the second coming of the Lord. Each divine witness contains a great proclamation to all the world—the title page of the Book of Mormon, and section 1, the Lord's preface to the Doctrine and Covenants. "This generation," said the Lord to Joseph Smith, "shall have my word through you" (D&C 5:10). And so it has through the Book of Mormon, the Doctrine and Covenants, and other modern revelations.

The Book of Mormon and the Doctrine and Covenants testify of each other. You cannot believe one and not the other. The Doctrine and Covenants is the binding link between the Book of Mormon and the continuing work of the Restoration through the Prophet Joseph Smith and his successors.

In the Doctrine and Covenants we learn of temple work, eternal families, the degrees of glory, Church organization, and many other great truths of the Restoration. "Search these commandments," said the Lord of the Doctrine and Covenants, "for they are true and faithful, and the prophecies and promises which are in them shall all be fulfilled. (D&C 1:37–38)

The Book of Mormon brings men to Christ. The Doctrine and Covenants brings men to Christ's kingdom, even The Church of Jesus Christ of Latter-day Saints, "the only true and living church upon the face of the whole earth" (D&C 1:30). I know that. The Book of Mormon is the "keystone" of our religion, and the Doctrine and Covenants is the capstone, with continuing latter-day revelation. The Lord has placed His stamp of approval on both the keystone and the capstone.

("The Book of Mormon and the Doctrine and Covenants", April 1987, Ezra Taft Benson, President of the Church)

Introduction

The Doctrine and Covenants is a collection of divine revelations and inspired declarations given for the establishment and regulation of the kingdom of God on the earth in the last days. Although most of the sections are directed to members of The Church of Jesus Christ of Latter-day Saints, the messages, warnings, and exhortations are for the benefit of all mankind and contain an invitation to all people everywhere to hear the voice of the Lord Jesus Christ, speaking to them for their temporal well-being and their everlasting salvation.

Most of the revelations in this compilation were received through Joseph Smith Jr., the first prophet and president of The Church of Jesus Christ of Latter-day Saints. Others were issued through some of his successors in the Presidency (see headings to D&C 135, 136, and 138, and Official Declarations 1 and 2).

The book of Doctrine and Covenants is one of the standard works of the Church in company with the Holy Bible, the Book of Mormon, and the Pearl of Great Price. However, the Doctrine and Covenants is unique because it is not a translation of an ancient document, but is of modern origin and was given of God through His chosen prophets for the restoration of His holy work and the establishment of the kingdom of God on the earth in these days. In the revelations, one hears the tender but firm voice of the Lord Jesus Christ, speaking anew in the dispensation of the fulness of times; and the work that is initiated herein is preparatory to His Second Coming, in fulfillment of and in concert with the words of all the holy prophets since the world began.

Joseph Smith Jr. was born December 23, 1805, in Sharon, Windsor County, Vermont. During his early life, he moved with his family to present-day Manchester, in western New York. It was while he was living there in the spring of 1820, when he was fourteen years of age, that he experienced his first vision, in which he was visited in person by God, the Eternal Father, and His Son Jesus Christ. He was told in this vision that the true Church of Jesus Christ that had been established in New Testament times, and which had administered the fulness of the gospel, was no longer on the earth. Other divine manifestations followed in which he was taught by many angels; it was shown to him that God had a special work for him to do on the earth and that through him the Church of Jesus Christ would be restored to the earth.

In the course of time, Joseph Smith was enabled by divine assistance to translate and publish the Book of Mormon. In the meantime he and Oliver Cowdery were ordained to the Aaronic Priesthood by John the Baptist in May 1829 (see D&C 13), and soon thereafter they were also ordained to the Melchizedek

Priesthood by the ancient Apostles Peter, James, and John (see D&C 27:12). Other ordinations followed in which priesthood keys were conferred by Moses, Elijah, Elias, and many ancient prophets (see D&C 110; 128:18, 21). These ordinations were, in fact, a restoration of divine authority to man on the earth. On April 6, 1830, under heavenly direction, the Prophet Joseph Smith organized the Church, and thus the true Church of Jesus Christ is once again operative as an institution among men, with authority to teach the gospel and administer the ordinances of salvation. (See D&C 20 and the Pearl of Great Price, Joseph Smith—History 1.)

These sacred revelations were received in answer to prayer, in times of need, and came out of real-life situations involving real people. The Prophet and his associates sought for divine guidance, and these revelations certify that they received it. In the revelations, one sees the restoration and unfolding of the gospel of Jesus Christ and the ushering in of the dispensation of the fulness of times. The westward movement of the Church from New York and Pennsylvania to Ohio, to Missouri, to Illinois, and finally to the Great Basin of western America and the mighty struggles of the Saints in attempting to build Zion on the earth in modern times are also shown forth in these revelations.

Several of the earlier sections involve matters regarding the translation and publication of the Book of Mormon (see sections 3, 5, 10, 17, and 19). Some later sections reflect the work of the Prophet Joseph Smith in making an inspired translation of the Bible, during which many of the great doctrinal sections were received (see, for example, sections 37, 45, 73, 76, 77, 86, 91, and 132, each of which has some direct relationship to the Bible translation).

In the revelations, the doctrines of the gospel are set forth with explanations about such fundamental matters as the nature of the Godhead, the origin of man, the reality of Satan, the purpose of mortality, the necessity for obedience, the need for repentance, the workings of the Holy Spirit, the ordinances and performances that pertain to salvation, the destiny of the earth, the future conditions of man after the Resurrection and the Judgment, the eternity of the marriage relationship, and the eternal nature of the family. Likewise, the gradual unfolding of the administrative structure of the Church is shown with the calling of bishops, the First Presidency, the Council of the Twelve, and the Seventy and the establishment of other presiding offices and quorums. Finally, the testimony that is given of Jesus Christ—His divinity, His majesty, His perfection, His love, and His redeeming power—makes this book of great value to the human family and "worth to the Church the riches of the whole Earth" (see heading to D&C 70).

The revelations were originally recorded by Joseph Smith's scribes, and Church members enthusiastically shared handwritten copies with each other. To create a more permanent record, scribes soon copied these revelations into manuscript record books, which Church leaders used in preparing the revelations to be printed. Joseph and the early Saints viewed the revelations as they did the Church: living, dynamic, and subject to refinement with additional revelation. They also recognized that unintentional errors had likely occurred through the process of copying the revelations and preparing them for publication. Thus, a Church conference asked Joseph Smith in 1831 to "correct those errors or mistakes which he may discover by the Holy Spirit."

After the revelations had been reviewed and corrected, Church members in Missouri began printing a book titled A Book of Commandments for the Government of the Church of Christ, which contained many of the Prophet's early revelations. This first attempt to publish the revelations ended, however, when a mob destroyed the Saints' printing office in Jackson County on July 20, 1833.

Upon hearing of the destruction of the Missouri printing office, Joseph Smith and other Church leaders began preparations to publish the revelations in Kirtland, Ohio. To again correct errors, clarify wording, and recognize developments in Church doctrine and organization, Joseph Smith oversaw the editing of the text of some revelations to prepare them for publication in 1835 as the Doctrine and Covenants of the Church of the Latter Day Saints. Joseph Smith authorized another edition of the Doctrine and Covenants, which was published only months after the Prophet's martyrdom in 1844.

The early Latter-day Saints prized the revelations and viewed them as messages from God. On one occasion in late 1831, several elders of the Church gave solemn testimony that the Lord had borne record to their souls of the truth of the revelations. This testimony was published in the 1835 edition of the Doctrine and Covenants as the written testimony of the Twelve Apostles:

TESTIMONY OF THE

TWELVE APOSTLES TO THE TRUTH OF THE

BOOK OF DOCTRINE AND COVENANTS

The Testimony of the Witnesses to the Book of the Lord's Commandments, which commandments He gave to His Church through Joseph Smith, Jun., who was appointed by the voice of the Church for this purpose:

We, therefore, feel willing to bear testimony to all the world of mankind, to every creature upon the face of the earth, that the Lord has borne record to our souls, through the Holy Ghost shed forth upon us, that these commandments were given by inspiration of God, and are profitable for all men and are verily true.

We give this testimony unto the world, the Lord being our helper; and it is through the grace of God the Father, and His Son, Jesus Christ, that we are permitted to have this privilege of bearing this testimony unto the world, in the which we rejoice exceedingly, praying the Lord always that the children of men may be profited thereby.

The names of the Twelve were:

- Thomas B. Marsh
- David W. Patten
- Brigham Young
- Heber C. Kimball
- Orson Hyde
- William E. McLellin
- Parley P. Pratt
- Luke S. Johnson
- William Smith
- Orson Pratt
- John F. Boynton
- Lyman E. Johnson

In successive editions of the Doctrine and Covenants, additional revelations or other matters of record have been added, as received and as accepted by competent assemblies or conferences of the Church. The 1876 edition, prepared by Elder Orson Pratt under Brigham Young's direction, arranged the revelations chronologically and supplied new headings with historical introductions.

Beginning with the 1835 edition, a series of seven theological lessons was also included; these were titled the Lectures on Faith. These had been prepared for use in the School of the Prophets in Kirtland, Ohio, from 1834 to 1835. Although profitable for doctrine and instruction, these lectures have been omitted from the Doctrine and Covenants since the 1921 edition because they were not given or presented as revelations to the whole Church.

In the 1981 edition of the Doctrine and Covenants, three documents were included for the first time. These are sections 137 and 138, setting forth the fundamentals of salvation for the dead; and Official Declaration 2, announcing that all worthy male members of the Church may be ordained to the priesthood without regard for race or color.

Each new edition of the Doctrine and Covenants has corrected past errors and added new information, particularly in the historical portions of the section headings. The present edition further refines dates and place-names and makes other corrections. These changes have been made to bring the material into conformity with the most accurate historical information. Other special features of this latest edition include revised maps showing the major geographical locations in which the revelations were received, plus improved photographs of Church historical sites, cross-references, section headings, and subject-matter summaries, all of which are designed to help readers to understand and rejoice in the message of the Lord as given in the Doctrine and Covenants. Information for the section headings has been taken from the Manuscript History of the Church and the published *History of the Church* (collectively referred to in the headings as Joseph Smith's history) and *The Joseph Smith Papers.*

Chronological Order of Contents

	March	Kirtland, Ohio	78
	April	Independence, Missouri	82, 83
	August	Hiram, Ohio	99
	September	Kirtland, Ohio	84
	November	Kirtland, Ohio	85
	December	Kirtland, Ohio	86, 87*, 88
1833	February	Kirtland, Ohio	89
	March	Kirtland, Ohio	90, 91, 92
	May	Kirtland, Ohio	93
	June	Kirtland, Ohio	95, 96
	August	Kirtland, Ohio	94, 97, 98
	October	Perrysburg, New York	100
	December	Kirtland, Ohio	101
1834	February	Kirtland, Ohio	102, 103
	April	Kirtland, Ohio	104*
	June	Fishing River, Missouri	105
	November	Kirtland, Ohio	106
1835	April	Kirtland, Ohio	107
	August	Kirtland, Ohio	134
	December	Kirtland, Ohio	108
1836	January	Kirtland, Ohio	137
	March	Kirtland, Ohio	109
	April	Kirtland, Ohio	110
	August	Salem, Massachusetts	111
1837	July	Kirtland, Ohio	112
1838	March	Far West, Missouri	113*
	April	Far West, Missouri	114, 115
	May	Spring Hill, Daviess Cnty, Missouri	116
	July	Far West, Missouri	117, 118, 119, 120
1839	March	Liberty Jail, Clay County, Missouri	121, 122, 123
1841	January	Nauvoo, Illinois	124
	March	Nauvoo, Illinois	125
	July	Nauvoo, Illinois	126
1842	September	Nauvoo, Illinois	127, 128
1843	February	Nauvoo, Illinois	129
	April	Ramus, Illinois	130
	May	Ramus, Illinois	131
	July	Nauvoo, Illinois	132
1844	June	Nauvoo, Illinois	135
1847	January	Winter Quarters (now Nebraska)	136
1890	October	Salt Lake City, Utah	Official Declaration 1
1918	October	Salt Lake City, Utah	138
1978	June	Salt Lake City, Utah	Official Declaration 2

Section 1

Revelation given through Joseph Smith the Prophet, on November 1, 1831, during a special conference of elders of the Church, held at Hiram, Ohio. Many revelations had been received from the Lord prior to this time, and the compilation of these for publication in book form was one of the principal subjects passed upon at the conference. This section constitutes the Lord's preface to the doctrines, covenants, and commandments given in this dispensation.

1–7, The voice of warning is to all people; 8–16, Apostasy and wickedness precede the Second Coming; 17–23, Joseph Smith is called to restore to earth the Lord's truths and powers; 24–33, The Book of Mormon is brought forth and the true Church is established; 34–36, Peace will be taken from the earth; 37–39, Search these commandments.

1 Hearken, O ye people of my church, saith the voice of him who dwells on high, and whose eyes are upon all men; yea, verily I say: Hearken ye people from afar; and ye that are upon the islands of the sea, listen together.

2 For verily the voice of the Lord is unto all men, and there is none to escape; and there is no eye that shall not see, neither ear that shall not hear, neither heart that shall not be penetrated.

3 And the rebellious shall be pierced with much sorrow; for their iniquities shall be spoken upon the housetops, and their secret acts shall be revealed.

4 And the voice of warning shall be unto all people, by the mouths of my disciples, whom I have chosen in these last days.

5 And they shall go forth and none shall stay them, for I the Lord have commanded them.

6 Behold, this is mine authority, and the authority of my servants, and my preface unto the book of my commandments, which I have given them to publish unto you, O inhabitants of the earth.

7 Wherefore, fear and tremble, O ye people, for what I the Lord have decreed in them shall be fulfilled.

8 And verily I say unto you, that they who go forth, bearing these tidings unto the inhabitants of the earth, to them is power given to seal both on earth and in heaven, the unbelieving and rebellious;

9 Yea, verily, to seal them up unto the day when the wrath of God shall be poured out upon the wicked without measure—

10 Unto the day when the Lord shall come to recompense unto every man according to his work, and measure to every man according to the measure which he has measured to his fellow man.

11 Wherefore the voice of the Lord is unto the ends of the earth, that all that will hear may hear:

12 Prepare ye, prepare ye for that which is to come, for the Lord is nigh;

13 And the anger of the Lord is kindled, and his sword is bathed in heaven, and it shall fall upon the inhabitants of the earth.

14 And the arm of the Lord shall be revealed; and the day cometh that they who will not hear the voice of the Lord, neither the voice of his servants, neither give heed to the words of the prophets and apostles, shall be cut off from among the people;

15 For they have strayed from mine ordinances, and have broken mine

everlasting covenant;

16 They seek not the Lord to establish his righteousness, but every man walketh in his own way, and after the image of his own god, whose image is in the likeness of the world, and whose substance is that of an idol, which waxeth old and shall perish in Babylon, even Babylon the great, which shall fall.

17 Wherefore, I the Lord, knowing the calamity which should come upon the inhabitants of the earth, called upon my servant Joseph Smith, Jun., and spake unto him from heaven, and gave him commandments;

18 And also gave commandments to others, that they should proclaim these things unto the world; and all this that it might be fulfilled, which was written by the prophets—

19 The weak things of the world shall come forth and break down the mighty and strong ones, that man should not counsel his fellow man, neither trust in the arm of flesh—

20 But that every man might speak in the name of God the Lord, even the Savior of the world;

21 That faith also might increase in the earth;

22 That mine everlasting covenant might be established;

23 That the fulness of my gospel might be proclaimed by the weak and the simple unto the ends of the world, and before kings and rulers.

24 Behold, I am God and have spoken it; these commandments are of me, and were given unto my servants in their weakness, after the manner of their language, that they might come to understanding.

25 And inasmuch as they erred it might be made known;

26 And inasmuch as they sought wisdom they might be instructed;

27 And inasmuch as they sinned they might be chastened, that they might repent;

28 And inasmuch as they were humble they might be made strong, and blessed from on high, and receive knowledge from time to time.

29 And after having received the record of the Nephites, yea, even my servant Joseph Smith, Jun., might have power to translate through the mercy of God, by the power of God, the Book of Mormon.

30 And also those to whom these commandments were given, might have power to lay the foundation of this church, and to bring it forth out of obscurity and out of darkness, the only true and living church upon the face of the whole earth, with which I, the Lord, am well pleased, speaking unto the church collectively and not individually—

31 For I the Lord cannot look upon sin with the least degree of allowance;

32 Nevertheless, he that repents and does the commandments of the Lord shall be forgiven;

33 And he that repents not, from him shall be taken even the light which he has received; for my Spirit shall not always strive with man, saith the Lord of Hosts.

34 And again, verily I say unto you, O inhabitants of the earth: I the Lord am willing to make these things known unto all flesh;

35 For I am no respecter of persons,

and will that all men shall know that the day speedily cometh; the hour is not yet, but is nigh at hand, when peace shall be taken from the earth, and the devil shall have power over his own dominion.

36 And also the Lord shall have power over his saints, and shall reign in their midst, and shall come down in judgment upon Idumea, or the world.

37 Search these commandments, for they are true and faithful, and the prophecies and promises which are in them shall all be fulfilled.

38 What I the Lord have spoken, I have spoken, and I excuse not myself; and though the heavens and the earth pass away, my word shall not pass away, but shall all be fulfilled, whether by mine own voice or by the voice of my servants, it is the same.

39 For behold, and lo, the Lord is God, and the Spirit beareth record, and the record is true, and the truth abideth forever and ever. Amen.

Section 2

An extract from Joseph Smith's history relating the words of the angel Moroni to Joseph Smith the Prophet, while in the house of the Prophet's father at Manchester, New York, on the evening of September 21, 1823. Moroni was the last of a long line of historians who had made the record that is now before the world as the Book of Mormon. (Compare Malachi 4:5–6; also sections 27:9; 110:13–16; and 128:18.)

1, Elijah is to reveal the priesthood; 2–3, The promises of the fathers are planted in the hearts of the children.

1 Behold, I will reveal unto you the Priesthood, by the hand of Elijah the prophet, before the coming of the great and dreadful day of the Lord.

2 And he shall plant in the hearts of the children the promises made to the fathers, and the hearts of the children shall turn to their fathers.

3 If it were not so, the whole earth would be utterly wasted at his coming.

Section 3

Revelation given to Joseph Smith the Prophet, at Harmony, Pennsylvania, July 1828, relating to the loss of 116 pages of manuscript translated from the first part of the Book of Mormon, which was called the book of Lehi. The Prophet had reluctantly allowed these pages to pass from his custody to that of Martin Harris, who had served for a brief period as scribe in the translation of the Book of Mormon. The revelation was given through the Urim and Thummim. (See section 10.)

1–4, The Lord's course is one eternal round; 5–15, Joseph Smith must repent or lose the gift to translate; 16–20, The Book of Mormon comes forth to save the seed of Lehi.

1 The works, and the designs, and the purposes of God cannot be frustrated, neither can they come to naught.

2 For God doth not walk in crooked paths, neither doth he turn to the right hand nor to the left, neither doth he vary from that which he hath said, therefore his paths are straight, and his course is one eternal round.

3 Remember, remember that it is not the work of God that is frustrated, but the work of men;

4 For although a man may have many revelations, and have power to do many mighty works, yet if he boasts in his own strength, and sets at naught the counsels of God, and follows after the dictates of his own will and carnal desires, he must fall and incur the vengeance of a just God upon him.

5 Behold, you have been entrusted with these things, but how strict were your commandments; and remember also the promises which were made to you, if you did not transgress them.

6 And behold, how oft you have transgressed the commandments and the laws of God, and have gone on in the persuasions of men.

7 For, behold, you should not have feared man more than God. Although men set at naught the counsels of God, and despise his words—

8 Yet you should have been faithful; and he would have extended his arm and supported you against all the fiery darts of the adversary; and he would have been with you in every time of trouble.

9 Behold, thou art Joseph, and thou wast chosen to do the work of the Lord, but because of transgression, if thou art not aware thou wilt fall.

10 But remember, God is merciful; therefore, repent of that which thou hast done which is contrary to the commandment which I gave you, and thou art still chosen, and art again called to the work;

11 Except thou do this, thou shalt be delivered up and become as other men, and have no more gift.

12 And when thou deliveredst up that which God had given thee sight and power to translate, thou deliveredst up that which was sacred into the hands of a wicked man,

13 Who has set at naught the counsels of God, and has broken the most sacred promises which were made before God, and has depended upon his own judgment and boasted in his own wisdom.

14 And this is the reason that thou hast lost thy privileges for a season—

15 For thou hast suffered the counsel of thy director to be trampled upon from the beginning.

16 Nevertheless, my work shall go forth, for inasmuch as the knowledge of a Savior has come unto the world, through the testimony of the Jews, even so shall the knowledge of a Savior come unto my people—

17 And to the Nephites, and the Jacobites, and the Josephites, and the Zoramites, through the testimony of their fathers—

18 And this testimony shall come to the knowledge of the Lamanites, and the Lemuelites, and the Ishmaelites, who dwindled in unbelief because of the iniquity of their fathers, whom the Lord has suffered to destroy their brethren the Nephites, because of their iniquities and their abominations.

19 And for this very purpose are these plates preserved, which contain these records—that the promises of the Lord might be fulfilled, which he made to his people;

20 And that the Lamanites might come to the knowledge of their fathers, and that they might know the promises of the Lord, and that they may believe the gospel and rely upon the merits of Jesus Christ, and be glorified through faith in his name, and that through their repentance they might be saved. Amen.

Section 4

Revelation given through Joseph Smith the Prophet to his father, Joseph Smith Sr., at Harmony, Pennsylvania, February 1829.

1–4, Valiant service saves the Lord's ministers; 5–6, Godly attributes qualify them for the ministry; 7, The things of God must be sought after.

1 Now behold, a marvelous work is about to come forth among the children of men.

2 Therefore, O ye that embark in the service of God, see that ye serve him with all your heart, might, mind and strength, that ye may stand blameless before God at the last day.

3 Therefore, if ye have desires to serve God ye are called to the work;

4 For behold the field is white already to harvest; and lo, he that thrusteth in his sickle with his might, the same layeth up in store that he perisheth not, but bringeth salvation to his soul;

5 And faith, hope, charity and love, with an eye single to the glory of God, qualify him for the work.

6 Remember faith, virtue, knowledge, temperance, patience, brotherly kindness, godliness, charity, humility, diligence.

7 Ask, and ye shall receive; knock, and it shall be opened unto you. Amen.

Section 5

Revelation given through Joseph Smith the Prophet, at Harmony, Pennsylvania, March 1829, at the request of Martin Harris.

1–10, This generation will receive the Lord's word through Joseph Smith; 11–18, Three witnesses will testify of the Book of Mormon; 19–20, The word of the Lord will be verified as in previous times; 21–35, Martin Harris may repent and be one of the witnesses.

1 Behold, I say unto you, that as my servant Martin Harris has desired a witness at my hand, that you, my servant Joseph Smith, Jun., have got the plates of which you have testified and borne record that you have received of me;

2 And now, behold, this shall you say unto him—he who spake unto you, said unto you: I, the Lord, am God, and have given these things unto you, my servant Joseph Smith, Jun., and have commanded you that you should stand as a witness of these things;

3 And I have caused you that you should enter into a covenant with me, that you should not show them except to those persons to whom I commanded you; and you have no power over them except I grant it unto you.

4 And you have a gift to translate the plates; and this is the first gift that I bestowed upon you; and I have commanded that you should pretend to no other gift until my purpose is fulfilled in this; for I will grant unto you no other gift until it is finished.

5 Verily, I say unto you, that woe shall come unto the inhabitants of the earth if they will not hearken unto my words;

6 For hereafter you shall be ordained and go forth and deliver my words unto the children of men.

7 Behold, if they will not believe my words, they would not believe you, my servant Joseph, if it were possible that you should show them all these things which I have committed unto you.

8 Oh, this unbelieving and stiffnecked generation—mine anger is kindled against them.

9 Behold, verily I say unto you, I have reserved those things which I have entrusted unto you, my servant Joseph, for a wise purpose in me, and it shall be made known unto future generations;

10 But this generation shall have my word through you;

11 And in addition to your testimony, the testimony of three of my servants, whom I shall call and ordain, unto whom I will show these things, and they shall go forth with my words that are given through you.

12 Yea, they shall know of a surety that these things are true, for from heaven will I declare it unto them.

13 I will give them power that they may behold and view these things as they are;

14 And to none else will I grant this power, to receive this same testimony among this generation, in this the beginning of the rising up and the coming forth of my church out of the wilderness—clear as the moon, and fair as the sun, and terrible as an army with banners.

15 And the testimony of three witnesses will I send forth of my word.

16 And behold, whosoever believeth

on my words, them will I visit with the manifestation of my Spirit; and they shall be born of me, even of water and of the Spirit—

17 And you must wait yet a little while, for ye are not yet ordained—

18 And their testimony shall also go forth unto the condemnation of this generation if they harden their hearts against them;

19 For a desolating scourge shall go forth among the inhabitants of the earth, and shall continue to be poured out from time to time, if they repent not, until the earth is empty, and the inhabitants thereof are consumed away and utterly destroyed by the brightness of my coming.

20 Behold, I tell you these things, even as I also told the people of the destruction of Jerusalem; and my word shall be verified at this time as it hath hitherto been verified.

21 And now I command you, my servant Joseph, to repent and walk more uprightly before me, and to yield to the persuasions of men no more;

22 And that you be firm in keeping the commandments wherewith I have commanded you; and if you do this, behold I grant unto you eternal life, even if you should be slain.

23 And now, again, I speak unto you, my servant Joseph, concerning the man that desires the witness—

24 Behold, I say unto him, he exalts himself and does not humble himself sufficiently before me; but if he will bow down before me, and humble himself in mighty prayer and faith, in the sincerity of his heart, then will I grant unto him a view of the things which he desires to see.

25 And then he shall say unto the people of this generation: Behold, I have seen the things which the Lord hath shown unto Joseph Smith, Jun., and I know of a surety that they are true, for I have seen them, for they have been shown unto me by the power of God and not of man.

26 And I the Lord command him, my servant Martin Harris, that he shall say no more unto them concerning these things, except he shall say: I have seen them, and they have been shown unto me by the power of God; and these are the words which he shall say.

27 But if he deny this he will break the covenant which he has before covenanted with me, and behold, he is condemned.

28 And now, except he humble himself and acknowledge unto me the things that he has done which are wrong, and covenant with me that he will keep my commandments, and exercise faith in me, behold, I say unto him, he shall have no such views, for I will grant unto him no views of the things of which I have spoken.

29 And if this be the case, I command you, my servant Joseph, that you shall say unto him, that he shall do no more, nor trouble me any more concerning this matter.

30 And if this be the case, behold, I say unto thee Joseph, when thou hast translated a few more pages thou shalt stop for a season, even until I command thee again; then thou mayest translate again.

31 And except thou do this, behold, thou shalt have no more gift, and I will take away the things which I have entrusted with thee.

32 And now, because I foresee the lying in wait to destroy thee, yea, I

foresee that if my servant Martin Harris humbleth not himself and receive a witness from my hand, that he will fall into transgression;

33 And there are many that lie in wait to destroy thee from off the face of the earth; and for this cause, that thy days may be prolonged, I have given unto thee these commandments.

34 Yea, for this cause I have said: Stop, and stand still until I command thee, and I will provide means whereby thou mayest accomplish the thing which I have commanded thee.

35 And if thou art faithful in keeping my commandments, thou shalt be lifted up at the last day. Amen.

Section 6

Revelation given to Joseph Smith the Prophet and Oliver Cowdery, at Harmony, Pennsylvania, April 1829. Oliver Cowdery began his labors as scribe in the translation of the Book of Mormon, April 7, 1829. He had already received a divine manifestation of the truth of the Prophet's testimony respecting the plates on which was engraved the Book of Mormon record. The Prophet inquired of the Lord through the Urim and Thummim and received this response.

1–6, Laborers in the Lord's field gain salvation; 7–13, There is no gift greater than the gift of salvation; 14–27, A witness of the truth comes by the power of the Spirit; 28–37, Look unto Christ, and do good continually.

1 A great and marvelous work is about to come forth unto the children of men.

2 Behold, I am God; give heed unto my word, which is quick and powerful, sharper than a two-edged sword, to the dividing asunder of both joints and marrow; therefore give heed unto my words.

3 Behold, the field is white already to harvest; therefore, whoso desireth to reap, let him thrust in his sickle with his might, and reap while the day lasts, that he may treasure up for his soul everlasting salvation in the kingdom of God.

4 Yea, whosoever will thrust in his sickle and reap, the same is called of God.

5 Therefore, if you will ask of me you shall receive; if you will knock it shall be opened unto you.

6 Now, as you have asked, behold, I say unto you, keep my commandments, and seek to bring forth and establish the cause of Zion;

7 Seek not for riches but for wisdom, and behold, the mysteries of God shall be unfolded unto you, and then shall you be made rich. Behold, he that hath eternal life is rich.

8 Verily, verily, I say unto you, even as you desire of me so it shall be unto you; and if you desire, you shall be the means of doing much good in this generation.

9 Say nothing but repentance unto this generation; keep my commandments, and assist to bring forth my work, according to my commandments, and you shall be blessed.

10 Behold thou hast a gift, and blessed art thou because of thy gift. Remember it is sacred and cometh from above—

11 And if thou wilt inquire, thou shalt know mysteries which are great and marvelous; therefore thou shalt exercise thy gift, that thou mayest find out mysteries, that thou mayest bring many to the knowledge of the truth, yea, convince them of the error of their ways.

12 Make not thy gift known unto any save it be those who are of thy faith. Trifle not with sacred things.

13 If thou wilt do good, yea, and hold out faithful to the end, thou shalt be saved in the kingdom of God, which is the greatest of all the gifts of God; for there is no gift greater than the gift of salvation.

14 Verily, verily, I say unto thee, blessed art thou for what thou hast done; for thou hast inquired of me, and behold, as often as thou hast inquired thou hast received instruction of my Spirit. If it had not been so, thou wouldst not have come to the place where thou art at this time.

15 Behold, thou knowest that thou hast inquired of me and I did enlighten thy mind; and now I tell thee these things

that thou mayest know that thou hast been enlightened by the Spirit of truth;

16 Yea, I tell thee, that thou mayest know that there is none else save God that knowest thy thoughts and the intents of thy heart.

17 I tell thee these things as a witness unto thee—that the words or the work which thou hast been writing are true.

18 Therefore be diligent; stand by my servant Joseph, faithfully, in whatsoever difficult circumstances he may be for the word's sake.

19 Admonish him in his faults, and also receive admonition of him. Be patient; be sober; be temperate; have patience, faith, hope and charity.

20 Behold, thou art Oliver, and I have spoken unto thee because of thy desires; therefore treasure up these words in thy heart. Be faithful and diligent in keeping the commandments of God, and I will encircle thee in the arms of my love.

21 Behold, I am Jesus Christ, the Son of God. I am the same that came unto mine own, and mine own received me not. I am the light which shineth in darkness, and the darkness comprehendeth it not.

22 Verily, verily, I say unto you, if you desire a further witness, cast your mind upon the night that you cried unto me in your heart, that you might know concerning the truth of these things.

23 Did I not speak peace to your mind concerning the matter? What greater witness can you have than from God?

24 And now, behold, you have received a witness; for if I have told you things which no man knoweth have you not received a witness?

25 And, behold, I grant unto you a gift, if you desire of me, to translate, even as my servant Joseph.

26 Verily, verily, I say unto you, that there are records which contain much of my gospel, which have been kept back because of the wickedness of the people;

27 And now I command you, that if you have good desires—a desire to lay up treasures for yourself in heaven—then shall you assist in bringing to light, with your gift, those parts of my scriptures which have been hidden because of iniquity.

28 And now, behold, I give unto you, and also unto my servant Joseph, the keys of this gift, which shall bring to light this ministry; and in the mouth of two or three witnesses shall every word be established.

29 Verily, verily, I say unto you, if they reject my words, and this part of my gospel and ministry, blessed are ye, for they can do no more unto you than unto me.

30 And even if they do unto you even as they have done unto me, blessed are ye, for you shall dwell with me in glory.

31 But if they reject not my words, which shall be established by the testimony which shall be given, blessed are they, and then shall ye have joy in the fruit of your labors.

32 Verily, verily, I say unto you, as I said unto my disciples, where two or three are gathered together in my name, as touching one thing, behold, there will I be in the midst of them—even so am I in the midst of you.

33 Fear not to do good, my sons, for whatsoever ye sow, that shall ye also reap; therefore, if ye sow good ye shall also reap good for your reward.

34 Therefore, fear not, little flock; do

good; let earth and hell combine against
you, for if ye are built upon my rock,
they cannot prevail.

35 Behold, I do not condemn you; go
your ways and sin no more; perform
with soberness the work which I have
commanded you.

36 Look unto me in every thought;
doubt not, fear not.

37 Behold the wounds which pierced
my side, and also the prints of the
nails in my hands and feet; be faithful,
keep my commandments, and ye shall
inherit the kingdom of heaven. Amen.

Section 7

Revelation given to Joseph Smith the Prophet and Oliver Cowdery, at Harmony, Pennsylvania, April 1829, when they inquired through the Urim and Thummim as to whether John, the beloved disciple, tarried in the flesh or had died. The revelation is a translated version of the record made on parchment by John and hidden up by himself.

1–3, John the Beloved will live until the Lord comes; 4–8, Peter, James, and John hold gospel keys.

1 And the Lord said unto me: John, my beloved, what desirest thou? For if you shall ask what you will, it shall be granted unto you.

2 And I said unto him: Lord, give unto me power over death, that I may live and bring souls unto thee.

3 And the Lord said unto me: Verily, verily, I say unto thee, because thou desirest this thou shalt tarry until I come in my glory, and shalt prophesy before nations, kindreds, tongues and people.

4 And for this cause the Lord said unto Peter: If I will that he tarry till I come, what is that to thee? For he desired of me that he might bring souls unto me, but thou desiredst that thou mightest speedily come unto me in my kingdom.

5 I say unto thee, Peter, this was a good desire; but my beloved has desired that he might do more, or a greater work yet among men than what he has before done.

6 Yea, he has undertaken a greater work; therefore I will make him as flaming fire and a ministering angel; he shall minister for those who shall be heirs of salvation who dwell on the earth.

7 And I will make thee to minister for him and for thy brother James; and unto you three I will give this power and the keys of this ministry until I come.

8 Verily I say unto you, ye shall both have according to your desires, for ye both joy in that which ye have desired.

Section 8

Revelation given through Joseph Smith the Prophet to Oliver Cowdery, at Harmony, Pennsylvania, April 1829. In the course of the translation of the Book of Mormon, Oliver, who continued to serve as scribe, writing at the Prophet's dictation, desired to be endowed with the gift of translation. The Lord responded to his supplication by granting this revelation.

1–5, Revelation comes by the power of the Holy Ghost; 6–12, Knowledge of the mysteries of God and the power to translate ancient records come by faith.

1 Oliver Cowdery, verily, verily, I say unto you, that assuredly as the Lord liveth, who is your God and your Redeemer, even so surely shall you receive a knowledge of whatsoever things you shall ask in faith, with an honest heart, believing that you shall receive a knowledge concerning the engravings of old records, which are ancient, which contain those parts of my scripture of which has been spoken by the manifestation of my Spirit.

2 Yea, behold, I will tell you in your mind and in your heart, by the Holy Ghost, which shall come upon you and which shall dwell in your heart.

3 Now, behold, this is the spirit of revelation; behold, this is the spirit by which Moses brought the children of Israel through the Red Sea on dry ground.

4 Therefore this is thy gift; apply unto it, and blessed art thou, for it shall deliver you out of the hands of your enemies, when, if it were not so, they would slay you and bring your soul to destruction.

5 Oh, remember these words, and keep my commandments. Remember, this is your gift.

6 Now this is not all thy gift; for you have another gift, which is the gift of Aaron; behold, it has told you many things;

7 Behold, there is no other power, save the power of God, that can cause this gift of Aaron to be with you.

8 Therefore, doubt not, for it is the gift of God; and you shall hold it in your hands, and do marvelous works; and no power shall be able to take it away out of your hands, for it is the work of God.

9 And, therefore, whatsoever you shall ask me to tell you by that means, that will I grant unto you, and you shall have knowledge concerning it.

10 Remember that without faith you can do nothing; therefore ask in faith. Trifle not with these things; do not ask for that which you ought not.

11 Ask that you may know the mysteries of God, and that you may translate and receive knowledge from all those ancient records which have been hid up, that are sacred; and according to your faith shall it be done unto you.

12 Behold, it is I that have spoken it; and I am the same that spake unto you from the beginning. Amen.

Section 9

Revelation given through Joseph Smith the Prophet to Oliver Cowdery, at Harmony, Pennsylvania, April 1829. Oliver is admonished to be patient and is urged to be content to write, for the time being, at the dictation of the translator, rather than to attempt to translate.

1–6, Other ancient records are yet to be translated; 7–14, The Book of Mormon is translated by study and by spiritual confirmation.

1 Behold, I say unto you, my son, that because you did not translate according to that which you desired of me, and did commence again to write for my servant, Joseph Smith, Jun., even so I would that ye should continue until you have finished this record, which I have entrusted unto him.

2 And then, behold, other records have I, that I will give unto you power that you may assist to translate.

3 Be patient, my son, for it is wisdom in me, and it is not expedient that you should translate at this present time.

4 Behold, the work which you are called to do is to write for my servant Joseph.

5 And, behold, it is because that you did not continue as you commenced, when you began to translate, that I have taken away this privilege from you.

6 Do not murmur, my son, for it is wisdom in me that I have dealt with you after this manner.

7 Behold, you have not understood; you have supposed that I would give it unto you, when you took no thought save it was to ask me.

8 But, behold, I say unto you, that you must study it out in your mind; then you must ask me if it be right, and if it is right I will cause that your bosom shall burn within you; therefore, you shall feel that it is right.

9 But if it be not right you shall have no such feelings, but you shall have a stupor of thought that shall cause you to forget the thing which is wrong; therefore, you cannot write that which is sacred save it be given you from me.

10 Now, if you had known this you could have translated; nevertheless, it is not expedient that you should translate now.

11 Behold, it was expedient when you commenced; but you feared, and the time is past, and it is not expedient now;

12 For, do you not behold that I have given unto my servant Joseph sufficient strength, whereby it is made up? And neither of you have I condemned.

13 Do this thing which I have commanded you, and you shall prosper. Be faithful, and yield to no temptation.

14 Stand fast in the work wherewith I have called you, and a hair of your head shall not be lost, and you shall be lifted up at the last day. Amen.

Section 10

Revelation given to Joseph Smith the Prophet, at Harmony, Pennsylvania, likely around April 1829, though portions may have been received as early as the summer of 1828. Herein the Lord informs Joseph of alterations made by wicked men in the 116 manuscript pages from the translation of the book of Lehi, in the Book of Mormon. These manuscript pages had been lost from the possession of Martin Harris, to whom the sheets had been temporarily entrusted. (See the heading to section 3.) The evil design was to await the expected retranslation of the matter covered by the stolen pages and then to discredit the translator by showing discrepancies created by the alterations. That this wicked purpose had been conceived by the evil one and was known to the Lord even while Mormon, the ancient Nephite historian, was making his abridgment of the accumulated plates, is shown in the Book of Mormon (see Words of Mormon 1:3–7).

1–26, Satan stirs up wicked men to oppose the Lord's work; 27–33, He seeks to destroy the souls of men; 34–52, The gospel is to go to the Lamanites and all nations through the Book of Mormon; 53–63, The Lord will establish His Church and His gospel among men; 64–70, He will gather the repentant into His Church and will save the obedient.

1 Now, behold, I say unto you, that because you delivered up those writings which you had power given unto you to translate by the means of the Urim and Thummim, into the hands of a wicked man, you have lost them.

2 And you also lost your gift at the same time, and your mind became darkened.

3 Nevertheless, it is now restored unto you again; therefore see that you are faithful and continue on unto the finishing of the remainder of the work of translation as you have begun.

4 Do not run faster or labor more than you have strength and means provided to enable you to translate; but be diligent unto the end.

5 Pray always, that you may come off conqueror; yea, that you may conquer Satan, and that you may escape the hands of the servants of Satan that do uphold his work.

6 Behold, they have sought to destroy you; yea, even the man in whom you have trusted has sought to destroy you.

7 And for this cause I said that he is a wicked man, for he has sought to take away the things wherewith you have been entrusted; and he has also sought to destroy your gift.

8 And because you have delivered the writings into his hands, behold, wicked men have taken them from you.

9 Therefore, you have delivered them up, yea, that which was sacred, unto wickedness.

10 And, behold, Satan hath put it into their hearts to alter the words which you have caused to be written, or which you have translated, which have gone out of your hands.

11 And behold, I say unto you, that because they have altered the words, they read contrary from that which you translated and caused to be written;

12 And, on this wise, the devil has sought to lay a cunning plan, that he may destroy this work;

13 For he hath put into their hearts to do this, that by lying they may say they have caught you in the words which you have pretended to translate.

14 Verily, I say unto you, that I will not

suffer that Satan shall accomplish his evil design in this thing.

15 For behold, he has put it into their hearts to get thee to tempt the Lord thy God, in asking to translate it over again.

16 And then, behold, they say and think in their hearts—We will see if God has given him power to translate; if so, he will also give him power again;

17 And if God giveth him power again, or if he translates again, or, in other words, if he bringeth forth the same words, behold, we have the same with us, and we have altered them;

18 Therefore they will not agree, and we will say that he has lied in his words, and that he has no gift, and that he has no power;

19 Therefore we will destroy him, and also the work; and we will do this that we may not be ashamed in the end, and that we may get glory of the world.

20 Verily, verily, I say unto you, that Satan has great hold upon their hearts; he stirreth them up to iniquity against that which is good;

21 And their hearts are corrupt, and full of wickedness and abominations; and they love darkness rather than light, because their deeds are evil; therefore they will not ask of me.

22 Satan stirreth them up, that he may lead their souls to destruction.

23 And thus he has laid a cunning plan, thinking to destroy the work of God; but I will require this at their hands, and it shall turn to their shame and condemnation in the day of judgment.

24 Yea, he stirreth up their hearts to anger against this work.

25 Yea, he saith unto them: Deceive and lie in wait to catch, that ye may destroy; behold, this is no harm. And thus he flattereth them, and telleth them that it is no sin to lie that they may catch a man in a lie, that they may destroy him.

26 And thus he flattereth them, and leadeth them along until he draggeth their souls down to hell; and thus he causeth them to catch themselves in their own snare.

27 And thus he goeth up and down, to and fro in the earth, seeking to destroy the souls of men.

28 Verily, verily, I say unto you, wo be unto him that lieth to deceive because he supposeth that another lieth to deceive, for such are not exempt from the justice of God.

29 Now, behold, they have altered these words, because Satan saith unto them: He hath deceived you—and thus he flattereth them away to do iniquity, to get thee to tempt the Lord thy God.

30 Behold, I say unto you, that you shall not translate again those words which have gone forth out of your hands;

31 For, behold, they shall not accomplish their evil designs in lying against those words. For, behold, if you should bring forth the same words they will say that you have lied and that you have pretended to translate, but that you have contradicted yourself.

32 And, behold, they will publish this, and Satan will harden the hearts of the people to stir them up to anger against you, that they will not believe my words.

33 Thus Satan thinketh to overpower your testimony in this generation, that the work may not come forth in this generation.

34 But behold, here is wisdom, and because I show unto you wisdom, and

give you commandments concerning these things, what you shall do, show it not unto the world until you have accomplished the work of translation.

35 Marvel not that I said unto you: Here is wisdom, show it not unto the world—for I said, show it not unto the world, that you may be preserved.

36 Behold, I do not say that you shall not show it unto the righteous;

37 But as you cannot always judge the righteous, or as you cannot always tell the wicked from the righteous, therefore I say unto you, hold your peace until I shall see fit to make all things known unto the world concerning the matter.

38 And now, verily I say unto you, that an account of those things that you have written, which have gone out of your hands, is engraven upon the plates of Nephi;

39 Yea, and you remember it was said in those writings that a more particular account was given of these things upon the plates of Nephi.

40 And now, because the account which is engraven upon the plates of Nephi is more particular concerning the things which, in my wisdom, I would bring to the knowledge of the people in this account—

41 Therefore, you shall translate the engravings which are on the plates of Nephi, down even till you come to the reign of king Benjamin, or until you come to that which you have translated, which you have retained;

42 And behold, you shall publish it as the record of Nephi; and thus I will confound those who have altered my words.

43 I will not suffer that they shall destroy my work; yea, I will show unto them that my wisdom is greater than the cunning of the devil.

44 Behold, they have only got a part, or an abridgment of the account of Nephi.

45 Behold, there are many things engraven upon the plates of Nephi which do throw greater views upon my gospel; therefore, it is wisdom in me that you should translate this first part of the engravings of Nephi, and send forth in this work.

46 And, behold, all the remainder of this work does contain all those parts of my gospel which my holy prophets, yea, and also my disciples, desired in their prayers should come forth unto this people.

47 And I said unto them, that it should be granted unto them according to their faith in their prayers;

48 Yea, and this was their faith—that my gospel, which I gave unto them that they might preach in their days, might come unto their brethren the Lamanites, and also all that had become Lamanites because of their dissensions.

49 Now, this is not all—their faith in their prayers was that this gospel should be made known also, if it were possible that other nations should possess this land;

50 And thus they did leave a blessing upon this land in their prayers, that whosoever should believe in this gospel in this land might have eternal life;

51 Yea, that it might be free unto all of whatsoever nation, kindred, tongue, or people they may be.

52 And now, behold, according to their faith in their prayers will I bring this part of my gospel to the knowledge of my people. Behold, I do not bring it to destroy that which they have received,

but to build it up.

53 And for this cause have I said: If this generation harden not their hearts, I will establish my church among them.

54 Now I do not say this to destroy my church, but I say this to build up my church;

55 Therefore, whosoever belongeth to my church need not fear, for such shall inherit the kingdom of heaven.

56 But it is they who do not fear me, neither keep my commandments but build up churches unto themselves to get gain, yea, and all those that do wickedly and build up the kingdom of the devil—yea, verily, verily, I say unto you, that it is they that I will disturb, and cause to tremble and shake to the center.

57 Behold, I am Jesus Christ, the Son of God. I came unto mine own, and mine own received me not.

58 I am the light which shineth in darkness, and the darkness comprehendeth it not.

59 I am he who said—Other sheep have I which are not of this fold—unto my disciples, and many there were that understood me not.

60 And I will show unto this people that I had other sheep, and that they were a branch of the house of Jacob;

61 And I will bring to light their marvelous works, which they did in my name;

62 Yea, and I will also bring to light my gospel which was ministered unto them, and, behold, they shall not deny that which you have received, but they shall build it up, and shall bring to light the true points of my doctrine, yea, and the only doctrine which is in me.

63 And this I do that I may establish my gospel, that there may not be so much contention; yea, Satan doth stir up the hearts of the people to contention concerning the points of my doctrine; and in these things they do err, for they do wrest the scriptures and do not understand them.

64 Therefore, I will unfold unto them this great mystery;

65 For, behold, I will gather them as a hen gathereth her chickens under her wings, if they will not harden their hearts;

66 Yea, if they will come, they may, and partake of the waters of life freely.

67 Behold, this is my doctrine—whosoever repenteth and cometh unto me, the same is my church.

68 Whosoever declareth more or less than this, the same is not of me, but is against me; therefore he is not of my church.

69 And now, behold, whosoever is of my church, and endureth of my church to the end, him will I establish upon my rock, and the gates of hell shall not prevail against them.

70 And now, remember the words of him who is the life and light of the world, your Redeemer, your Lord and your God. Amen.

Section 11

Revelation given through Joseph Smith the Prophet to his brother Hyrum Smith, at Harmony, Pennsylvania, May 1829. This revelation was received through the Urim and Thummim in answer to Joseph's supplication and inquiry. Joseph Smith's history suggests that this revelation was received after the restoration of the Aaronic Priesthood.

1–6, Laborers in the vineyard will gain salvation; 7–14, Seek wisdom, cry repentance, trust in the Spirit; 15–22, Keep the commandments, and study the Lord's word; 23–27, Deny not the spirit of revelation and of prophecy; 28–30, Those who receive Christ become the sons of God.

1 A great and marvelous work is about to come forth among the children of men.

2 Behold, I am God; give heed to my word, which is quick and powerful, sharper than a two-edged sword, to the dividing asunder of both joints and marrow; therefore give heed unto my word.

3 Behold, the field is white already to harvest; therefore, whoso desireth to reap let him thrust in his sickle with his might, and reap while the day lasts, that he may treasure up for his soul everlasting salvation in the kingdom of God.

4 Yea, whosoever will thrust in his sickle and reap, the same is called of God.

5 Therefore, if you will ask of me you shall receive; if you will knock it shall be opened unto you.

6 Now, as you have asked, behold, I say unto you, keep my commandments, and seek to bring forth and establish the cause of Zion.

7 Seek not for riches but for wisdom; and, behold, the mysteries of God shall be unfolded unto you, and then shall you be made rich. Behold, he that hath eternal life is rich.

8 Verily, verily, I say unto you, even as you desire of me so it shall be done unto you; and, if you desire, you shall be the means of doing much good in this generation.

9 Say nothing but repentance unto this generation. Keep my commandments, and assist to bring forth my work, according to my commandments, and you shall be blessed.

10 Behold, thou hast a gift, or thou shalt have a gift if thou wilt desire of me in faith, with an honest heart, believing in the power of Jesus Christ, or in my power which speaketh unto thee;

11 For, behold, it is I that speak; behold, I am the light which shineth in darkness, and by my power I give these words unto thee.

12 And now, verily, verily, I say unto thee, put your trust in that Spirit which leadeth to do good—yea, to do justly, to walk humbly, to judge righteously; and this is my Spirit.

13 Verily, verily, I say unto you, I will impart unto you of my Spirit, which shall enlighten your mind, which shall fill your soul with joy;

14 And then shall ye know, or by this shall you know, all things whatsoever you desire of me, which are pertaining unto things of righteousness, in faith believing in me that you shall receive.

15 Behold, I command you that you need not suppose that you are called to preach until you are called.

16 Wait a little longer, until you shall
have my word, my rock, my church,
and my gospel, that you may know of a
surety my doctrine.

17 And then, behold, according to your
desires, yea, even according to your
faith shall it be done unto you.

18 Keep my commandments; hold your
peace; appeal unto my Spirit;

19 Yea, cleave unto me with all your
heart, that you may assist in bringing
to light those things of which has
been spoken—yea, the translation of
my work; be patient until you shall
accomplish it.

20 Behold, this is your work, to keep
my commandments, yea, with all your
might, mind and strength.

21 Seek not to declare my word, but
first seek to obtain my word, and then
shall your tongue be loosed; then, if you
desire, you shall have my Spirit and my
word, yea, the power of God unto the
convincing of men.

22 But now hold your peace; study my
word which hath gone forth among
the children of men, and also study my
word which shall come forth among the
children of men, or that which is now
translating, yea, until you have obtained
all which I shall grant unto the children
of men in this generation, and then shall
all things be added thereto.

23 Behold thou art Hyrum, my son;
seek the kingdom of God, and all things
shall be added according to that which
is just.

24 Build upon my rock, which is my
gospel;

25 Deny not the spirit of revelation, nor
the spirit of prophecy, for wo unto him
that denieth these things;

26 Therefore, treasure up in your heart
until the time which is in my wisdom
that you shall go forth.

27 Behold, I speak unto all who have
good desires, and have thrust in their
sickle to reap.

28 Behold, I am Jesus Christ, the Son
of God. I am the life and the light of the
world.

29 I am the same who came unto mine
own and mine own received me not;

30 But verily, verily, I say unto you, that
as many as receive me, to them will I
give power to become the sons of God,
even to them that believe on my name.
Amen.

Section 12

Revelation given through Joseph Smith the Prophet to Joseph Knight Sr., at Harmony, Pennsylvania, May 1829. Joseph Knight believed the declarations of Joseph Smith concerning his possession of the Book of Mormon plates and the work of translation then in progress and several times had given material assistance to Joseph Smith and his scribe, which enabled them to continue translating. At Joseph Knight's request, the Prophet inquired of the Lord and received the revelation.

1–6, Laborers in the vineyard are to gain salvation; 7–9, All who desire and are qualified may assist in the Lord's work.

1 A great and marvelous work is about to come forth among the children of men.

2 Behold, I am God; give heed to my word, which is quick and powerful, sharper than a two-edged sword, to the dividing asunder of both joints and marrow; therefore, give heed unto my word.

3 Behold, the field is white already to harvest; therefore, whoso desireth to reap let him thrust in his sickle with his might, and reap while the day lasts, that he may treasure up for his soul everlasting salvation in the kingdom of God.

4 Yea, whosoever will thrust in his sickle and reap, the same is called of God.

5 Therefore, if you will ask of me you shall receive; if you will knock it shall be opened unto you.

6 Now, as you have asked, behold, I say unto you, keep my commandments, and seek to bring forth and establish the cause of Zion.

7 Behold, I speak unto you, and also to all those who have desires to bring forth and establish this work;

8 And no one can assist in this work except he shall be humble and full of love, having faith, hope, and charity, being temperate in all things, whatsoever shall be entrusted to his care.

9 Behold, I am the light and the life of the world, that speak these words, therefore give heed with your might, and then you are called. Amen.

Section 13

An extract from Joseph Smith's history recounting the ordination of the Prophet and Oliver Cowdery to the Aaronic Priesthood near Harmony, Pennsylvania, May 15, 1829. The ordination was done by the hands of an angel who announced himself as John, the same that is called John the Baptist in the New Testament. The angel explained that he was acting under the direction of Peter, James, and John, the ancient Apostles, who held the keys of the higher priesthood, which was called the Priesthood of Melchizedek. The promise was given to Joseph and Oliver that in due time this higher priesthood would be conferred upon them. (See section 27:7–8, 12.)

The keys and powers of the Aaronic Priesthood are set forth.

1 Upon you my fellow servants, in the name of Messiah I confer the Priesthood of Aaron, which holds the keys of the ministering of angels, and of the gospel of repentance, and of baptism by immersion for the remission of sins; and this shall never be taken again from the earth, until the sons of Levi do offer again an offering unto the Lord in righteousness.

Section 14

Revelation given through Joseph Smith the Prophet to David Whitmer, at Fayette, New York, June 1829. The Whitmer family had become greatly interested in the translating of the Book of Mormon. The Prophet established his residence at the home of Peter Whitmer Sr., where he dwelt until the work of translation was carried to completion and the copyright on the forthcoming book was secured. Three of the Whitmer sons, each having received a testimony as to the genuineness of the work, became deeply concerned over the matter of their individual duty. This revelation and the two following (sections 15 and 16) were given in answer to an inquiry through the Urim and Thummim. David Whitmer later became one of the Three Witnesses to the Book of Mormon.

1–6, Laborers in the vineyard will gain salvation; 7–8, Eternal life is the greatest of God's gifts; 9–11, Christ created the heavens and the earth.

1 A great and marvelous work is about to come forth unto the children of men.

2 Behold, I am God; give heed to my word, which is quick and powerful, sharper than a two-edged sword, to the dividing asunder of both joints and marrow; therefore give heed unto my word.

3 Behold, the field is white already to harvest; therefore, whoso desireth to reap let him thrust in his sickle with his might, and reap while the day lasts, that he may treasure up for his soul everlasting salvation in the kingdom of God.

4 Yea, whosoever will thrust in his sickle and reap, the same is called of God.

5 Therefore, if you will ask of me you shall receive; if you will knock it shall be opened unto you.

6 Seek to bring forth and establish my Zion. Keep my commandments in all things.

7 And, if you keep my commandments and endure to the end you shall have eternal life, which gift is the greatest of all the gifts of God.

8 And it shall come to pass, that if you shall ask the Father in my name, in faith believing, you shall receive the Holy Ghost, which giveth utterance, that you may stand as a witness of the things of which you shall both hear and see, and also that you may declare repentance unto this generation.

9 Behold, I am Jesus Christ, the Son of the living God, who created the heavens and the earth, a light which cannot be hid in darkness;

10 Wherefore, I must bring forth the fulness of my gospel from the Gentiles unto the house of Israel.

11 And behold, thou art David, and thou art called to assist; which thing if ye do, and are faithful, ye shall be blessed both spiritually and temporally, and great shall be your reward. Amen.

Section 15

Revelation given through Joseph Smith the Prophet to John Whitmer, at Fayette, New York, June 1829 (see the heading to section 14). The message is intimately and impressively personal in that the Lord tells of what was known only to John Whitmer and Himself. John Whitmer later became one of the Eight Witnesses to the Book of Mormon.

1–2, The Lord's arm is over all the earth; 3–6, To preach the gospel and save souls is the thing of most worth.

1 Hearken, my servant John, and listen to the words of Jesus Christ, your Lord and your Redeemer.

2 For behold, I speak unto you with sharpness and with power, for mine arm is over all the earth.

3 And I will tell you that which no man knoweth save me and thee alone—

4 For many times you have desired of me to know that which would be of the most worth unto you.

5 Behold, blessed are you for this thing, and for speaking my words which I have given you according to my commandments.

6 And now, behold, I say unto you, that the thing which will be of the most worth unto you will be to declare repentance unto this people, that you may bring souls unto me, that you may rest with them in the kingdom of my Father. Amen.

Section 16

Revelation given through Joseph Smith the Prophet to Peter Whitmer Jr., at Fayette, New York, June 1829 (see the heading to section 14). Peter Whitmer Jr. later became one of the Eight Witnesses to the Book of Mormon.

1–2, The Lord's arm is over all the earth; 3–6, To preach the gospel and save souls is the thing of most worth.

1 Hearken, my servant Peter, and listen to the words of Jesus Christ, your Lord and your Redeemer.

2 For behold, I speak unto you with sharpness and with power, for mine arm is over all the earth.

3 And I will tell you that which no man knoweth save me and thee alone—

4 For many times you have desired of me to know that which would be of the most worth unto you.

5 Behold, blessed are you for this thing, and for speaking my words which I have given unto you according to my commandments.

6 And now, behold, I say unto you, that the thing which will be of the most worth unto you will be to declare repentance unto this people, that you may bring souls unto me, that you may rest with them in the kingdom of my Father. Amen.

Section 17

Revelation given through Joseph Smith the Prophet to Oliver Cowdery, David Whitmer, and Martin Harris, at Fayette, New York, June 1829, prior to their viewing the engraved plates that contained the Book of Mormon record. Joseph and his scribe, Oliver Cowdery, had learned from the translation of the Book of Mormon plates that three special witnesses would be designated (see Ether 5:2–4; 2 Nephi 11:3; 27:12). Oliver Cowdery, David Whitmer, and Martin Harris were moved upon by an inspired desire to be the three special witnesses. The Prophet inquired of the Lord, and this revelation was given in answer through the Urim and Thummim.

1–4, By faith the Three Witnesses will see the plates and other sacred items; 5–9, Christ bears testimony of the divinity of the Book of Mormon.

1 Behold, I say unto you, that you must rely upon my word, which if you do with full purpose of heart, you shall have a view of the plates, and also of the breastplate, the sword of Laban, the Urim and Thummim, which were given to the brother of Jared upon the mount, when he talked with the Lord face to face, and the miraculous directors which were given to Lehi while in the wilderness, on the borders of the Red Sea.

2 And it is by your faith that you shall obtain a view of them, even by that faith which was had by the prophets of old.

3 And after that you have obtained faith, and have seen them with your eyes, you shall testify of them, by the power of God;

4 And this you shall do that my servant Joseph Smith, Jun., may not be destroyed, that I may bring about my righteous purposes unto the children of men in this work.

5 And ye shall testify that you have seen them, even as my servant Joseph Smith, Jun., has seen them; for it is by my power that he has seen them, and it is because he had faith.

6 And he has translated the book, even that part which I have commanded him, and as your Lord and your God liveth it is true.

7 Wherefore, you have received the same power, and the same faith, and the same gift like unto him;

8 And if you do these last commandments of mine, which I have given you, the gates of hell shall not prevail against you; for my grace is sufficient for you, and you shall be lifted up at the last day.

9 And I, Jesus Christ, your Lord and your God, have spoken it unto you, that I might bring about my righteous purposes unto the children of men. Amen.

Section 18

Revelation to Joseph Smith the Prophet, Oliver Cowdery, and David Whitmer, given at Fayette, New York, June 1829. According to the Prophet, this revelation made known "the calling of twelve apostles in these last days, and also instructions relative to building up the Church."

1–5, Scriptures show how to build up the Church; 6–8, The world is ripening in iniquity; 9–16, The worth of souls is great; 17–25, To gain salvation, men must take upon themselves the name of Christ; 26–36, The calling and mission of the Twelve are revealed; 37–39, Oliver Cowdery and David Whitmer are to search out the Twelve; 40–47, To gain salvation, men must repent, be baptized, and keep the commandments.

1 Now, behold, because of the thing which you, my servant Oliver Cowdery, have desired to know of me, I give unto you these words:

2 Behold, I have manifested unto you, by my Spirit in many instances, that the things which you have written are true; wherefore you know that they are true.

3 And if you know that they are true, behold, I give unto you a commandment, that you rely upon the things which are written;

4 For in them are all things written concerning the foundation of my church, my gospel, and my rock.

5 Wherefore, if you shall build up my church, upon the foundation of my gospel and my rock, the gates of hell shall not prevail against you.

6 Behold, the world is ripening in iniquity; and it must needs be that the children of men are stirred up unto repentance, both the Gentiles and also the house of Israel.

7 Wherefore, as thou hast been baptized by the hands of my servant Joseph Smith, Jun., according to that which I have commanded him, he hath fulfilled the thing which I commanded him.

8 And now, marvel not that I have called him unto mine own purpose, which purpose is known in me; wherefore, if he shall be diligent in keeping my commandments he shall be blessed unto eternal life; and his name is Joseph.

9 And now, Oliver Cowdery, I speak unto you, and also unto David Whitmer, by the way of commandment; for, behold, I command all men everywhere to repent, and I speak unto you, even as unto Paul mine apostle, for you are called even with that same calling with which he was called.

10 Remember the worth of souls is great in the sight of God;

11 For, behold, the Lord your Redeemer suffered death in the flesh; wherefore he suffered the pain of all men, that all men might repent and come unto him.

12 And he hath risen again from the dead, that he might bring all men unto him, on conditions of repentance.

13 And how great is his joy in the soul that repenteth!

14 Wherefore, you are called to cry repentance unto this people.

15 And if it so be that you should labor all your days in crying repentance unto this people, and bring, save it be one soul unto me, how great shall be your joy with him in the kingdom of my Father!

16 And now, if your joy will be great with one soul that you have brought

unto me into the kingdom of my Father, how great will be your joy if you should bring many souls unto me!

17 Behold, you have my gospel before you, and my rock, and my salvation.

18 Ask the Father in my name in faith, believing that you shall receive, and you shall have the Holy Ghost, which manifesteth all things which are expedient unto the children of men.

19 And if you have not faith, hope, and charity, you can do nothing.

20 Contend against no church, save it be the church of the devil.

21 Take upon you the name of Christ, and speak the truth in soberness.

22 And as many as repent and are baptized in my name, which is Jesus Christ, and endure to the end, the same shall be saved.

23 Behold, Jesus Christ is the name which is given of the Father, and there is none other name given whereby man can be saved;

24 Wherefore, all men must take upon them the name which is given of the Father, for in that name shall they be called at the last day;

25 Wherefore, if they know not the name by which they are called, they cannot have place in the kingdom of my Father.

26 And now, behold, there are others who are called to declare my gospel, both unto Gentile and unto Jew;

27 Yea, even twelve; and the Twelve shall be my disciples, and they shall take upon them my name; and the Twelve are they who shall desire to take upon them my name with full purpose of heart.

28 And if they desire to take upon them my name with full purpose of heart, they are called to go into all the world to preach my gospel unto every creature.

29 And they are they who are ordained of me to baptize in my name, according to that which is written;

30 And you have that which is written before you; wherefore, you must perform it according to the words which are written.

31 And now I speak unto you, the Twelve—Behold, my grace is sufficient for you; you must walk uprightly before me and sin not.

32 And, behold, you are they who are ordained of me to ordain priests and teachers; to declare my gospel, according to the power of the Holy Ghost which is in you, and according to the callings and gifts of God unto men;

33 And I, Jesus Christ, your Lord and your God, have spoken it.

34 These words are not of men nor of man, but of me; wherefore, you shall testify they are of me and not of man;

35 For it is my voice which speaketh them unto you; for they are given by my Spirit unto you, and by my power you can read them one to another; and save it were by my power you could not have them;

36 Wherefore, you can testify that you have heard my voice, and know my words.

37 And now, behold, I give unto you, Oliver Cowdery, and also unto David Whitmer, that you shall search out the Twelve, who shall have the desires of which I have spoken;

38 And by their desires and their works you shall know them.

39 And when you have found them you shall show these things unto them.

40 And you shall fall down and worship the Father in my name.

41 And you must preach unto the world, saying: You must repent and be baptized, in the name of Jesus Christ;

42 For all men must repent and be baptized, and not only men, but women, and children who have arrived at the years of accountability.

43 And now, after that you have received this, you must keep my commandments in all things;

44 And by your hands I will work a marvelous work among the children of men, unto the convincing of many of their sins, that they may come unto repentance, and that they may come unto the kingdom of my Father.

45 Wherefore, the blessings which I give unto you are above all things.

46 And after that you have received this, if you keep not my commandments you cannot be saved in the kingdom of my Father.

47 Behold, I, Jesus Christ, your Lord and your God, and your Redeemer, by the power of my Spirit have spoken it. Amen.

Section 19

Revelation given through Joseph Smith, at Manchester, New York, likely in the summer of 1829. In his history, the Prophet introduces it as "a commandment of God and not of man, to Martin Harris, given by him who is Eternal."

1–3, Christ has all power; 4–5, All men must repent or suffer; 6–12, Eternal punishment is God's punishment; 13–20, Christ suffered for all, that they might not suffer if they would repent; 21–28, Preach the gospel of repentance; 29–41, Declare glad tidings.

1 I am Alpha and Omega, Christ the Lord; yea, even I am he, the beginning and the end, the Redeemer of the world.

2 I, having accomplished and finished the will of him whose I am, even the Father, concerning me—having done this that I might subdue all things unto myself—

3 Retaining all power, even to the destroying of Satan and his works at the end of the world, and the last great day of judgment, which I shall pass upon the inhabitants thereof, judging every man according to his works and the deeds which he hath done.

4 And surely every man must repent or suffer, for I, God, am endless.

5 Wherefore, I revoke not the judgments which I shall pass, but woes shall go forth, weeping, wailing and gnashing of teeth, yea, to those who are found on my left hand.

6 Nevertheless, it is not written that there shall be no end to this torment, but it is written endless torment.

7 Again, it is written eternal damnation; wherefore it is more express than other scriptures, that it might work upon the hearts of the children of men, altogether for my name's glory.

8 Wherefore, I will explain unto you this mystery, for it is meet unto you to know even as mine apostles.

9 I speak unto you that are chosen in this thing, even as one, that you may enter into my rest.

10 For, behold, the mystery of godliness, how great is it! For, behold, I am endless, and the punishment which is given from my hand is endless punishment, for Endless is my name. Wherefore—

11 Eternal punishment is God's punishment.

12 Endless punishment is God's punishment.

13 Wherefore, I command you to repent, and keep the commandments which you have received by the hand of my servant Joseph Smith, Jun., in my name;

14 And it is by my almighty power that you have received them;

15 Therefore I command you to repent—repent, lest I smite you by the rod of my mouth, and by my wrath, and by my anger, and your sufferings be sore—how sore you know not, how exquisite you know not, yea, how hard to bear you know not.

16 For behold, I, God, have suffered these things for all, that they might not suffer if they would repent;

17 But if they would not repent they must suffer even as I;

18 Which suffering caused myself, even God, the greatest of all, to tremble because of pain, and to bleed at every pore, and to suffer both body and

spirit—and would that I might not drink the bitter cup, and shrink—

19 Nevertheless, glory be to the Father, and I partook and finished my preparations unto the children of men.

20 Wherefore, I command you again to repent, lest I humble you with my almighty power; and that you confess your sins, lest you suffer these punishments of which I have spoken, of which in the smallest, yea, even in the least degree you have tasted at the time I withdrew my Spirit.

21 And I command you that you preach naught but repentance, and show not these things unto the world until it is wisdom in me.

22 For they cannot bear meat now, but milk they must receive; wherefore, they must not know these things, lest they perish.

23 Learn of me, and listen to my words; walk in the meekness of my Spirit, and you shall have peace in me.

24 I am Jesus Christ; I came by the will of the Father, and I do his will.

25 And again, I command thee that thou shalt not covet thy neighbor's wife; nor seek thy neighbor's life.

26 And again, I command thee that thou shalt not covet thine own property, but impart it freely to the printing of the Book of Mormon, which contains the truth and the word of God—

27 Which is my word to the Gentile, that soon it may go to the Jew, of whom the Lamanites are a remnant, that they may believe the gospel, and look not for a Messiah to come who has already come.

28 And again, I command thee that thou shalt pray vocally as well as in thy heart; yea, before the world as well as in secret, in public as well as in private.

29 And thou shalt declare glad tidings, yea, publish it upon the mountains, and upon every high place, and among every people that thou shalt be permitted to see.

30 And thou shalt do it with all humility, trusting in me, reviling not against revilers.

31 And of tenets thou shalt not talk, but thou shalt declare repentance and faith on the Savior, and remission of sins by baptism, and by fire, yea, even the Holy Ghost.

32 Behold, this is a great and the last commandment which I shall give unto you concerning this matter; for this shall suffice for thy daily walk, even unto the end of thy life.

33 And misery thou shalt receive if thou wilt slight these counsels, yea, even the destruction of thyself and property.

34 Impart a portion of thy property, yea, even part of thy lands, and all save the support of thy family.

35 Pay the debt thou hast contracted with the printer. Release thyself from bondage.

36 Leave thy house and home, except when thou shalt desire to see thy family;

37 And speak freely to all; yea, preach, exhort, declare the truth, even with a loud voice, with a sound of rejoicing, crying—Hosanna, hosanna, blessed be the name of the Lord God!

38 Pray always, and I will pour out my Spirit upon you, and great shall be your blessing—yea, even more than if you should obtain treasures of earth and corruptibleness to the extent thereof.

39 Behold, canst thou read this without
rejoicing and lifting up thy heart for
gladness?

40 Or canst thou run about longer as a
blind guide?

41 Or canst thou be humble and meek,
and conduct thyself wisely before me?
Yea, come unto me thy Savior. Amen.

Section 20

Revelation on Church organization and government, given through Joseph Smith the Prophet, at or near Fayette, New York. Portions of this revelation may have been given as early as summer 1829. The complete revelation, known at the time as the Articles and Covenants, was likely recorded soon after April 6, 1830 (the day the Church was organized). The Prophet wrote, "We obtained of Him [Jesus Christ] the following, by the spirit of prophecy and revelation; which not only gave us much information, but also pointed out to us the precise day upon which, according to His will and commandment, we should proceed to organize His Church once more here upon the earth."

1–16, The Book of Mormon proves the divinity of the latter-day work; 17–28, The doctrines of creation, fall, atonement, and baptism are affirmed; 29–37, Laws governing repentance, justification, sanctification, and baptism are set forth; 38–67, Duties of elders, priests, teachers, and deacons are summarized; 68–74, Duties of members, blessing of children, and the mode of baptism are revealed; 75–84, Sacramental prayers and regulations governing Church membership are given.

1 The rise of the Church of Christ in these last days, being one thousand eight hundred and thirty years since the coming of our Lord and Savior Jesus Christ in the flesh, it being regularly organized and established agreeable to the laws of our country, by the will and commandments of God, in the fourth month, and on the sixth day of the month which is called April—

2 Which commandments were given to Joseph Smith, Jun., who was called of God, and ordained an apostle of Jesus Christ, to be the first elder of this church;

3 And to Oliver Cowdery, who was also called of God, an apostle of Jesus Christ, to be the second elder of this church, and ordained under his hand;

4 And this according to the grace of our Lord and Savior Jesus Christ, to whom be all glory, both now and forever. Amen.

5 After it was truly manifested unto this first elder that he had received a remission of his sins, he was entangled again in the vanities of the world;

6 But after repenting, and humbling himself sincerely, through faith, God ministered unto him by an holy angel, whose countenance was as lightning, and whose garments were pure and white above all other whiteness;

7 And gave unto him commandments which inspired him;

8 And gave him power from on high, by the means which were before prepared, to translate the Book of Mormon;

9 Which contains a record of a fallen people, and the fulness of the gospel of Jesus Christ to the Gentiles and to the Jews also;

10 Which was given by inspiration, and is confirmed to others by the ministering of angels, and is declared unto the world by them—

11 Proving to the world that the holy scriptures are true, and that God does inspire men and call them to his holy work in this age and generation, as well as in generations of old;

12 Thereby showing that he is the same God yesterday, today, and forever. Amen.

13 Therefore, having so great witnesses, by them shall the world be judged, even as many as shall hereafter come to a knowledge of this work.

14 And those who receive it in faith, and work righteousness, shall receive a crown of eternal life;

15 But those who harden their hearts in unbelief, and reject it, it shall turn to their own condemnation—

16 For the Lord God has spoken it; and we, the elders of the church, have heard and bear witness to the words of the glorious Majesty on high, to whom be glory forever and ever. Amen.

17 By these things we know that there is a God in heaven, who is infinite and eternal, from everlasting to everlasting the same unchangeable God, the framer of heaven and earth, and all things which are in them;

18 And that he created man, male and female, after his own image and in his own likeness, created he them;

19 And gave unto them commandments that they should love and serve him, the only living and true God, and that he should be the only being whom they should worship.

20 But by the transgression of these holy laws man became sensual and devilish, and became fallen man.

21 Wherefore, the Almighty God gave his Only Begotten Son, as it is written in those scriptures which have been given of him.

22 He suffered temptations but gave no heed unto them.

23 He was crucified, died, and rose again the third day;

24 And ascended into heaven, to sit down on the right hand of the Father, to reign with almighty power according to the will of the Father;

25 That as many as would believe and be baptized in his holy name, and endure in faith to the end, should be saved—

26 Not only those who believed after he came in the meridian of time, in the flesh, but all those from the beginning, even as many as were before he came, who believed in the words of the holy prophets, who spake as they were inspired by the gift of the Holy Ghost, who truly testified of him in all things, should have eternal life,

27 As well as those who should come after, who should believe in the gifts and callings of God by the Holy Ghost, which beareth record of the Father and of the Son;

28 Which Father, Son, and Holy Ghost are one God, infinite and eternal, without end. Amen.

29 And we know that all men must repent and believe on the name of Jesus Christ, and worship the Father in his name, and endure in faith on his name to the end, or they cannot be saved in the kingdom of God.

30 And we know that justification through the grace of our Lord and Savior Jesus Christ is just and true;

31 And we know also, that sanctification through the grace of our Lord and Savior Jesus Christ is just and true, to all those who love and serve God with all their mights, minds, and strength.

32 But there is a possibility that man may fall from grace and depart from the living God;

33 Therefore let the church take heed and pray always, lest they fall into temptation;

34 Yea, and even let those who are sanctified take heed also.

35 And we know that these things are true and according to the revelations of John, neither adding to, nor diminishing from the prophecy of his book, the holy scriptures, or the revelations of God which shall come hereafter by the gift and power of the Holy Ghost, the voice of God, or the ministering of angels.

36 And the Lord God has spoken it; and honor, power and glory be rendered to his holy name, both now and ever. Amen.

37 And again, by way of commandment to the church concerning the manner of baptism—All those who humble themselves before God, and desire to be baptized, and come forth with broken hearts and contrite spirits, and witness before the church that they have truly repented of all their sins, and are willing to take upon them the name of Jesus Christ, having a determination to serve him to the end, and truly manifest by their works that they have received of the Spirit of Christ unto the remission of their sins, shall be received by baptism into his church.

38 The duty of the elders, priests, teachers, deacons, and members of the church of Christ—An apostle is an elder, and it is his calling to baptize;

39 And to ordain other elders, priests, teachers, and deacons;

40 And to administer bread and wine—the emblems of the flesh and blood of Christ—

41 And to confirm those who are baptized into the church, by the laying on of hands for the baptism of fire and the Holy Ghost, according to the scriptures;

42 And to teach, expound, exhort, baptize, and watch over the church;

43 And to confirm the church by the laying on of the hands, and the giving of the Holy Ghost;

44 And to take the lead of all meetings.

45 The elders are to conduct the meetings as they are led by the Holy Ghost, according to the commandments and revelations of God.

46 The priest's duty is to preach, teach, expound, exhort, and baptize, and administer the sacrament,

47 And visit the house of each member, and exhort them to pray vocally and in secret and attend to all family duties.

48 And he may also ordain other priests, teachers, and deacons.

49 And he is to take the lead of meetings when there is no elder present;

50 But when there is an elder present, he is only to preach, teach, expound, exhort, and baptize,

51 And visit the house of each member, exhorting them to pray vocally and in secret and attend to all family duties.

52 In all these duties the priest is to assist the elder if occasion requires.

53 The teacher's duty is to watch over the church always, and be with and strengthen them;

54 And see that there is no iniquity in the church, neither hardness with each other, neither lying, backbiting, nor evil speaking;

55 And see that the church meet together often, and also see that all the members do their duty.

56 And he is to take the lead of meetings in the absence of the elder or priest—

57 And is to be assisted always, in all his duties in the church, by the deacons, if occasion requires.

58 But neither teachers nor deacons have authority to baptize, administer the sacrament, or lay on hands;

59 They are, however, to warn, expound, exhort, and teach, and invite all to come unto Christ.

60 Every elder, priest, teacher, or deacon is to be ordained according to the gifts and callings of God unto him; and he is to be ordained by the power of the Holy Ghost, which is in the one who ordains him.

61 The several elders composing this church of Christ are to meet in conference once in three months, or from time to time as said conferences shall direct or appoint;

62 And said conferences are to do whatever church business is necessary to be done at the time.

63 The elders are to receive their licenses from other elders, by vote of the church to which they belong, or from the conferences.

64 Each priest, teacher, or deacon, who is ordained by a priest, may take a certificate from him at the time, which certificate, when presented to an elder, shall entitle him to a license, which shall authorize him to perform the duties of his calling, or he may receive it from a conference.

65 No person is to be ordained to any office in this church, where there is a regularly organized branch of the same, without the vote of that church;

66 But the presiding elders, traveling bishops, high councilors, high priests, and elders, may have the privilege of ordaining, where there is no branch of the church that a vote may be called.

67 Every president of the high priesthood (or presiding elder), bishop, high councilor, and high priest, is to be ordained by the direction of a high council or general conference.

68 The duty of the members after they are received by baptism—The elders or priests are to have a sufficient time to expound all things concerning the church of Christ to their understanding, previous to their partaking of the sacrament and being confirmed by the laying on of the hands of the elders, so that all things may be done in order.

69 And the members shall manifest before the church, and also before the elders, by a godly walk and conversation, that they are worthy of it, that there may be works and faith agreeable to the holy scriptures—walking in holiness before the Lord.

70 Every member of the church of Christ having children is to bring them unto the elders before the church, who are to lay their hands upon them in the name of Jesus Christ, and bless them in his name.

71 No one can be received into the church of Christ unless he has arrived unto the years of accountability before God, and is capable of repentance.

72 Baptism is to be administered in the following manner unto all those who repent—

73 The person who is called of God and has authority from Jesus Christ to baptize, shall go down into the water with the person who has presented himself or herself for baptism, and shall say, calling him or her by name: Having been commissioned of Jesus Christ, I baptize you in the name of the Father, and of the Son, and of the Holy Ghost. Amen.

74 Then shall he immerse him or her in the water, and come forth again out of the water.

75 It is expedient that the church meet together often to partake of bread and wine in the remembrance of the Lord Jesus;

76 And the elder or priest shall administer it; and after this manner shall he administer it—he shall kneel with the church and call upon the Father in solemn prayer, saying:

77 O God, the Eternal Father, we ask thee in the name of thy Son, Jesus Christ, to bless and sanctify this bread to the souls of all those who partake of it, that they may eat in remembrance of the body of thy Son, and witness unto thee, O God, the Eternal Father, that they are willing to take upon them the name of thy Son, and always remember him and keep his commandments which he has given them; that they may always have his Spirit to be with them. Amen.

78 The manner of administering the wine—he shall take the cup also, and say:

79 O God, the Eternal Father, we ask thee in the name of thy Son, Jesus Christ, to bless and sanctify this wine to the souls of all those who drink of it, that they may do it in remembrance of the blood of thy Son, which was shed for them; that they may witness unto thee, O God, the Eternal Father, that they do always remember him, that they may have his Spirit to be with them. Amen.

80 Any member of the church of Christ transgressing, or being overtaken in a fault, shall be dealt with as the scriptures direct.

81 It shall be the duty of the several churches, composing the church of Christ, to send one or more of their teachers to attend the several conferences held by the elders of the church,

82 With a list of the names of the several members uniting themselves with the church since the last conference; or send by the hand of some priest; so that a regular list of all the names of the whole church may be kept in a book by one of the elders, whomsoever the other elders shall appoint from time to time;

83 And also, if any have been expelled from the church, so that their names may be blotted out of the general church record of names.

84 All members removing from the church where they reside, if going to a church where they are not known, may take a letter certifying that they are regular members and in good standing, which certificate may be signed by any elder or priest if the member receiving the letter is personally acquainted with the elder or priest, or it may be signed by the teachers or deacons of the church.

Section 21

Revelation given to Joseph Smith the Prophet, at Fayette, New York, April 6, 1830. This revelation was given at the organization of the Church, on the date named, in the home of Peter Whitmer Sr. Six men, who had previously been baptized, participated. By unanimous vote these persons expressed their desire and determination to organize, according to the commandment of God (see section 20). They also voted to accept and sustain Joseph Smith Jr. and Oliver Cowdery as the presiding officers of the Church. With the laying on of hands, Joseph then ordained Oliver an elder of the Church, and Oliver similarly ordained Joseph. After administration of the sacrament, Joseph and Oliver laid hands upon the participants individually for the bestowal of the Holy Ghost and for the confirmation of each as a member of the Church.

1–3, Joseph Smith is called to be a seer, translator, prophet, apostle, and elder; 4–8, His word will guide the cause of Zion; 9–12, The Saints will believe his words as he speaks by the Comforter.

1 Behold, there shall be a record kept among you; and in it thou shalt be called a seer, a translator, a prophet, an apostle of Jesus Christ, an elder of the church through the will of God the Father, and the grace of your Lord Jesus Christ,

2 Being inspired of the Holy Ghost to lay the foundation thereof, and to build it up unto the most holy faith.

3 Which church was organized and established in the year of your Lord eighteen hundred and thirty, in the fourth month, and on the sixth day of the month which is called April.

4 Wherefore, meaning the church, thou shalt give heed unto all his words and commandments which he shall give unto you as he receiveth them, walking in all holiness before me;

5 For his word ye shall receive, as if from mine own mouth, in all patience and faith.

6 For by doing these things the gates of hell shall not prevail against you; yea, and the Lord God will disperse the powers of darkness from before you, and cause the heavens to shake for your good, and his name's glory.

7 For thus saith the Lord God: Him have I inspired to move the cause of Zion in mighty power for good, and his diligence I know, and his prayers I have heard.

8 Yea, his weeping for Zion I have seen, and I will cause that he shall mourn for her no longer; for his days of rejoicing are come unto the remission of his sins, and the manifestations of my blessings upon his works.

9 For, behold, I will bless all those who labor in my vineyard with a mighty blessing, and they shall believe on his words, which are given him through me by the Comforter, which manifesteth that Jesus was crucified by sinful men for the sins of the world, yea, for the remission of sins unto the contrite heart.

10 Wherefore it behooveth me that he should be ordained by you, Oliver Cowdery mine apostle;

11 This being an ordinance unto you, that you are an elder under his hand, he being the first unto you, that you might be an elder unto this church of Christ, bearing my name—

12 And the first preacher of this church unto the church, and before the world, yea, before the Gentiles; yea, and thus saith the Lord God, lo, lo! to the Jews also. Amen.

Section 22

Revelation given through Joseph Smith the Prophet, at Manchester, New York, April 16, 1830. This revelation was given to the Church in consequence of some who had previously been baptized desiring to unite with the Church without rebaptism.

1, Baptism is a new and everlasting covenant; 2–4, Authoritative baptism is required.

1 Behold, I say unto you that all old covenants have I caused to be done away in this thing; and this is a new and an everlasting covenant, even that which was from the beginning.

2 Wherefore, although a man should be baptized an hundred times it availeth him nothing, for you cannot enter in at the strait gate by the law of Moses, neither by your dead works.

3 For it is because of your dead works that I have caused this last covenant and this church to be built up unto me, even as in days of old.

4 Wherefore, enter ye in at the gate, as I have commanded, and seek not to counsel your God. Amen.

Section 23

A series of five revelations given through Joseph Smith the Prophet, at Manchester, New York, April 1830, to Oliver Cowdery, Hyrum Smith, Samuel H. Smith, Joseph Smith Sr., and Joseph Knight Sr. As the result of earnest desire on the part of the five persons named to know of their respective duties, the Prophet inquired of the Lord and received a revelation for each person.

1–7, These early disciples are called to preach, exhort, and strengthen the Church.

1 Behold, I speak unto you, Oliver, a few words. Behold, thou art blessed, and art under no condemnation. But beware of pride, lest thou shouldst enter into temptation.

2 Make known thy calling unto the church, and also before the world, and thy heart shall be opened to preach the truth from henceforth and forever. Amen.

3 Behold, I speak unto you, Hyrum, a few words; for thou also art under no condemnation, and thy heart is opened, and thy tongue loosed; and thy calling is to exhortation, and to strengthen the church continually. Wherefore thy duty is unto the church forever, and this because of thy family. Amen.

4 Behold, I speak a few words unto you, Samuel; for thou also art under no condemnation, and thy calling is to exhortation, and to strengthen the church; and thou art not as yet called to preach before the world. Amen.

5 Behold, I speak a few words unto you, Joseph; for thou also art under no condemnation, and thy calling also is to exhortation, and to strengthen the church; and this is thy duty from henceforth and forever. Amen.

6 Behold, I manifest unto you, Joseph Knight, by these words, that you must take up your cross, in the which you must pray vocally before the world as well as in secret, and in your family, and among your friends, and in all places.

7 And, behold, it is your duty to unite with the true church, and give your language to exhortation continually, that you may receive the reward of the laborer. Amen.

Section 24

Revelation given to Joseph Smith the Prophet and Oliver Cowdery, at Harmony, Pennsylvania, July 1830. Though less than four months had elapsed since the Church was organized, persecution had become intense, and the leaders had to seek safety in partial seclusion. The following three revelations were given at this time to strengthen, encourage, and instruct them.

1–9, Joseph Smith is called to translate, preach, and expound scriptures; 10–12, Oliver Cowdery is called to preach the gospel; 13–19, The law is revealed relative to miracles, cursings, casting off the dust of one's feet, and going without purse or scrip.

1 Behold, thou wast called and chosen to write the Book of Mormon, and to my ministry; and I have lifted thee up out of thine afflictions, and have counseled thee, that thou hast been delivered from all thine enemies, and thou hast been delivered from the powers of Satan and from darkness!

2 Nevertheless, thou art not excusable in thy transgressions; nevertheless, go thy way and sin no more.

3 Magnify thine office; and after thou hast sowed thy fields and secured them, go speedily unto the church which is in Colesville, Fayette, and Manchester, and they shall support thee; and I will bless them both spiritually and temporally;

4 But if they receive thee not, I will send upon them a cursing instead of a blessing.

5 And thou shalt continue in calling upon God in my name, and writing the things which shall be given thee by the Comforter, and expounding all scriptures unto the church.

6 And it shall be given thee in the very moment what thou shalt speak and write, and they shall hear it, or I will send unto them a cursing instead of a blessing.

7 For thou shalt devote all thy service in Zion; and in this thou shalt have strength.

8 Be patient in afflictions, for thou shalt have many; but endure them, for, lo, I am with thee, even unto the end of thy days.

9 And in temporal labors thou shalt not have strength, for this is not thy calling. Attend to thy calling and thou shalt have wherewith to magnify thine office, and to expound all scriptures, and continue in laying on of the hands and confirming the churches.

10 And thy brother Oliver shall continue in bearing my name before the world, and also to the church. And he shall not suppose that he can say enough in my cause; and lo, I am with him to the end.

11 In me he shall have glory, and not of himself, whether in weakness or in strength, whether in bonds or free;

12 And at all times, and in all places, he shall open his mouth and declare my gospel as with the voice of a trump, both day and night. And I will give unto him strength such as is not known among men.

13 Require not miracles, except I shall command you, except casting out devils, healing the sick, and against poisonous serpents, and against deadly poisons;

14 And these things ye shall not do, except it be required of you by them who desire it, that the scriptures might be fulfilled; for ye shall do according to that which is written.

15 And in whatsoever place ye shall enter, and they receive you not in my

name, ye shall leave a cursing instead of a blessing, by casting off the dust of your feet against them as a testimony, and cleansing your feet by the wayside.

16 And it shall come to pass that whosoever shall lay their hands upon you by violence, ye shall command to be smitten in my name; and, behold, I will smite them according to your words, in mine own due time.

17 And whosoever shall go to law with thee shall be cursed by the law.

18 And thou shalt take no purse nor scrip, neither staves, neither two coats, for the church shall give unto thee in the very hour what thou needest for food and for raiment, and for shoes and for money, and for scrip.

19 For thou art called to prune my vineyard with a mighty pruning, yea, even for the last time; yea, and also all those whom thou hast ordained, and they shall do even according to this pattern. Amen.

Section 25

Revelation given through Joseph Smith the Prophet, at Harmony, Pennsylvania, July 1830 (see the heading to section 24). This revelation manifests the will of the Lord to Emma Smith, the Prophet's wife.

1–6, Emma Smith, an elect lady, is called to aid and comfort her husband; 7–11, She is also called to write, to expound scriptures, and to select hymns; 12–14, The song of the righteous is a prayer unto the Lord; 15–16, Principles of obedience in this revelation are applicable to all.

1 Hearken unto the voice of the Lord your God, while I speak unto you, Emma Smith, my daughter; for verily I say unto you, all those who receive my gospel are sons and daughters in my kingdom.

2 A revelation I give unto you concerning my will; and if thou art faithful and walk in the paths of virtue before me, I will preserve thy life, and thou shalt receive an inheritance in Zion.

3 Behold, thy sins are forgiven thee, and thou art an elect lady, whom I have called.

4 Murmur not because of the things which thou hast not seen, for they are withheld from thee and from the world, which is wisdom in me in a time to come.

5 And the office of thy calling shall be for a comfort unto my servant, Joseph Smith, Jun., thy husband, in his afflictions, with consoling words, in the spirit of meekness.

6 And thou shalt go with him at the time of his going, and be unto him for a scribe, while there is no one to be a scribe for him, that I may send my servant, Oliver Cowdery, whithersoever I will.

7 And thou shalt be ordained under his hand to expound scriptures, and to exhort the church, according as it shall be given thee by my Spirit.

8 For he shall lay his hands upon thee, and thou shalt receive the Holy Ghost, and thy time shall be given to writing, and to learning much.

9 And thou needest not fear, for thy husband shall support thee in the church; for unto them is his calling, that all things might be revealed unto them, whatsoever I will, according to their faith.

10 And verily I say unto thee that thou shalt lay aside the things of this world, and seek for the things of a better.

11 And it shall be given thee, also, to make a selection of sacred hymns, as it shall be given thee, which is pleasing unto me, to be had in my church.

12 For my soul delighteth in the song of the heart; yea, the song of the righteous is a prayer unto me, and it shall be answered with a blessing upon their heads.

13 Wherefore, lift up thy heart and rejoice, and cleave unto the covenants which thou hast made.

14 Continue in the spirit of meekness, and beware of pride. Let thy soul delight in thy husband, and the glory which shall come upon him.

15 Keep my commandments continually, and a crown of righteousness thou shalt receive. And except thou do this, where I am you cannot come.

16 And verily, verily, I say unto you, that this is my voice unto all. Amen.

Section 26

Revelation given to Joseph Smith the Prophet, Oliver Cowdery, and John Whitmer, at Harmony, Pennsylvania, July 1830 (see the heading to section 24).

1, They are instructed to study the scriptures and to preach; 2, The law of common consent is affirmed.

1 Behold, I say unto you that you shall let your time be devoted to the studying of the scriptures, and to preaching, and to confirming the church at Colesville, and to performing your labors on the land, such as is required, until after you shall go to the west to hold the next conference; and then it shall be made known what you shall do.

2 And all things shall be done by common consent in the church, by much prayer and faith, for all things you shall receive by faith. Amen.

Section 27

Revelation given to Joseph Smith the Prophet, at Harmony, Pennsylvania, August 1830. In preparation for a religious service at which the sacrament of bread and wine was to be administered, Joseph set out to procure wine. He was met by a heavenly messenger and received this revelation, a portion of which was written at the time and the remainder in the September following. Water is now used instead of wine in the sacramental services of the Church.

1–4, The emblems to be used in partaking of the sacrament are set forth; 5–14, Christ and His servants from all dispensations are to partake of the sacrament; 15–18, Put on the whole armor of God.

1 Listen to the voice of Jesus Christ, your Lord, your God, and your Redeemer, whose word is quick and powerful.

2 For, behold, I say unto you, that it mattereth not what ye shall eat or what ye shall drink when ye partake of the sacrament, if it so be that ye do it with an eye single to my glory—remembering unto the Father my body which was laid down for you, and my blood which was shed for the remission of your sins.

3 Wherefore, a commandment I give unto you, that you shall not purchase wine neither strong drink of your enemies;

4 Wherefore, you shall partake of none except it is made new among you; yea, in this my Father's kingdom which shall be built up on the earth.

5 Behold, this is wisdom in me; wherefore, marvel not, for the hour cometh that I will drink of the fruit of the vine with you on the earth, and with Moroni, whom I have sent unto you to reveal the Book of Mormon, containing the fulness of my everlasting gospel, to whom I have committed the keys of the record of the stick of Ephraim;

6 And also with Elias, to whom I have committed the keys of bringing to pass the restoration of all things spoken by the mouth of all the holy prophets since the world began, concerning the last days;

7 And also John the son of Zacharias, which Zacharias he (Elias) visited and gave promise that he should have a son, and his name should be John, and he should be filled with the spirit of Elias;

8 Which John I have sent unto you, my servants, Joseph Smith, Jun., and Oliver Cowdery, to ordain you unto the first priesthood which you have received, that you might be called and ordained even as Aaron;

9 And also Elijah, unto whom I have committed the keys of the power of turning the hearts of the fathers to the children, and the hearts of the children to the fathers, that the whole earth may not be smitten with a curse;

10 And also with Joseph and Jacob, and Isaac, and Abraham, your fathers, by whom the promises remain;

11 And also with Michael, or Adam, the father of all, the prince of all, the ancient of days;

12 And also with Peter, and James, and John, whom I have sent unto you, by whom I have ordained you and confirmed you to be apostles, and especial witnesses of my name, and bear the keys of your ministry and of the same things which I revealed unto them;

13 Unto whom I have committed the keys of my kingdom, and a dispensation of the gospel for the last times; and for the fulness of times, in the which I will

gather together in one all things, both which are in heaven, and which are on earth;

14 And also with all those whom my Father hath given me out of the world.

15 Wherefore, lift up your hearts and rejoice, and gird up your loins, and take upon you my whole armor, that ye may be able to withstand the evil day, having done all, that ye may be able to stand.

16 Stand, therefore, having your loins girt about with truth, having on the breastplate of righteousness, and your feet shod with the preparation of the gospel of peace, which I have sent mine angels to commit unto you;

17 Taking the shield of faith wherewith ye shall be able to quench all the fiery darts of the wicked;

18 And take the helmet of salvation, and the sword of my Spirit, which I will pour out upon you, and my word which I reveal unto you, and be agreed as touching all things whatsoever ye ask of me, and be faithful until I come, and ye shall be caught up, that where I am ye shall be also. Amen.

Section 28

Revelation given through Joseph Smith the Prophet to Oliver Cowdery, at Fayette, New York, September 1830. Hiram Page, a member of the Church, had a certain stone and professed to be receiving revelations by its aid concerning the upbuilding of Zion and the order of the Church. Several members had been deceived by these claims, and even Oliver Cowdery was wrongly influenced thereby. Just prior to an appointed conference, the Prophet inquired earnestly of the Lord concerning the matter, and this revelation followed.

1–7, Joseph Smith holds the keys of the mysteries, and only he receives revelations for the Church; 8–10, Oliver Cowdery is to preach to the Lamanites; 11–16, Satan deceived Hiram Page and gave him false revelations.

1 Behold, I say unto thee, Oliver, that it shall be given unto thee that thou shalt be heard by the church in all things whatsoever thou shalt teach them by the Comforter, concerning the revelations and commandments which I have given.

2 But, behold, verily, verily, I say unto thee, no one shall be appointed to receive commandments and revelations in this church excepting my servant Joseph Smith, Jun., for he receiveth them even as Moses.

3 And thou shalt be obedient unto the things which I shall give unto him, even as Aaron, to declare faithfully the commandments and the revelations, with power and authority unto the church.

4 And if thou art led at any time by the Comforter to speak or teach, or at all times by the way of commandment unto the church, thou mayest do it.

5 But thou shalt not write by way of commandment, but by wisdom;

6 And thou shalt not command him who is at thy head, and at the head of the church;

7 For I have given him the keys of the mysteries, and the revelations which are sealed, until I shall appoint unto them another in his stead.

8 And now, behold, I say unto you that you shall go unto the Lamanites and preach my gospel unto them; and inasmuch as they receive thy teachings thou shalt cause my church to be established among them; and thou shalt have revelations, but write them not by way of commandment.

9 And now, behold, I say unto you that it is not revealed, and no man knoweth where the city Zion shall be built, but it shall be given hereafter. Behold, I say unto you that it shall be on the borders by the Lamanites.

10 Thou shalt not leave this place until after the conference; and my servant Joseph shall be appointed to preside over the conference by the voice of it, and what he saith to thee thou shalt tell.

11 And again, thou shalt take thy brother, Hiram Page, between him and thee alone, and tell him that those things which he hath written from that stone are not of me and that Satan deceiveth him;

12 For, behold, these things have not been appointed unto him, neither shall anything be appointed unto any of this church contrary to the church covenants.

13 For all things must be done in order, and by common consent in the church, by the prayer of faith.

14 And thou shalt assist to settle all these things, according to the covenants

of the church, before thou shalt take thy journey among the Lamanites.

15 And it shall be given thee from the time thou shalt go, until the time thou shalt return, what thou shalt do.

16 And thou must open thy mouth at all times, declaring my gospel with the sound of rejoicing. Amen.

Section 29

Revelation given through Joseph Smith the Prophet, in the presence of six elders, at Fayette, New York, September 1830. This revelation was given some days prior to the conference, beginning September 26, 1830.

1–8, Christ gathers His elect; 9–11, His coming ushers in the Millennium; 12–13, The Twelve will judge all Israel; 14–21, Signs, plagues, and desolations will precede the Second Coming; 22–28, The last resurrection and final judgment follow the Millennium; 29–35, All things are spiritual unto the Lord; 36–39, The devil and his hosts were cast out of heaven to tempt man; 40–45, The Fall and Atonement bring salvation; 46–50, Little children are redeemed through the Atonement.

1 Listen to the voice of Jesus Christ, your Redeemer, the Great I AM, whose arm of mercy hath atoned for your sins;

2 Who will gather his people even as a hen gathereth her chickens under her wings, even as many as will hearken to my voice and humble themselves before me, and call upon me in mighty prayer.

3 Behold, verily, verily, I say unto you, that at this time your sins are forgiven you, therefore ye receive these things; but remember to sin no more, lest perils shall come upon you.

4 Verily, I say unto you that ye are chosen out of the world to declare my gospel with the sound of rejoicing, as with the voice of a trump.

5 Lift up your hearts and be glad, for I am in your midst, and am your advocate with the Father; and it is his good will to give you the kingdom.

6 And, as it is written—Whatsoever ye shall ask in faith, being united in prayer according to my command, ye shall receive.

7 And ye are called to bring to pass the gathering of mine elect; for mine elect hear my voice and harden not their hearts;

8 Wherefore the decree hath gone forth from the Father that they shall be gathered in unto one place upon the face of this land, to prepare their hearts and be prepared in all things against the day when tribulation and desolation are sent forth upon the wicked.

9 For the hour is nigh and the day soon at hand when the earth is ripe; and all the proud and they that do wickedly shall be as stubble; and I will burn them up, saith the Lord of Hosts, that wickedness shall not be upon the earth;

10 For the hour is nigh, and that which was spoken by mine apostles must be fulfilled; for as they spoke so shall it come to pass;

11 For I will reveal myself from heaven with power and great glory, with all the hosts thereof, and dwell in righteousness with men on earth a thousand years, and the wicked shall not stand.

12 And again, verily, verily, I say unto you, and it hath gone forth in a firm decree, by the will of the Father, that mine apostles, the Twelve which were with me in my ministry at Jerusalem, shall stand at my right hand at the day of my coming in a pillar of fire, being clothed with robes of righteousness, with crowns upon their heads, in glory even as I am, to judge the whole house of Israel, even as many as have loved me and kept my commandments, and none else.

13 For a trump shall sound both long and loud, even as upon Mount Sinai, and all the earth shall quake, and they shall come forth—yea, even the dead which died in me, to receive a crown of

righteousness, and to be clothed upon, even as I am, to be with me, that we may be one.

14 But, behold, I say unto you that before this great day shall come the sun shall be darkened, and the moon shall be turned into blood, and the stars shall fall from heaven, and there shall be greater signs in heaven above and in the earth beneath;

15 And there shall be weeping and wailing among the hosts of men;

16 And there shall be a great hailstorm sent forth to destroy the crops of the earth.

17 And it shall come to pass, because of the wickedness of the world, that I will take vengeance upon the wicked, for they will not repent; for the cup of mine indignation is full; for behold, my blood shall not cleanse them if they hear me not.

18 Wherefore, I the Lord God will send forth flies upon the face of the earth, which shall take hold of the inhabitants thereof, and shall eat their flesh, and shall cause maggots to come in upon them;

19 And their tongues shall be stayed that they shall not utter against me; and their flesh shall fall from off their bones, and their eyes from their sockets;

20 And it shall come to pass that the beasts of the forest and the fowls of the air shall devour them up.

21 And the great and abominable church, which is the whore of all the earth, shall be cast down by devouring fire, according as it is spoken by the mouth of Ezekiel the prophet, who spoke of these things, which have not come to pass but surely must, as I live, for abominations shall not reign.

22 And again, verily, verily, I say unto you that when the thousand years are ended, and men again begin to deny their God, then will I spare the earth but for a little season;

23 And the end shall come, and the heaven and the earth shall be consumed and pass away, and there shall be a new heaven and a new earth.

24 For all old things shall pass away, and all things shall become new, even the heaven and the earth, and all the fulness thereof, both men and beasts, the fowls of the air, and the fishes of the sea;

25 And not one hair, neither mote, shall be lost, for it is the workmanship of mine hand.

26 But, behold, verily I say unto you, before the earth shall pass away, Michael, mine archangel, shall sound his trump, and then shall all the dead awake, for their graves shall be opened, and they shall come forth—yea, even all.

27 And the righteous shall be gathered on my right hand unto eternal life; and the wicked on my left hand will I be ashamed to own before the Father;

28 Wherefore I will say unto them—Depart from me, ye cursed, into everlasting fire, prepared for the devil and his angels.

29 And now, behold, I say unto you, never at any time have I declared from mine own mouth that they should return, for where I am they cannot come, for they have no power.

30 But remember that all my judgments are not given unto men; and as the words have gone forth out of my mouth even so shall they be fulfilled, that the first shall be last, and that the last shall be first in all things whatsoever I have created by the word of my power, which

is the power of my Spirit.

31 For by the power of my Spirit created I them; yea, all things both spiritual and temporal—

32 First spiritual, secondly temporal, which is the beginning of my work; and again, first temporal, and secondly spiritual, which is the last of my work—

33 Speaking unto you that you may naturally understand; but unto myself my works have no end, neither beginning; but it is given unto you that ye may understand, because ye have asked it of me and are agreed.

34 Wherefore, verily I say unto you that all things unto me are spiritual, and not at any time have I given unto you a law which was temporal; neither any man, nor the children of men; neither Adam, your father, whom I created.

35 Behold, I gave unto him that he should be an agent unto himself; and I gave unto him commandment, but no temporal commandment gave I unto him, for my commandments are spiritual; they are not natural nor temporal, neither carnal nor sensual.

36 And it came to pass that Adam, being tempted of the devil—for, behold, the devil was before Adam, for he rebelled against me, saying, Give me thine honor, which is my power; and also a third part of the hosts of heaven turned he away from me because of their agency;

37 And they were thrust down, and thus came the devil and his angels;

38 And, behold, there is a place prepared for them from the beginning, which place is hell.

39 And it must needs be that the devil should tempt the children of men, or they could not be agents unto themselves; for if they never should have bitter they could not know the sweet—

40 Wherefore, it came to pass that the devil tempted Adam, and he partook of the forbidden fruit and transgressed the commandment, wherein he became subject to the will of the devil, because he yielded unto temptation.

41 Wherefore, I, the Lord God, caused that he should be cast out from the Garden of Eden, from my presence, because of his transgression, wherein he became spiritually dead, which is the first death, even that same death which is the last death, which is spiritual, which shall be pronounced upon the wicked when I shall say: Depart, ye cursed.

42 But, behold, I say unto you that I, the Lord God, gave unto Adam and unto his seed, that they should not die as to the temporal death, until I, the Lord God, should send forth angels to declare unto them repentance and redemption, through faith on the name of mine Only Begotten Son.

43 And thus did I, the Lord God, appoint unto man the days of his probation—that by his natural death he might be raised in immortality unto eternal life, even as many as would believe;

44 And they that believe not unto eternal damnation; for they cannot be redeemed from their spiritual fall, because they repent not;

45 For they love darkness rather than light, and their deeds are evil, and they receive their wages of whom they list to obey.

46 But behold, I say unto you, that little children are redeemed from the foundation of the world through mine Only Begotten;

47 Wherefore, they cannot sin, for
power is not given unto Satan to tempt
little children, until they begin to
become accountable before me;

48 For it is given unto them even as I
will, according to mine own pleasure,
that great things may be required at the
hand of their fathers.

49 And, again, I say unto you, that
whoso having knowledge, have I not
commanded to repent?

50 And he that hath no understanding,
it remaineth in me to do according as it
is written. And now I declare no more
unto you at this time. Amen.

Section 30

Revelation given through Joseph Smith the Prophet to David Whitmer, Peter Whitmer Jr., and John Whitmer, at Fayette, New York, September 1830, following the three-day conference at Fayette, but before the elders of the Church had separated. Originally this material was published as three revelations; it was combined into one section by the Prophet for the 1835 edition of the Doctrine and Covenants.

1–4, David Whitmer is chastened for failure to serve diligently; 5–8, Peter Whitmer Jr. is to accompany Oliver Cowdery on a mission to the Lamanites; 9–11, John Whitmer is called to preach the gospel.

1 Behold, I say unto you, David, that you have feared man and have not relied on me for strength as you ought.

2 But your mind has been on the things of the earth more than on the things of me, your Maker, and the ministry whereunto you have been called; and you have not given heed unto my Spirit, and to those who were set over you, but have been persuaded by those whom I have not commanded.

3 Wherefore, you are left to inquire for yourself at my hand, and ponder upon the things which you have received.

4 And your home shall be at your father's house, until I give unto you further commandments. And you shall attend to the ministry in the church, and before the world, and in the regions round about. Amen.

5 Behold, I say unto you, Peter, that you shall take your journey with your brother Oliver; for the time has come that it is expedient in me that you shall open your mouth to declare my gospel; therefore, fear not, but give heed unto the words and advice of your brother, which he shall give you.

6 And be you afflicted in all his afflictions, ever lifting up your heart unto me in prayer and faith, for his and your deliverance; for I have given unto him power to build up my church among the Lamanites;

7 And none have I appointed to be his counselor over him in the church, concerning church matters, except it is his brother, Joseph Smith, Jun.

8 Wherefore, give heed unto these things and be diligent in keeping my commandments, and you shall be blessed unto eternal life. Amen.

9 Behold, I say unto you, my servant John, that thou shalt commence from this time forth to proclaim my gospel, as with the voice of a trump.

10 And your labor shall be at your brother Philip Burroughs', and in that region round about, yea, wherever you can be heard, until I command you to go from hence.

11 And your whole labor shall be in Zion, with all your soul, from henceforth; yea, you shall ever open your mouth in my cause, not fearing what man can do, for I am with you. Amen.

Section 31

Revelation given through Joseph Smith the Prophet to Thomas B. Marsh, September 1830. The occasion was immediately following a conference of the Church (see the heading to section 30). Thomas B. Marsh had been baptized earlier in the month and had been ordained an elder in the Church before this revelation was given.

1–6, Thomas B. Marsh is called to preach the gospel and is assured of his family's well-being; 7–13, He is counseled to be patient, pray always, and follow the Comforter.

1 Thomas, my son, blessed are you because of your faith in my work.

2 Behold, you have had many afflictions because of your family; nevertheless, I will bless you and your family, yea, your little ones; and the day cometh that they will believe and know the truth and be one with you in my church.

3 Lift up your heart and rejoice, for the hour of your mission is come; and your tongue shall be loosed, and you shall declare glad tidings of great joy unto this generation.

4 You shall declare the things which have been revealed to my servant, Joseph Smith, Jun. You shall begin to preach from this time forth, yea, to reap in the field which is white already to be burned.

5 Therefore, thrust in your sickle with all your soul, and your sins are forgiven you, and you shall be laden with sheaves upon your back, for the laborer is worthy of his hire. Wherefore, your family shall live.

6 Behold, verily I say unto you, go from them only for a little time, and declare my word, and I will prepare a place for them.

7 Yea, I will open the hearts of the people, and they will receive you. And I will establish a church by your hand;

8 And you shall strengthen them and prepare them against the time when they shall be gathered.

9 Be patient in afflictions, revile not against those that revile. Govern your house in meekness, and be steadfast.

10 Behold, I say unto you that you shall be a physician unto the church, but not unto the world, for they will not receive you.

11 Go your way whithersoever I will, and it shall be given you by the Comforter what you shall do and whither you shall go.

12 Pray always, lest you enter into temptation and lose your reward.

13 Be faithful unto the end, and lo, I am with you. These words are not of man nor of men, but of me, even Jesus Christ, your Redeemer, by the will of the Father. Amen.

Section 32

Revelation given through Joseph Smith the Prophet to Parley P. Pratt and Ziba Peterson, in Manchester, New York, early October 1830. Great interest and desires were felt by the elders respecting the Lamanites, of whose predicted blessings the Church had learned from the Book of Mormon. In consequence, supplication was made that the Lord would indicate His will as to whether elders should be sent at that time to the Indian tribes in the West. The revelation followed.

1–3, Parley P. Pratt and Ziba Peterson are called to preach to the Lamanites and to accompany Oliver Cowdery and Peter Whitmer Jr.; 4–5, They are to pray for an understanding of the scriptures.

1 And now concerning my servant Parley P. Pratt, behold, I say unto him that as I live I will that he shall declare my gospel and learn of me, and be meek and lowly of heart.

2 And that which I have appointed unto him is that he shall go with my servants, Oliver Cowdery and Peter Whitmer, Jun., into the wilderness among the Lamanites.

3 And Ziba Peterson also shall go with them; and I myself will go with them and be in their midst; and I am their advocate with the Father, and nothing shall prevail against them.

4 And they shall give heed to that which is written, and pretend to no other revelation; and they shall pray always that I may unfold the same to their understanding.

5 And they shall give heed unto these words and trifle not, and I will bless them. Amen.

Section 33

Revelation given through Joseph Smith the Prophet to Ezra Thayre and Northrop Sweet, at Fayette, New York, October 1830. In introducing this revelation, Joseph Smith's history affirms that "the Lord ... is ever ready to instruct such as diligently seek in faith."

1–4, Laborers are called to declare the gospel in the eleventh hour; 5–6, The Church is established, and the elect are to be gathered; 7–10, Repent, for the kingdom of heaven is at hand; 11–15, The Church is built upon the gospel rock; 16–18, Prepare for the coming of the Bridegroom.

1 Behold, I say unto you, my servants Ezra and Northrop, open ye your ears and hearken to the voice of the Lord your God, whose word is quick and powerful, sharper than a two-edged sword, to the dividing asunder of the joints and marrow, soul and spirit; and is a discerner of the thoughts and intents of the heart.

2 For verily, verily, I say unto you that ye are called to lift up your voices as with the sound of a trump, to declare my gospel unto a crooked and perverse generation.

3 For behold, the field is white already to harvest; and it is the eleventh hour, and the last time that I shall call laborers into my vineyard.

4 And my vineyard has become corrupted every whit; and there is none which doeth good save it be a few; and they err in many instances because of priestcrafts, all having corrupt minds.

5 And verily, verily, I say unto you, that this church have I established and called forth out of the wilderness.

6 And even so will I gather mine elect from the four quarters of the earth, even as many as will believe in me, and hearken unto my voice.

7 Yea, verily, verily, I say unto you, that the field is white already to harvest; wherefore, thrust in your sickles, and reap with all your might, mind, and strength.

8 Open your mouths and they shall be filled, and you shall become even as Nephi of old, who journeyed from Jerusalem in the wilderness.

9 Yea, open your mouths and spare not, and you shall be laden with sheaves upon your backs, for lo, I am with you.

10 Yea, open your mouths and they shall be filled, saying: Repent, repent, and prepare ye the way of the Lord, and make his paths straight; for the kingdom of heaven is at hand;

11 Yea, repent and be baptized, every one of you, for a remission of your sins; yea, be baptized even by water, and then cometh the baptism of fire and of the Holy Ghost.

12 Behold, verily, verily, I say unto you, this is my gospel; and remember that they shall have faith in me or they can in nowise be saved;

13 And upon this rock I will build my church; yea, upon this rock ye are built, and if ye continue, the gates of hell shall not prevail against you.

14 And ye shall remember the church articles and covenants to keep them.

15 And whoso having faith you shall confirm in my church, by the laying on of the hands, and I will bestow the gift of the Holy Ghost upon them.

16 And the Book of Mormon and the holy scriptures are given of me for your instruction; and the power of my Spirit

quickeneth all things.

17 Wherefore, be faithful, praying always, having your lamps trimmed and burning, and oil with you, that you may be ready at the coming of the Bridegroom—

18 For behold, verily, verily, I say unto you, that I come quickly. Even so. Amen.

Section 34

Revelation given through Joseph Smith the Prophet to Orson Pratt, at Fayette, New York, November 4, 1830. Brother Pratt was nineteen years old at the time. He had been converted and baptized when he first heard the preaching of the restored gospel by his older brother, Parley P. Pratt, six weeks before. This revelation was received in the Peter Whitmer Sr. home.

1–4, The faithful become the sons of God through the Atonement; 5–9, The preaching of the gospel prepares the way for the Second Coming; 10–12, Prophecy comes by the power of the Holy Ghost.

1 My son Orson, hearken and hear and behold what I, the Lord God, shall say unto you, even Jesus Christ your Redeemer;

2 The light and the life of the world, a light which shineth in darkness and the darkness comprehendeth it not;

3 Who so loved the world that he gave his own life, that as many as would believe might become the sons of God. Wherefore you are my son;

4 And blessed are you because you have believed;

5 And more blessed are you because you are called of me to preach my gospel—

6 To lift up your voice as with the sound of a trump, both long and loud, and cry repentance unto a crooked and perverse generation, preparing the way of the Lord for his second coming.

7 For behold, verily, verily, I say unto you, the time is soon at hand that I shall come in a cloud with power and great glory.

8 And it shall be a great day at the time of my coming, for all nations shall tremble.

9 But before that great day shall come, the sun shall be darkened, and the moon be turned into blood; and the stars shall refuse their shining, and some shall fall, and great destructions await the wicked.

10 Wherefore, lift up your voice and spare not, for the Lord God hath spoken; therefore prophesy, and it shall be given by the power of the Holy Ghost.

11 And if you are faithful, behold, I am with you until I come—

12 And verily, verily, I say unto you, I come quickly. I am your Lord and your Redeemer. Even so. Amen.

Section 35

Revelation given to Joseph Smith the Prophet and Sidney Rigdon, at or near Fayette, New York, December 7, 1830. At this time, the Prophet was engaged almost daily in making a translation of the Bible. The translation was begun as early as June 1830, and both Oliver Cowdery and John Whitmer had served as scribes. Since they had now been called to other duties, Sidney Rigdon was called by divine appointment to serve as the Prophet's scribe in this work (see verse 20). As a preface to the record of this revelation, Joseph Smith's history states: "In December Sidney Rigdon came [from Ohio] to inquire of the Lord, and with him came Edward Partridge. ... Shortly after the arrival of these two brethren, thus spake the Lord."

1–2, How men may become the sons of God; 3–7, Sidney Rigdon is called to baptize and to confer the Holy Ghost; 8–12, Signs and miracles are wrought by faith; 13–16, The Lord's servants will thresh the nations by the power of the Spirit; 17–19, Joseph Smith holds the keys of the mysteries; 20–21, The elect will abide the day of the Lord's coming; 22–27, Israel will be saved.

1 Listen to the voice of the Lord your God, even Alpha and Omega, the beginning and the end, whose course is one eternal round, the same today as yesterday, and forever.

2 I am Jesus Christ, the Son of God, who was crucified for the sins of the world, even as many as will believe on my name, that they may become the sons of God, even one in me as I am one in the Father, as the Father is one in me, that we may be one.

3 Behold, verily, verily, I say unto my servant Sidney, I have looked upon thee and thy works. I have heard thy prayers, and prepared thee for a greater work.

4 Thou art blessed, for thou shalt do great things. Behold thou wast sent forth, even as John, to prepare the way before me, and before Elijah which should come, and thou knewest it not.

5 Thou didst baptize by water unto repentance, but they received not the Holy Ghost;

6 But now I give unto thee a commandment, that thou shalt baptize by water, and they shall receive the Holy Ghost by the laying on of the hands, even as the apostles of old.

7 And it shall come to pass that there shall be a great work in the land, even among the Gentiles, for their folly and their abominations shall be made manifest in the eyes of all people.

8 For I am God, and mine arm is not shortened; and I will show miracles, signs, and wonders, unto all those who believe on my name.

9 And whoso shall ask it in my name in faith, they shall cast out devils; they shall heal the sick; they shall cause the blind to receive their sight, and the deaf to hear, and the dumb to speak, and the lame to walk.

10 And the time speedily cometh that great things are to be shown forth unto the children of men;

11 But without faith shall not anything be shown forth except desolations upon Babylon, the same which has made all nations drink of the wine of the wrath of her fornication.

12 And there are none that doeth good except those who are ready to receive the fulness of my gospel, which I have sent forth unto this generation.

13 Wherefore, I call upon the weak things of the world, those who are unlearned and despised, to thresh the nations by the power of my Spirit;

14 And their arm shall be my arm, and I will be their shield and their buckler; and I will gird up their loins, and they shall fight manfully for me; and their enemies shall be under their feet; and I will let fall the sword in their behalf, and by the fire of mine indignation will I preserve them.

15 And the poor and the meek shall have the gospel preached unto them, and they shall be looking forth for the time of my coming, for it is nigh at hand—

16 And they shall learn the parable of the fig tree, for even now already summer is nigh.

17 And I have sent forth the fulness of my gospel by the hand of my servant Joseph; and in weakness have I blessed him;

18 And I have given unto him the keys of the mystery of those things which have been sealed, even things which were from the foundation of the world, and the things which shall come from this time until the time of my coming, if he abide in me, and if not, another will I plant in his stead.

19 Wherefore, watch over him that his faith fail not, and it shall be given by the Comforter, the Holy Ghost, that knoweth all things.

20 And a commandment I give unto thee—that thou shalt write for him; and the scriptures shall be given, even as they are in mine own bosom, to the salvation of mine own elect;

21 For they will hear my voice, and shall see me, and shall not be asleep, and shall abide the day of my coming; for they shall be purified, even as I am pure.

22 And now I say unto you, tarry with him, and he shall journey with you; forsake him not, and surely these things shall be fulfilled.

23 And inasmuch as ye do not write, behold, it shall be given unto him to prophesy; and thou shalt preach my gospel and call on the holy prophets to prove his words, as they shall be given him.

24 Keep all the commandments and covenants by which ye are bound; and I will cause the heavens to shake for your good, and Satan shall tremble and Zion shall rejoice upon the hills and flourish;

25 And Israel shall be saved in mine own due time; and by the keys which I have given shall they be led, and no more be confounded at all.

26 Lift up your hearts and be glad, your redemption draweth nigh.

27 Fear not, little flock, the kingdom is yours until I come. Behold, I come quickly. Even so. Amen.

Section 36

Revelation given through Joseph Smith the Prophet to Edward Partridge, near Fayette, New York, December 9, 1830 (see the heading to section 35). Joseph Smith's history states that Edward Partridge "was a pattern of piety, and one of the Lord's great men."

1–3, The Lord lays His hand upon Edward Partridge by the hand of Sidney Rigdon; 4–8, Every man who receives the gospel and the priesthood is to be called to go forth and preach.

1 Thus saith the Lord God, the Mighty One of Israel: Behold, I say unto you, my servant Edward, that you are blessed, and your sins are forgiven you, and you are called to preach my gospel as with the voice of a trump;

2 And I will lay my hand upon you by the hand of my servant Sidney Rigdon, and you shall receive my Spirit, the Holy Ghost, even the Comforter, which shall teach you the peaceable things of the kingdom;

3 And you shall declare it with a loud voice, saying: Hosanna, blessed be the name of the most high God.

4 And now this calling and commandment give I unto you concerning all men—

5 That as many as shall come before my servants Sidney Rigdon and Joseph Smith, Jun., embracing this calling and commandment, shall be ordained and sent forth to preach the everlasting gospel among the nations—

6 Crying repentance, saying: Save yourselves from this untoward generation, and come forth out of the fire, hating even the garments spotted with the flesh.

7 And this commandment shall be given unto the elders of my church, that every man which will embrace it with singleness of heart may be ordained and sent forth, even as I have spoken.

8 I am Jesus Christ, the Son of God; wherefore, gird up your loins and I will suddenly come to my temple. Even so. Amen.

Section 37

Revelation given to Joseph Smith the Prophet and Sidney Rigdon, near Fayette, New York, December 1830. Herein is given the first commandment concerning a gathering in this dispensation.

1–4, The Saints are called to gather at the Ohio.

1 Behold, I say unto you that it is not expedient in me that ye should translate any more until ye shall go to the Ohio, and this because of the enemy and for your sakes.

2 And again, I say unto you that ye shall not go until ye have preached my gospel in those parts, and have strengthened up the church whithersoever it is found, and more especially in Colesville; for, behold, they pray unto me in much faith.

3 And again, a commandment I give unto the church, that it is expedient in me that they should assemble together at the Ohio, against the time that my servant Oliver Cowdery shall return unto them.

4 Behold, here is wisdom, and let every man choose for himself until I come. Even so. Amen.

Section 38

Revelation given through Joseph Smith the Prophet, at Fayette, New York, January 2, 1831. The occasion was a conference of the Church.

1–6, Christ created all things; 7–8, He is in the midst of His Saints, who will soon see Him; 9–12, All flesh is corrupted before Him; 13–22, He has reserved a land of promise for His Saints in time and in eternity; 23–27, The Saints are commanded to be one and esteem each other as brethren; 28–29, Wars are predicted; 30–33, The Saints are to be given power from on high and to go forth among all nations; 34–42, The Church is commanded to care for the poor and needy and to seek the riches of eternity.

1 Thus saith the Lord your God, even Jesus Christ, the Great I AM, Alpha and Omega, the beginning and the end, the same which looked upon the wide expanse of eternity, and all the seraphic hosts of heaven, before the world was made;

2 The same which knoweth all things, for all things are present before mine eyes;

3 I am the same which spake, and the world was made, and all things came by me.

4 I am the same which have taken the Zion of Enoch into mine own bosom; and verily, I say, even as many as have believed in my name, for I am Christ, and in mine own name, by the virtue of the blood which I have spilt, have I pleaded before the Father for them.

5 But behold, the residue of the wicked have I kept in chains of darkness until the judgment of the great day, which shall come at the end of the earth;

6 And even so will I cause the wicked to be kept, that will not hear my voice but harden their hearts, and wo, wo, wo, is their doom.

7 But behold, verily, verily, I say unto you that mine eyes are upon you. I am in your midst and ye cannot see me;

8 But the day soon cometh that ye shall see me, and know that I am; for the veil of darkness shall soon be rent, and he that is not purified shall not abide the day.

9 Wherefore, gird up your loins and be prepared. Behold, the kingdom is yours, and the enemy shall not overcome.

10 Verily I say unto you, ye are clean, but not all; and there is none else with whom I am well pleased;

11 For all flesh is corrupted before me; and the powers of darkness prevail upon the earth, among the children of men, in the presence of all the hosts of heaven—

12 Which causeth silence to reign, and all eternity is pained, and the angels are waiting the great command to reap down the earth, to gather the tares that they may be burned; and, behold, the enemy is combined.

13 And now I show unto you a mystery, a thing which is had in secret chambers, to bring to pass even your destruction in process of time, and ye knew it not;

14 But now I tell it unto you, and ye are blessed, not because of your iniquity, neither your hearts of unbelief; for verily some of you are guilty before me, but I will be merciful unto your weakness.

15 Therefore, be ye strong from henceforth; fear not, for the kingdom is yours.

16 And for your salvation I give unto you a commandment, for I have

heard your prayers, and the poor have complained before me, and the rich have I made, and all flesh is mine, and I am no respecter of persons.

17 And I have made the earth rich, and behold it is my footstool, wherefore, again I will stand upon it.

18 And I hold forth and deign to give unto you greater riches, even a land of promise, a land flowing with milk and honey, upon which there shall be no curse when the Lord cometh;

19 And I will give it unto you for the land of your inheritance, if you seek it with all your hearts.

20 And this shall be my covenant with you, ye shall have it for the land of your inheritance, and for the inheritance of your children forever, while the earth shall stand, and ye shall possess it again in eternity, no more to pass away.

21 But, verily I say unto you that in time ye shall have no king nor ruler, for I will be your king and watch over you.

22 Wherefore, hear my voice and follow me, and you shall be a free people, and ye shall have no laws but my laws when I come, for I am your lawgiver, and what can stay my hand?

23 But, verily I say unto you, teach one another according to the office wherewith I have appointed you;

24 And let every man esteem his brother as himself, and practice virtue and holiness before me.

25 And again I say unto you, let every man esteem his brother as himself.

26 For what man among you having twelve sons, and is no respecter of them, and they serve him obediently, and he saith unto the one: Be thou clothed in robes and sit thou here; and to the other: Be thou clothed in rags and sit thou there—and looketh upon his sons and saith I am just?

27 Behold, this I have given unto you as a parable, and it is even as I am. I say unto you, be one; and if ye are not one ye are not mine.

28 And again, I say unto you that the enemy in the secret chambers seeketh your lives.

29 Ye hear of wars in far countries, and you say that there will soon be great wars in far countries, but ye know not the hearts of men in your own land.

30 I tell you these things because of your prayers; wherefore, treasure up wisdom in your bosoms, lest the wickedness of men reveal these things unto you by their wickedness, in a manner which shall speak in your ears with a voice louder than that which shall shake the earth; but if ye are prepared ye shall not fear.

31 And that ye might escape the power of the enemy, and be gathered unto me a righteous people, without spot and blameless—

32 Wherefore, for this cause I gave unto you the commandment that ye should go to the Ohio; and there I will give unto you my law; and there you shall be endowed with power from on high;

33 And from thence, whosoever I will shall go forth among all nations, and it shall be told them what they shall do; for I have a great work laid up in store, for Israel shall be saved, and I will lead them whithersoever I will, and no power shall stay my hand.

34 And now, I give unto the church in these parts a commandment, that certain men among them shall be appointed, and they shall be appointed by the voice of the church;

35 And they shall look to the poor and the needy, and administer to their relief that they shall not suffer; and send them forth to the place which I have commanded them;

36 And this shall be their work, to govern the affairs of the property of this church.

37 And they that have farms that cannot be sold, let them be left or rented as seemeth them good.

38 See that all things are preserved; and when men are endowed with power from on high and sent forth, all these things shall be gathered unto the bosom of the church.

39 And if ye seek the riches which it is the will of the Father to give unto you, ye shall be the richest of all people, for ye shall have the riches of eternity; and it must needs be that the riches of the earth are mine to give; but beware of pride, lest ye become as the Nephites of old.

40 And again, I say unto you, I give unto you a commandment, that every man, both elder, priest, teacher, and also member, go to with his might, with the labor of his hands, to prepare and accomplish the things which I have commanded.

41 And let your preaching be the warning voice, every man to his neighbor, in mildness and in meekness.

42 And go ye out from among the wicked. Save yourselves. Be ye clean that bear the vessels of the Lord. Even so. Amen.

Section 39

Revelation given through Joseph Smith the Prophet to James Covel, at Fayette, New York, January 5, 1831. James Covel, who had been a Methodist minister for about forty years, covenanted with the Lord that he would obey any command that the Lord would give to him through Joseph the Prophet.

1–4, The Saints have power to become the sons of God; 5–6, To receive the gospel is to receive Christ; 7–14, James Covel is commanded to be baptized and labor in the Lord's vineyard; 15–21, The Lord's servants are to preach the gospel before the Second Coming; 22–24, Those who receive the gospel will be gathered in time and in eternity.

1 Hearken and listen to the voice of him who is from all eternity to all eternity, the Great I AM, even Jesus Christ—

2 The light and the life of the world; a light which shineth in darkness and the darkness comprehendeth it not;

3 The same which came in the meridian of time unto mine own, and mine own received me not;

4 But to as many as received me, gave I power to become my sons; and even so will I give unto as many as will receive me, power to become my sons.

5 And verily, verily, I say unto you, he that receiveth my gospel receiveth me; and he that receiveth not my gospel receiveth not me.

6 And this is my gospel—repentance and baptism by water, and then cometh the baptism of fire and the Holy Ghost, even the Comforter, which showeth all things, and teacheth the peaceable things of the kingdom.

7 And now, behold, I say unto you, my servant James, I have looked upon thy works and I know thee.

8 And verily I say unto thee, thine heart is now right before me at this time; and, behold, I have bestowed great blessings upon thy head;

9 Nevertheless, thou hast seen great sorrow, for thou hast rejected me many times because of pride and the cares of the world.

10 But, behold, the days of thy deliverance are come, if thou wilt hearken to my voice, which saith unto thee: Arise and be baptized, and wash away your sins, calling on my name, and you shall receive my Spirit, and a blessing so great as you never have known.

11 And if thou do this, I have prepared thee for a greater work. Thou shalt preach the fulness of my gospel, which I have sent forth in these last days, the covenant which I have sent forth to recover my people, which are of the house of Israel.

12 And it shall come to pass that power shall rest upon thee; thou shalt have great faith, and I will be with thee and go before thy face.

13 Thou art called to labor in my vineyard, and to build up my church, and to bring forth Zion, that it may rejoice upon the hills and flourish.

14 Behold, verily, verily, I say unto thee, thou art not called to go into the eastern countries, but thou art called to go to the Ohio.

15 And inasmuch as my people shall assemble themselves at the Ohio, I have kept in store a blessing such as is not known among the children of men, and it shall be poured forth upon their heads. And from thence men shall go forth into all nations.

16 Behold, verily, verily, I say unto you, that the people in Ohio call upon me in much faith, thinking I will stay my hand in judgment upon the nations, but I cannot deny my word.

17 Wherefore lay to with your might and call faithful laborers into my vineyard, that it may be pruned for the last time.

18 And inasmuch as they do repent and receive the fulness of my gospel, and become sanctified, I will stay mine hand in judgment.

19 Wherefore, go forth, crying with a loud voice, saying: The kingdom of heaven is at hand; crying: Hosanna! blessed be the name of the Most High God.

20 Go forth baptizing with water, preparing the way before my face for the time of my coming;

21 For the time is at hand; the day or the hour no man knoweth; but it surely shall come.

22 And he that receiveth these things receiveth me; and they shall be gathered unto me in time and in eternity.

23 And again, it shall come to pass that on as many as ye shall baptize with water, ye shall lay your hands, and they shall receive the gift of the Holy Ghost, and shall be looking forth for the signs of my coming, and shall know me.

24 Behold, I come quickly. Even so. Amen.

Section 40

Revelation given to Joseph Smith the Prophet and Sidney Rigdon, at Fayette, New York, January 6, 1831. Preceding the record of this revelation, the Prophet's history states, "As James [Covel] rejected the word of the Lord, and returned to his former principles and people, the Lord gave unto me and Sidney Rigdon the following revelation" (see section 39).

1–3, Fear of persecution and cares of the world cause rejection of the gospel.

1 Behold, verily I say unto you, that the heart of my servant James Covel was right before me, for he covenanted with me that he would obey my word.

2 And he received the word with gladness, but straightway Satan tempted him; and the fear of persecution and the cares of the world caused him to reject the word.

3 Wherefore he broke my covenant, and it remaineth with me to do with him as seemeth me good. Amen.

Section 41

Revelation given through Joseph Smith the Prophet to the Church, at Kirtland, Ohio, February 4, 1831. This revelation instructs the Prophet and Church elders to pray to receive God's "law" (see section 42). Joseph Smith had just arrived in Kirtland from New York, and Leman Copley, a Church member in nearby Thompson, Ohio, "requested Brother Joseph and Sidney [Rigdon] ... live with him and he would furnish them houses and provisions." The following revelation clarifies where Joseph and Sidney should live and also calls Edward Partridge to be the Church's first bishop.

1–3, The elders will govern the Church by the spirit of revelation; 4–6, True disciples will receive and keep the Lord's law; 7–12, Edward Partridge is named as a bishop unto the Church.

1 Hearken and hear, O ye my people, saith the Lord and your God, ye whom I delight to bless with the greatest of all blessings, ye that hear me; and ye that hear me not will I curse, that have professed my name, with the heaviest of all cursings.

2 Hearken, O ye elders of my church whom I have called, behold I give unto you a commandment, that ye shall assemble yourselves together to agree upon my word;

3 And by the prayer of your faith ye shall receive my law, that ye may know how to govern my church and have all things right before me.

4 And I will be your ruler when I come; and behold, I come quickly, and ye shall see that my law is kept.

5 He that receiveth my law and doeth it, the same is my disciple; and he that saith he receiveth it and doeth it not, the same is not my disciple, and shall be cast out from among you;

6 For it is not meet that the things which belong to the children of the kingdom should be given to them that are not worthy, or to dogs, or the pearls to be cast before swine.

7 And again, it is meet that my servant Joseph Smith, Jun., should have a house built, in which to live and translate.

8 And again, it is meet that my servant Sidney Rigdon should live as seemeth him good, inasmuch as he keepeth my commandments.

9 And again, I have called my servant Edward Partridge; and I give a commandment, that he should be appointed by the voice of the church, and ordained a bishop unto the church, to leave his merchandise and to spend all his time in the labors of the church;

10 To see to all things as it shall be appointed unto him in my laws in the day that I shall give them.

11 And this because his heart is pure before me, for he is like unto Nathanael of old, in whom there is no guile.

12 These words are given unto you, and they are pure before me; wherefore, beware how you hold them, for they are to be answered upon your souls in the day of judgment. Even so. Amen.

Section 42

Revelation given in two parts through Joseph Smith the Prophet, at Kirtland, Ohio, February 9 and 23, 1831. The first part, consisting of verses 1 through 72, was received in the presence of twelve elders and in fulfillment of the Lord's promise previously made that the "law" would be given in Ohio (see section 38:32). The second portion consists of verses 73 through 93. The Prophet specifies this revelation as "embracing the law of the Church."

1–10, The elders are called to preach the gospel, baptize converts, and build up the Church; 11–12, They must be called and ordained and are to teach the principles of the gospel found in the scriptures; 13–17, They are to teach and prophesy by the power of the Spirit; 18–29, The Saints are commanded not to kill, steal, lie, lust, commit adultery, or speak evil against others; 30–39, Laws governing the consecration of properties are set forth; 40–42, Pride and idleness are condemned; 43–52, The sick are to be healed through administrations and by faith; 53–60, The scriptures govern the Church and are to be proclaimed to the world; 61–69, The site of the New Jerusalem and the mysteries of the kingdom will be revealed; 70–73, Consecrated properties are to be used to support Church officers; 74–93, Laws governing fornication, adultery, killing, stealing, and confession of sins are set forth.

1 Hearken, O ye elders of my church, who have assembled yourselves together in my name, even Jesus Christ the Son of the living God, the Savior of the world; inasmuch as ye believe on my name and keep my commandments.

2 Again I say unto you, hearken and hear and obey the law which I shall give unto you.

3 For verily I say, as ye have assembled yourselves together according to the commandment wherewith I commanded you, and are agreed as touching this one thing, and have asked the Father in my name, even so ye shall receive.

4 Behold, verily I say unto you, I give unto you this first commandment, that ye shall go forth in my name, every one of you, excepting my servants Joseph Smith, Jun., and Sidney Rigdon.

5 And I give unto them a commandment that they shall go forth for a little season, and it shall be given by the power of the Spirit when they shall return.

6 And ye shall go forth in the power of my Spirit, preaching my gospel, two by two, in my name, lifting up your voices as with the sound of a trump, declaring my word like unto angels of God.

7 And ye shall go forth baptizing with water, saying: Repent ye, repent ye, for the kingdom of heaven is at hand.

8 And from this place ye shall go forth into the regions westward; and inasmuch as ye shall find them that will receive you ye shall build up my church in every region—

9 Until the time shall come when it shall be revealed unto you from on high, when the city of the New Jerusalem shall be prepared, that ye may be gathered in one, that ye may be my people and I will be your God.

10 And again, I say unto you, that my servant Edward Partridge shall stand in the office whereunto I have appointed him. And it shall come to pass, that if he transgress another shall be appointed in his stead. Even so. Amen.

11 Again I say unto you, that it shall not be given to any one to go forth to preach my gospel, or to build up my church, except he be ordained by some one who has authority, and it is known to the

church that he has authority and has been regularly ordained by the heads of the church.

12 And again, the elders, priests and teachers of this church shall teach the principles of my gospel, which are in the Bible and the Book of Mormon, in the which is the fulness of the gospel.

13 And they shall observe the covenants and church articles to do them, and these shall be their teachings, as they shall be directed by the Spirit.

14 And the Spirit shall be given unto you by the prayer of faith; and if ye receive not the Spirit ye shall not teach.

15 And all this ye shall observe to do as I have commanded concerning your teaching, until the fulness of my scriptures is given.

16 And as ye shall lift up your voices by the Comforter, ye shall speak and prophesy as seemeth me good;

17 For, behold, the Comforter knoweth all things, and beareth record of the Father and of the Son.

18 And now, behold, I speak unto the church. Thou shalt not kill; and he that kills shall not have forgiveness in this world, nor in the world to come.

19 And again, I say, thou shalt not kill; but he that killeth shall die.

20 Thou shalt not steal; and he that stealeth and will not repent shall be cast out.

21 Thou shalt not lie; he that lieth and will not repent shall be cast out.

22 Thou shalt love thy wife with all thy heart, and shalt cleave unto her and none else.

23 And he that looketh upon a woman to lust after her shall deny the faith, and shall not have the Spirit; and if he repents not he shall be cast out.

24 Thou shalt not commit adultery; and he that committeth adultery, and repenteth not, shall be cast out.

25 But he that has committed adultery and repents with all his heart, and forsaketh it, and doeth it no more, thou shalt forgive;

26 But if he doeth it again, he shall not be forgiven, but shall be cast out.

27 Thou shalt not speak evil of thy neighbor, nor do him any harm.

28 Thou knowest my laws concerning these things are given in my scriptures; he that sinneth and repenteth not shall be cast out.

29 If thou lovest me thou shalt serve me and keep all my commandments.

30 And behold, thou wilt remember the poor, and consecrate of thy properties for their support that which thou hast to impart unto them, with a covenant and a deed which cannot be broken.

31 And inasmuch as ye impart of your substance unto the poor, ye will do it unto me; and they shall be laid before the bishop of my church and his counselors, two of the elders, or high priests, such as he shall appoint or has appointed and set apart for that purpose.

32 And it shall come to pass, that after they are laid before the bishop of my church, and after that he has received these testimonies concerning the consecration of the properties of my church, that they cannot be taken from the church, agreeable to my commandments, every man shall be made accountable unto me, a steward over his own property, or that which he

has received by consecration, as much as is sufficient for himself and family.

33 And again, if there shall be properties in the hands of the church, or any individuals of it, more than is necessary for their support after this first consecration, which is a residue to be consecrated unto the bishop, it shall be kept to administer to those who have not, from time to time, that every man who has need may be amply supplied and receive according to his wants.

34 Therefore, the residue shall be kept in my storehouse, to administer to the poor and the needy, as shall be appointed by the high council of the church, and the bishop and his council;

35 And for the purpose of purchasing lands for the public benefit of the church, and building houses of worship, and building up of the New Jerusalem which is hereafter to be revealed—

36 That my covenant people may be gathered in one in that day when I shall come to my temple. And this I do for the salvation of my people.

37 And it shall come to pass, that he that sinneth and repenteth not shall be cast out of the church, and shall not receive again that which he has consecrated unto the poor and the needy of my church, or in other words, unto me—

38 For inasmuch as ye do it unto the least of these, ye do it unto me.

39 For it shall come to pass, that which I spake by the mouths of my prophets shall be fulfilled; for I will consecrate of the riches of those who embrace my gospel among the Gentiles unto the poor of my people who are of the house of Israel.

40 And again, thou shalt not be proud in thy heart; let all thy garments be plain, and their beauty the beauty of the work of thine own hands;

41 And let all things be done in cleanliness before me.

42 Thou shalt not be idle; for he that is idle shall not eat the bread nor wear the garments of the laborer.

43 And whosoever among you are sick, and have not faith to be healed, but believe, shall be nourished with all tenderness, with herbs and mild food, and that not by the hand of an enemy.

44 And the elders of the church, two or more, shall be called, and shall pray for and lay their hands upon them in my name; and if they die they shall die unto me, and if they live they shall live unto me.

45 Thou shalt live together in love, insomuch that thou shalt weep for the loss of them that die, and more especially for those that have not hope of a glorious resurrection.

46 And it shall come to pass that those that die in me shall not taste of death, for it shall be sweet unto them;

47 And they that die not in me, wo unto them, for their death is bitter.

48 And again, it shall come to pass that he that hath faith in me to be healed, and is not appointed unto death, shall be healed.

49 He who hath faith to see shall see.

50 He who hath faith to hear shall hear.

51 The lame who hath faith to leap shall leap.

52 And they who have not faith to do these things, but believe in me, have power to become my sons; and inasmuch as they break not my laws

thou shalt bear their infirmities.

53 Thou shalt stand in the place of thy stewardship.

54 Thou shalt not take thy brother's garment; thou shalt pay for that which thou shalt receive of thy brother.

55 And if thou obtainest more than that which would be for thy support, thou shalt give it into my storehouse, that all things may be done according to that which I have said.

56 Thou shalt ask, and my scriptures shall be given as I have appointed, and they shall be preserved in safety;

57 And it is expedient that thou shouldst hold thy peace concerning them, and not teach them until ye have received them in full.

58 And I give unto you a commandment that then ye shall teach them unto all men; for they shall be taught unto all nations, kindreds, tongues and people.

59 Thou shalt take the things which thou hast received, which have been given unto thee in my scriptures for a law, to be my law to govern my church;

60 And he that doeth according to these things shall be saved, and he that doeth them not shall be damned if he so continue.

61 If thou shalt ask, thou shalt receive revelation upon revelation, knowledge upon knowledge, that thou mayest know the mysteries and peaceable things—that which bringeth joy, that which bringeth life eternal.

62 Thou shalt ask, and it shall be revealed unto you in mine own due time where the New Jerusalem shall be built.

63 And behold, it shall come to pass that my servants shall be sent forth to the east and to the west, to the north and to the south.

64 And even now, let him that goeth to the east teach them that shall be converted to flee to the west, and this in consequence of that which is coming on the earth, and of secret combinations.

65 Behold, thou shalt observe all these things, and great shall be thy reward; for unto you it is given to know the mysteries of the kingdom, but unto the world it is not given to know them.

66 Ye shall observe the laws which ye have received and be faithful.

67 And ye shall hereafter receive church covenants, such as shall be sufficient to establish you, both here and in the New Jerusalem.

68 Therefore, he that lacketh wisdom, let him ask of me, and I will give him liberally and upbraid him not.

69 Lift up your hearts and rejoice, for unto you the kingdom, or in other words, the keys of the church have been given. Even so. Amen.

70 The priests and teachers shall have their stewardships, even as the members.

71 And the elders or high priests who are appointed to assist the bishop as counselors in all things, are to have their families supported out of the property which is consecrated to the bishop, for the good of the poor, and for other purposes, as before mentioned;

72 Or they are to receive a just remuneration for all their services, either a stewardship or otherwise, as may be thought best or decided by the counselors and bishop.

73 And the bishop, also, shall receive

his support, or a just remuneration for all his services in the church.

74 Behold, verily I say unto you, that whatever persons among you, having put away their companions for the cause of fornication, or in other words, if they shall testify before you in all lowliness of heart that this is the case, ye shall not cast them out from among you;

75 But if ye shall find that any persons have left their companions for the sake of adultery, and they themselves are the offenders, and their companions are living, they shall be cast out from among you.

76 And again, I say unto you, that ye shall be watchful and careful, with all inquiry, that ye receive none such among you if they are married;

77 And if they are not married, they shall repent of all their sins or ye shall not receive them.

78 And again, every person who belongeth to this church of Christ, shall observe to keep all the commandments and covenants of the church.

79 And it shall come to pass, that if any persons among you shall kill they shall be delivered up and dealt with according to the laws of the land; for remember that he hath no forgiveness; and it shall be proved according to the laws of the land.

80 And if any man or woman shall commit adultery, he or she shall be tried before two elders of the church, or more, and every word shall be established against him or her by two witnesses of the church, and not of the enemy; but if there are more than two witnesses it is better.

81 But he or she shall be condemned by the mouth of two witnesses; and the elders shall lay the case before the church, and the church shall lift up their hands against him or her, that they may be dealt with according to the law of God.

82 And if it can be, it is necessary that the bishop be present also.

83 And thus ye shall do in all cases which shall come before you.

84 And if a man or woman shall rob, he or she shall be delivered up unto the law of the land.

85 And if he or she shall steal, he or she shall be delivered up unto the law of the land.

86 And if he or she shall lie, he or she shall be delivered up unto the law of the land.

87 And if he or she do any manner of iniquity, he or she shall be delivered up unto the law, even that of God.

88 And if thy brother or sister offend thee, thou shalt take him or her between him or her and thee alone; and if he or she confess thou shalt be reconciled.

89 And if he or she confess not thou shalt deliver him or her up unto the church, not to the members, but to the elders. And it shall be done in a meeting, and that not before the world.

90 And if thy brother or sister offend many, he or she shall be chastened before many.

91 And if any one offend openly, he or she shall be rebuked openly, that he or she may be ashamed. And if he or she confess not, he or she shall be delivered up unto the law of God.

92 If any shall offend in secret, he or she shall be rebuked in secret, that he or she may have opportunity to confess in

secret to him or her whom he or she has offended, and to God, that the church may not speak reproachfully of him or her.

93 And thus shall ye conduct in all things.

Section 43

Revelation given through Joseph Smith the Prophet, at Kirtland, Ohio, in February 1831. At this time some members of the Church were disturbed by people making false claims as revelators. The Prophet inquired of the Lord and received this communication addressed to the elders of the Church. The first part deals with matters of Church polity; the latter part contains a warning that the elders are to give to the nations of the earth.

1–7, Revelations and commandments come only through the one appointed; 8–14, The Saints are sanctified by acting in all holiness before the Lord; 15–22, Elders are sent forth to cry repentance and prepare men for the great day of the Lord; 23–28, The Lord calls upon men by His own voice and through the forces of nature; 29–35, The Millennium and the binding of Satan will come.

1 O hearken, ye elders of my church, and give ear to the words which I shall speak unto you.

2 For behold, verily, verily, I say unto you, that ye have received a commandment for a law unto my church, through him whom I have appointed unto you to receive commandments and revelations from my hand.

3 And this ye shall know assuredly—that there is none other appointed unto you to receive commandments and revelations until he be taken, if he abide in me.

4 But verily, verily, I say unto you, that none else shall be appointed unto this gift except it be through him; for if it be taken from him he shall not have power except to appoint another in his stead.

5 And this shall be a law unto you, that ye receive not the teachings of any that shall come before you as revelations or commandments;

6 And this I give unto you that you may not be deceived, that you may know they are not of me.

7 For verily I say unto you, that he that is ordained of me shall come in at the gate and be ordained as I have told you before, to teach those revelations which you have received and shall receive through him whom I have appointed.

8 And now, behold, I give unto you a commandment, that when ye are assembled together ye shall instruct and edify each other, that ye may know how to act and direct my church, how to act upon the points of my law and commandments, which I have given.

9 And thus ye shall become instructed in the law of my church, and be sanctified by that which ye have received, and ye shall bind yourselves to act in all holiness before me—

10 That inasmuch as ye do this, glory shall be added to the kingdom which ye have received. Inasmuch as ye do it not, it shall be taken, even that which ye have received.

11 Purge ye out the iniquity which is among you; sanctify yourselves before me;

12 And if ye desire the glories of the kingdom, appoint ye my servant Joseph Smith, Jun., and uphold him before me by the prayer of faith.

13 And again, I say unto you, that if ye desire the mysteries of the kingdom, provide for him food and raiment, and whatsoever thing he needeth to accomplish the work wherewith I have commanded him;

14 And if ye do it not he shall remain unto them that have received him, that I may reserve unto myself a pure people

before me.

15 Again I say, hearken ye elders of my church, whom I have appointed: Ye are not sent forth to be taught, but to teach the children of men the things which I have put into your hands by the power of my Spirit;

16 And ye are to be taught from on high. Sanctify yourselves and ye shall be endowed with power, that ye may give even as I have spoken.

17 Hearken ye, for, behold, the great day of the Lord is nigh at hand.

18 For the day cometh that the Lord shall utter his voice out of heaven; the heavens shall shake and the earth shall tremble, and the trump of God shall sound both long and loud, and shall say to the sleeping nations: Ye saints arise and live; ye sinners stay and sleep until I shall call again.

19 Wherefore gird up your loins lest ye be found among the wicked.

20 Lift up your voices and spare not. Call upon the nations to repent, both old and young, both bond and free, saying: Prepare yourselves for the great day of the Lord;

21 For if I, who am a man, do lift up my voice and call upon you to repent, and ye hate me, what will ye say when the day cometh when the thunders shall utter their voices from the ends of the earth, speaking to the ears of all that live, saying—Repent, and prepare for the great day of the Lord?

22 Yea, and again, when the lightnings shall streak forth from the east unto the west, and shall utter forth their voices unto all that live, and make the ears of all tingle that hear, saying these words—Repent ye, for the great day of the Lord is come?

23 And again, the Lord shall utter his voice out of heaven, saying: Hearken, O ye nations of the earth, and hear the words of that God who made you.

24 O, ye nations of the earth, how often would I have gathered you together as a hen gathereth her chickens under her wings, but ye would not!

25 How oft have I called upon you by the mouth of my servants, and by the ministering of angels, and by mine own voice, and by the voice of thunderings, and by the voice of lightnings, and by the voice of tempests, and by the voice of earthquakes, and great hailstorms, and by the voice of famines and pestilences of every kind, and by the great sound of a trump, and by the voice of judgment, and by the voice of mercy all the day long, and by the voice of glory and honor and the riches of eternal life, and would have saved you with an everlasting salvation, but ye would not!

26 Behold, the day has come, when the cup of the wrath of mine indignation is full.

27 Behold, verily I say unto you, that these are the words of the Lord your God.

28 Wherefore, labor ye, labor ye in my vineyard for the last time—for the last time call upon the inhabitants of the earth.

29 For in mine own due time will I come upon the earth in judgment, and my people shall be redeemed and shall reign with me on earth.

30 For the great Millennium, of which I have spoken by the mouth of my servants, shall come.

31 For Satan shall be bound, and when he is loosed again he shall only reign for a little season, and then cometh the end

of the earth.

32 And he that liveth in righteousness shall be changed in the twinkling of an eye, and the earth shall pass away so as by fire.

33 And the wicked shall go away into unquenchable fire, and their end no man knoweth on earth, nor ever shall know, until they come before me in judgment.

34 Hearken ye to these words. Behold, I am Jesus Christ, the Savior of the world. Treasure these things up in your hearts, and let the solemnities of eternity rest upon your minds.

35 Be sober. Keep all my commandments. Even so. Amen.

Section 44

Revelation given to Joseph Smith the Prophet and Sidney Rigdon, at Kirtland, Ohio, in the latter part of February 1831. In compliance with the requirement herein set forth, the Church appointed a conference to be held early in the month of June following.

1–3, Elders are to assemble in conference; 4–6, They are to organize according to the laws of the land and to care for the poor.

1 Behold, thus saith the Lord unto you my servants, it is expedient in me that the elders of my church should be called together, from the east and from the west, and from the north and from the south, by letter or some other way.

2 And it shall come to pass, that inasmuch as they are faithful, and exercise faith in me, I will pour out my Spirit upon them in the day that they assemble themselves together.

3 And it shall come to pass that they shall go forth into the regions round about, and preach repentance unto the people.

4 And many shall be converted, insomuch that ye shall obtain power to organize yourselves according to the laws of man;

5 That your enemies may not have power over you; that you may be preserved in all things; that you may be enabled to keep my laws; that every bond may be broken wherewith the enemy seeketh to destroy my people.

6 Behold, I say unto you, that ye must visit the poor and the needy and administer to their relief, that they may be kept until all things may be done according to my law which ye have received. Amen.

Section 45

Revelation given through Joseph Smith the Prophet to the Church, at Kirtland, Ohio, March 7, 1831. Prefacing the record of this revelation, Joseph Smith's history states that "at this age of the Church ... many false reports ... and foolish stories, were published ... and circulated, ... to prevent people from investigating the work, or embracing the faith. ... But to the joy of the Saints, ... I received the following."

1–5, Christ is our advocate with the Father; 6–10, The gospel is a messenger to prepare the way before the Lord; 11–15, Enoch and his brethren were received by the Lord unto Himself; 16–23, Christ revealed signs of His coming as given on the Mount of Olives; 24–38, The gospel will be restored, the times of the Gentiles will be fulfilled, and a desolating sickness will cover the land; 39–47, Signs, wonders, and the Resurrection are to attend the Second Coming; 48–53, Christ will stand on the Mount of Olives, and the Jews will see the wounds in His hands and feet; 54–59, The Lord will reign during the Millennium; 60–62, The Prophet is instructed to begin the translation of the New Testament, through which important information will be made known; 63–75, The Saints are commanded to gather and build the New Jerusalem, to which people from all nations will come.

1 Hearken, O ye people of my church, to whom the kingdom has been given; hearken ye and give ear to him who laid the foundation of the earth, who made the heavens and all the hosts thereof, and by whom all things were made which live, and move, and have a being.

2 And again I say, hearken unto my voice, lest death shall overtake you; in an hour when ye think not the summer shall be past, and the harvest ended, and your souls not saved.

3 Listen to him who is the advocate with the Father, who is pleading your cause before him—

4 Saying: Father, behold the sufferings and death of him who did no sin, in whom thou wast well pleased; behold the blood of thy Son which was shed, the blood of him whom thou gavest that thyself might be glorified;

5 Wherefore, Father, spare these my brethren that believe on my name, that they may come unto me and have everlasting life.

6 Hearken, O ye people of my church, and ye elders listen together, and hear my voice while it is called today, and harden not your hearts;

7 For verily I say unto you that I am Alpha and Omega, the beginning and the end, the light and the life of the world—a light that shineth in darkness and the darkness comprehendeth it not.

8 I came unto mine own, and mine own received me not; but unto as many as received me gave I power to do many miracles, and to become the sons of God; and even unto them that believed on my name gave I power to obtain eternal life.

9 And even so I have sent mine everlasting covenant into the world, to be a light to the world, and to be a standard for my people, and for the Gentiles to seek to it, and to be a messenger before my face to prepare the way before me.

10 Wherefore, come ye unto it, and with him that cometh I will reason as with men in days of old, and I will show unto you my strong reasoning.

11 Wherefore, hearken ye together and let me show unto you even my wisdom—the wisdom of him whom ye say is the God of Enoch, and his brethren,

12 Who were separated from the earth,

and were received unto myself—a city reserved until a day of righteousness shall come—a day which was sought for by all holy men, and they found it not because of wickedness and abominations;

13 And confessed they were strangers and pilgrims on the earth;

14 But obtained a promise that they should find it and see it in their flesh.

15 Wherefore, hearken and I will reason with you, and I will speak unto you and prophesy, as unto men in days of old.

16 And I will show it plainly as I showed it unto my disciples as I stood before them in the flesh, and spake unto them, saying: As ye have asked of me concerning the signs of my coming, in the day when I shall come in my glory in the clouds of heaven, to fulfil the promises that I have made unto your fathers,

17 For as ye have looked upon the long absence of your spirits from your bodies to be a bondage, I will show unto you how the day of redemption shall come, and also the restoration of the scattered Israel.

18 And now ye behold this temple which is in Jerusalem, which ye call the house of God, and your enemies say that this house shall never fall.

19 But, verily I say unto you, that desolation shall come upon this generation as a thief in the night, and this people shall be destroyed and scattered among all nations.

20 And this temple which ye now see shall be thrown down that there shall not be left one stone upon another.

21 And it shall come to pass, that this generation of Jews shall not pass away until every desolation which I have told you concerning them shall come to pass.

22 Ye say that ye know that the end of the world cometh; ye say also that ye know that the heavens and the earth shall pass away;

23 And in this ye say truly, for so it is; but these things which I have told you shall not pass away until all shall be fulfilled.

24 And this I have told you concerning Jerusalem; and when that day shall come, shall a remnant be scattered among all nations;

25 But they shall be gathered again; but they shall remain until the times of the Gentiles be fulfilled.

26 And in that day shall be heard of wars and rumors of wars, and the whole earth shall be in commotion, and men's hearts shall fail them, and they shall say that Christ delayeth his coming until the end of the earth.

27 And the love of men shall wax cold, and iniquity shall abound.

28 And when the times of the Gentiles is come in, a light shall break forth among them that sit in darkness, and it shall be the fulness of my gospel;

29 But they receive it not; for they perceive not the light, and they turn their hearts from me because of the precepts of men.

30 And in that generation shall the times of the Gentiles be fulfilled.

31 And there shall be men standing in that generation, that shall not pass until they shall see an overflowing scourge; for a desolating sickness shall cover the land.

32 But my disciples shall stand in holy

places, and shall not be moved; but among the wicked, men shall lift up their voices and curse God and die.

33 And there shall be earthquakes also in divers places, and many desolations; yet men will harden their hearts against me, and they will take up the sword, one against another, and they will kill one another.

34 And now, when I the Lord had spoken these words unto my disciples, they were troubled.

35 And I said unto them: Be not troubled, for, when all these things shall come to pass, ye may know that the promises which have been made unto you shall be fulfilled.

36 And when the light shall begin to break forth, it shall be with them like unto a parable which I will show you—

37 Ye look and behold the fig trees, and ye see them with your eyes, and ye say when they begin to shoot forth, and their leaves are yet tender, that summer is now nigh at hand;

38 Even so it shall be in that day when they shall see all these things, then shall they know that the hour is nigh.

39 And it shall come to pass that he that feareth me shall be looking forth for the great day of the Lord to come, even for the signs of the coming of the Son of Man.

40 And they shall see signs and wonders, for they shall be shown forth in the heavens above, and in the earth beneath.

41 And they shall behold blood, and fire, and vapors of smoke.

42 And before the day of the Lord shall come, the sun shall be darkened, and the moon be turned into blood, and the stars fall from heaven.

43 And the remnant shall be gathered unto this place;

44 And then they shall look for me, and, behold, I will come; and they shall see me in the clouds of heaven, clothed with power and great glory; with all the holy angels; and he that watches not for me shall be cut off.

45 But before the arm of the Lord shall fall, an angel shall sound his trump, and the saints that have slept shall come forth to meet me in the cloud.

46 Wherefore, if ye have slept in peace blessed are you; for as you now behold me and know that I am, even so shall ye come unto me and your souls shall live, and your redemption shall be perfected; and the saints shall come forth from the four quarters of the earth.

47 Then shall the arm of the Lord fall upon the nations.

48 And then shall the Lord set his foot upon this mount, and it shall cleave in twain, and the earth shall tremble, and reel to and fro, and the heavens also shall shake.

49 And the Lord shall utter his voice, and all the ends of the earth shall hear it; and the nations of the earth shall mourn, and they that have laughed shall see their folly.

50 And calamity shall cover the mocker, and the scorner shall be consumed; and they that have watched for iniquity shall be hewn down and cast into the fire.

51 And then shall the Jews look upon me and say: What are these wounds in thine hands and in thy feet?

52 Then shall they know that I am the Lord; for I will say unto them: These wounds are the wounds with which

I was wounded in the house of my friends. I am he who was lifted up. I am Jesus that was crucified. I am the Son of God.

53 And then shall they weep because of their iniquities; then shall they lament because they persecuted their king.

54 And then shall the heathen nations be redeemed, and they that knew no law shall have part in the first resurrection; and it shall be tolerable for them.

55 And Satan shall be bound, that he shall have no place in the hearts of the children of men.

56 And at that day, when I shall come in my glory, shall the parable be fulfilled which I spake concerning the ten virgins.

57 For they that are wise and have received the truth, and have taken the Holy Spirit for their guide, and have not been deceived—verily I say unto you, they shall not be hewn down and cast into the fire, but shall abide the day.

58 And the earth shall be given unto them for an inheritance; and they shall multiply and wax strong, and their children shall grow up without sin unto salvation.

59 For the Lord shall be in their midst, and his glory shall be upon them, and he will be their king and their lawgiver.

60 And now, behold, I say unto you, it shall not be given unto you to know any further concerning this chapter, until the New Testament be translated, and in it all these things shall be made known;

61 Wherefore I give unto you that ye may now translate it, that ye may be prepared for the things to come.

62 For verily I say unto you, that great things await you;

63 Ye hear of wars in foreign lands; but, behold, I say unto you, they are nigh, even at your doors, and not many years hence ye shall hear of wars in your own lands.

64 Wherefore I, the Lord, have said, gather ye out from the eastern lands, assemble ye yourselves together ye elders of my church; go ye forth into the western countries, call upon the inhabitants to repent, and inasmuch as they do repent, build up churches unto me.

65 And with one heart and with one mind, gather up your riches that ye may purchase an inheritance which shall hereafter be appointed unto you.

66 And it shall be called the New Jerusalem, a land of peace, a city of refuge, a place of safety for the saints of the Most High God;

67 And the glory of the Lord shall be there, and the terror of the Lord also shall be there, insomuch that the wicked will not come unto it, and it shall be called Zion.

68 And it shall come to pass among the wicked, that every man that will not take his sword against his neighbor must needs flee unto Zion for safety.

69 And there shall be gathered unto it out of every nation under heaven; and it shall be the only people that shall not be at war one with another.

70 And it shall be said among the wicked: Let us not go up to battle against Zion, for the inhabitants of Zion are terrible; wherefore we cannot stand.

71 And it shall come to pass that the righteous shall be gathered out from among all nations, and shall come to Zion, singing with songs of everlasting

joy.

72 And now I say unto you, keep these things from going abroad unto the world until it is expedient in me, that ye may accomplish this work in the eyes of the people, and in the eyes of your enemies, that they may not know your works until ye have accomplished the thing which I have commanded you;

73 That when they shall know it, that they may consider these things.

74 For when the Lord shall appear he shall be terrible unto them, that fear may seize upon them, and they shall stand afar off and tremble.

75 And all nations shall be afraid because of the terror of the Lord, and the power of his might. Even so. Amen.

Section 46

Revelation given through Joseph Smith the Prophet to the Church, at Kirtland, Ohio, March 8, 1831. In this early time of the Church, a unified pattern for the conducting of Church services had not yet developed. However, a custom of admitting only members and earnest investigators to the sacrament meetings and other assemblies of the Church had become somewhat general. This revelation expresses the will of the Lord relative to governing and conducting meetings and His direction on seeking and discerning the gifts of the Spirit.

1–2, Elders are to conduct meetings as guided by the Holy Spirit; 3–6, Truth seekers should not be excluded from sacramental services; 7–12, Ask of God and seek the gifts of the Spirit; 13–26, An enumeration of some of these gifts is given; 27–33, Church leaders are given power to discern the gifts of the Spirit.

1 Hearken, O ye people of my church; for verily I say unto you that these things were spoken unto you for your profit and learning.

2 But notwithstanding those things which are written, it always has been given to the elders of my church from the beginning, and ever shall be, to conduct all meetings as they are directed and guided by the Holy Spirit.

3 Nevertheless ye are commanded never to cast any one out from your public meetings, which are held before the world.

4 Ye are also commanded not to cast any one who belongeth to the church out of your sacrament meetings; nevertheless, if any have trespassed, let him not partake until he makes reconciliation.

5 And again I say unto you, ye shall not cast any out of your sacrament meetings who are earnestly seeking the kingdom—I speak this concerning those who are not of the church.

6 And again I say unto you, concerning your confirmation meetings, that if there be any that are not of the church, that are earnestly seeking after the kingdom, ye shall not cast them out.

7 But ye are commanded in all things to ask of God, who giveth liberally; and that which the Spirit testifies unto you even so I would that ye should do in all holiness of heart, walking uprightly before me, considering the end of your salvation, doing all things with prayer and thanksgiving, that ye may not be seduced by evil spirits, or doctrines of devils, or the commandments of men; for some are of men, and others of devils.

8 Wherefore, beware lest ye are deceived; and that ye may not be deceived seek ye earnestly the best gifts, always remembering for what they are given;

9 For verily I say unto you, they are given for the benefit of those who love me and keep all my commandments, and him that seeketh so to do; that all may be benefited that seek or that ask of me, that ask and not for a sign that they may consume it upon their lusts.

10 And again, verily I say unto you, I would that ye should always remember, and always retain in your minds what those gifts are, that are given unto the church.

11 For all have not every gift given unto them; for there are many gifts, and to every man is given a gift by the Spirit of God.

12 To some is given one, and to some is given another, that all may be profited thereby.

13 To some it is given by the Holy Ghost to know that Jesus Christ is the Son of God, and that he was crucified for the sins of the world.

14 To others it is given to believe on their words, that they also might have eternal life if they continue faithful.

15 And again, to some it is given by the Holy Ghost to know the differences of administration, as it will be pleasing unto the same Lord, according as the Lord will, suiting his mercies according to the conditions of the children of men.

16 And again, it is given by the Holy Ghost to some to know the diversities of operations, whether they be of God, that the manifestations of the Spirit may be given to every man to profit withal.

17 And again, verily I say unto you, to some is given, by the Spirit of God, the word of wisdom.

18 To another is given the word of knowledge, that all may be taught to be wise and to have knowledge.

19 And again, to some it is given to have faith to be healed;

20 And to others it is given to have faith to heal.

21 And again, to some is given the working of miracles;

22 And to others it is given to prophesy;

23 And to others the discerning of spirits.

24 And again, it is given to some to speak with tongues;

25 And to another is given the interpretation of tongues.

26 And all these gifts come from God, for the benefit of the children of God.

27 And unto the bishop of the church, and unto such as God shall appoint and ordain to watch over the church and to be elders unto the church, are to have it given unto them to discern all those gifts lest there shall be any among you professing and yet be not of God.

28 And it shall come to pass that he that asketh in Spirit shall receive in Spirit;

29 That unto some it may be given to have all those gifts, that there may be a head, in order that every member may be profited thereby.

30 He that asketh in the Spirit asketh according to the will of God; wherefore it is done even as he asketh.

31 And again, I say unto you, all things must be done in the name of Christ, whatsoever you do in the Spirit;

32 And ye must give thanks unto God in the Spirit for whatsoever blessing ye are blessed with.

33 And ye must practice virtue and holiness before me continually. Even so. Amen.

Section 47

Revelation given through Joseph Smith the Prophet, at Kirtland, Ohio, March 8, 1831. John Whitmer, who had already served as a clerk to the Prophet, initially hesitated when he was asked to serve as the Church historian and recorder, replacing Oliver Cowdery. He wrote, "I would rather not do it but observed that the will of the Lord be done, and if he desires it, I desire that he would manifest it through Joseph the Seer." After Joseph Smith received this revelation, John Whitmer accepted and served in his appointed office.

1–4, John Whitmer is designated to keep the history of the Church and to write for the Prophet.

1 Behold, it is expedient in me that my servant John should write and keep a regular history, and assist you, my servant Joseph, in transcribing all things which shall be given you, until he is called to further duties.

2 Again, verily I say unto you that he can also lift up his voice in meetings, whenever it shall be expedient.

3 And again, I say unto you that it shall be appointed unto him to keep the church record and history continually; for Oliver Cowdery I have appointed to another office.

4 Wherefore, it shall be given him, inasmuch as he is faithful, by the Comforter, to write these things. Even so. Amen.

Section 48

Revelation given through Joseph Smith the Prophet, at Kirtland, Ohio, March 10, 1831. The Prophet had inquired of the Lord as to the mode of procedure in procuring lands for the settlement of the Saints. This was an important matter in view of the migration of members of the Church from the eastern United States, in obedience to the Lord's command that they should assemble in Ohio (see sections 37:1–3; 45:64).

1–3, The Saints in Ohio are to share their lands with their brethren; 4–6, The Saints are to purchase lands, build a city, and follow the counsel of their presiding officers.

1 It is necessary that ye should remain for the present time in your places of abode, as it shall be suitable to your circumstances.

2 And inasmuch as ye have lands, ye shall impart to the eastern brethren;

3 And inasmuch as ye have not lands, let them buy for the present time in those regions round about, as seemeth them good, for it must needs be necessary that they have places to live for the present time.

4 It must needs be necessary that ye save all the money that ye can, and that ye obtain all that ye can in righteousness, that in time ye may be enabled to purchase land for an inheritance, even the city.

5 The place is not yet to be revealed; but after your brethren come from the east there are to be certain men appointed, and to them it shall be given to know the place, or to them it shall be revealed.

6 And they shall be appointed to purchase the lands, and to make a commencement to lay the foundation of the city; and then shall ye begin to be gathered with your families, every man according to his family, according to his circumstances, and as is appointed to him by the presidency and the bishop of the church, according to the laws and commandments which ye have received, and which ye shall hereafter receive. Even so. Amen.

Section 49

Revelation given through Joseph Smith the Prophet to Sidney Rigdon, Parley P. Pratt, and Leman Copley, at Kirtland, Ohio, May 7, 1831. Leman Copley had embraced the gospel but still held to some of the teachings of the Shakers (United Society of Believers in Christ's Second Appearing), to which he had formerly belonged. Some of the beliefs of the Shakers were that Christ's Second Coming had already occurred and that He had appeared in the form of a woman, Ann Lee. They did not consider baptism by water essential. They rejected marriage and believed in a life of total celibacy. Some Shakers also forbade the eating of meat. In prefacing this revelation, Joseph Smith's history states, "In order to have [a] more perfect understanding on the subject, I inquired of the Lord, and received the following." The revelation refutes some of the basic concepts of the Shaker group. The aforementioned brethren took a copy of the revelation to the Shaker community (near Cleveland, Ohio) and read it to them in its entirety, but it was rejected.

1–7, The day and hour of Christ's coming will remain unknown until He comes; 8–14, Men must repent, believe the gospel, and obey the ordinances to gain salvation; 15–16, Marriage is ordained of God; 17–21, The eating of meat is approved; 22–28, Zion will flourish and the Lamanites blossom as the rose before the Second Coming.

1 Hearken unto my word, my servants Sidney, and Parley, and Leman; for behold, verily I say unto you, that I give unto you a commandment that you shall go and preach my gospel which ye have received, even as ye have received it, unto the Shakers.

2 Behold, I say unto you, that they desire to know the truth in part, but not all, for they are not right before me and must needs repent.

3 Wherefore, I send you, my servants Sidney and Parley, to preach the gospel unto them.

4 And my servant Leman shall be ordained unto this work, that he may reason with them, not according to that which he has received of them, but according to that which shall be taught him by you my servants; and by so doing I will bless him, otherwise he shall not prosper.

5 Thus saith the Lord; for I am God, and have sent mine Only Begotten Son into the world for the redemption of the world, and have decreed that he that receiveth him shall be saved, and he that receiveth him not shall be damned—

6 And they have done unto the Son of Man even as they listed; and he has taken his power on the right hand of his glory, and now reigneth in the heavens, and will reign till he descends on the earth to put all enemies under his feet, which time is nigh at hand—

7 I, the Lord God, have spoken it; but the hour and the day no man knoweth, neither the angels in heaven, nor shall they know until he comes.

8 Wherefore, I will that all men shall repent, for all are under sin, except those which I have reserved unto myself, holy men that ye know not of.

9 Wherefore, I say unto you that I have sent unto you mine everlasting covenant, even that which was from the beginning.

10 And that which I have promised I have so fulfilled, and the nations of the earth shall bow to it; and, if not of themselves, they shall come down, for that which is now exalted of itself shall be laid low of power.

11 Wherefore, I give unto you a commandment that ye go among this people, and say unto them, like unto

mine apostle of old, whose name was Peter:

12 Believe on the name of the Lord Jesus, who was on the earth, and is to come, the beginning and the end;

13 Repent and be baptized in the name of Jesus Christ, according to the holy commandment, for the remission of sins;

14 And whoso doeth this shall receive the gift of the Holy Ghost, by the laying on of the hands of the elders of the church.

15 And again, verily I say unto you, that whoso forbiddeth to marry is not ordained of God, for marriage is ordained of God unto man.

16 Wherefore, it is lawful that he should have one wife, and they twain shall be one flesh, and all this that the earth might answer the end of its creation;

17 And that it might be filled with the measure of man, according to his creation before the world was made.

18 And whoso forbiddeth to abstain from meats, that man should not eat the same, is not ordained of God;

19 For, behold, the beasts of the field and the fowls of the air, and that which cometh of the earth, is ordained for the use of man for food and for raiment, and that he might have in abundance.

20 But it is not given that one man should possess that which is above another, wherefore the world lieth in sin.

21 And wo be unto man that sheddeth blood or that wasteth flesh and hath no need.

22 And again, verily I say unto you, that the Son of Man cometh not in the form of a woman, neither of a man traveling on the earth.

23 Wherefore, be not deceived, but continue in steadfastness, looking forth for the heavens to be shaken, and the earth to tremble and to reel to and fro as a drunken man, and for the valleys to be exalted, and for the mountains to be made low, and for the rough places to become smooth—and all this when the angel shall sound his trumpet.

24 But before the great day of the Lord shall come, Jacob shall flourish in the wilderness, and the Lamanites shall blossom as the rose.

25 Zion shall flourish upon the hills and rejoice upon the mountains, and shall be assembled together unto the place which I have appointed.

26 Behold, I say unto you, go forth as I have commanded you; repent of all your sins; ask and ye shall receive; knock and it shall be opened unto you.

27 Behold, I will go before you and be your rearward; and I will be in your midst, and you shall not be confounded.

28 Behold, I am Jesus Christ, and I come quickly. Even so. Amen.

Section 50

Revelation given through Joseph Smith the Prophet, at Kirtland, Ohio, May 9, 1831. Joseph Smith's history states that some of the elders did not understand the manifestations of different spirits abroad in the earth and that this revelation was given in response to his special inquiry on the matter. So-called spiritual phenomena were not uncommon among the members, some of whom claimed to be receiving visions and revelations.

1–5, Many false spirits are abroad in the earth; 6–9, Wo unto the hypocrites and those who are cut off from the Church; 10–14, Elders are to preach the gospel by the Spirit; 15–22, Both preachers and hearers need to be enlightened by the Spirit; 23–25, That which doth not edify is not of God; 26–28, The faithful are possessors of all things; 29–36, The prayers of the purified are answered; 37–46, Christ is the Good Shepherd and the Stone of Israel.

1 Hearken, O ye elders of my church, and give ear to the voice of the living God; and attend to the words of wisdom which shall be given unto you, according as ye have asked and are agreed as touching the church, and the spirits which have gone abroad in the earth.

2 Behold, verily I say unto you, that there are many spirits which are false spirits, which have gone forth in the earth, deceiving the world.

3 And also Satan hath sought to deceive you, that he might overthrow you.

4 Behold, I, the Lord, have looked upon you, and have seen abominations in the church that profess my name.

5 But blessed are they who are faithful and endure, whether in life or in death, for they shall inherit eternal life.

6 But wo unto them that are deceivers and hypocrites, for, thus saith the Lord, I will bring them to judgment.

7 Behold, verily I say unto you, there are hypocrites among you, who have deceived some, which has given the adversary power; but behold such shall be reclaimed;

8 But the hypocrites shall be detected and shall be cut off, either in life or in death, even as I will; and wo unto them who are cut off from my church, for the same are overcome of the world.

9 Wherefore, let every man beware lest he do that which is not in truth and righteousness before me.

10 And now come, saith the Lord, by the Spirit, unto the elders of his church, and let us reason together, that ye may understand;

11 Let us reason even as a man reasoneth one with another face to face.

12 Now, when a man reasoneth he is understood of man, because he reasoneth as a man; even so will I, the Lord, reason with you that you may understand.

13 Wherefore, I the Lord ask you this question—unto what were ye ordained?

14 To preach my gospel by the Spirit, even the Comforter which was sent forth to teach the truth.

15 And then received ye spirits which ye could not understand, and received them to be of God; and in this are ye justified?

16 Behold ye shall answer this question yourselves; nevertheless, I will be merciful unto you; he that is weak among you hereafter shall be made strong.

17 Verily I say unto you, he that is ordained of me and sent forth to preach the word of truth by the Comforter, in the Spirit of truth, doth he preach it by the Spirit of truth or some other way?

18 And if it be by some other way it is not of God.

19 And again, he that receiveth the word of truth, doth he receive it by the Spirit of truth or some other way?

20 If it be some other way it is not of God.

21 Therefore, why is it that ye cannot understand and know, that he that receiveth the word by the Spirit of truth receiveth it as it is preached by the Spirit of truth?

22 Wherefore, he that preacheth and he that receiveth, understand one another, and both are edified and rejoice together.

23 And that which doth not edify is not of God, and is darkness.

24 That which is of God is light; and he that receiveth light, and continueth in God, receiveth more light; and that light groweth brighter and brighter until the perfect day.

25 And again, verily I say unto you, and I say it that you may know the truth, that you may chase darkness from among you;

26 He that is ordained of God and sent forth, the same is appointed to be the greatest, notwithstanding he is the least and the servant of all.

27 Wherefore, he is possessor of all things; for all things are subject unto him, both in heaven and on the earth, the life and the light, the Spirit and the power, sent forth by the will of the Father through Jesus Christ, his Son.

28 But no man is possessor of all things except he be purified and cleansed from all sin.

29 And if ye are purified and cleansed from all sin, ye shall ask whatsoever you will in the name of Jesus and it shall be done.

30 But know this, it shall be given you what you shall ask; and as ye are appointed to the head, the spirits shall be subject unto you.

31 Wherefore, it shall come to pass, that if you behold a spirit manifested that you cannot understand, and you receive not that spirit, ye shall ask of the Father in the name of Jesus; and if he give not unto you that spirit, then you may know that it is not of God.

32 And it shall be given unto you, power over that spirit; and you shall proclaim against that spirit with a loud voice that it is not of God—

33 Not with railing accusation, that ye be not overcome, neither with boasting nor rejoicing, lest you be seized therewith.

34 He that receiveth of God, let him account it of God; and let him rejoice that he is accounted of God worthy to receive.

35 And by giving heed and doing these things which ye have received, and which ye shall hereafter receive—and the kingdom is given you of the Father, and power to overcome all things which are not ordained of him—

36 And behold, verily I say unto you, blessed are you who are now hearing these words of mine from the mouth of my servant, for your sins are forgiven you.

37 Let my servant Joseph Wakefield, in whom I am well pleased, and my

servant Parley P. Pratt go forth among the churches and strengthen them by the word of exhortation;

38 And also my servant John Corrill, or as many of my servants as are ordained unto this office, and let them labor in the vineyard; and let no man hinder them doing that which I have appointed unto them—

39 Wherefore, in this thing my servant Edward Partridge is not justified; nevertheless let him repent and he shall be forgiven.

40 Behold, ye are little children and ye cannot bear all things now; ye must grow in grace and in the knowledge of the truth.

41 Fear not, little children, for you are mine, and I have overcome the world, and you are of them that my Father hath given me;

42 And none of them that my Father hath given me shall be lost.

43 And the Father and I are one. I am in the Father and the Father in me; and inasmuch as ye have received me, ye are in me and I in you.

44 Wherefore, I am in your midst, and I am the good shepherd, and the stone of Israel. He that buildeth upon this rock shall never fall.

45 And the day cometh that you shall hear my voice and see me, and know that I am.

46 Watch, therefore, that ye may be ready. Even so. Amen.

Section 51

Revelation given through Joseph Smith the Prophet, at Thompson, Ohio, May 20, 1831. At this time the Saints migrating from the eastern states began to arrive in Ohio, and it became necessary to make definite arrangements for their settlement. As this undertaking belonged particularly to the bishop's office, Bishop Edward Partridge sought instruction on the matter, and the Prophet inquired of the Lord.

1–8, Edward Partridge is appointed to regulate stewardships and properties; 9–12, The Saints are to deal honestly and receive alike; 13–15, They are to have a bishop's storehouse and to organize properties according to the Lord's law; 16–20, Ohio is to be a temporary gathering place.

1 Hearken unto me, saith the Lord your God, and I will speak unto my servant Edward Partridge, and give unto him directions; for it must needs be that he receive directions how to organize this people.

2 For it must needs be that they be organized according to my laws; if otherwise, they will be cut off.

3 Wherefore, let my servant Edward Partridge, and those whom he has chosen, in whom I am well pleased, appoint unto this people their portions, every man equal according to his family, according to his circumstances and his wants and needs.

4 And let my servant Edward Partridge, when he shall appoint a man his portion, give unto him a writing that shall secure unto him his portion, that he shall hold it, even this right and this inheritance in the church, until he transgresses and is not accounted worthy by the voice of the church, according to the laws and covenants of the church, to belong to the church.

5 And if he shall transgress and is not accounted worthy to belong to the church, he shall not have power to claim that portion which he has consecrated unto the bishop for the poor and needy of my church; therefore, he shall not retain the gift, but shall only have claim on that portion that is deeded unto him.

6 And thus all things shall be made sure, according to the laws of the land.

7 And let that which belongs to this people be appointed unto this people.

8 And the money which is left unto this people—let there be an agent appointed unto this people, to take the money to provide food and raiment, according to the wants of this people.

9 And let every man deal honestly, and be alike among this people, and receive alike, that ye may be one, even as I have commanded you.

10 And let that which belongeth to this people not be taken and given unto that of another church.

11 Wherefore, if another church would receive money of this church, let them pay unto this church again according as they shall agree;

12 And this shall be done through the bishop or the agent, which shall be appointed by the voice of the church.

13 And again, let the bishop appoint a storehouse unto this church; and let all things both in money and in meat, which are more than is needful for the wants of this people, be kept in the hands of the bishop.

14 And let him also reserve unto himself for his own wants, and for the wants of his family, as he shall be employed in doing this business.

15 And thus I grant unto this people a privilege of organizing themselves

according to my laws.

16 And I consecrate unto them this land for a little season, until I, the Lord, shall provide for them otherwise, and command them to go hence;

17 And the hour and the day is not given unto them, wherefore let them act upon this land as for years, and this shall turn unto them for their good.

18 Behold, this shall be an example unto my servant Edward Partridge, in other places, in all churches.

19 And whoso is found a faithful, a just, and a wise steward shall enter into the joy of his Lord, and shall inherit eternal life.

20 Verily, I say unto you, I am Jesus Christ, who cometh quickly, in an hour you think not. Even so. Amen.

Section 52

Revelation given through Joseph Smith the Prophet to the elders of the Church, at Kirtland, Ohio, June 6, 1831. A conference had been held at Kirtland, beginning on the 3rd and closing on the 6th of June. At this conference the first distinctive ordinations to the office of high priest were made, and certain manifestations of false and deceiving spirits were discerned and rebuked.

1–2, The next conference is designated to be held in Missouri; 3–8, Appointments of certain elders to travel together are made; 9–11, The elders are to teach what the apostles and prophets have written; 12–21, Those enlightened by the Spirit bring forth fruits of praise and wisdom; 22–44, Various elders are appointed to go forth preaching the gospel while traveling to Missouri for the conference.

1 Behold, thus saith the Lord unto the elders whom he hath called and chosen in these last days, by the voice of his Spirit—

2 Saying: I, the Lord, will make known unto you what I will that ye shall do from this time until the next conference, which shall be held in Missouri, upon the land which I will consecrate unto my people, which are a remnant of Jacob, and those who are heirs according to the covenant.

3 Wherefore, verily I say unto you, let my servants Joseph Smith, Jun., and Sidney Rigdon take their journey as soon as preparations can be made to leave their homes, and journey to the land of Missouri.

4 And inasmuch as they are faithful unto me, it shall be made known unto them what they shall do;

5 And it shall also, inasmuch as they are faithful, be made known unto them the land of your inheritance.

6 And inasmuch as they are not faithful, they shall be cut off, even as I will, as seemeth me good.

7 And again, verily I say unto you, let my servant Lyman Wight and my servant John Corrill take their journey speedily;

8 And also my servant John Murdock, and my servant Hyrum Smith, take their journey unto the same place by the way of Detroit.

9 And let them journey from thence preaching the word by the way, saying none other things than that which the prophets and apostles have written, and that which is taught them by the Comforter through the prayer of faith.

10 Let them go two by two, and thus let them preach by the way in every congregation, baptizing by water, and the laying on of the hands by the water's side.

11 For thus saith the Lord, I will cut my work short in righteousness, for the days come that I will send forth judgment unto victory.

12 And let my servant Lyman Wight beware, for Satan desireth to sift him as chaff.

13 And behold, he that is faithful shall be made ruler over many things.

14 And again, I will give unto you a pattern in all things, that ye may not be deceived; for Satan is abroad in the land, and he goeth forth deceiving the nations—

15 Wherefore he that prayeth, whose spirit is contrite, the same is accepted of me if he obey mine ordinances.

16 He that speaketh, whose spirit is contrite, whose language is meek and

edifieth, the same is of God if he obey mine ordinances.

17 And again, he that trembleth under my power shall be made strong, and shall bring forth fruits of praise and wisdom, according to the revelations and truths which I have given you.

18 And again, he that is overcome and bringeth not forth fruits, even according to this pattern, is not of me.

19 Wherefore, by this pattern ye shall know the spirits in all cases under the whole heavens.

20 And the days have come; according to men's faith it shall be done unto them.

21 Behold, this commandment is given unto all the elders whom I have chosen.

22 And again, verily I say unto you, let my servant Thomas B. Marsh and my servant Ezra Thayre take their journey also, preaching the word by the way unto this same land.

23 And again, let my servant Isaac Morley and my servant Ezra Booth take their journey, also preaching the word by the way unto this same land.

24 And again, let my servants Edward Partridge and Martin Harris take their journey with my servants Sidney Rigdon and Joseph Smith, Jun.

25 Let my servants David Whitmer and Harvey Whitlock also take their journey, and preach by the way unto this same land.

26 And let my servants Parley P. Pratt and Orson Pratt take their journey, and preach by the way, even unto this same land.

27 And let my servants Solomon Hancock and Simeon Carter also take their journey unto this same land, and preach by the way.

28 Let my servants Edson Fuller and Jacob Scott also take their journey.

29 Let my servants Levi W. Hancock and Zebedee Coltrin also take their journey.

30 Let my servants Reynolds Cahoon and Samuel H. Smith also take their journey.

31 Let my servants Wheeler Baldwin and William Carter also take their journey.

32 And let my servants Newel Knight and Selah J. Griffin both be ordained, and also take their journey.

33 Yea, verily I say, let all these take their journey unto one place, in their several courses, and one man shall not build upon another's foundation, neither journey in another's track.

34 He that is faithful, the same shall be kept and blessed with much fruit.

35 And again, I say unto you, let my servants Joseph Wakefield and Solomon Humphrey take their journey into the eastern lands;

36 Let them labor with their families, declaring none other things than the prophets and apostles, that which they have seen and heard and most assuredly believe, that the prophecies may be fulfilled.

37 In consequence of transgression, let that which was bestowed upon Heman Basset be taken from him, and placed upon the head of Simonds Ryder.

38 And again, verily I say unto you, let Jared Carter be ordained a priest, and also George James be ordained a priest.

39 Let the residue of the elders watch over the churches, and declare the word in the regions round about them; and let them labor with their own hands that there be no idolatry nor wickedness practiced.

40 And remember in all things the poor and the needy, the sick and the afflicted, for he that doeth not these things, the same is not my disciple.

41 And again, let my servants Joseph Smith, Jun., and Sidney Rigdon and Edward Partridge take with them a recommend from the church. And let there be one obtained for my servant Oliver Cowdery also.

42 And thus, even as I have said, if ye are faithful ye shall assemble yourselves together to rejoice upon the land of Missouri, which is the land of your inheritance, which is now the land of your enemies.

43 But, behold, I, the Lord, will hasten the city in its time, and will crown the faithful with joy and with rejoicing.

44 Behold, I am Jesus Christ, the Son of God, and I will lift them up at the last day. Even so. Amen.

Section 53

Revelation given through Joseph Smith the Prophet to Algernon Sidney Gilbert, at Kirtland, Ohio, June 8, 1831. At Sidney Gilbert's request, the Prophet inquired of the Lord as to Brother Gilbert's work and appointment in the Church.

1–3, Sidney Gilbert's calling and election in the Church is to be ordained an elder; 4–7, He is also to serve as a bishop's agent.

1 Behold, I say unto you, my servant Sidney Gilbert, that I have heard your prayers; and you have called upon me that it should be made known unto you, of the Lord your God, concerning your calling and election in the church, which I, the Lord, have raised up in these last days.

2 Behold, I, the Lord, who was crucified for the sins of the world, give unto you a commandment that you shall forsake the world.

3 Take upon you mine ordination, even that of an elder, to preach faith and repentance and remission of sins, according to my word, and the reception of the Holy Spirit by the laying on of hands;

4 And also to be an agent unto this church in the place which shall be appointed by the bishop, according to commandments which shall be given hereafter.

5 And again, verily I say unto you, you shall take your journey with my servants Joseph Smith, Jun., and Sidney Rigdon.

6 Behold, these are the first ordinances which you shall receive; and the residue shall be made known in a time to come, according to your labor in my vineyard.

7 And again, I would that ye should learn that he only is saved who endureth unto the end. Even so. Amen.

Section 54

Revelation given through Joseph Smith the Prophet to Newel Knight, at Kirtland, Ohio, June 10, 1831. Members of the Church living in Thompson, Ohio, were divided on questions having to do with the consecration of properties. Selfishness and greed were manifest. Following his mission to the Shakers (see the heading to section 49), Leman Copley had broken his covenant to consecrate his large farm as a place of inheritance for the Saints arriving from Colesville, New York. As a consequence, Newel Knight (leader of the members living in Thompson) and other elders had come to the Prophet asking how to proceed. The Prophet inquired of the Lord and received this revelation, which commands the members in Thompson to leave Leman Copley's farm and journey to Missouri.

1–6, The Saints must keep the gospel covenant to gain mercy; 7–10, They must be patient in tribulation.

1 Behold, thus saith the Lord, even Alpha and Omega, the beginning and the end, even he who was crucified for the sins of the world—

2 Behold, verily, verily, I say unto you, my servant Newel Knight, you shall stand fast in the office whereunto I have appointed you.

3 And if your brethren desire to escape their enemies, let them repent of all their sins, and become truly humble before me and contrite.

4 And as the covenant which they made unto me has been broken, even so it has become void and of none effect.

5 And wo to him by whom this offense cometh, for it had been better for him that he had been drowned in the depth of the sea.

6 But blessed are they who have kept the covenant and observed the commandment, for they shall obtain mercy.

7 Wherefore, go to now and flee the land, lest your enemies come upon you; and take your journey, and appoint whom you will to be your leader, and to pay moneys for you.

8 And thus you shall take your journey into the regions westward, unto the land of Missouri, unto the borders of the Lamanites.

9 And after you have done journeying, behold, I say unto you, seek ye a living like unto men, until I prepare a place for you.

10 And again, be patient in tribulation until I come; and, behold, I come quickly, and my reward is with me, and they who have sought me early shall find rest to their souls. Even so. Amen.

Section 55

Revelation given through Joseph Smith the Prophet to William W. Phelps, at Kirtland, Ohio, June 14, 1831. William W. Phelps, a printer, and his family had just arrived at Kirtland, and the Prophet sought the Lord for information concerning him.

1–3, William W. Phelps is called and chosen to be baptized, to be ordained an elder, and to preach the gospel; 4, He is also to write books for children in Church schools; 5–6, He is to travel to Missouri, which will be the area of his labors.

1 Behold, thus saith the Lord unto you, my servant William, yea, even the Lord of the whole earth, thou art called and chosen; and after thou hast been baptized by water, which if you do with an eye single to my glory, you shall have a remission of your sins and a reception of the Holy Spirit by the laying on of hands;

2 And then thou shalt be ordained by the hand of my servant Joseph Smith, Jun., to be an elder unto this church, to preach repentance and remission of sins by way of baptism in the name of Jesus Christ, the Son of the living God.

3 And on whomsoever you shall lay your hands, if they are contrite before me, you shall have power to give the Holy Spirit.

4 And again, you shall be ordained to assist my servant Oliver Cowdery to do the work of printing, and of selecting and writing books for schools in this church, that little children also may receive instruction before me as is pleasing unto me.

5 And again, verily I say unto you, for this cause you shall take your journey with my servants Joseph Smith, Jun., and Sidney Rigdon, that you may be planted in the land of your inheritance to do this work.

6 And again, let my servant Joseph Coe also take his journey with them. The residue shall be made known hereafter, even as I will. Amen.

Section 56

Revelation given through Joseph Smith the Prophet, at Kirtland, Ohio, June 15, 1831. This revelation chastises Ezra Thayre for not obeying a former revelation (the "commandment" referred to in verse 8), which Joseph Smith had received for him, instructing Thayre concerning his duties on Frederick G. Williams' farm, where he lived. The following revelation also revokes Thayre's call to travel to Missouri with Thomas B. Marsh (see section 52:22).

1–2, The Saints must take up their cross and follow the Lord to gain salvation; 3–13, The Lord commands and revokes, and the disobedient are cast off; 14–17, Wo unto the rich who will not help the poor, and wo unto the poor whose hearts are not broken; 18–20, Blessed are the poor who are pure in heart, for they will inherit the earth.

1 Hearken, O ye people who profess my name, saith the Lord your God; for behold, mine anger is kindled against the rebellious, and they shall know mine arm and mine indignation, in the day of visitation and of wrath upon the nations.

2 And he that will not take up his cross and follow me, and keep my commandments, the same shall not be saved.

3 Behold, I, the Lord, command; and he that will not obey shall be cut off in mine own due time, after I have commanded and the commandment is broken.

4 Wherefore I, the Lord, command and revoke, as it seemeth me good; and all this to be answered upon the heads of the rebellious, saith the Lord.

5 Wherefore, I revoke the commandment which was given unto my servants Thomas B. Marsh and Ezra Thayre, and give a new commandment unto my servant Thomas, that he shall take up his journey speedily to the land of Missouri, and my servant Selah J. Griffin shall also go with him.

6 For behold, I revoke the commandment which was given unto my servants Selah J. Griffin and Newel Knight, in consequence of the stiffneckedness of my people which are in Thompson, and their rebellions.

7 Wherefore, let my servant Newel Knight remain with them; and as many as will go may go, that are contrite before me, and be led by him to the land which I have appointed.

8 And again, verily I say unto you, that my servant Ezra Thayre must repent of his pride, and of his selfishness, and obey the former commandment which I have given him concerning the place upon which he lives.

9 And if he will do this, as there shall be no divisions made upon the land, he shall be appointed still to go to the land of Missouri;

10 Otherwise he shall receive the money which he has paid, and shall leave the place, and shall be cut off out of my church, saith the Lord God of hosts;

11 And though the heaven and the earth pass away, these words shall not pass away, but shall be fulfilled.

12 And if my servant Joseph Smith, Jun., must needs pay the money, behold, I, the Lord, will pay it unto him again in the land of Missouri, that those of whom he shall receive may be rewarded again according to that which they do;

13 For according to that which they do they shall receive, even in lands for their inheritance.

14 Behold, thus saith the Lord unto my

people—you have many things to do and to repent of; for behold, your sins have come up unto me, and are not pardoned, because you seek to counsel in your own ways.

15 And your hearts are not satisfied. And ye obey not the truth, but have pleasure in unrighteousness.

16 Wo unto you rich men, that will not give your substance to the poor, for your riches will canker your souls; and this shall be your lamentation in the day of visitation, and of judgment, and of indignation: The harvest is past, the summer is ended, and my soul is not saved!

17 Wo unto you poor men, whose hearts are not broken, whose spirits are not contrite, and whose bellies are not satisfied, and whose hands are not stayed from laying hold upon other men's goods, whose eyes are full of greediness, and who will not labor with your own hands!

18 But blessed are the poor who are pure in heart, whose hearts are broken, and whose spirits are contrite, for they shall see the kingdom of God coming in power and great glory unto their deliverance; for the fatness of the earth shall be theirs.

19 For behold, the Lord shall come, and his recompense shall be with him, and he shall reward every man, and the poor shall rejoice;

20 And their generations shall inherit the earth from generation to generation, forever and ever. And now I make an end of speaking unto you. Even so. Amen.

Section 57

Revelation given through Joseph Smith the Prophet, in Zion, Jackson County, Missouri, July 20, 1831. In compliance with the Lord's command to travel to Missouri, where He would reveal "the land of your inheritance" (section 52), the elders had journeyed from Ohio to Missouri's western border. Joseph Smith contemplated the state of the Lamanites and wondered: "When will the wilderness blossom as the rose? When will Zion be built up in her glory, and where will Thy temple stand, unto which all nations shall come in the last days?" Subsequently he received this revelation.

1–3, Independence, Missouri, is the place for the City of Zion and the temple; 4–7, The Saints are to purchase lands and receive inheritances in that area; 8–16, Sidney Gilbert is to establish a store, William W. Phelps is to be a printer, and Oliver Cowdery is to edit material for publication.

1 Hearken, O ye elders of my church, saith the Lord your God, who have assembled yourselves together, according to my commandments, in this land, which is the land of Missouri, which is the land which I have appointed and consecrated for the gathering of the saints.

2 Wherefore, this is the land of promise, and the place for the city of Zion.

3 And thus saith the Lord your God, if you will receive wisdom here is wisdom. Behold, the place which is now called Independence is the center place; and a spot for the temple is lying westward, upon a lot which is not far from the courthouse.

4 Wherefore, it is wisdom that the land should be purchased by the saints, and also every tract lying westward, even unto the line running directly between Jew and Gentile;

5 And also every tract bordering by the prairies, inasmuch as my disciples are enabled to buy lands. Behold, this is wisdom, that they may obtain it for an everlasting inheritance.

6 And let my servant Sidney Gilbert stand in the office to which I have appointed him, to receive moneys, to be an agent unto the church, to buy land in all the regions round about, inasmuch as can be done in righteousness, and as wisdom shall direct.

7 And let my servant Edward Partridge stand in the office to which I have appointed him, and divide unto the saints their inheritance, even as I have commanded; and also those whom he has appointed to assist him.

8 And again, verily I say unto you, let my servant Sidney Gilbert plant himself in this place, and establish a store, that he may sell goods without fraud, that he may obtain money to buy lands for the good of the saints, and that he may obtain whatsoever things the disciples may need to plant them in their inheritance.

9 And also let my servant Sidney Gilbert obtain a license—behold here is wisdom, and whoso readeth let him understand—that he may send goods also unto the people, even by whom he will as clerks employed in his service;

10 And thus provide for my saints, that my gospel may be preached unto those who sit in darkness and in the region and shadow of death.

11 And again, verily I say unto you, let my servant William W. Phelps be planted in this place, and be established as a printer unto the church.

12 And lo, if the world receive his writings—behold here is wisdom—let him obtain whatsoever he can obtain in righteousness, for the good of the saints.

13 And let my servant Oliver Cowdery assist him, even as I have commanded, in whatsoever place I shall appoint unto him, to copy, and to correct, and select, that all things may be right before me, as it shall be proved by the Spirit through him.

14 And thus let those of whom I have spoken be planted in the land of Zion, as speedily as can be, with their families, to do those things even as I have spoken.

15 And now concerning the gathering—Let the bishop and the agent make preparations for those families which have been commanded to come to this land, as soon as possible, and plant them in their inheritance.

16 And unto the residue of both elders and members further directions shall be given hereafter. Even so. Amen.

Section 58

Revelation given through Joseph Smith the Prophet, in Zion, Jackson County, Missouri, August 1, 1831. Earlier, on the first Sabbath after the arrival of the Prophet and his party in Jackson County, Missouri, a religious service had been held, and two members had been received by baptism. During that week, some of the Colesville Saints from the Thompson Branch and others arrived (see section 54). Many were eager to learn the will of the Lord concerning them in the new place of gathering.

1–5, Those who endure tribulation will be crowned with glory; 6–12, The Saints are to prepare for the marriage of the Lamb and the supper of the Lord; 13–18, Bishops are judges in Israel; 19–23, The Saints are to obey the laws of the land; 24–29, Men should use their agency to do good; 30–33, The Lord commands and revokes; 34–43, To repent, men must confess and forsake their sins; 44–58, The Saints are to purchase their inheritance and gather in Missouri; 59–65, The gospel must be preached unto every creature.

1 Hearken, O ye elders of my church, and give ear to my word, and learn of me what I will concerning you, and also concerning this land unto which I have sent you.

2 For verily I say unto you, blessed is he that keepeth my commandments, whether in life or in death; and he that is faithful in tribulation, the reward of the same is greater in the kingdom of heaven.

3 Ye cannot behold with your natural eyes, for the present time, the design of your God concerning those things which shall come hereafter, and the glory which shall follow after much tribulation.

4 For after much tribulation come the blessings. Wherefore the day cometh that ye shall be crowned with much glory; the hour is not yet, but is nigh at hand.

5 Remember this, which I tell you before, that you may lay it to heart, and receive that which is to follow.

6 Behold, verily I say unto you, for this cause I have sent you—that you might be obedient, and that your hearts might be prepared to bear testimony of the things which are to come;

7 And also that you might be honored in laying the foundation, and in bearing record of the land upon which the Zion of God shall stand;

8 And also that a feast of fat things might be prepared for the poor; yea, a feast of fat things, of wine on the lees well refined, that the earth may know that the mouths of the prophets shall not fail;

9 Yea, a supper of the house of the Lord, well prepared, unto which all nations shall be invited.

10 First, the rich and the learned, the wise and the noble;

11 And after that cometh the day of my power; then shall the poor, the lame, and the blind, and the deaf, come in unto the marriage of the Lamb, and partake of the supper of the Lord, prepared for the great day to come.

12 Behold, I, the Lord, have spoken it.

13 And that the testimony might go forth from Zion, yea, from the mouth of the city of the heritage of God—

14 Yea, for this cause I have sent you hither, and have selected my servant Edward Partridge, and have appointed unto him his mission in this land.

15 But if he repent not of his sins, which

are unbelief and blindness of heart, let him take heed lest he fall.

16 Behold his mission is given unto him, and it shall not be given again.

17 And whoso standeth in this mission is appointed to be a judge in Israel, like as it was in ancient days, to divide the lands of the heritage of God unto his children;

18 And to judge his people by the testimony of the just, and by the assistance of his counselors, according to the laws of the kingdom which are given by the prophets of God.

19 For verily I say unto you, my law shall be kept on this land.

20 Let no man think he is ruler; but let God rule him that judgeth, according to the counsel of his own will, or, in other words, him that counseleth or sitteth upon the judgment seat.

21 Let no man break the laws of the land, for he that keepeth the laws of God hath no need to break the laws of the land.

22 Wherefore, be subject to the powers that be, until he reigns whose right it is to reign, and subdues all enemies under his feet.

23 Behold, the laws which ye have received from my hand are the laws of the church, and in this light ye shall hold them forth. Behold, here is wisdom.

24 And now, as I spake concerning my servant Edward Partridge, this land is the land of his residence, and those whom he has appointed for his counselors; and also the land of the residence of him whom I have appointed to keep my storehouse;

25 Wherefore, let them bring their families to this land, as they shall counsel between themselves and me.

26 For behold, it is not meet that I should command in all things; for he that is compelled in all things, the same is a slothful and not a wise servant; wherefore he receiveth no reward.

27 Verily I say, men should be anxiously engaged in a good cause, and do many things of their own free will, and bring to pass much righteousness;

28 For the power is in them, wherein they are agents unto themselves. And inasmuch as men do good they shall in nowise lose their reward.

29 But he that doeth not anything until he is commanded, and receiveth a commandment with doubtful heart, and keepeth it with slothfulness, the same is damned.

30 Who am I that made man, saith the Lord, that will hold him guiltless that obeys not my commandments?

31 Who am I, saith the Lord, that have promised and have not fulfilled?

32 I command and men obey not; I revoke and they receive not the blessing.

33 Then they say in their hearts: This is not the work of the Lord, for his promises are not fulfilled. But wo unto such, for their reward lurketh beneath, and not from above.

34 And now I give unto you further directions concerning this land.

35 It is wisdom in me that my servant Martin Harris should be an example unto the church, in laying his moneys before the bishop of the church.

36 And also, this is a law unto every man that cometh unto this land to receive an inheritance; and he shall do

with his moneys according as the law directs.

37 And it is wisdom also that there should be lands purchased in Independence, for the place of the storehouse, and also for the house of the printing.

38 And other directions concerning my servant Martin Harris shall be given him of the Spirit, that he may receive his inheritance as seemeth him good;

39 And let him repent of his sins, for he seeketh the praise of the world.

40 And also let my servant William W. Phelps stand in the office to which I have appointed him, and receive his inheritance in the land;

41 And also he hath need to repent, for I, the Lord, am not well pleased with him, for he seeketh to excel, and he is not sufficiently meek before me.

42 Behold, he who has repented of his sins, the same is forgiven, and I, the Lord, remember them no more.

43 By this ye may know if a man repenteth of his sins—behold, he will confess them and forsake them.

44 And now, verily, I say concerning the residue of the elders of my church, the time has not yet come, for many years, for them to receive their inheritance in this land, except they desire it through the prayer of faith, only as it shall be appointed unto them of the Lord.

45 For, behold, they shall push the people together from the ends of the earth.

46 Wherefore, assemble yourselves together; and they who are not appointed to stay in this land, let them preach the gospel in the regions round about; and after that let them return to their homes.

47 Let them preach by the way, and bear testimony of the truth in all places, and call upon the rich, the high and the low, and the poor to repent.

48 And let them build up churches, inasmuch as the inhabitants of the earth will repent.

49 And let there be an agent appointed by the voice of the church, unto the church in Ohio, to receive moneys to purchase lands in Zion.

50 And I give unto my servant Sidney Rigdon a commandment, that he shall write a description of the land of Zion, and a statement of the will of God, as it shall be made known by the Spirit unto him;

51 And an epistle and subscription, to be presented unto all the churches to obtain moneys, to be put into the hands of the bishop, of himself or the agent, as seemeth him good or as he shall direct, to purchase lands for an inheritance for the children of God.

52 For, behold, verily I say unto you, the Lord willeth that the disciples and the children of men should open their hearts, even to purchase this whole region of country, as soon as time will permit.

53 Behold, here is wisdom. Let them do this lest they receive none inheritance, save it be by the shedding of blood.

54 And again, inasmuch as there is land obtained, let there be workmen sent forth of all kinds unto this land, to labor for the saints of God.

55 Let all these things be done in order; and let the privileges of the lands be made known from time to time, by the bishop or the agent of the church.

56 And let the work of the gathering be not in haste, nor by flight; but let it be done as it shall be counseled by the elders of the church at the conferences, according to the knowledge which they receive from time to time.

57 And let my servant Sidney Rigdon consecrate and dedicate this land, and the spot for the temple, unto the Lord.

58 And let a conference meeting be called; and after that let my servants Sidney Rigdon and Joseph Smith, Jun., return, and also Oliver Cowdery with them, to accomplish the residue of the work which I have appointed unto them in their own land, and the residue as shall be ruled by the conferences.

59 And let no man return from this land except he bear record by the way, of that which he knows and most assuredly believes.

60 Let that which has been bestowed upon Ziba Peterson be taken from him; and let him stand as a member in the church, and labor with his own hands, with the brethren, until he is sufficiently chastened for all his sins; for he confesseth them not, and he thinketh to hide them.

61 Let the residue of the elders of this church, who are coming to this land, some of whom are exceedingly blessed even above measure, also hold a conference upon this land.

62 And let my servant Edward Partridge direct the conference which shall be held by them.

63 And let them also return, preaching the gospel by the way, bearing record of the things which are revealed unto them.

64 For, verily, the sound must go forth from this place into all the world, and unto the uttermost parts of the earth—the gospel must be preached unto every creature, with signs following them that believe.

65 And behold the Son of Man cometh. Amen.

Section 59

Revelation given through Joseph Smith the Prophet, in Zion, Jackson County, Missouri, August 7, 1831. Preceding this revelation, the land was consecrated, as the Lord had directed, and the site for the future temple was dedicated. On the day this revelation was received, Polly Knight, the wife of Joseph Knight Sr., died, the first Church member to die in Zion. Early members characterized this revelation as "instructing the Saints how to keep the sabbath and how to fast and pray."

1–4, The faithful Saints in Zion will be blessed; 5–8, They are to love and serve the Lord and keep His commandments; 9–19, By keeping the Lord's day holy, the Saints are blessed temporally and spiritually; 20–24, The righteous are promised peace in this world and eternal life in the world to come.

1 Behold, blessed, saith the Lord, are they who have come up unto this land with an eye single to my glory, according to my commandments.

2 For those that live shall inherit the earth, and those that die shall rest from all their labors, and their works shall follow them; and they shall receive a crown in the mansions of my Father, which I have prepared for them.

3 Yea, blessed are they whose feet stand upon the land of Zion, who have obeyed my gospel; for they shall receive for their reward the good things of the earth, and it shall bring forth in its strength.

4 And they shall also be crowned with blessings from above, yea, and with commandments not a few, and with revelations in their time—they that are faithful and diligent before me.

5 Wherefore, I give unto them a commandment, saying thus: Thou shalt love the Lord thy God with all thy heart, with all thy might, mind, and strength; and in the name of Jesus Christ thou shalt serve him.

6 Thou shalt love thy neighbor as thyself. Thou shalt not steal; neither commit adultery, nor kill, nor do anything like unto it.

7 Thou shalt thank the Lord thy God in all things.

8 Thou shalt offer a sacrifice unto the Lord thy God in righteousness, even that of a broken heart and a contrite spirit.

9 And that thou mayest more fully keep thyself unspotted from the world, thou shalt go to the house of prayer and offer up thy sacraments upon my holy day;

10 For verily this is a day appointed unto you to rest from your labors, and to pay thy devotions unto the Most High;

11 Nevertheless thy vows shall be offered up in righteousness on all days and at all times;

12 But remember that on this, the Lord's day, thou shalt offer thine oblations and thy sacraments unto the Most High, confessing thy sins unto thy brethren, and before the Lord.

13 And on this day thou shalt do none other thing, only let thy food be prepared with singleness of heart that thy fasting may be perfect, or, in other words, that thy joy may be full.

14 Verily, this is fasting and prayer, or in other words, rejoicing and prayer.

15 And inasmuch as ye do these things with thanksgiving, with cheerful hearts and countenances, not with much laughter, for this is sin, but with a glad heart and a cheerful countenance—

16 Verily I say, that inasmuch as ye do this, the fulness of the earth is yours, the beasts of the field and the fowls of the air, and that which climbeth upon the trees and walketh upon the earth;

17 Yea, and the herb, and the good things which come of the earth, whether for food or for raiment, or for houses, or for barns, or for orchards, or for gardens, or for vineyards;

18 Yea, all things which come of the earth, in the season thereof, are made for the benefit and the use of man, both to please the eye and to gladden the heart;

19 Yea, for food and for raiment, for taste and for smell, to strengthen the body and to enliven the soul.

20 And it pleaseth God that he hath given all these things unto man; for unto this end were they made to be used, with judgment, not to excess, neither by extortion.

21 And in nothing doth man offend God, or against none is his wrath kindled, save those who confess not his hand in all things, and obey not his commandments.

22 Behold, this is according to the law and the prophets; wherefore, trouble me no more concerning this matter.

23 But learn that he who doeth the works of righteousness shall receive his reward, even peace in this world, and eternal life in the world to come.

24 I, the Lord, have spoken it, and the Spirit beareth record. Amen.

Section 60

Revelation given through Joseph Smith the Prophet, in Independence, Jackson County, Missouri, August 8, 1831. On this occasion the elders who had traveled to Jackson County and participated in the dedication of the land and the temple site desired to know what they were to do.

1–9, The elders are to preach the gospel in the congregations of the wicked; 10–14, They should not idle away their time, nor bury their talents; 15–17, They may wash their feet as a testimony against those who reject the gospel.

1 Behold, thus saith the Lord unto the elders of his church, who are to return speedily to the land from whence they came: Behold, it pleaseth me, that you have come up hither;

2 But with some I am not well pleased, for they will not open their mouths, but they hide the talent which I have given unto them, because of the fear of man. Wo unto such, for mine anger is kindled against them.

3 And it shall come to pass, if they are not more faithful unto me, it shall be taken away, even that which they have.

4 For I, the Lord, rule in the heavens above, and among the armies of the earth; and in the day when I shall make up my jewels, all men shall know what it is that bespeaketh the power of God.

5 But, verily, I will speak unto you concerning your journey unto the land from whence you came. Let there be a craft made, or bought, as seemeth you good, it mattereth not unto me, and take your journey speedily for the place which is called St. Louis.

6 And from thence let my servants, Sidney Rigdon, Joseph Smith, Jun., and Oliver Cowdery, take their journey for Cincinnati;

7 And in this place let them lift up their voice and declare my word with loud voices, without wrath or doubting, lifting up holy hands upon them. For I am able to make you holy, and your sins are forgiven you.

8 And let the residue take their journey from St. Louis, two by two, and preach the word, not in haste, among the congregations of the wicked, until they return to the churches from whence they came.

9 And all this for the good of the churches; for this intent have I sent them.

10 And let my servant Edward Partridge impart of the money which I have given him, a portion unto mine elders who are commanded to return;

11 And he that is able, let him return it by the way of the agent; and he that is not, of him it is not required.

12 And now I speak of the residue who are to come unto this land.

13 Behold, they have been sent to preach my gospel among the congregations of the wicked; wherefore, I give unto them a commandment, thus: Thou shalt not idle away thy time, neither shalt thou bury thy talent that it may not be known.

14 And after thou hast come up unto the land of Zion, and hast proclaimed my word, thou shalt speedily return, proclaiming my word among the congregations of the wicked, not in haste, neither in wrath nor with strife.

15 And shake off the dust of thy feet against those who receive thee not, not in their presence, lest thou provoke them, but in secret; and wash thy feet, as a testimony against them in the day

of judgment.

16 Behold, this is sufficient for you, and the will of him who hath sent you.

17 And by the mouth of my servant Joseph Smith, Jun., it shall be made known concerning Sidney Rigdon and Oliver Cowdery. The residue hereafter. Even so. Amen.

Section 61

Revelation given through Joseph Smith the Prophet, on the bank of the Missouri River, McIlwaine's Bend, August 12, 1831. On their return trip to Kirtland, the Prophet and ten elders had traveled down the Missouri River in canoes. On the third day of the journey, many dangers were experienced. Elder William W. Phelps, in a daylight vision, saw the destroyer riding in power upon the face of the waters.

1–12, The Lord has decreed many destructions upon the waters; 13–22, The waters were cursed by John, and the destroyer rides upon their face; 23–29, Some have power to command the waters; 30–35, Elders are to journey two by two and preach the gospel; 36–39, They are to prepare for the coming of the Son of Man.

1 Behold, and hearken unto the voice of him who has all power, who is from everlasting to everlasting, even Alpha and Omega, the beginning and the end.

2 Behold, verily thus saith the Lord unto you, O ye elders of my church, who are assembled upon this spot, whose sins are now forgiven you, for I, the Lord, forgive sins, and am merciful unto those who confess their sins with humble hearts;

3 But verily I say unto you, that it is not needful for this whole company of mine elders to be moving swiftly upon the waters, whilst the inhabitants on either side are perishing in unbelief.

4 Nevertheless, I suffered it that ye might bear record; behold, there are many dangers upon the waters, and more especially hereafter;

5 For I, the Lord, have decreed in mine anger many destructions upon the waters; yea, and especially upon these waters.

6 Nevertheless, all flesh is in mine hand, and he that is faithful among you shall not perish by the waters.

7 Wherefore, it is expedient that my servant Sidney Gilbert and my servant William W. Phelps be in haste upon their errand and mission.

8 Nevertheless, I would not suffer that ye should part until you were chastened for all your sins, that you might be one, that you might not perish in wickedness;

9 But now, verily I say, it behooveth me that ye should part. Wherefore let my servants Sidney Gilbert and William W. Phelps take their former company, and let them take their journey in haste that they may fill their mission, and through faith they shall overcome;

10 And inasmuch as they are faithful they shall be preserved, and I, the Lord, will be with them.

11 And let the residue take that which is needful for clothing.

12 Let my servant Sidney Gilbert take that which is not needful with him, as you shall agree.

13 And now, behold, for your good I gave unto you a commandment concerning these things; and I, the Lord, will reason with you as with men in days of old.

14 Behold, I, the Lord, in the beginning blessed the waters; but in the last days, by the mouth of my servant John, I cursed the waters.

15 Wherefore, the days will come that no flesh shall be safe upon the waters.

16 And it shall be said in days to come that none is able to go up to the land of Zion upon the waters, but he that is upright in heart.

17 And, as I, the Lord, in the beginning cursed the land, even so in the last days have I blessed it, in its time, for the use of my saints, that they may partake the fatness thereof.

18 And now I give unto you a commandment that what I say unto one I say unto all, that you shall forewarn your brethren concerning these waters, that they come not in journeying upon them, lest their faith fail and they are caught in snares;

19 I, the Lord, have decreed, and the destroyer rideth upon the face thereof, and I revoke not the decree.

20 I, the Lord, was angry with you yesterday, but today mine anger is turned away.

21 Wherefore, let those concerning whom I have spoken, that should take their journey in haste—again I say unto you, let them take their journey in haste.

22 And it mattereth not unto me, after a little, if it so be that they fill their mission, whether they go by water or by land; let this be as it is made known unto them according to their judgments hereafter.

23 And now, concerning my servants, Sidney Rigdon, Joseph Smith, Jun., and Oliver Cowdery, let them come not again upon the waters, save it be upon the canal, while journeying unto their homes; or in other words they shall not come upon the waters to journey, save upon the canal.

24 Behold, I, the Lord, have appointed a way for the journeying of my saints; and behold, this is the way—that after they leave the canal they shall journey by land, inasmuch as they are commanded to journey and go up unto the land of Zion;

25 And they shall do like unto the children of Israel, pitching their tents by the way.

26 And, behold, this commandment you shall give unto all your brethren.

27 Nevertheless, unto whom is given power to command the waters, unto him it is given by the Spirit to know all his ways;

28 Wherefore, let him do as the Spirit of the living God commandeth him, whether upon the land or upon the waters, as it remaineth with me to do hereafter.

29 And unto you is given the course for the saints, or the way for the saints of the camp of the Lord, to journey.

30 And again, verily I say unto you, my servants, Sidney Rigdon, Joseph Smith, Jun., and Oliver Cowdery, shall not open their mouths in the congregations of the wicked until they arrive at Cincinnati;

31 And in that place they shall lift up their voices unto God against that people, yea, unto him whose anger is kindled against their wickedness, a people who are well-nigh ripened for destruction.

32 And from thence let them journey for the congregations of their brethren, for their labors even now are wanted more abundantly among them than among the congregations of the wicked.

33 And now, concerning the residue, let them journey and declare the word among the congregations of the wicked, inasmuch as it is given;

34 And inasmuch as they do this they shall rid their garments, and they shall be spotless before me.

35 And let them journey together, or two by two, as seemeth them good,

only let my servant Reynolds Cahoon, and my servant Samuel H. Smith, with whom I am well pleased, be not separated until they return to their homes, and this for a wise purpose in me.

36 And now, verily I say unto you, and what I say unto one I say unto all, be of good cheer, little children; for I am in your midst, and I have not forsaken you;

37 And inasmuch as you have humbled yourselves before me, the blessings of the kingdom are yours.

38 Gird up your loins and be watchful and be sober, looking forth for the coming of the Son of Man, for he cometh in an hour you think not.

39 Pray always that you enter not into temptation, that you may abide the day of his coming, whether in life or in death. Even so. Amen.

Section 62

Revelation given through Joseph Smith the Prophet, on the bank of the Missouri River at Chariton, Missouri, August 13, 1831. On this day the Prophet and his group, who were on their way from Independence to Kirtland, met several elders who were on their way to the land of Zion, and, after joyful salutations, received this revelation.

1–3, Testimonies are recorded in heaven; 4–9, The elders are to travel and preach according to judgment and as directed by the Spirit.

1 Behold, and hearken, O ye elders of my church, saith the Lord your God, even Jesus Christ, your advocate, who knoweth the weakness of man and how to succor them who are tempted.

2 And verily mine eyes are upon those who have not as yet gone up unto the land of Zion; wherefore your mission is not yet full.

3 Nevertheless, ye are blessed, for the testimony which ye have borne is recorded in heaven for the angels to look upon; and they rejoice over you, and your sins are forgiven you.

4 And now continue your journey. Assemble yourselves upon the land of Zion; and hold a meeting and rejoice together, and offer a sacrament unto the Most High.

5 And then you may return to bear record, yea, even altogether, or two by two, as seemeth you good, it mattereth not unto me; only be faithful, and declare glad tidings unto the inhabitants of the earth, or among the congregations of the wicked.

6 Behold, I, the Lord, have brought you together that the promise might be fulfilled, that the faithful among you should be preserved and rejoice together in the land of Missouri. I, the Lord, promise the faithful and cannot lie.

7 I, the Lord, am willing, if any among you desire to ride upon horses, or upon mules, or in chariots, he shall receive this blessing, if he receive it from the hand of the Lord, with a thankful heart in all things.

8 These things remain with you to do according to judgment and the directions of the Spirit.

9 Behold, the kingdom is yours. And behold, and lo, I am with the faithful always. Even so. Amen.

Section 63

Revelation given through Joseph Smith the Prophet, at Kirtland, Ohio, August 30, 1831. The Prophet, Sidney Rigdon, and Oliver Cowdery had arrived in Kirtland on August 27 from their visit to Missouri. Joseph Smith's history describes this revelation: "In these infant days of the Church, there was a great anxiety to obtain the word of the Lord upon every subject that in any way concerned our salvation; and as the land of Zion was now the most important temporal object in view, I enquired of the Lord for further information upon the gathering of the Saints, and the purchase of the land, and other matters."

1–6, A day of wrath will come upon the wicked; 7–12, Signs come by faith; 13–19, The adulterous in heart will deny the faith and be cast into the lake of fire; 20, The faithful will receive an inheritance upon the transfigured earth; 21, A full account of the events on the Mount of Transfiguration has not yet been revealed; 22–23, The obedient receive the mysteries of the kingdom; 24–31, Inheritances in Zion are to be purchased; 32–35, The Lord decrees wars, and the wicked slay the wicked; 36–48, The Saints are to gather to Zion and provide moneys to build it up; 49–54, Blessings are assured the faithful at the Second Coming, in the Resurrection, and during the Millennium; 55–58, This is a day of warning; 59–66, The Lord's name is taken in vain by those who use it without authority.

1 Hearken, O ye people, and open your hearts and give ear from afar; and listen, you that call yourselves the people of the Lord, and hear the word of the Lord and his will concerning you.

2 Yea, verily, I say, hear the word of him whose anger is kindled against the wicked and rebellious;

3 Who willeth to take even them whom he will take, and preserveth in life them whom he will preserve;

4 Who buildeth up at his own will and pleasure; and destroyeth when he pleases, and is able to cast the soul down to hell.

5 Behold, I, the Lord, utter my voice, and it shall be obeyed.

6 Wherefore, verily I say, let the wicked take heed, and let the rebellious fear and tremble; and let the unbelieving hold their lips, for the day of wrath shall come upon them as a whirlwind, and all flesh shall know that I am God.

7 And he that seeketh signs shall see signs, but not unto salvation.

8 Verily, I say unto you, there are those among you who seek signs, and there have been such even from the beginning;

9 But, behold, faith cometh not by signs, but signs follow those that believe.

10 Yea, signs come by faith, not by the will of men, nor as they please, but by the will of God.

11 Yea, signs come by faith, unto mighty works, for without faith no man pleaseth God; and with whom God is angry he is not well pleased; wherefore, unto such he showeth no signs, only in wrath unto their condemnation.

12 Wherefore, I, the Lord, am not pleased with those among you who have sought after signs and wonders for faith, and not for the good of men unto my glory.

13 Nevertheless, I give commandments, and many have turned away from my commandments and have not kept them.

14 There were among you adulterers and adulteresses; some of whom have

turned away from you, and others remain with you that hereafter shall be revealed.

15 Let such beware and repent speedily, lest judgment shall come upon them as a snare, and their folly shall be made manifest, and their works shall follow them in the eyes of the people.

16 And verily I say unto you, as I have said before, he that looketh on a woman to lust after her, or if any shall commit adultery in their hearts, they shall not have the Spirit, but shall deny the faith and shall fear.

17 Wherefore, I, the Lord, have said that the fearful, and the unbelieving, and all liars, and whosoever loveth and maketh a lie, and the whoremonger, and the sorcerer, shall have their part in that lake which burneth with fire and brimstone, which is the second death.

18 Verily I say, that they shall not have part in the first resurrection.

19 And now behold, I, the Lord, say unto you that ye are not justified, because these things are among you.

20 Nevertheless, he that endureth in faith and doeth my will, the same shall overcome, and shall receive an inheritance upon the earth when the day of transfiguration shall come;

21 When the earth shall be transfigured, even according to the pattern which was shown unto mine apostles upon the mount; of which account the fulness ye have not yet received.

22 And now, verily I say unto you, that as I said that I would make known my will unto you, behold I will make it known unto you, not by the way of commandment, for there are many who observe not to keep my commandments.

23 But unto him that keepeth my commandments I will give the mysteries of my kingdom, and the same shall be in him a well of living water, springing up unto everlasting life.

24 And now, behold, this is the will of the Lord your God concerning his saints, that they should assemble themselves together unto the land of Zion, not in haste, lest there should be confusion, which bringeth pestilence.

25 Behold, the land of Zion—I, the Lord, hold it in mine own hands;

26 Nevertheless, I, the Lord, render unto Cæsar the things which are Cæsar's.

27 Wherefore, I the Lord will that you should purchase the lands, that you may have advantage of the world, that you may have claim on the world, that they may not be stirred up unto anger.

28 For Satan putteth it into their hearts to anger against you, and to the shedding of blood.

29 Wherefore, the land of Zion shall not be obtained but by purchase or by blood, otherwise there is none inheritance for you.

30 And if by purchase, behold you are blessed;

31 And if by blood, as you are forbidden to shed blood, lo, your enemies are upon you, and ye shall be scourged from city to city, and from synagogue to synagogue, and but few shall stand to receive an inheritance.

32 I, the Lord, am angry with the wicked; I am holding my Spirit from the inhabitants of the earth.

33 I have sworn in my wrath, and decreed wars upon the face of the earth, and the wicked shall slay the wicked,

and fear shall come upon every man;

34 And the saints also shall hardly escape; nevertheless, I, the Lord, am with them, and will come down in heaven from the presence of my Father and consume the wicked with unquenchable fire.

35 And behold, this is not yet, but by and by.

36 Wherefore, seeing that I, the Lord, have decreed all these things upon the face of the earth, I will that my saints should be assembled upon the land of Zion;

37 And that every man should take righteousness in his hands and faithfulness upon his loins, and lift a warning voice unto the inhabitants of the earth; and declare both by word and by flight that desolation shall come upon the wicked.

38 Wherefore, let my disciples in Kirtland arrange their temporal concerns, who dwell upon this farm.

39 Let my servant Titus Billings, who has the care thereof, dispose of the land, that he may be prepared in the coming spring to take his journey up unto the land of Zion, with those that dwell upon the face thereof, excepting those whom I shall reserve unto myself, that shall not go until I shall command them.

40 And let all the moneys which can be spared, it mattereth not unto me whether it be little or much, be sent up unto the land of Zion, unto them whom I have appointed to receive.

41 Behold, I, the Lord, will give unto my servant Joseph Smith, Jun., power that he shall be enabled to discern by the Spirit those who shall go up unto the land of Zion, and those of my disciples who shall tarry.

42 Let my servant Newel K. Whitney retain his store, or in other words, the store, yet for a little season.

43 Nevertheless, let him impart all the money which he can impart, to be sent up unto the land of Zion.

44 Behold, these things are in his own hands, let him do according to wisdom.

45 Verily I say, let him be ordained as an agent unto the disciples that shall tarry, and let him be ordained unto this power;

46 And now speedily visit the churches, expounding these things unto them, with my servant Oliver Cowdery. Behold, this is my will, obtaining moneys even as I have directed.

47 He that is faithful and endureth shall overcome the world.

48 He that sendeth up treasures unto the land of Zion shall receive an inheritance in this world, and his works shall follow him, and also a reward in the world to come.

49 Yea, and blessed are the dead that die in the Lord, from henceforth, when the Lord shall come, and old things shall pass away, and all things become new, they shall rise from the dead and shall not die after, and shall receive an inheritance before the Lord, in the holy city.

50 And he that liveth when the Lord shall come, and hath kept the faith, blessed is he; nevertheless, it is appointed to him to die at the age of man.

51 Wherefore, children shall grow up until they become old; old men shall die; but they shall not sleep in the dust, but they shall be changed in the twinkling of an eye.

52 Wherefore, for this cause preached the apostles unto the world the resurrection of the dead.

53 These things are the things that ye must look for; and, speaking after the manner of the Lord, they are now nigh at hand, and in a time to come, even in the day of the coming of the Son of Man.

54 And until that hour there will be foolish virgins among the wise; and at that hour cometh an entire separation of the righteous and the wicked; and in that day will I send mine angels to pluck out the wicked and cast them into unquenchable fire.

55 And now behold, verily I say unto you, I, the Lord, am not pleased with my servant Sidney Rigdon; he exalted himself in his heart, and received not counsel, but grieved the Spirit;

56 Wherefore his writing is not acceptable unto the Lord, and he shall make another; and if the Lord receive it not, behold he standeth no longer in the office to which I have appointed him.

57 And again, verily I say unto you, those who desire in their hearts, in meekness, to warn sinners to repentance, let them be ordained unto this power.

58 For this is a day of warning, and not a day of many words. For I, the Lord, am not to be mocked in the last days.

59 Behold, I am from above, and my power lieth beneath. I am over all, and in all, and through all, and search all things, and the day cometh that all things shall be subject unto me.

60 Behold, I am Alpha and Omega, even Jesus Christ.

61 Wherefore, let all men beware how they take my name in their lips—

62 For behold, verily I say, that many there be who are under this condemnation, who use the name of the Lord, and use it in vain, having not authority.

63 Wherefore, let the church repent of their sins, and I, the Lord, will own them; otherwise they shall be cut off.

64 Remember that that which cometh from above is sacred, and must be spoken with care, and by constraint of the Spirit; and in this there is no condemnation, and ye receive the Spirit through prayer; wherefore, without this there remaineth condemnation.

65 Let my servants, Joseph Smith, Jun., and Sidney Rigdon, seek them a home, as they are taught through prayer by the Spirit.

66 These things remain to overcome through patience, that such may receive a more exceeding and eternal weight of glory, otherwise, a greater condemnation. Amen.

Section 64

Revelation given through Joseph Smith the Prophet to the elders of the Church, at Kirtland, Ohio, September 11, 1831. The Prophet was preparing to move to Hiram, Ohio, to renew his work on the translation of the Bible, which had been laid aside while he had been in Missouri. A company of brethren who had been commanded to journey to Zion (Missouri) was earnestly engaged in making preparations to leave in October. At this busy time, the revelation was received.

1–11, The Saints are commanded to forgive one another, lest there remain in them the greater sin; 12–22, The unrepentant are to be brought before the Church; 23–25, He that is tithed will not be burned at the Lord's coming; 26–32, The Saints are warned against debt; 33–36, The rebellious will be cut off out of Zion; 37–40, The Church will judge the nations; 41–43, Zion will flourish.

1 Behold, thus saith the Lord your God unto you, O ye elders of my church, hearken ye and hear, and receive my will concerning you.

2 For verily I say unto you, I will that ye should overcome the world; wherefore I will have compassion upon you.

3 There are those among you who have sinned; but verily I say, for this once, for mine own glory, and for the salvation of souls, I have forgiven you your sins.

4 I will be merciful unto you, for I have given unto you the kingdom.

5 And the keys of the mysteries of the kingdom shall not be taken from my servant Joseph Smith, Jun., through the means I have appointed, while he liveth, inasmuch as he obeyeth mine ordinances.

6 There are those who have sought occasion against him without cause;

7 Nevertheless, he has sinned; but verily I say unto you, I, the Lord, forgive sins unto those who confess their sins before me and ask forgiveness, who have not sinned unto death.

8 My disciples, in days of old, sought occasion against one another and forgave not one another in their hearts; and for this evil they were afflicted and sorely chastened.

9 Wherefore, I say unto you, that ye ought to forgive one another; for he that forgiveth not his brother his trespasses standeth condemned before the Lord; for there remaineth in him the greater sin.

10 I, the Lord, will forgive whom I will forgive, but of you it is required to forgive all men.

11 And ye ought to say in your hearts—let God judge between me and thee, and reward thee according to thy deeds.

12 And him that repenteth not of his sins, and confesseth them not, ye shall bring before the church, and do with him as the scripture saith unto you, either by commandment or by revelation.

13 And this ye shall do that God may be glorified—not because ye forgive not, having not compassion, but that ye may be justified in the eyes of the law, that ye may not offend him who is your lawgiver—

14 Verily I say, for this cause ye shall do these things.

15 Behold, I, the Lord, was angry with him who was my servant Ezra Booth, and also my servant Isaac Morley, for they kept not the law, neither the commandment;

16 They sought evil in their hearts, and I, the Lord, withheld my Spirit. They condemned for evil that thing in which there was no evil; nevertheless I have forgiven my servant Isaac Morley.

17 And also my servant Edward Partridge, behold, he hath sinned, and Satan seeketh to destroy his soul; but when these things are made known unto them, and they repent of the evil, they shall be forgiven.

18 And now, verily I say that it is expedient in me that my servant Sidney Gilbert, after a few weeks, shall return upon his business, and to his agency in the land of Zion;

19 And that which he hath seen and heard may be made known unto my disciples, that they perish not. And for this cause have I spoken these things.

20 And again, I say unto you, that my servant Isaac Morley may not be tempted above that which he is able to bear, and counsel wrongfully to your hurt, I gave commandment that his farm should be sold.

21 I will not that my servant Frederick G. Williams should sell his farm, for I, the Lord, will to retain a strong hold in the land of Kirtland, for the space of five years, in the which I will not overthrow the wicked, that thereby I may save some.

22 And after that day, I, the Lord, will not hold any guilty that shall go with an open heart up to the land of Zion; for I, the Lord, require the hearts of the children of men.

23 Behold, now it is called today until the coming of the Son of Man, and verily it is a day of sacrifice, and a day for the tithing of my people; for he that is tithed shall not be burned at his coming.

24 For after today cometh the burning—this is speaking after the manner of the Lord—for verily I say, tomorrow all the proud and they that do wickedly shall be as stubble; and I will burn them up, for I am the Lord of Hosts; and I will not spare any that remain in Babylon.

25 Wherefore, if ye believe me, ye will labor while it is called today.

26 And it is not meet that my servants, Newel K. Whitney and Sidney Gilbert, should sell their store and their possessions here; for this is not wisdom until the residue of the church, which remaineth in this place, shall go up unto the land of Zion.

27 Behold, it is said in my laws, or forbidden, to get in debt to thine enemies;

28 But behold, it is not said at any time that the Lord should not take when he please, and pay as seemeth him good.

29 Wherefore, as ye are agents, ye are on the Lord's errand; and whatever ye do according to the will of the Lord is the Lord's business.

30 And he hath set you to provide for his saints in these last days, that they may obtain an inheritance in the land of Zion.

31 And behold, I, the Lord, declare unto you, and my words are sure and shall not fail, that they shall obtain it.

32 But all things must come to pass in their time.

33 Wherefore, be not weary in well-doing, for ye are laying the foundation of a great work. And out of small things proceedeth that which is great.

34 Behold, the Lord requireth the heart and a willing mind; and the willing and obedient shall eat the good of the land of

Zion in these last days.

35 And the rebellious shall be cut off out of the land of Zion, and shall be sent away, and shall not inherit the land.

36 For, verily I say that the rebellious are not of the blood of Ephraim, wherefore they shall be plucked out.

37 Behold, I, the Lord, have made my church in these last days like unto a judge sitting on a hill, or in a high place, to judge the nations.

38 For it shall come to pass that the inhabitants of Zion shall judge all things pertaining to Zion.

39 And liars and hypocrites shall be proved by them, and they who are not apostles and prophets shall be known.

40 And even the bishop, who is a judge, and his counselors, if they are not faithful in their stewardships shall be condemned, and others shall be planted in their stead.

41 For, behold, I say unto you that Zion shall flourish, and the glory of the Lord shall be upon her;

42 And she shall be an ensign unto the people, and there shall come unto her out of every nation under heaven.

43 And the day shall come when the nations of the earth shall tremble because of her, and shall fear because of her terrible ones. The Lord hath spoken it. Amen.

Section 65

Revelation on prayer given through Joseph Smith the Prophet, at Hiram, Ohio, October 30, 1831.

1–2, The keys of the kingdom of God are committed to man on earth, and the gospel cause will triumph; 3–6, The millennial kingdom of heaven will come and join the kingdom of God on earth.

1 Hearken, and lo, a voice as of one sent down from on high, who is mighty and powerful, whose going forth is unto the ends of the earth, yea, whose voice is unto men—Prepare ye the way of the Lord, make his paths straight.

2 The keys of the kingdom of God are committed unto man on the earth, and from thence shall the gospel roll forth unto the ends of the earth, as the stone which is cut out of the mountain without hands shall roll forth, until it has filled the whole earth.

3 Yea, a voice crying—Prepare ye the way of the Lord, prepare ye the supper of the Lamb, make ready for the Bridegroom.

4 Pray unto the Lord, call upon his holy name, make known his wonderful works among the people.

5 Call upon the Lord, that his kingdom may go forth upon the earth, that the inhabitants thereof may receive it, and be prepared for the days to come, in the which the Son of Man shall come down in heaven, clothed in the brightness of his glory, to meet the kingdom of God which is set up on the earth.

6 Wherefore, may the kingdom of God go forth, that the kingdom of heaven may come, that thou, O God, mayest be glorified in heaven so on earth, that thine enemies may be subdued; for thine is the honor, power and glory, forever and ever. Amen.

Section 66

Revelation given through Joseph Smith the Prophet, at Hiram, Ohio, October 29, 1831. William E. McLellin had petitioned the Lord in secret to make known through the Prophet the answer to five questions, which were unknown to Joseph Smith. At McLellin's request, the Prophet inquired of the Lord and received this revelation.

1–4, The everlasting covenant is the fulness of the gospel; 5–8, Elders are to preach, testify, and reason with the people; 9–13, Faithful ministerial service ensures an inheritance of eternal life.

1 Behold, thus saith the Lord unto my servant William E. McLellin—Blessed are you, inasmuch as you have turned away from your iniquities, and have received my truths, saith the Lord your Redeemer, the Savior of the world, even of as many as believe on my name.

2 Verily I say unto you, blessed are you for receiving mine everlasting covenant, even the fulness of my gospel, sent forth unto the children of men, that they might have life and be made partakers of the glories which are to be revealed in the last days, as it was written by the prophets and apostles in days of old.

3 Verily I say unto you, my servant William, that you are clean, but not all; repent, therefore, of those things which are not pleasing in my sight, saith the Lord, for the Lord will show them unto you.

4 And now, verily, I, the Lord, will show unto you what I will concerning you, or what is my will concerning you.

5 Behold, verily I say unto you, that it is my will that you should proclaim my gospel from land to land, and from city to city, yea, in those regions round about where it has not been proclaimed.

6 Tarry not many days in this place; go not up unto the land of Zion as yet; but inasmuch as you can send, send; otherwise, think not of thy property.

7 Go unto the eastern lands, bear testimony in every place, unto every people and in their synagogues, reasoning with the people.

8 Let my servant Samuel H. Smith go with you, and forsake him not, and give him thine instructions; and he that is faithful shall be made strong in every place; and I, the Lord, will go with you.

9 Lay your hands upon the sick, and they shall recover. Return not till I, the Lord, shall send you. Be patient in affliction. Ask, and ye shall receive; knock, and it shall be opened unto you.

10 Seek not to be cumbered. Forsake all unrighteousness. Commit not adultery—a temptation with which thou hast been troubled.

11 Keep these sayings, for they are true and faithful; and thou shalt magnify thine office, and push many people to Zion with songs of everlasting joy upon their heads.

12 Continue in these things even unto the end, and you shall have a crown of eternal life at the right hand of my Father, who is full of grace and truth.

13 Verily, thus saith the Lord your God, your Redeemer, even Jesus Christ. Amen.

Section 67

Revelation given through Joseph Smith the Prophet, at Hiram, Ohio, early November 1831. The occasion was that of a special conference, and the publication of the revelations already received from the Lord through the Prophet was considered and acted upon (see the heading to section 1). William W. Phelps had recently established the Church printing press in Independence, Missouri. The conference decided to publish the revelations in the Book of Commandments and to print 10,000 copies (which because of unforeseen difficulties was later reduced to 3,000 copies). Many of the brethren bore solemn testimony that the revelations then compiled for publication were verily true, as was witnessed by the Holy Ghost shed forth upon them. Joseph Smith's history records that after the revelation known as section 1 had been received, some conversation was had concerning the language used in the revelations. The present revelation followed.

1–3, The Lord hears the prayers of and watches over His elders; 4–9, He challenges the wisest person to duplicate the least of His revelations; 10–14, Faithful elders will be quickened by the Spirit and see the face of God.

1 Behold and hearken, O ye elders of my church, who have assembled yourselves together, whose prayers I have heard, and whose hearts I know, and whose desires have come up before me.

2 Behold and lo, mine eyes are upon you, and the heavens and the earth are in mine hands, and the riches of eternity are mine to give.

3 Ye endeavored to believe that ye should receive the blessing which was offered unto you; but behold, verily I say unto you there were fears in your hearts, and verily this is the reason that ye did not receive.

4 And now I, the Lord, give unto you a testimony of the truth of these commandments which are lying before you.

5 Your eyes have been upon my servant Joseph Smith, Jun., and his language you have known, and his imperfections you have known; and you have sought in your hearts knowledge that you might express beyond his language; this you also know.

6 Now, seek ye out of the Book of Commandments, even the least that is among them, and appoint him that is the most wise among you;

7 Or, if there be any among you that shall make one like unto it, then ye are justified in saying that ye do not know that they are true;

8 But if ye cannot make one like unto it, ye are under condemnation if ye do not bear record that they are true.

9 For ye know that there is no unrighteousness in them, and that which is righteous cometh down from above, from the Father of lights.

10 And again, verily I say unto you that it is your privilege, and a promise I give unto you that have been ordained unto this ministry, that inasmuch as you strip yourselves from jealousies and fears, and humble yourselves before me, for ye are not sufficiently humble, the veil shall be rent and you shall see me and know that I am—not with the carnal neither natural mind, but with the spiritual.

11 For no man has seen God at any time in the flesh, except quickened by the Spirit of God.

12 Neither can any natural man abide the presence of God, neither after the carnal mind.

13 Ye are not able to abide the presence of God now, neither the ministering of

angels; wherefore, continue in patience until ye are perfected.

14 Let not your minds turn back; and when ye are worthy, in mine own due time, ye shall see and know that which was conferred upon you by the hands of my servant Joseph Smith, Jun. Amen.

Section 68

Revelation given through Joseph Smith the Prophet, at Hiram, Ohio, November 1, 1831, in response to prayer that the mind of the Lord be made known concerning Orson Hyde, Luke S. Johnson, Lyman E. Johnson, and William E. McLellin. Although part of this revelation was directed toward these four men, much of the content pertains to the whole Church. This revelation was expanded under Joseph Smith's direction when it was published in the 1835 edition of the Doctrine and Covenants.

1–5, The words of the elders when moved upon by the Holy Ghost are scripture; 6–12, Elders are to preach and baptize, and signs will follow true believers; 13–24, The firstborn among the sons of Aaron may serve as the Presiding Bishop (that is, hold the keys of presidency as a bishop) under the direction of the First Presidency; 25–28, Parents are commanded to teach the gospel to their children; 29–35, The Saints are to observe the Sabbath, labor diligently, and pray.

1 My servant, Orson Hyde, was called by his ordination to proclaim the everlasting gospel, by the Spirit of the living God, from people to people, and from land to land, in the congregations of the wicked, in their synagogues, reasoning with and expounding all scriptures unto them.

2 And, behold, and lo, this is an ensample unto all those who were ordained unto this priesthood, whose mission is appointed unto them to go forth—

3 And this is the ensample unto them, that they shall speak as they are moved upon by the Holy Ghost.

4 And whatsoever they shall speak when moved upon by the Holy Ghost shall be scripture, shall be the will of the Lord, shall be the mind of the Lord, shall be the word of the Lord, shall be the voice of the Lord, and the power of God unto salvation.

5 Behold, this is the promise of the Lord unto you, O ye my servants.

6 Wherefore, be of good cheer, and do not fear, for I the Lord am with you, and will stand by you; and ye shall bear record of me, even Jesus Christ, that I am the Son of the living God, that I was, that I am, and that I am to come.

7 This is the word of the Lord unto you, my servant Orson Hyde, and also unto my servant Luke Johnson, and unto my servant Lyman Johnson, and unto my servant William E. McLellin, and unto all the faithful elders of my church—

8 Go ye into all the world, preach the gospel to every creature, acting in the authority which I have given you, baptizing in the name of the Father, and of the Son, and of the Holy Ghost.

9 And he that believeth and is baptized shall be saved, and he that believeth not shall be damned.

10 And he that believeth shall be blest with signs following, even as it is written.

11 And unto you it shall be given to know the signs of the times, and the signs of the coming of the Son of Man;

12 And of as many as the Father shall bear record, to you shall be given power to seal them up unto eternal life. Amen.

13 And now, concerning the items in addition to the covenants and commandments, they are these—

14 There remain hereafter, in the due time of the Lord, other bishops to be set apart unto the church, to minister even according to the first;

15 Wherefore they shall be high priests

who are worthy, and they shall be appointed by the First Presidency of the Melchizedek Priesthood, except they be literal descendants of Aaron.

16 And if they be literal descendants of Aaron they have a legal right to the bishopric, if they are the firstborn among the sons of Aaron;

17 For the firstborn holds the right of the presidency over this priesthood, and the keys or authority of the same.

18 No man has a legal right to this office, to hold the keys of this priesthood, except he be a literal descendant and the firstborn of Aaron.

19 But, as a high priest of the Melchizedek Priesthood has authority to officiate in all the lesser offices he may officiate in the office of bishop when no literal descendant of Aaron can be found, provided he is called and set apart and ordained unto this power, under the hands of the First Presidency of the Melchizedek Priesthood.

20 And a literal descendant of Aaron, also, must be designated by this Presidency, and found worthy, and anointed, and ordained under the hands of this Presidency, otherwise they are not legally authorized to officiate in their priesthood.

21 But, by virtue of the decree concerning their right of the priesthood descending from father to son, they may claim their anointing if at any time they can prove their lineage, or do ascertain it by revelation from the Lord under the hands of the above named Presidency.

22 And again, no bishop or high priest who shall be set apart for this ministry shall be tried or condemned for any crime, save it be before the First Presidency of the church;

23 And inasmuch as he is found guilty before this Presidency, by testimony that cannot be impeached, he shall be condemned;

24 And if he repent he shall be forgiven, according to the covenants and commandments of the church.

25 And again, inasmuch as parents have children in Zion, or in any of her stakes which are organized, that teach them not to understand the doctrine of repentance, faith in Christ the Son of the living God, and of baptism and the gift of the Holy Ghost by the laying on of the hands, when eight years old, the sin be upon the heads of the parents.

26 For this shall be a law unto the inhabitants of Zion, or in any of her stakes which are organized.

27 And their children shall be baptized for the remission of their sins when eight years old, and receive the laying on of the hands.

28 And they shall also teach their children to pray, and to walk uprightly before the Lord.

29 And the inhabitants of Zion shall also observe the Sabbath day to keep it holy.

30 And the inhabitants of Zion also shall remember their labors, inasmuch as they are appointed to labor, in all faithfulness; for the idler shall be had in remembrance before the Lord.

31 Now, I, the Lord, am not well pleased with the inhabitants of Zion, for there are idlers among them; and their children are also growing up in wickedness; they also seek not earnestly the riches of eternity, but their eyes are full of greediness.

32 These things ought not to be, and must be done away from among them; wherefore, let my servant Oliver

Cowdery carry these sayings unto the land of Zion.

33 And a commandment I give unto them—that he that observeth not his prayers before the Lord in the season thereof, let him be had in remembrance before the judge of my people.

34 These sayings are true and faithful; wherefore, transgress them not, neither take therefrom.

35 Behold, I am Alpha and Omega, and I come quickly. Amen.

Section 69

Revelation given through Joseph Smith the Prophet, at Hiram, Ohio, November 11, 1831. The compilation of revelations intended for early publication had been passed upon at the special conference of November 1–2. On November 3, the revelation herein appearing as section 133, later called the Appendix, was added. Oliver Cowdery had previously been appointed to carry the manuscript of the compiled revelations and commandments to Independence, Missouri, for printing. He was also to take with him money that had been contributed for the building up of the Church in Missouri. This revelation instructs John Whitmer to accompany Oliver Cowdery and also directs Whitmer to travel and collect historical material in his calling as Church historian and recorder.

1–2, John Whitmer is to accompany Oliver Cowdery to Missouri; 3–8, He is also to preach and to collect, record, and write historical data.

1 Hearken unto me, saith the Lord your God, for my servant Oliver Cowdery's sake. It is not wisdom in me that he should be entrusted with the commandments and the moneys which he shall carry unto the land of Zion, except one go with him who will be true and faithful.

2 Wherefore, I, the Lord, will that my servant, John Whitmer, should go with my servant Oliver Cowdery;

3 And also that he shall continue in writing and making a history of all the important things which he shall observe and know concerning my church;

4 And also that he receive counsel and assistance from my servant Oliver Cowdery and others.

5 And also, my servants who are abroad in the earth should send forth the accounts of their stewardships to the land of Zion;

6 For the land of Zion shall be a seat and a place to receive and do all these things.

7 Nevertheless, let my servant John Whitmer travel many times from place to place, and from church to church, that he may the more easily obtain knowledge—

8 Preaching and expounding, writing, copying, selecting, and obtaining all things which shall be for the good of the church, and for the rising generations that shall grow up on the land of Zion, to possess it from generation to generation, forever and ever. Amen

Section 70

Revelation given through Joseph Smith the Prophet, at Hiram, Ohio, November 12, 1831. The Prophet's history states that four special conferences were held from the 1st to the 12th of November, inclusive. In the last of these assemblies, the great importance of the revelations that would later be published as the Book of Commandments and then the Doctrine and Covenants was considered. This revelation was given after the conference voted that the revelations were "worth to the Church the riches of the whole Earth." Joseph Smith's history refers to the revelations as "the foundation of the Church in these last days, and a benefit to the world, showing that the keys of the mysteries of the kingdom of our Savior are again entrusted to man."

1–5, Stewards are appointed to publish the revelations; 6–13, Those who labor in spiritual things are worthy of their hire; 14–18, The Saints should be equal in temporal things.

1 Behold, and hearken, O ye inhabitants of Zion, and all ye people of my church who are afar off, and hear the word of the Lord which I give unto my servant Joseph Smith, Jun., and also unto my servant Martin Harris, and also unto my servant Oliver Cowdery, and also unto my servant John Whitmer, and also unto my servant Sidney Rigdon, and also unto my servant William W. Phelps, by the way of commandment unto them.

2 For I give unto them a commandment; wherefore hearken and hear, for thus saith the Lord unto them—

3 I, the Lord, have appointed them, and ordained them to be stewards over the revelations and commandments which I have given unto them, and which I shall hereafter give unto them;

4 And an account of this stewardship will I require of them in the day of judgment.

5 Wherefore, I have appointed unto them, and this is their business in the church of God, to manage them and the concerns thereof, yea, the benefits thereof.

6 Wherefore, a commandment I give unto them, that they shall not give these things unto the church, neither unto the world;

7 Nevertheless, inasmuch as they receive more than is needful for their necessities and their wants, it shall be given into my storehouse;

8 And the benefits shall be consecrated unto the inhabitants of Zion, and unto their generations, inasmuch as they become heirs according to the laws of the kingdom.

9 Behold, this is what the Lord requires of every man in his stewardship, even as I, the Lord, have appointed or shall hereafter appoint unto any man.

10 And behold, none are exempt from this law who belong to the church of the living God;

11 Yea, neither the bishop, neither the agent who keepeth the Lord's storehouse, neither he who is appointed in a stewardship over temporal things.

12 He who is appointed to administer spiritual things, the same is worthy of his hire, even as those who are appointed to a stewardship to administer in temporal things;

13 Yea, even more abundantly, which abundance is multiplied unto them through the manifestations of the Spirit.

14 Nevertheless, in your temporal things you shall be equal, and this not grudgingly, otherwise the abundance of

the manifestations of the Spirit shall be withheld.

15 Now, this commandment I give unto my servants for their benefit while they remain, for a manifestation of my blessings upon their heads, and for a reward of their diligence and for their security;

16 For food and for raiment; for an inheritance; for houses and for lands, in whatsoever circumstances I, the Lord, shall place them, and whithersoever I, the Lord, shall send them.

17 For they have been faithful over many things, and have done well inasmuch as they have not sinned.

18 Behold, I, the Lord, am merciful and will bless them, and they shall enter into the joy of these things. Even so. Amen.

Section 71

Revelation given to Joseph Smith the Prophet and Sidney Rigdon, at Hiram, Ohio, December 1, 1831. The Prophet had continued to translate the Bible with Sidney Rigdon as his scribe until this revelation was received, at which time it was temporarily laid aside so as to enable them to fulfill the instruction given herein. The brethren were to go forth to preach in order to allay the unfriendly feelings that had developed against the Church as a result of the publication of letters written by Ezra Booth, who had apostatized.

1–4, Joseph Smith and Sidney Rigdon are sent forth to proclaim the gospel; 5–11, Enemies of the Saints will be confounded.

1 Behold, thus saith the Lord unto you my servants Joseph Smith, Jun., and Sidney Rigdon, that the time has verily come that it is necessary and expedient in me that you should open your mouths in proclaiming my gospel, the things of the kingdom, expounding the mysteries thereof out of the scriptures, according to that portion of Spirit and power which shall be given unto you, even as I will.

2 Verily I say unto you, proclaim unto the world in the regions round about, and in the church also, for the space of a season, even until it shall be made known unto you.

3 Verily this is a mission for a season, which I give unto you.

4 Wherefore, labor ye in my vineyard. Call upon the inhabitants of the earth, and bear record, and prepare the way for the commandments and revelations which are to come.

5 Now, behold this is wisdom; whoso readeth, let him understand and receive also;

6 For unto him that receiveth it shall be given more abundantly, even power.

7 Wherefore, confound your enemies; call upon them to meet you both in public and in private; and inasmuch as ye are faithful their shame shall be made manifest.

8 Wherefore, let them bring forth their strong reasons against the Lord.

9 Verily, thus saith the Lord unto you—there is no weapon that is formed against you shall prosper;

10 And if any man lift his voice against you he shall be confounded in mine own due time.

11 Wherefore, keep my commandments; they are true and faithful. Even so. Amen.

Section 72

Revelation given through Joseph Smith the Prophet, at Kirtland, Ohio, December 4, 1831. Several elders and members had assembled to learn their duty and to be further edified in the teachings of the Church. This section is a compilation of three revelations received on the same day. Verses 1 through 8 make known the calling of Newel K. Whitney as a bishop. He was then called and ordained, after which verses 9 through 23 were received, giving additional information as to a bishop's duties. Thereafter, verses 24 through 26 were given, providing instructions concerning the gathering to Zion.

1–8, Elders are to render an account of their stewardship unto the bishop; 9–15, The bishop keeps the storehouse and cares for the poor and needy; 16–26, Bishops are to certify the worthiness of elders.

1 Hearken, and listen to the voice of the Lord, O ye who have assembled yourselves together, who are the high priests of my church, to whom the kingdom and power have been given.

2 For verily thus saith the Lord, it is expedient in me for a bishop to be appointed unto you, or of you, unto the church in this part of the Lord's vineyard.

3 And verily in this thing ye have done wisely, for it is required of the Lord, at the hand of every steward, to render an account of his stewardship, both in time and in eternity.

4 For he who is faithful and wise in time is accounted worthy to inherit the mansions prepared for him of my Father.

5 Verily I say unto you, the elders of the church in this part of my vineyard shall render an account of their stewardship unto the bishop, who shall be appointed of me in this part of my vineyard.

6 These things shall be had on record, to be handed over unto the bishop in Zion.

7 And the duty of the bishop shall be made known by the commandments which have been given, and the voice of the conference.

8 And now, verily I say unto you, my servant Newel K. Whitney is the man who shall be appointed and ordained unto this power. This is the will of the Lord your God, your Redeemer. Even so. Amen.

9 The word of the Lord, in addition to the law which has been given, making known the duty of the bishop who has been ordained unto the church in this part of the vineyard, which is verily this—

10 To keep the Lord's storehouse; to receive the funds of the church in this part of the vineyard;

11 To take an account of the elders as before has been commanded; and to administer to their wants, who shall pay for that which they receive, inasmuch as they have wherewith to pay;

12 That this also may be consecrated to the good of the church, to the poor and needy.

13 And he who hath not wherewith to pay, an account shall be taken and handed over to the bishop of Zion, who shall pay the debt out of that which the Lord shall put into his hands.

14 And the labors of the faithful who labor in spiritual things, in administering the gospel and the things of the kingdom unto the church, and unto the world, shall answer the debt unto the bishop in Zion;

15 Thus it cometh out of the church, for according to the law every man that cometh up to Zion must lay all things before the bishop in Zion.

16 And now, verily I say unto you, that as every elder in this part of the vineyard must give an account of his stewardship unto the bishop in this part of the vineyard—

17 A certificate from the judge or bishop in this part of the vineyard, unto the bishop in Zion, rendereth every man acceptable, and answereth all things, for an inheritance, and to be received as a wise steward and as a faithful laborer;

18 Otherwise he shall not be accepted of the bishop of Zion.

19 And now, verily I say unto you, let every elder who shall give an account unto the bishop of the church in this part of the vineyard be recommended by the church or churches, in which he labors, that he may render himself and his accounts approved in all things.

20 And again, let my servants who are appointed as stewards over the literary concerns of my church have claim for assistance upon the bishop or bishops in all things—

21 That the revelations may be published, and go forth unto the ends of the earth; that they also may obtain funds which shall benefit the church in all things;

22 That they also may render themselves approved in all things, and be accounted as wise stewards.

23 And now, behold, this shall be an ensample for all the extensive branches of my church, in whatsoever land they shall be established. And now I make an end of my sayings. Amen.

24 A few words in addition to the laws of the kingdom, respecting the members of the church—they that are appointed by the Holy Spirit to go up unto Zion, and they who are privileged to go up unto Zion—

25 Let them carry up unto the bishop a certificate from three elders of the church, or a certificate from the bishop;

26 Otherwise he who shall go up unto the land of Zion shall not be accounted as a wise steward. This is also an ensample. Amen.

Section 73

Revelation given to Joseph Smith the Prophet and Sidney Rigdon, at Hiram, Ohio, January 10, 1832. Since the early part of the preceding December, the Prophet and Sidney had been engaged in preaching, and by this means much was accomplished in diminishing the unfavorable feelings that had arisen against the Church (see the heading to section 71).

1–2, Elders are to continue to preach; 3–6, Joseph Smith and Sidney Rigdon are to continue to translate the Bible until it is finished.

1 For verily, thus saith the Lord, it is expedient in me that they should continue preaching the gospel, and in exhortation to the churches in the regions round about, until conference;

2 And then, behold, it shall be made known unto them, by the voice of the conference, their several missions.

3 Now, verily I say unto you my servants, Joseph Smith, Jun., and Sidney Rigdon, saith the Lord, it is expedient to translate again;

4 And, inasmuch as it is practicable, to preach in the regions round about until conference; and after that it is expedient to continue the work of translation until it be finished.

5 And let this be a pattern unto the elders until further knowledge, even as it is written.

6 Now I give no more unto you at this time. Gird up your loins and be sober. Even so. Amen.

Section 74

Revelation given to Joseph Smith the Prophet, at Wayne County, New York, in 1830. Even before the organization of the Church, questions had arisen about the proper mode of baptism, leading the Prophet to seek answers on the subject. Joseph Smith's history states that this revelation is an explanation of 1 Corinthians 7:14, a scripture that had often been used to justify infant baptism.

1–5, Paul counsels the Church of his day not to keep the law of Moses; 6–7, Little children are holy and are sanctified through the Atonement.

1 For the unbelieving husband is sanctified by the wife, and the unbelieving wife is sanctified by the husband; else were your children unclean, but now are they holy.

2 Now, in the days of the apostles the law of circumcision was had among all the Jews who believed not the gospel of Jesus Christ.

3 And it came to pass that there arose a great contention among the people concerning the law of circumcision, for the unbelieving husband was desirous that his children should be circumcised and become subject to the law of Moses, which law was fulfilled.

4 And it came to pass that the children, being brought up in subjection to the law of Moses, gave heed to the traditions of their fathers and believed not the gospel of Christ, wherein they became unholy.

5 Wherefore, for this cause the apostle wrote unto the church, giving unto them a commandment, not of the Lord, but of himself, that a believer should not be united to an unbeliever; except the law of Moses should be done away among them,

6 That their children might remain without circumcision; and that the tradition might be done away, which saith that little children are unholy; for it was had among the Jews;

7 But little children are holy, being sanctified through the atonement of Jesus Christ; and this is what the scriptures mean.

Section 75

Revelation given through Joseph Smith the Prophet, at Amherst, Ohio, January 25, 1832. This section comprises two separate revelations (the first in verses 1 through 22 and the second in verses 23 through 36) given on the same day. The occasion was a conference at which Joseph Smith was sustained and ordained President of the High Priesthood. Certain elders desired to learn more about their immediate duties. These revelations followed.

1–5, Faithful elders who preach the gospel will gain eternal life; 6–12, Pray to receive the Comforter, who teaches all things; 13–22, Elders will sit in judgment on those who reject their message; 23–36, Families of missionaries are to receive help from the Church.

1 Verily, verily, I say unto you, I who speak even by the voice of my Spirit, even Alpha and Omega, your Lord and your God—

2 Hearken, O ye who have given your names to go forth to proclaim my gospel, and to prune my vineyard.

3 Behold, I say unto you that it is my will that you should go forth and not tarry, neither be idle but labor with your might—

4 Lifting up your voices as with the sound of a trump, proclaiming the truth according to the revelations and commandments which I have given you.

5 And thus, if ye are faithful ye shall be laden with many sheaves, and crowned with honor, and glory, and immortality, and eternal life.

6 Therefore, verily I say unto my servant William E. McLellin, I revoke the commission which I gave unto him to go unto the eastern countries;

7 And I give unto him a new commission and a new commandment, in the which I, the Lord, chasten him for the murmurings of his heart;

8 And he sinned; nevertheless, I forgive him and say unto him again, Go ye into the south countries.

9 And let my servant Luke Johnson go with him, and proclaim the things which I have commanded them—

10 Calling on the name of the Lord for the Comforter, which shall teach them all things that are expedient for them—

11 Praying always that they faint not; and inasmuch as they do this, I will be with them even unto the end.

12 Behold, this is the will of the Lord your God concerning you. Even so. Amen.

13 And again, verily thus saith the Lord, let my servant Orson Hyde and my servant Samuel H. Smith take their journey into the eastern countries, and proclaim the things which I have commanded them; and inasmuch as they are faithful, lo, I will be with them even unto the end.

14 And again, verily I say unto my servant Lyman Johnson, and unto my servant Orson Pratt, they shall also take their journey into the eastern countries; and behold, and lo, I am with them also, even unto the end.

15 And again, I say unto my servant Asa Dodds, and unto my servant Calves Wilson, that they also shall take their journey unto the western countries, and proclaim my gospel, even as I have commanded them.

16 And he who is faithful shall overcome all things, and shall be lifted

up at the last day.

17 And again, I say unto my servant Major N. Ashley, and my servant Burr Riggs, let them take their journey also into the south country.

18 Yea, let all those take their journey, as I have commanded them, going from house to house, and from village to village, and from city to city.

19 And in whatsoever house ye enter, and they receive you, leave your blessing upon that house.

20 And in whatsoever house ye enter, and they receive you not, ye shall depart speedily from that house, and shake off the dust of your feet as a testimony against them.

21 And you shall be filled with joy and gladness; and know this, that in the day of judgment you shall be judges of that house, and condemn them;

22 And it shall be more tolerable for the heathen in the day of judgment, than for that house; therefore, gird up your loins and be faithful, and ye shall overcome all things, and be lifted up at the last day. Even so. Amen.

23 And again, thus saith the Lord unto you, O ye elders of my church, who have given your names that you might know his will concerning you—

24 Behold, I say unto you, that it is the duty of the church to assist in supporting the families of those, and also to support the families of those who are called and must needs be sent unto the world to proclaim the gospel unto the world.

25 Wherefore, I, the Lord, give unto you this commandment, that ye obtain places for your families, inasmuch as your brethren are willing to open their hearts.

26 And let all such as can obtain places for their families, and support of the church for them, not fail to go into the world, whether to the east or to the west, or to the north, or to the south.

27 Let them ask and they shall receive, knock and it shall be opened unto them, and be made known from on high, even by the Comforter, whither they shall go.

28 And again, verily I say unto you, that every man who is obliged to provide for his own family, let him provide, and he shall in nowise lose his crown; and let him labor in the church.

29 Let every man be diligent in all things. And the idler shall not have place in the church, except he repent and mend his ways.

30 Wherefore, let my servant Simeon Carter and my servant Emer Harris be united in the ministry;

31 And also my servant Ezra Thayre and my servant Thomas B. Marsh;

32 Also my servant Hyrum Smith and my servant Reynolds Cahoon;

33 And also my servant Daniel Stanton and my servant Seymour Brunson;

34 And also my servant Sylvester Smith and my servant Gideon Carter;

35 And also my servant Ruggles Eames and my servant Stephen Burnett;

36 And also my servant Micah B. Welton and also my servant Eden Smith. Even so. Amen.

Section 76

A vision given to Joseph Smith the Prophet and Sidney Rigdon, at Hiram, Ohio, February 16, 1832. Prefacing the record of this vision, Joseph Smith's history states: "Upon my return from Amherst conference, I resumed the translation of the Scriptures. From sundry revelations which had been received, it was apparent that many important points touching the salvation of man had been taken from the Bible, or lost before it was compiled. It appeared self-evident from what truths were left, that if God rewarded every one according to the deeds done in the body the term 'Heaven,' as intended for the Saints' eternal home, must include more kingdoms than one. Accordingly, ... while translating St. John's Gospel, myself and Elder Rigdon saw the following vision." At the time this vision was given, the Prophet was translating John 5:29.

1–4, The Lord is God; 5–10, The mysteries of the kingdom will be revealed to all the faithful; 11–17, All will come forth in the resurrection of the just or the unjust; 18–24, The inhabitants of many worlds are begotten sons and daughters unto God through the Atonement of Jesus Christ; 25–29, An angel of God fell and became the devil; 30–49, Sons of perdition suffer eternal damnation; all others gain some degree of salvation; 50–70, The glory and reward of exalted beings in the celestial kingdom is described; 71–80, Those who will inherit the terrestrial kingdom are described; 81–113, The status of those in the telestial, terrestrial, and celestial glories is explained; 114–19, The faithful may see and understand the mysteries of God's kingdom by the power of the Holy Spirit.

1 Hear, O ye heavens, and give ear, O earth, and rejoice ye inhabitants thereof, for the Lord is God, and beside him there is no Savior.

2 Great is his wisdom, marvelous are his ways, and the extent of his doings none can find out.

3 His purposes fail not, neither are there any who can stay his hand.

4 From eternity to eternity he is the same, and his years never fail.

5 For thus saith the Lord—I, the Lord, am merciful and gracious unto those who fear me, and delight to honor those who serve me in righteousness and in truth unto the end.

6 Great shall be their reward and eternal shall be their glory.

7 And to them will I reveal all mysteries, yea, all the hidden mysteries of my kingdom from days of old, and for ages to come, will I make known unto them the good pleasure of my will concerning all things pertaining to my kingdom.

8 Yea, even the wonders of eternity shall they know, and things to come will I show them, even the things of many generations.

9 And their wisdom shall be great, and their understanding reach to heaven; and before them the wisdom of the wise shall perish, and the understanding of the prudent shall come to naught.

10 For by my Spirit will I enlighten them, and by my power will I make known unto them the secrets of my will—yea, even those things which eye has not seen, nor ear heard, nor yet entered into the heart of man.

11 We, Joseph Smith, Jun., and Sidney Rigdon, being in the Spirit on the sixteenth day of February, in the year of our Lord one thousand eight hundred and thirty-two—

12 By the power of the Spirit our eyes

were opened and our understandings were enlightened, so as to see and understand the things of God—

13 Even those things which were from the beginning before the world was, which were ordained of the Father, through his Only Begotten Son, who was in the bosom of the Father, even from the beginning;

14 Of whom we bear record; and the record which we bear is the fulness of the gospel of Jesus Christ, who is the Son, whom we saw and with whom we conversed in the heavenly vision.

15 For while we were doing the work of translation, which the Lord had appointed unto us, we came to the twenty-ninth verse of the fifth chapter of John, which was given unto us as follows—

16 Speaking of the resurrection of the dead, concerning those who shall hear the voice of the Son of Man:

17 And shall come forth; they who have done good, in the resurrection of the just; and they who have done evil, in the resurrection of the unjust.

18 Now this caused us to marvel, for it was given unto us of the Spirit.

19 And while we meditated upon these things, the Lord touched the eyes of our understandings and they were opened, and the glory of the Lord shone round about.

20 And we beheld the glory of the Son, on the right hand of the Father, and received of his fulness;

21 And saw the holy angels, and them who are sanctified before his throne, worshiping God, and the Lamb, who worship him forever and ever.

22 And now, after the many testimonies which have been given of him, this is the testimony, last of all, which we give of him: That he lives!

23 For we saw him, even on the right hand of God; and we heard the voice bearing record that he is the Only Begotten of the Father—

24 That by him, and through him, and of him, the worlds are and were created, and the inhabitants thereof are begotten sons and daughters unto God.

25 And this we saw also, and bear record, that an angel of God who was in authority in the presence of God, who rebelled against the Only Begotten Son whom the Father loved and who was in the bosom of the Father, was thrust down from the presence of God and the Son,

26 And was called Perdition, for the heavens wept over him—he was Lucifer, a son of the morning.

27 And we beheld, and lo, he is fallen! is fallen, even a son of the morning!

28 And while we were yet in the Spirit, the Lord commanded us that we should write the vision; for we beheld Satan, that old serpent, even the devil, who rebelled against God, and sought to take the kingdom of our God and his Christ—

29 Wherefore, he maketh war with the saints of God, and encompasseth them round about.

30 And we saw a vision of the sufferings of those with whom he made war and overcame, for thus came the voice of the Lord unto us:

31 Thus saith the Lord concerning all those who know my power, and have been made partakers thereof, and suffered themselves through the power of the devil to be overcome, and to deny

the truth and defy my power—

32 They are they who are the sons of perdition, of whom I say that it had been better for them never to have been born;

33 For they are vessels of wrath, doomed to suffer the wrath of God, with the devil and his angels in eternity;

34 Concerning whom I have said there is no forgiveness in this world nor in the world to come—

35 Having denied the Holy Spirit after having received it, and having denied the Only Begotten Son of the Father, having crucified him unto themselves and put him to an open shame.

36 These are they who shall go away into the lake of fire and brimstone, with the devil and his angels—

37 And the only ones on whom the second death shall have any power;

38 Yea, verily, the only ones who shall not be redeemed in the due time of the Lord, after the sufferings of his wrath.

39 For all the rest shall be brought forth by the resurrection of the dead, through the triumph and the glory of the Lamb, who was slain, who was in the bosom of the Father before the worlds were made.

40 And this is the gospel, the glad tidings, which the voice out of the heavens bore record unto us—

41 That he came into the world, even Jesus, to be crucified for the world, and to bear the sins of the world, and to sanctify the world, and to cleanse it from all unrighteousness;

42 That through him all might be saved whom the Father had put into his power and made by him;

43 Who glorifies the Father, and saves all the works of his hands, except those sons of perdition who deny the Son after the Father has revealed him.

44 Wherefore, he saves all except them—they shall go away into everlasting punishment, which is endless punishment, which is eternal punishment, to reign with the devil and his angels in eternity, where their worm dieth not, and the fire is not quenched, which is their torment—

45 And the end thereof, neither the place thereof, nor their torment, no man knows;

46 Neither was it revealed, neither is, neither will be revealed unto man, except to them who are made partakers thereof;

47 Nevertheless, I, the Lord, show it by vision unto many, but straightway shut it up again;

48 Wherefore, the end, the width, the height, the depth, and the misery thereof, they understand not, neither any man except those who are ordained unto this condemnation.

49 And we heard the voice, saying: Write the vision, for lo, this is the end of the vision of the sufferings of the ungodly.

50 And again we bear record—for we saw and heard, and this is the testimony of the gospel of Christ concerning them who shall come forth in the resurrection of the just—

51 They are they who received the testimony of Jesus, and believed on his name and were baptized after the manner of his burial, being buried in the water in his name, and this according to the commandment which he has given—

52 That by keeping the commandments they might be washed and cleansed from all their sins, and receive the Holy Spirit by the laying on of the hands of him who is ordained and sealed unto this power;

53 And who overcome by faith, and are sealed by the Holy Spirit of promise, which the Father sheds forth upon all those who are just and true.

54 They are they who are the church of the Firstborn.

55 They are they into whose hands the Father has given all things—

56 They are they who are priests and kings, who have received of his fulness, and of his glory;

57 And are priests of the Most High, after the order of Melchizedek, which was after the order of Enoch, which was after the order of the Only Begotten Son.

58 Wherefore, as it is written, they are gods, even the sons of God—

59 Wherefore, all things are theirs, whether life or death, or things present, or things to come, all are theirs and they are Christ's, and Christ is God's.

60 And they shall overcome all things.

61 Wherefore, let no man glory in man, but rather let him glory in God, who shall subdue all enemies under his feet.

62 These shall dwell in the presence of God and his Christ forever and ever.

63 These are they whom he shall bring with him, when he shall come in the clouds of heaven to reign on the earth over his people.

64 These are they who shall have part in the first resurrection.

65 These are they who shall come forth in the resurrection of the just.

66 These are they who are come unto Mount Zion, and unto the city of the living God, the heavenly place, the holiest of all.

67 These are they who have come to an innumerable company of angels, to the general assembly and church of Enoch, and of the Firstborn.

68 These are they whose names are written in heaven, where God and Christ are the judge of all.

69 These are they who are just men made perfect through Jesus the mediator of the new covenant, who wrought out this perfect atonement through the shedding of his own blood.

70 These are they whose bodies are celestial, whose glory is that of the sun, even the glory of God, the highest of all, whose glory the sun of the firmament is written of as being typical.

71 And again, we saw the terrestrial world, and behold and lo, these are they who are of the terrestrial, whose glory differs from that of the church of the Firstborn who have received the fulness of the Father, even as that of the moon differs from the sun in the firmament.

72 Behold, these are they who died without law;

73 And also they who are the spirits of men kept in prison, whom the Son visited, and preached the gospel unto them, that they might be judged according to men in the flesh;

74 Who received not the testimony of Jesus in the flesh, but afterwards received it.

75 These are they who are honorable men of the earth, who were blinded by

the craftiness of men.

76 These are they who receive of his glory, but not of his fulness.

77 These are they who receive of the presence of the Son, but not of the fulness of the Father.

78 Wherefore, they are bodies terrestrial, and not bodies celestial, and differ in glory as the moon differs from the sun.

79 These are they who are not valiant in the testimony of Jesus; wherefore, they obtain not the crown over the kingdom of our God.

80 And now this is the end of the vision which we saw of the terrestrial, that the Lord commanded us to write while we were yet in the Spirit.

81 And again, we saw the glory of the telestial, which glory is that of the lesser, even as the glory of the stars differs from that of the glory of the moon in the firmament.

82 These are they who received not the gospel of Christ, neither the testimony of Jesus.

83 These are they who deny not the Holy Spirit.

84 These are they who are thrust down to hell.

85 These are they who shall not be redeemed from the devil until the last resurrection, until the Lord, even Christ the Lamb, shall have finished his work.

86 These are they who receive not of his fulness in the eternal world, but of the Holy Spirit through the ministration of the terrestrial;

87 And the terrestrial through the ministration of the celestial.

88 And also the telestial receive it of the administering of angels who are appointed to minister for them, or who are appointed to be ministering spirits for them; for they shall be heirs of salvation.

89 And thus we saw, in the heavenly vision, the glory of the telestial, which surpasses all understanding;

90 And no man knows it except him to whom God has revealed it.

91 And thus we saw the glory of the terrestrial which excels in all things the glory of the telestial, even in glory, and in power, and in might, and in dominion.

92 And thus we saw the glory of the celestial, which excels in all things—where God, even the Father, reigns upon his throne forever and ever;

93 Before whose throne all things bow in humble reverence, and give him glory forever and ever.

94 They who dwell in his presence are the church of the Firstborn; and they see as they are seen, and know as they are known, having received of his fulness and of his grace;

95 And he makes them equal in power, and in might, and in dominion.

96 And the glory of the celestial is one, even as the glory of the sun is one.

97 And the glory of the terrestrial is one, even as the glory of the moon is one.

98 And the glory of the telestial is one, even as the glory of the stars is one; for as one star differs from another star in glory, even so differs one from another in glory in the telestial world;

99 For these are they who are of Paul, and of Apollos, and of Cephas.

100 These are they who say they are some of one and some of another—some of Christ and some of John, and some of Moses, and some of Elias, and some of Esaias, and some of Isaiah, and some of Enoch;

101 But received not the gospel, neither the testimony of Jesus, neither the prophets, neither the everlasting covenant.

102 Last of all, these all are they who will not be gathered with the saints, to be caught up unto the church of the Firstborn, and received into the cloud.

103 These are they who are liars, and sorcerers, and adulterers, and whoremongers, and whosoever loves and makes a lie.

104 These are they who suffer the wrath of God on earth.

105 These are they who suffer the vengeance of eternal fire.

106 These are they who are cast down to hell and suffer the wrath of Almighty God, until the fulness of times, when Christ shall have subdued all enemies under his feet, and shall have perfected his work;

107 When he shall deliver up the kingdom, and present it unto the Father, spotless, saying: I have overcome and have trodden the wine-press alone, even the wine-press of the fierceness of the wrath of Almighty God.

108 Then shall he be crowned with the crown of his glory, to sit on the throne of his power to reign forever and ever.

109 But behold, and lo, we saw the glory and the inhabitants of the telestial world, that they were as innumerable as the stars in the firmament of heaven, or as the sand upon the seashore;

110 And heard the voice of the Lord saying: These all shall bow the knee, and every tongue shall confess to him who sits upon the throne forever and ever;

111 For they shall be judged according to their works, and every man shall receive according to his own works, his own dominion, in the mansions which are prepared;

112 And they shall be servants of the Most High; but where God and Christ dwell they cannot come, worlds without end.

113 This is the end of the vision which we saw, which we were commanded to write while we were yet in the Spirit.

114 But great and marvelous are the works of the Lord, and the mysteries of his kingdom which he showed unto us, which surpass all understanding in glory, and in might, and in dominion;

115 Which he commanded us we should not write while we were yet in the Spirit, and are not lawful for man to utter;

116 Neither is man capable to make them known, for they are only to be seen and understood by the power of the Holy Spirit, which God bestows on those who love him, and purify themselves before him;

117 To whom he grants this privilege of seeing and knowing for themselves;

118 That through the power and manifestation of the Spirit, while in the flesh, they may be able to bear his presence in the world of glory.

119 And to God and the Lamb be glory, and honor, and dominion forever and ever. Amen.

Section 77

Revelation given to Joseph Smith the Prophet, at Hiram, Ohio, about March 1832. Joseph Smith's history states, "In connection with the translation of the Scriptures, I received the following explanation of the Revelation of St. John."

1–4, Beasts have spirits and will dwell in eternal felicity; 5–7, This earth has a temporal existence of 7,000 years; 8–10, Various angels restore the gospel and minister on earth; 11, The sealing of the 144,000; 12–14, Christ will come in the beginning of the seventh thousand years; 15, Two prophets will be raised up to the Jewish nation.

1 Q. What is the sea of glass spoken of by John, 4th chapter, and 6th verse of the Revelation?A. It is the earth, in its sanctified, immortal, and eternal state.

2 Q. What are we to understand by the four beasts, spoken of in the same verse?A. They are figurative expressions, used by the Revelator, John, in describing heaven, the paradise of God, the happiness of man, and of beasts, and of creeping things, and of the fowls of the air; that which is spiritual being in the likeness of that which is temporal; and that which is temporal in the likeness of that which is spiritual; the spirit of man in the likeness of his person, as also the spirit of the beast, and every other creature which God has created.

3 Q. Are the four beasts limited to individual beasts, or do they represent classes or orders?A. They are limited to four individual beasts, which were shown to John, to represent the glory of the classes of beings in their destined order or sphere of creation, in the enjoyment of their eternal felicity.

4 Q. What are we to understand by the eyes and wings, which the beasts had?A. Their eyes are a representation of light and knowledge, that is, they are full of knowledge; and their wings are a representation of power, to move, to act, etc.

5 Q. What are we to understand by the four and twenty elders, spoken of by John?A. We are to understand that these elders whom John saw, were elders who had been faithful in the work of the ministry and were dead; who belonged to the seven churches, and were then in the paradise of God.

6 Q. What are we to understand by the book which John saw, which was sealed on the back with seven seals?A. We are to understand that it contains the revealed will, mysteries, and the works of God; the hidden things of his economy concerning this earth during the seven thousand years of its continuance, or its temporal existence.

7 Q. What are we to understand by the seven seals with which it was sealed?A. We are to understand that the first seal contains the things of the first thousand years, and the second also of the second thousand years, and so on until the seventh.

8 Q. What are we to understand by the four angels, spoken of in the 7th chapter and 1st verse of Revelation?A. We are to understand that they are four angels sent forth from God, to whom is given power over the four parts of the earth, to save life and to destroy; these are they who have the everlasting gospel to commit to every nation, kindred, tongue, and people; having power to shut up the heavens, to seal up unto life, or to cast down to the regions of darkness.

9 Q. What are we to understand by the angel ascending from the east, Revelation 7th chapter and 2nd verse?A. We are to understand that the angel ascending from the east is he

to whom is given the seal of the living God over the twelve tribes of Israel; wherefore, he crieth unto the four angels having the everlasting gospel, saying: Hurt not the earth, neither the sea, nor the trees, till we have sealed the servants of our God in their foreheads. And, if you will receive it, this is Elias which was to come to gather together the tribes of Israel and restore all things.

10 Q. What time are the things spoken of in this chapter to be accomplished?A. They are to be accomplished in the sixth thousand years, or the opening of the sixth seal.

11 Q. What are we to understand by sealing the one hundred and forty-four thousand, out of all the tribes of Israel—twelve thousand out of every tribe?A. We are to understand that those who are sealed are high priests, ordained unto the holy order of God, to administer the everlasting gospel; for they are they who are ordained out of every nation, kindred, tongue, and people, by the angels to whom is given power over the nations of the earth, to bring as many as will come to the church of the Firstborn.

12 Q. What are we to understand by the sounding of the trumpets, mentioned in the 8th chapter of Revelation?A. We are to understand that as God made the world in six days, and on the seventh day he finished his work, and sanctified it, and also formed man out of the dust of the earth, even so, in the beginning of the seventh thousand years will the Lord God sanctify the earth, and complete the salvation of man, and judge all things, and shall redeem all things, except that which he hath not put into his power, when he shall have sealed all things, unto the end of all things; and the sounding of the trumpets of the seven angels are the preparing and finishing of his work, in the beginning of the seventh thousand years—the preparing of the way before the time of his coming.

13 Q. When are the things to be accomplished, which are written in the 9th chapter of Revelation?A. They are to be accomplished after the opening of the seventh seal, before the coming of Christ.

14 Q. What are we to understand by the little book which was eaten by John, as mentioned in the 10th chapter of Revelation?A. We are to understand that it was a mission, and an ordinance, for him to gather the tribes of Israel; behold, this is Elias, who, as it is written, must come and restore all things.

15 Q. What is to be understood by the two witnesses, in the eleventh chapter of Revelation?A. They are two prophets that are to be raised up to the Jewish nation in the last days, at the time of the restoration, and to prophesy to the Jews after they are gathered and have built the city of Jerusalem in the land of their fathers.

Section 78

Revelation given through Joseph Smith the Prophet, at Kirtland, Ohio, March 1, 1832. On that day, the Prophet and other leaders had assembled to discuss Church business. This revelation originally instructed the Prophet, Sidney Rigdon, and Newel K. Whitney to travel to Missouri and organize the Church's mercantile and publishing endeavors by creating a "firm" that would oversee these efforts, generating funds for the establishment of Zion and for the benefit of the poor. This firm, known as the United Firm, was organized in April 1832 and disbanded in 1834 (see section 82). Sometime after its dissolution, under the direction of Joseph Smith, the phrase "the affairs of the storehouse for the poor" replaced "mercantile and publishing establishments" in the revelation, and the word "order" replaced the word "firm."

1–4, The Saints should organize and establish a storehouse; 5–12, Wise use of their properties will lead to salvation; 13–14, The Church should be independent of earthly powers; 15–16, Michael (Adam) serves under the direction of the Holy One (Christ); 17–22, Blessed are the faithful, for they will inherit all things.

1 The Lord spake unto Joseph Smith, Jun., saying: Hearken unto me, saith the Lord your God, who are ordained unto the high priesthood of my church, who have assembled yourselves together;

2 And listen to the counsel of him who has ordained you from on high, who shall speak in your ears the words of wisdom, that salvation may be unto you in that thing which you have presented before me, saith the Lord God.

3 For verily I say unto you, the time has come, and is now at hand; and behold, and lo, it must needs be that there be an organization of my people, in regulating and establishing the affairs of the storehouse for the poor of my people, both in this place and in the land of Zion—

4 For a permanent and everlasting establishment and order unto my church, to advance the cause, which ye have espoused, to the salvation of man, and to the glory of your Father who is in heaven;

5 That you may be equal in the bonds of heavenly things, yea, and earthly things also, for the obtaining of heavenly things.

6 For if ye are not equal in earthly things ye cannot be equal in obtaining heavenly things;

7 For if you will that I give unto you a place in the celestial world, you must prepare yourselves by doing the things which I have commanded you and required of you.

8 And now, verily thus saith the Lord, it is expedient that all things be done unto my glory, by you who are joined together in this order;

9 Or, in other words, let my servant Newel K. Whitney and my servant Joseph Smith, Jun., and my servant Sidney Rigdon sit in council with the saints which are in Zion;

10 Otherwise Satan seeketh to turn their hearts away from the truth, that they become blinded and understand not the things which are prepared for them.

11 Wherefore, a commandment I give unto you, to prepare and organize yourselves by a bond or everlasting covenant that cannot be broken.

12 And he who breaketh it shall lose his office and standing in the church, and shall be delivered over to the buffetings of Satan until the day of redemption.

13 Behold, this is the preparation wherewith I prepare you, and the foundation, and the ensample which I give unto you, whereby you may accomplish the commandments which are given you;

14 That through my providence, notwithstanding the tribulation which shall descend upon you, that the church may stand independent above all other creatures beneath the celestial world;

15 That you may come up unto the crown prepared for you, and be made rulers over many kingdoms, saith the Lord God, the Holy One of Zion, who hath established the foundations of Adam-ondi-Ahman;

16 Who hath appointed Michael your prince, and established his feet, and set him upon high, and given unto him the keys of salvation under the counsel and direction of the Holy One, who is without beginning of days or end of life.

17 Verily, verily, I say unto you, ye are little children, and ye have not as yet understood how great blessings the Father hath in his own hands and prepared for you;

18 And ye cannot bear all things now; nevertheless, be of good cheer, for I will lead you along. The kingdom is yours and the blessings thereof are yours, and the riches of eternity are yours.

19 And he who receiveth all things with thankfulness shall be made glorious; and the things of this earth shall be added unto him, even an hundred fold, yea, more.

20 Wherefore, do the things which I have commanded you, saith your Redeemer, even the Son Ahman, who prepareth all things before he taketh you;

21 For ye are the church of the Firstborn, and he will take you up in a cloud, and appoint every man his portion.

22 And he that is a faithful and wise steward shall inherit all things. Amen.

Section 79

Revelation given through Joseph Smith the Prophet, at Hiram, Ohio, March 12, 1832.

1–4, Jared Carter is called to preach the gospel by the Comforter.

1 Verily I say unto you, that it is my will that my servant Jared Carter should go again into the eastern countries, from place to place, and from city to city, in the power of the ordination wherewith he has been ordained, proclaiming glad tidings of great joy, even the everlasting gospel.

2 And I will send upon him the Comforter, which shall teach him the truth and the way whither he shall go;

3 And inasmuch as he is faithful, I will crown him again with sheaves.

4 Wherefore, let your heart be glad, my servant Jared Carter, and fear not, saith your Lord, even Jesus Christ. Amen.

Section 80

Revelation given through Joseph Smith the Prophet to Stephen Burnett, at Hiram, Ohio, March 7, 1832.

1–5, Stephen Burnett and Eden Smith are called to preach in whatever place they choose.

1 Verily, thus saith the Lord unto you my servant Stephen Burnett: Go ye, go ye into the world and preach the gospel to every creature that cometh under the sound of your voice.

2 And inasmuch as you desire a companion, I will give unto you my servant Eden Smith.

3 Wherefore, go ye and preach my gospel, whether to the north or to the south, to the east or to the west, it mattereth not, for ye cannot go amiss.

4 Therefore, declare the things which ye have heard, and verily believe, and know to be true.

5 Behold, this is the will of him who hath called you, your Redeemer, even Jesus Christ. Amen.

Section 81

Revelation given through Joseph Smith the Prophet, at Hiram, Ohio, March 15, 1832. Frederick G. Williams is called to be a high priest and a counselor in the Presidency of the High Priesthood. The historical records show that when this revelation was received in March 1832, it called Jesse Gause to the office of counselor to Joseph Smith in the Presidency. However, when he failed to continue in a manner consistent with this appointment, the call was subsequently transferred to Frederick G. Williams. The revelation (dated March 1832) should be regarded as a step toward the formal organization of the First Presidency, specifically calling for the office of counselor in that body and explaining the dignity of the appointment. Brother Gause served for a time but was excommunicated from the Church in December 1832. Brother Williams was ordained to the specified office on March 18, 1833.

1–2, The keys of the kingdom are always held by the First Presidency; 3–7, If Frederick G. Williams is faithful in his ministry, he will have eternal life.

1 Verily, verily, I say unto you my servant Frederick G. Williams: Listen to the voice of him who speaketh, to the word of the Lord your God, and hearken to the calling wherewith you are called, even to be a high priest in my church, and a counselor unto my servant Joseph Smith, Jun.;

2 Unto whom I have given the keys of the kingdom, which belong always unto the Presidency of the High Priesthood:

3 Therefore, verily I acknowledge him and will bless him, and also thee, inasmuch as thou art faithful in counsel, in the office which I have appointed unto you, in prayer always, vocally and in thy heart, in public and in private, also in thy ministry in proclaiming the gospel in the land of the living, and among thy brethren.

4 And in doing these things thou wilt do the greatest good unto thy fellow beings, and wilt promote the glory of him who is your Lord.

5 Wherefore, be faithful; stand in the office which I have appointed unto you; succor the weak, lift up the hands which hang down, and strengthen the feeble knees.

6 And if thou art faithful unto the end thou shalt have a crown of immortality, and eternal life in the mansions which I have prepared in the house of my Father.

7 Behold, and lo, these are the words of Alpha and Omega, even Jesus Christ. Amen.

Section 82

Revelation given to Joseph Smith the Prophet, in Independence, Jackson County, Missouri, April 26, 1832. The occasion was a council of high priests and elders of the Church. At the council, Joseph Smith was sustained as the President of the High Priesthood, to which office he had previously been ordained at a conference of high priests, elders, and members, at Amherst, Ohio, January 25, 1832 (see the heading to section 75). This revelation reiterates instructions given in an earlier revelation (section 78) to establish a firm—known as the United Firm (under Joseph Smith's direction, the term "order" later replaced "firm")—to govern the Church's mercantile and publishing endeavors.

1–4, Where much is given, much is required; 5–7, Darkness reigns in the world; 8–13, The Lord is bound when we do what He says; 14–18, Zion must increase in beauty and holiness; 19–24, Every man should seek the interest of his neighbor.

1 Verily, verily, I say unto you, my servants, that inasmuch as you have forgiven one another your trespasses, even so I, the Lord, forgive you.

2 Nevertheless, there are those among you who have sinned exceedingly; yea, even all of you have sinned; but verily I say unto you, beware from henceforth, and refrain from sin, lest sore judgments fall upon your heads.

3 For of him unto whom much is given much is required; and he who sins against the greater light shall receive the greater condemnation.

4 Ye call upon my name for revelations, and I give them unto you; and inasmuch as ye keep not my sayings, which I give unto you, ye become transgressors; and justice and judgment are the penalty which is affixed unto my law.

5 Therefore, what I say unto one I say unto all: Watch, for the adversary spreadeth his dominions, and darkness reigneth;

6 And the anger of God kindleth against the inhabitants of the earth; and none doeth good, for all have gone out of the way.

7 And now, verily I say unto you, I, the Lord, will not lay any sin to your charge; go your ways and sin no more; but unto that soul who sinneth shall the former sins return, saith the Lord your God.

8 And again, I say unto you, I give unto you a new commandment, that you may understand my will concerning you;

9 Or, in other words, I give unto you directions how you may act before me, that it may turn to you for your salvation.

10 I, the Lord, am bound when ye do what I say; but when ye do not what I say, ye have no promise.

11 Therefore, verily I say unto you, that it is expedient for my servants Edward Partridge and Newel K. Whitney, A. Sidney Gilbert and Sidney Rigdon, and my servant Joseph Smith, and John Whitmer and Oliver Cowdery, and W. W. Phelps and Martin Harris to be bound together by a bond and covenant that cannot be broken by transgression, except judgment shall immediately follow, in your several stewardships—

12 To manage the affairs of the poor, and all things pertaining to the bishopric both in the land of Zion and in the land of Kirtland;

13 For I have consecrated the land of Kirtland in mine own due time for the benefit of the saints of the Most High, and for a stake to Zion.

14 For Zion must increase in beauty,
and in holiness; her borders must
be enlarged; her stakes must be
strengthened; yea, verily I say unto you,
Zion must arise and put on her beautiful
garments.

15 Therefore, I give unto you this
commandment, that ye bind yourselves
by this covenant, and it shall be done
according to the laws of the Lord.

16 Behold, here is wisdom also in me
for your good.

17 And you are to be equal, or in other
words, you are to have equal claims
on the properties, for the benefit
of managing the concerns of your
stewardships, every man according to
his wants and his needs, inasmuch as
his wants are just—

18 And all this for the benefit of the
church of the living God, that every
man may improve upon his talent, that
every man may gain other talents, yea,
even an hundred fold, to be cast into
the Lord's storehouse, to become the
common property of the whole church—

19 Every man seeking the interest of his
neighbor, and doing all things with an
eye single to the glory of God.

20 This order I have appointed to be an
everlasting order unto you, and unto
your successors, inasmuch as you sin
not.

21 And the soul that sins against this
covenant, and hardeneth his heart
against it, shall be dealt with according
to the laws of my church, and shall be
delivered over to the buffetings of Satan
until the day of redemption.

22 And now, verily I say unto you,
and this is wisdom, make unto
yourselves friends with the mammon
of unrighteousness, and they will not
destroy you.

23 Leave judgment alone with me, for it
is mine and I will repay. Peace be with
you; my blessings continue with you.

24 For even yet the kingdom is yours,
and shall be forever, if you fall not from
your steadfastness. Even so. Amen.

Section 83

Revelation given through Joseph Smith the Prophet, at Independence, Missouri, April 30, 1832. This revelation was received as the Prophet sat in council with his brethren.

1–4, Women and children have claim upon their husbands and fathers for their support; 5–6, Widows and orphans have claim upon the Church for their support.

1 Verily, thus saith the Lord, in addition to the laws of the church concerning women and children, those who belong to the church, who have lost their husbands or fathers:

2 Women have claim on their husbands for their maintenance, until their husbands are taken; and if they are not found transgressors they shall have fellowship in the church.

3 And if they are not faithful they shall not have fellowship in the church; yet they may remain upon their inheritances according to the laws of the land.

4 All children have claim upon their parents for their maintenance until they are of age.

5 And after that, they have claim upon the church, or in other words upon the Lord's storehouse, if their parents have not wherewith to give them inheritances.

6 And the storehouse shall be kept by the consecrations of the church; and widows and orphans shall be provided for, as also the poor. Amen.

Section 84

Revelation given through Joseph Smith the Prophet, at Kirtland, Ohio, September 22 and 23, 1832. During the month of September, elders had begun to return from their missions in the eastern states and to make reports of their labors. It was while they were together in this season of joy that the following communication was received. The Prophet designated it a revelation on priesthood.

1–5, The New Jerusalem and the temple will be built in Missouri; 6–17, The line of priesthood from Moses to Adam is given; 18–25, The greater priesthood holds the key of the knowledge of God; 26–32, The lesser priesthood holds the key of the ministering of angels and of the preparatory gospel; 33–44, Men gain eternal life through the oath and covenant of the priesthood; 45–53, The Spirit of Christ enlightens men, and the world lies in sin; 54–61, The Saints must testify of those things they have received; 62–76, They are to preach the gospel, and signs will follow; 77–91, Elders are to go forth without purse or scrip, and the Lord will care for their needs; 92–97, Plagues and cursings await those who reject the gospel; 98–102, The new song of the redemption of Zion is given; 103–10, Let every man stand in his own office and labor in his own calling; 111–20, The Lord's servants are to proclaim the abomination of desolation of the last days.

1 A revelation of Jesus Christ unto his servant Joseph Smith, Jun., and six elders, as they united their hearts and lifted their voices on high.

2 Yea, the word of the Lord concerning his church, established in the last days for the restoration of his people, as he has spoken by the mouth of his prophets, and for the gathering of his saints to stand upon Mount Zion, which shall be the city of New Jerusalem.

3 Which city shall be built, beginning at the temple lot, which is appointed by the finger of the Lord, in the western boundaries of the State of Missouri, and dedicated by the hand of Joseph Smith, Jun., and others with whom the Lord was well pleased.

4 Verily this is the word of the Lord, that the city New Jerusalem shall be built by the gathering of the saints, beginning at this place, even the place of the temple, which temple shall be reared in this generation.

5 For verily this generation shall not all pass away until an house shall be built unto the Lord, and a cloud shall rest upon it, which cloud shall be even the glory of the Lord, which shall fill the house.

6 And the sons of Moses, according to the Holy Priesthood which he received under the hand of his father-in-law, Jethro;

7 And Jethro received it under the hand of Caleb;

8 And Caleb received it under the hand of Elihu;

9 And Elihu under the hand of Jeremy;

10 And Jeremy under the hand of Gad;

11 And Gad under the hand of Esaias;

12 And Esaias received it under the hand of God.

13 Esaias also lived in the days of Abraham, and was blessed of him—

14 Which Abraham received the priesthood from Melchizedek, who received it through the lineage of his fathers, even till Noah;

15 And from Noah till Enoch, through the lineage of their fathers;

16 And from Enoch to Abel, who was slain by the conspiracy of his brother, who received the priesthood by the commandments of God, by the hand of his father Adam, who was the first man—

17 Which priesthood continueth in the church of God in all generations, and is without beginning of days or end of years.

18 And the Lord confirmed a priesthood also upon Aaron and his seed, throughout all their generations, which priesthood also continueth and abideth forever with the priesthood which is after the holiest order of God.

19 And this greater priesthood administereth the gospel and holdeth the key of the mysteries of the kingdom, even the key of the knowledge of God.

20 Therefore, in the ordinances thereof, the power of godliness is manifest.

21 And without the ordinances thereof, and the authority of the priesthood, the power of godliness is not manifest unto men in the flesh;

22 For without this no man can see the face of God, even the Father, and live.

23 Now this Moses plainly taught to the children of Israel in the wilderness, and sought diligently to sanctify his people that they might behold the face of God;

24 But they hardened their hearts and could not endure his presence; therefore, the Lord in his wrath, for his anger was kindled against them, swore that they should not enter into his rest while in the wilderness, which rest is the fulness of his glory.

25 Therefore, he took Moses out of their midst, and the Holy Priesthood also;

26 And the lesser priesthood continued, which priesthood holdeth the key of the ministering of angels and the preparatory gospel;

27 Which gospel is the gospel of repentance and of baptism, and the remission of sins, and the law of carnal commandments, which the Lord in his wrath caused to continue with the house of Aaron among the children of Israel until John, whom God raised up, being filled with the Holy Ghost from his mother's womb.

28 For he was baptized while he was yet in his childhood, and was ordained by the angel of God at the time he was eight days old unto this power, to overthrow the kingdom of the Jews, and to make straight the way of the Lord before the face of his people, to prepare them for the coming of the Lord, in whose hand is given all power.

29 And again, the offices of elder and bishop are necessary appendages belonging unto the high priesthood.

30 And again, the offices of teacher and deacon are necessary appendages belonging to the lesser priesthood, which priesthood was confirmed upon Aaron and his sons.

31 Therefore, as I said concerning the sons of Moses—for the sons of Moses and also the sons of Aaron shall offer an acceptable offering and sacrifice in the house of the Lord, which house shall be built unto the Lord in this generation, upon the consecrated spot as I have appointed—

32 And the sons of Moses and of Aaron shall be filled with the glory of the Lord, upon Mount Zion in the Lord's house, whose sons are ye; and also many whom I have called and sent forth to build up my church.

33 For whoso is faithful unto the obtaining these two priesthoods

of which I have spoken, and the magnifying their calling, are sanctified by the Spirit unto the renewing of their bodies.

34 They become the sons of Moses and of Aaron and the seed of Abraham, and the church and kingdom, and the elect of God.

35 And also all they who receive this priesthood receive me, saith the Lord;

36 For he that receiveth my servants receiveth me;

37 And he that receiveth me receiveth my Father;

38 And he that receiveth my Father receiveth my Father's kingdom; therefore all that my Father hath shall be given unto him.

39 And this is according to the oath and covenant which belongeth to the priesthood.

40 Therefore, all those who receive the priesthood, receive this oath and covenant of my Father, which he cannot break, neither can it be moved.

41 But whoso breaketh this covenant after he hath received it, and altogether turneth therefrom, shall not have forgiveness of sins in this world nor in the world to come.

42 And wo unto all those who come not unto this priesthood which ye have received, which I now confirm upon you who are present this day, by mine own voice out of the heavens; and even I have given the heavenly hosts and mine angels charge concerning you.

43 And I now give unto you a commandment to beware concerning yourselves, to give diligent heed to the words of eternal life.

44 For you shall live by every word that proceedeth forth from the mouth of God.

45 For the word of the Lord is truth, and whatsoever is truth is light, and whatsoever is light is Spirit, even the Spirit of Jesus Christ.

46 And the Spirit giveth light to every man that cometh into the world; and the Spirit enlighteneth every man through the world, that hearkeneth to the voice of the Spirit.

47 And every one that hearkeneth to the voice of the Spirit cometh unto God, even the Father.

48 And the Father teacheth him of the covenant which he has renewed and confirmed upon you, which is confirmed upon you for your sakes, and not for your sakes only, but for the sake of the whole world.

49 And the whole world lieth in sin, and groaneth under darkness and under the bondage of sin.

50 And by this you may know they are under the bondage of sin, because they come not unto me.

51 For whoso cometh not unto me is under the bondage of sin.

52 And whoso receiveth not my voice is not acquainted with my voice, and is not of me.

53 And by this you may know the righteous from the wicked, and that the whole world groaneth under sin and darkness even now.

54 And your minds in times past have been darkened because of unbelief, and because you have treated lightly the things you have received—

55 Which vanity and unbelief have

brought the whole church under condemnation.

56 And this condemnation resteth upon the children of Zion, even all.

57 And they shall remain under this condemnation until they repent and remember the new covenant, even the Book of Mormon and the former commandments which I have given them, not only to say, but to do according to that which I have written—

58 That they may bring forth fruit meet for their Father's kingdom; otherwise there remaineth a scourge and judgment to be poured out upon the children of Zion.

59 For shall the children of the kingdom pollute my holy land? Verily, I say unto you, Nay.

60 Verily, verily, I say unto you who now hear my words, which are my voice, blessed are ye inasmuch as you receive these things;

61 For I will forgive you of your sins with this commandment—that you remain steadfast in your minds in solemnity and the spirit of prayer, in bearing testimony to all the world of those things which are communicated unto you.

62 Therefore, go ye into all the world; and unto whatsoever place ye cannot go ye shall send, that the testimony may go from you into all the world unto every creature.

63 And as I said unto mine apostles, even so I say unto you, for you are mine apostles, even God's high priests; ye are they whom my Father hath given me; ye are my friends;

64 Therefore, as I said unto mine apostles I say unto you again, that every soul who believeth on your words, and is baptized by water for the remission of sins, shall receive the Holy Ghost.

65 And these signs shall follow them that believe—

66 In my name they shall do many wonderful works;

67 In my name they shall cast out devils;

68 In my name they shall heal the sick;

69 In my name they shall open the eyes of the blind, and unstop the ears of the deaf;

70 And the tongue of the dumb shall speak;

71 And if any man shall administer poison unto them it shall not hurt them;

72 And the poison of a serpent shall not have power to harm them.

73 But a commandment I give unto them, that they shall not boast themselves of these things, neither speak them before the world; for these things are given unto you for your profit and for salvation.

74 Verily, verily, I say unto you, they who believe not on your words, and are not baptized in water in my name, for the remission of their sins, that they may receive the Holy Ghost, shall be damned, and shall not come into my Father's kingdom where my Father and I am.

75 And this revelation unto you, and commandment, is in force from this very hour upon all the world, and the gospel is unto all who have not received it.

76 But, verily I say unto all those to whom the kingdom has been given—from you it must be preached unto

them, that they shall repent of their former evil works; for they are to be upbraided for their evil hearts of unbelief, and your brethren in Zion for their rebellion against you at the time I sent you.

77 And again I say unto you, my friends, for from henceforth I shall call you friends, it is expedient that I give unto you this commandment, that ye become even as my friends in days when I was with them, traveling to preach the gospel in my power;

78 For I suffered them not to have purse or scrip, neither two coats.

79 Behold, I send you out to prove the world, and the laborer is worthy of his hire.

80 And any man that shall go and preach this gospel of the kingdom, and fail not to continue faithful in all things, shall not be weary in mind, neither darkened, neither in body, limb, nor joint; and a hair of his head shall not fall to the ground unnoticed. And they shall not go hungry, neither athirst.

81 Therefore, take ye no thought for the morrow, for what ye shall eat, or what ye shall drink, or wherewithal ye shall be clothed.

82 For, consider the lilies of the field, how they grow, they toil not, neither do they spin; and the kingdoms of the world, in all their glory, are not arrayed like one of these.

83 For your Father, who is in heaven, knoweth that you have need of all these things.

84 Therefore, let the morrow take thought for the things of itself.

85 Neither take ye thought beforehand what ye shall say; but treasure up in your minds continually the words of life, and it shall be given you in the very hour that portion that shall be meted unto every man.

86 Therefore, let no man among you, for this commandment is unto all the faithful who are called of God in the church unto the ministry, from this hour take purse or scrip, that goeth forth to proclaim this gospel of the kingdom.

87 Behold, I send you out to reprove the world of all their unrighteous deeds, and to teach them of a judgment which is to come.

88 And whoso receiveth you, there I will be also, for I will go before your face. I will be on your right hand and on your left, and my Spirit shall be in your hearts, and mine angels round about you, to bear you up.

89 Whoso receiveth you receiveth me; and the same will feed you, and clothe you, and give you money.

90 And he who feeds you, or clothes you, or gives you money, shall in nowise lose his reward.

91 And he that doeth not these things is not my disciple; by this you may know my disciples.

92 He that receiveth you not, go away from him alone by yourselves, and cleanse your feet even with water, pure water, whether in heat or in cold, and bear testimony of it unto your Father which is in heaven, and return not again unto that man.

93 And in whatsoever village or city ye enter, do likewise.

94 Nevertheless, search diligently and spare not; and wo unto that house, or that village or city that rejecteth you, or your words, or your testimony concerning me.

95 Wo, I say again, unto that house, or that village or city that rejecteth you, or your words, or your testimony of me;

96 For I, the Almighty, have laid my hands upon the nations, to scourge them for their wickedness.

97 And plagues shall go forth, and they shall not be taken from the earth until I have completed my work, which shall be cut short in righteousness—

98 Until all shall know me, who remain, even from the least unto the greatest, and shall be filled with the knowledge of the Lord, and shall see eye to eye, and shall lift up their voice, and with the voice together sing this new song, saying:

99The Lord hath brought again Zion;The Lord hath redeemed his people, Israel,According to the election of grace,Which was brought to pass by the faithAnd covenant of their fathers.

100The Lord hath redeemed his people;And Satan is bound and time is no longer.The Lord hath gathered all things in one.The Lord hath brought down Zion from above.The Lord hath brought up Zion from beneath.

101The earth hath travailed and brought forth her strength;And truth is established in her bowels;And the heavens have smiled upon her;And she is clothed with the glory of her God;For he stands in the midst of his people.

102Glory, and honor, and power, and might,Be ascribed to our God; for he is full of mercy,Justice, grace and truth, and peace,Forever and ever, Amen.

103 And again, verily, verily, I say unto you, it is expedient that every man who goes forth to proclaim mine everlasting gospel, that inasmuch as they have families, and receive money by gift, that they should send it unto them or make use of it for their benefit, as the Lord shall direct them, for thus it seemeth me good.

104 And let all those who have not families, who receive money, send it up unto the bishop in Zion, or unto the bishop in Ohio, that it may be consecrated for the bringing forth of the revelations and the printing thereof, and for establishing Zion.

105 And if any man shall give unto any of you a coat, or a suit, take the old and cast it unto the poor, and go on your way rejoicing.

106 And if any man among you be strong in the Spirit, let him take with him him that is weak, that he may be edified in all meekness, that he may become strong also.

107 Therefore, take with you those who are ordained unto the lesser priesthood, and send them before you to make appointments, and to prepare the way, and to fill appointments that you yourselves are not able to fill.

108 Behold, this is the way that mine apostles, in ancient days, built up my church unto me.

109 Therefore, let every man stand in his own office, and labor in his own calling; and let not the head say unto the feet it hath no need of the feet; for without the feet how shall the body be able to stand?

110 Also the body hath need of every member, that all may be edified together, that the system may be kept perfect.

111 And behold, the high priests should travel, and also the elders, and also the lesser priests; but the deacons and teachers should be appointed to watch over the church, to be standing ministers unto the church.

112 And the bishop, Newel K. Whitney, also should travel round about and among all the churches, searching after the poor to administer to their wants by humbling the rich and the proud.

113 He should also employ an agent to take charge and to do his secular business as he shall direct.

114 Nevertheless, let the bishop go unto the city of New York, also to the city of Albany, and also to the city of Boston, and warn the people of those cities with the sound of the gospel, with a loud voice, of the desolation and utter abolishment which await them if they do reject these things.

115 For if they do reject these things the hour of their judgment is nigh, and their house shall be left unto them desolate.

116 Let him trust in me and he shall not be confounded; and a hair of his head shall not fall to the ground unnoticed.

117 And verily I say unto you, the rest of my servants, go ye forth as your circumstances shall permit, in your several callings, unto the great and notable cities and villages, reproving the world in righteousness of all their unrighteous and ungodly deeds, setting forth clearly and understandingly the desolation of abomination in the last days.

118 For, with you saith the Lord Almighty, I will rend their kingdoms; I will not only shake the earth, but the starry heavens shall tremble.

119 For I, the Lord, have put forth my hand to exert the powers of heaven; ye cannot see it now, yet a little while and ye shall see it, and know that I am, and that I will come and reign with my people.

120 I am Alpha and Omega, the beginning and the end. Amen.

Section 85

Revelation given through Joseph Smith the Prophet, at Kirtland, Ohio, November 27, 1832. This section is an extract from a letter of the Prophet to William W. Phelps, who was living in Independence, Missouri. It answers questions about those Saints who had moved to Zion but who had not followed the commandment to consecrate their properties and had thus not received their inheritances according to the established order in the Church.

1–5, Inheritances in Zion are to be received through consecration; 6–12, One mighty and strong will give the Saints their inheritance in Zion.

1 It is the duty of the Lord's clerk, whom he has appointed, to keep a history, and a general church record of all things that transpire in Zion, and of all those who consecrate properties, and receive inheritances legally from the bishop;

2 And also their manner of life, their faith, and works; and also of the apostates who apostatize after receiving their inheritances.

3 It is contrary to the will and commandment of God that those who receive not their inheritance by consecration, agreeable to his law, which he has given, that he may tithe his people, to prepare them against the day of vengeance and burning, should have their names enrolled with the people of God.

4 Neither is their genealogy to be kept, or to be had where it may be found on any of the records or history of the church.

5 Their names shall not be found, neither the names of the fathers, nor the names of the children written in the book of the law of God, saith the Lord of Hosts.

6 Yea, thus saith the still small voice, which whispereth through and pierceth all things, and often times it maketh my bones to quake while it maketh manifest, saying:

7 And it shall come to pass that I, the Lord God, will send one mighty and strong, holding the scepter of power in his hand, clothed with light for a covering, whose mouth shall utter words, eternal words; while his bowels shall be a fountain of truth, to set in order the house of God, and to arrange by lot the inheritances of the saints whose names are found, and the names of their fathers, and of their children, enrolled in the book of the law of God;

8 While that man, who was called of God and appointed, that putteth forth his hand to steady the ark of God, shall fall by the shaft of death, like as a tree that is smitten by the vivid shaft of lightning.

9 And all they who are not found written in the book of remembrance shall find none inheritance in that day, but they shall be cut asunder, and their portion shall be appointed them among unbelievers, where are wailing and gnashing of teeth.

10 These things I say not of myself; therefore, as the Lord speaketh, he will also fulfil.

11 And they who are of the High Priesthood, whose names are not found written in the book of the law, or that are found to have apostatized, or to have been cut off from the church, as well as the lesser priesthood, or the members, in that day shall not find an inheritance among the saints of the Most High;

12 Therefore, it shall be done unto them as unto the children of the priest, as will be found recorded in the second chapter and sixty-first and second verses of Ezra.

Section 86

Revelation given through Joseph Smith the Prophet, at Kirtland, Ohio, December 6, 1832. This revelation was received while the Prophet was reviewing and editing the manuscript of the translation of the Bible.

1–7, The Lord gives the meaning of the parable of the wheat and tares; 8–11, He explains priesthood blessings to those who are lawful heirs according to the flesh.

1 Verily, thus saith the Lord unto you my servants, concerning the parable of the wheat and of the tares:

2 Behold, verily I say, the field was the world, and the apostles were the sowers of the seed;

3 And after they have fallen asleep the great persecutor of the church, the apostate, the whore, even Babylon, that maketh all nations to drink of her cup, in whose hearts the enemy, even Satan, sitteth to reign—behold he soweth the tares; wherefore, the tares choke the wheat and drive the church into the wilderness.

4 But behold, in the last days, even now while the Lord is beginning to bring forth the word, and the blade is springing up and is yet tender—

5 Behold, verily I say unto you, the angels are crying unto the Lord day and night, who are ready and waiting to be sent forth to reap down the fields;

6 But the Lord saith unto them, pluck not up the tares while the blade is yet tender (for verily your faith is weak), lest you destroy the wheat also.

7 Therefore, let the wheat and the tares grow together until the harvest is fully ripe; then ye shall first gather out the wheat from among the tares, and after the gathering of the wheat, behold and lo, the tares are bound in bundles, and the field remaineth to be burned.

8 Therefore, thus saith the Lord unto you, with whom the priesthood hath continued through the lineage of your fathers—

9 For ye are lawful heirs, according to the flesh, and have been hid from the world with Christ in God—

10 Therefore your life and the priesthood have remained, and must needs remain through you and your lineage until the restoration of all things spoken by the mouths of all the holy prophets since the world began.

11 Therefore, blessed are ye if ye continue in my goodness, a light unto the Gentiles, and through this priesthood, a savior unto my people Israel. The Lord hath said it. Amen.

Section 87

Revelation and prophecy on war, given through Joseph Smith the Prophet, at or near Kirtland, Ohio, December 25, 1832. At this time disputes in the United States over slavery and South Carolina's nullification of federal tariffs were prevalent. Joseph Smith's history states that "appearances of troubles among the nations" were becoming "more visible" to the Prophet "than they had previously been since the Church began her journey out of the wilderness."

1–4, War is foretold between the Northern States and the Southern States; 5–8, Great calamities will fall upon all the inhabitants of the earth.

1 Verily, thus saith the Lord concerning the wars that will shortly come to pass, beginning at the rebellion of South Carolina, which will eventually terminate in the death and misery of many souls;

2 And the time will come that war will be poured out upon all nations, beginning at this place.

3 For behold, the Southern States shall be divided against the Northern States, and the Southern States will call on other nations, even the nation of Great Britain, as it is called, and they shall also call upon other nations, in order to defend themselves against other nations; and then war shall be poured out upon all nations.

4 And it shall come to pass, after many days, slaves shall rise up against their masters, who shall be marshaled and disciplined for war.

5 And it shall come to pass also that the remnants who are left of the land will marshal themselves, and shall become exceedingly angry, and shall vex the Gentiles with a sore vexation.

6 And thus, with the sword and by bloodshed the inhabitants of the earth shall mourn; and with famine, and plague, and earthquake, and the thunder of heaven, and the fierce and vivid lightning also, shall the inhabitants of the earth be made to feel the wrath, and indignation, and chastening hand of an Almighty God, until the consumption decreed hath made a full end of all nations;

7 That the cry of the saints, and of the blood of the saints, shall cease to come up into the ears of the Lord of Sabaoth, from the earth, to be avenged of their enemies.

8 Wherefore, stand ye in holy places, and be not moved, until the day of the Lord come; for behold, it cometh quickly, saith the Lord. Amen.

Section 88

Revelation given through Joseph Smith the Prophet at Kirtland, Ohio, December 27 and 28, 1832, and January 3, 1833. The Prophet designated it as the "'olive leaf' ... plucked from the Tree of Paradise, the Lord's message of peace to us." The revelation was given after high priests at a conference prayed "separately and vocally to the Lord to reveal his will unto us concerning the upbuilding of Zion."

1–5, Faithful Saints receive that Comforter, which is the promise of eternal life; 6–13, All things are controlled and governed by the Light of Christ; 14–16, The Resurrection comes through the Redemption; 17–31, Obedience to celestial, terrestrial, or telestial law prepares men for those respective kingdoms and glories; 32–35, Those who will to abide in sin remain filthy still; 36–41, All kingdoms are governed by law; 42–45, God has given a law unto all things; 46–50, Man will comprehend even God; 51–61, The parable of the man sending his servants into the field and visiting them in turn; 62–73, Draw near unto the Lord, and ye will see His face; 74–80, Sanctify yourselves and teach one another the doctrines of the kingdom; 81–85, Every man who has been warned should warn his neighbor; 86–94, Signs, upheavals of the elements, and angels prepare the way for the coming of the Lord; 95–102, Angelic trumps call forth the dead in their order; 103–16, Angelic trumps proclaim the restoration of the gospel, the fall of Babylon, and the battle of the great God; 117–26, Seek learning, establish a house of God (a temple), and clothe yourselves with the bond of charity; 127–41, The order of the School of the Prophets is set forth, including the ordinance of washing of feet.

1 Verily, thus saith the Lord unto you who have assembled yourselves together to receive his will concerning you:

2 Behold, this is pleasing unto your Lord, and the angels rejoice over you; the alms of your prayers have come up into the ears of the Lord of Sabaoth, and are recorded in the book of the names of the sanctified, even them of the celestial world.

3 Wherefore, I now send upon you another Comforter, even upon you my friends, that it may abide in your hearts, even the Holy Spirit of promise; which other Comforter is the same that I promised unto my disciples, as is recorded in the testimony of John.

4 This Comforter is the promise which I give unto you of eternal life, even the glory of the celestial kingdom;

5 Which glory is that of the church of the Firstborn, even of God, the holiest of all, through Jesus Christ his Son—

6 He that ascended up on high, as also he descended below all things, in that he comprehended all things, that he might be in all and through all things, the light of truth;

7 Which truth shineth. This is the light of Christ. As also he is in the sun, and the light of the sun, and the power thereof by which it was made.

8 As also he is in the moon, and is the light of the moon, and the power thereof by which it was made;

9 As also the light of the stars, and the power thereof by which they were made;

10 And the earth also, and the power thereof, even the earth upon which you stand.

11 And the light which shineth, which giveth you light, is through him who enlighteneth your eyes, which is the same light that quickeneth your understandings;

12 Which light proceedeth forth from the presence of God to fill the immensity of space—

13 The light which is in all things, which giveth life to all things, which is the law by which all things are governed, even the power of God who sitteth upon his throne, who is in the bosom of eternity, who is in the midst of all things.

14 Now, verily I say unto you, that through the redemption which is made for you is brought to pass the resurrection from the dead.

15 And the spirit and the body are the soul of man.

16 And the resurrection from the dead is the redemption of the soul.

17 And the redemption of the soul is through him that quickeneth all things, in whose bosom it is decreed that the poor and the meek of the earth shall inherit it.

18 Therefore, it must needs be sanctified from all unrighteousness, that it may be prepared for the celestial glory;

19 For after it hath filled the measure of its creation, it shall be crowned with glory, even with the presence of God the Father;

20 That bodies who are of the celestial kingdom may possess it forever and ever; for, for this intent was it made and created, and for this intent are they sanctified.

21 And they who are not sanctified through the law which I have given unto you, even the law of Christ, must inherit another kingdom, even that of a terrestrial kingdom, or that of a telestial kingdom.

22 For he who is not able to abide the law of a celestial kingdom cannot abide a celestial glory.

23 And he who cannot abide the law of a terrestrial kingdom cannot abide a terrestrial glory.

24 And he who cannot abide the law of a telestial kingdom cannot abide a telestial glory; therefore he is not meet for a kingdom of glory. Therefore he must abide a kingdom which is not a kingdom of glory.

25 And again, verily I say unto you, the earth abideth the law of a celestial kingdom, for it filleth the measure of its creation, and transgresseth not the law—

26 Wherefore, it shall be sanctified; yea, notwithstanding it shall die, it shall be quickened again, and shall abide the power by which it is quickened, and the righteous shall inherit it.

27 For notwithstanding they die, they also shall rise again, a spiritual body.

28 They who are of a celestial spirit shall receive the same body which was a natural body; even ye shall receive your bodies, and your glory shall be that glory by which your bodies are quickened.

29 Ye who are quickened by a portion of the celestial glory shall then receive of the same, even a fulness.

30 And they who are quickened by a portion of the terrestrial glory shall then receive of the same, even a fulness.

31 And also they who are quickened by a portion of the telestial glory shall then receive of the same, even a fulness.

32 And they who remain shall also be quickened; nevertheless, they shall return again to their own place, to enjoy

that which they are willing to receive, because they were not willing to enjoy that which they might have received.

33 For what doth it profit a man if a gift is bestowed upon him, and he receive not the gift? Behold, he rejoices not in that which is given unto him, neither rejoices in him who is the giver of the gift.

34 And again, verily I say unto you, that which is governed by law is also preserved by law and perfected and sanctified by the same.

35 That which breaketh a law, and abideth not by law, but seeketh to become a law unto itself, and willeth to abide in sin, and altogether abideth in sin, cannot be sanctified by law, neither by mercy, justice, nor judgment. Therefore, they must remain filthy still.

36 All kingdoms have a law given;

37 And there are many kingdoms; for there is no space in the which there is no kingdom; and there is no kingdom in which there is no space, either a greater or a lesser kingdom.

38 And unto every kingdom is given a law; and unto every law there are certain bounds also and conditions.

39 All beings who abide not in those conditions are not justified.

40 For intelligence cleaveth unto intelligence; wisdom receiveth wisdom; truth embraceth truth; virtue loveth virtue; light cleaveth unto light; mercy hath compassion on mercy and claimeth her own; justice continueth its course and claimeth its own; judgment goeth before the face of him who sitteth upon the throne and governeth and executeth all things.

41 He comprehendeth all things, and all things are before him, and all things are round about him; and he is above all things, and in all things, and is through all things, and is round about all things; and all things are by him, and of him, even God, forever and ever.

42 And again, verily I say unto you, he hath given a law unto all things, by which they move in their times and their seasons;

43 And their courses are fixed, even the courses of the heavens and the earth, which comprehend the earth and all the planets.

44 And they give light to each other in their times and in their seasons, in their minutes, in their hours, in their days, in their weeks, in their months, in their years—all these are one year with God, but not with man.

45 The earth rolls upon her wings, and the sun giveth his light by day, and the moon giveth her light by night, and the stars also give their light, as they roll upon their wings in their glory, in the midst of the power of God.

46 Unto what shall I liken these kingdoms, that ye may understand?

47 Behold, all these are kingdoms, and any man who hath seen any or the least of these hath seen God moving in his majesty and power.

48 I say unto you, he hath seen him; nevertheless, he who came unto his own was not comprehended.

49 The light shineth in darkness, and the darkness comprehendeth it not; nevertheless, the day shall come when you shall comprehend even God, being quickened in him and by him.

50 Then shall ye know that ye have seen me, that I am, and that I am the true light that is in you, and that you are in me; otherwise ye could not abound.

51 Behold, I will liken these kingdoms unto a man having a field, and he sent forth his servants into the field to dig in the field.

52 And he said unto the first: Go ye and labor in the field, and in the first hour I will come unto you, and ye shall behold the joy of my countenance.

53 And he said unto the second: Go ye also into the field, and in the second hour I will visit you with the joy of my countenance.

54 And also unto the third, saying: I will visit you;

55 And unto the fourth, and so on unto the twelfth.

56 And the lord of the field went unto the first in the first hour, and tarried with him all that hour, and he was made glad with the light of the countenance of his lord.

57 And then he withdrew from the first that he might visit the second also, and the third, and the fourth, and so on unto the twelfth.

58 And thus they all received the light of the countenance of their lord, every man in his hour, and in his time, and in his season—

59 Beginning at the first, and so on unto the last, and from the last unto the first, and from the first unto the last;

60 Every man in his own order, until his hour was finished, even according as his lord had commanded him, that his lord might be glorified in him, and he in his lord, that they all might be glorified.

61 Therefore, unto this parable I will liken all these kingdoms, and the inhabitants thereof—every kingdom in its hour, and in its time, and in its season, even according to the decree which God hath made.

62 And again, verily I say unto you, my friends, I leave these sayings with you to ponder in your hearts, with this commandment which I give unto you, that ye shall call upon me while I am near—

63 Draw near unto me and I will draw near unto you; seek me diligently and ye shall find me; ask, and ye shall receive; knock, and it shall be opened unto you.

64 Whatsoever ye ask the Father in my name it shall be given unto you, that is expedient for you;

65 And if ye ask anything that is not expedient for you, it shall turn unto your condemnation.

66 Behold, that which you hear is as the voice of one crying in the wilderness—in the wilderness, because you cannot see him—my voice, because my voice is Spirit; my Spirit is truth; truth abideth and hath no end; and if it be in you it shall abound.

67 And if your eye be single to my glory, your whole bodies shall be filled with light, and there shall be no darkness in you; and that body which is filled with light comprehendeth all things.

68 Therefore, sanctify yourselves that your minds become single to God, and the days will come that you shall see him; for he will unveil his face unto you, and it shall be in his own time, and in his own way, and according to his own will.

69 Remember the great and last promise which I have made unto you; cast away your idle thoughts and your excess of laughter far from you.

70 Tarry ye, tarry ye in this place, and call a solemn assembly, even of those who are the first laborers in this last kingdom.

71 And let those whom they have warned in their traveling call on the Lord, and ponder the warning in their hearts which they have received, for a little season.

72 Behold, and lo, I will take care of your flocks, and will raise up elders and send unto them.

73 Behold, I will hasten my work in its time.

74 And I give unto you, who are the first laborers in this last kingdom, a commandment that you assemble yourselves together, and organize yourselves, and prepare yourselves, and sanctify yourselves; yea, purify your hearts, and cleanse your hands and your feet before me, that I may make you clean;

75 That I may testify unto your Father, and your God, and my God, that you are clean from the blood of this wicked generation; that I may fulfil this promise, this great and last promise, which I have made unto you, when I will.

76 Also, I give unto you a commandment that ye shall continue in prayer and fasting from this time forth.

77 And I give unto you a commandment that you shall teach one another the doctrine of the kingdom.

78 Teach ye diligently and my grace shall attend you, that you may be instructed more perfectly in theory, in principle, in doctrine, in the law of the gospel, in all things that pertain unto the kingdom of God, that are expedient for you to understand;

79 Of things both in heaven and in the earth, and under the earth; things which have been, things which are, things which must shortly come to pass; things which are at home, things which are abroad; the wars and the perplexities of the nations, and the judgments which are on the land; and a knowledge also of countries and of kingdoms—

80 That ye may be prepared in all things when I shall send you again to magnify the calling whereunto I have called you, and the mission with which I have commissioned you.

81 Behold, I sent you out to testify and warn the people, and it becometh every man who hath been warned to warn his neighbor.

82 Therefore, they are left without excuse, and their sins are upon their own heads.

83 He that seeketh me early shall find me, and shall not be forsaken.

84 Therefore, tarry ye, and labor diligently, that you may be perfected in your ministry to go forth among the Gentiles for the last time, as many as the mouth of the Lord shall name, to bind up the law and seal up the testimony, and to prepare the saints for the hour of judgment which is to come;

85 That their souls may escape the wrath of God, the desolation of abomination which awaits the wicked, both in this world and in the world to come. Verily, I say unto you, let those who are not the first elders continue in the vineyard until the mouth of the Lord shall call them, for their time is not yet come; their garments are not clean from the blood of this generation.

86 Abide ye in the liberty wherewith ye are made free; entangle not yourselves in sin, but let your hands be clean, until the Lord comes.

87 For not many days hence and the earth shall tremble and reel to and fro as a drunken man; and the sun shall hide his face, and shall refuse to give light;

and the moon shall be bathed in blood; and the stars shall become exceedingly angry, and shall cast themselves down as a fig that falleth from off a fig tree.

88 And after your testimony cometh wrath and indignation upon the people.

89 For after your testimony cometh the testimony of earthquakes, that shall cause groanings in the midst of her, and men shall fall upon the ground and shall not be able to stand.

90 And also cometh the testimony of the voice of thunderings, and the voice of lightnings, and the voice of tempests, and the voice of the waves of the sea heaving themselves beyond their bounds.

91 And all things shall be in commotion; and surely, men's hearts shall fail them; for fear shall come upon all people.

92 And angels shall fly through the midst of heaven, crying with a loud voice, sounding the trump of God, saying: Prepare ye, prepare ye, O inhabitants of the earth; for the judgment of our God is come. Behold, and lo, the Bridegroom cometh; go ye out to meet him.

93 And immediately there shall appear a great sign in heaven, and all people shall see it together.

94 And another angel shall sound his trump, saying: That great church, the mother of abominations, that made all nations drink of the wine of the wrath of her fornication, that persecuteth the saints of God, that shed their blood—she who sitteth upon many waters, and upon the islands of the sea—behold, she is the tares of the earth; she is bound in bundles; her bands are made strong, no man can loose them; therefore, she is ready to be burned. And he shall sound his trump both long and loud, and all nations shall hear it.

95 And there shall be silence in heaven for the space of half an hour; and immediately after shall the curtain of heaven be unfolded, as a scroll is unfolded after it is rolled up, and the face of the Lord shall be unveiled;

96 And the saints that are upon the earth, who are alive, shall be quickened and be caught up to meet him.

97 And they who have slept in their graves shall come forth, for their graves shall be opened; and they also shall be caught up to meet him in the midst of the pillar of heaven—

98 They are Christ's, the first fruits, they who shall descend with him first, and they who are on the earth and in their graves, who are first caught up to meet him; and all this by the voice of the sounding of the trump of the angel of God.

99 And after this another angel shall sound, which is the second trump; and then cometh the redemption of those who are Christ's at his coming; who have received their part in that prison which is prepared for them, that they might receive the gospel, and be judged according to men in the flesh.

100 And again, another trump shall sound, which is the third trump; and then come the spirits of men who are to be judged, and are found under condemnation;

101 And these are the rest of the dead; and they live not again until the thousand years are ended, neither again, until the end of the earth.

102 And another trump shall sound, which is the fourth trump, saying: There are found among those who are to remain until that great and last day, even the end, who shall remain filthy still.

103 And another trump shall sound, which is the fifth trump, which is the fifth angel who committeth the everlasting gospel—flying through the midst of heaven, unto all nations, kindreds, tongues, and people;

104 And this shall be the sound of his trump, saying to all people, both in heaven and in earth, and that are under the earth—for every ear shall hear it, and every knee shall bow, and every tongue shall confess, while they hear the sound of the trump, saying: Fear God, and give glory to him who sitteth upon the throne, forever and ever; for the hour of his judgment is come.

105 And again, another angel shall sound his trump, which is the sixth angel, saying: She is fallen who made all nations drink of the wine of the wrath of her fornication; she is fallen, is fallen!

106 And again, another angel shall sound his trump, which is the seventh angel, saying: It is finished; it is finished! The Lamb of God hath overcome and trodden the wine-press alone, even the wine-press of the fierceness of the wrath of Almighty God.

107 And then shall the angels be crowned with the glory of his might, and the saints shall be filled with his glory, and receive their inheritance and be made equal with him.

108 And then shall the first angel again sound his trump in the ears of all living, and reveal the secret acts of men, and the mighty works of God in the first thousand years.

109 And then shall the second angel sound his trump, and reveal the secret acts of men, and the thoughts and intents of their hearts, and the mighty works of God in the second thousand years—

110 And so on, until the seventh angel shall sound his trump; and he shall stand forth upon the land and upon the sea, and swear in the name of him who sitteth upon the throne, that there shall be time no longer; and Satan shall be bound, that old serpent, who is called the devil, and shall not be loosed for the space of a thousand years.

111 And then he shall be loosed for a little season, that he may gather together his armies.

112 And Michael, the seventh angel, even the archangel, shall gather together his armies, even the hosts of heaven.

113 And the devil shall gather together his armies; even the hosts of hell, and shall come up to battle against Michael and his armies.

114 And then cometh the battle of the great God; and the devil and his armies shall be cast away into their own place, that they shall not have power over the saints any more at all.

115 For Michael shall fight their battles, and shall overcome him who seeketh the throne of him who sitteth upon the throne, even the Lamb.

116 This is the glory of God, and the sanctified; and they shall not any more see death.

117 Therefore, verily I say unto you, my friends, call your solemn assembly, as I have commanded you.

118 And as all have not faith, seek ye diligently and teach one another words of wisdom; yea, seek ye out of the best books words of wisdom; seek learning, even by study and also by faith.

119 Organize yourselves; prepare every needful thing; and establish a house, even a house of prayer, a house of fasting, a house of faith, a house of learning, a house of glory, a house of

order, a house of God;

120 That your incomings may be in the name of the Lord; that your outgoings may be in the name of the Lord; that all your salutations may be in the name of the Lord, with uplifted hands unto the Most High.

121 Therefore, cease from all your light speeches, from all laughter, from all your lustful desires, from all your pride and light-mindedness, and from all your wicked doings.

122 Appoint among yourselves a teacher, and let not all be spokesmen at once; but let one speak at a time and let all listen unto his sayings, that when all have spoken that all may be edified of all, and that every man may have an equal privilege.

123 See that ye love one another; cease to be covetous; learn to impart one to another as the gospel requires.

124 Cease to be idle; cease to be unclean; cease to find fault one with another; cease to sleep longer than is needful; retire to thy bed early, that ye may not be weary; arise early, that your bodies and your minds may be invigorated.

125 And above all things, clothe yourselves with the bond of charity, as with a mantle, which is the bond of perfectness and peace.

126 Pray always, that ye may not faint, until I come. Behold, and lo, I will come quickly, and receive you unto myself. Amen.

127 And again, the order of the house prepared for the presidency of the school of the prophets, established for their instruction in all things that are expedient for them, even for all the officers of the church, or in other words, those who are called to the ministry in the church, beginning at the high priests, even down to the deacons—

128 And this shall be the order of the house of the presidency of the school: He that is appointed to be president, or teacher, shall be found standing in his place, in the house which shall be prepared for him.

129 Therefore, he shall be first in the house of God, in a place that the congregation in the house may hear his words carefully and distinctly, not with loud speech.

130 And when he cometh into the house of God, for he should be first in the house—behold, this is beautiful, that he may be an example—

131 Let him offer himself in prayer upon his knees before God, in token or remembrance of the everlasting covenant.

132 And when any shall come in after him, let the teacher arise, and, with uplifted hands to heaven, yea, even directly, salute his brother or brethren with these words:

133 Art thou a brother or brethren? I salute you in the name of the Lord Jesus Christ, in token or remembrance of the everlasting covenant, in which covenant I receive you to fellowship, in a determination that is fixed, immovable, and unchangeable, to be your friend and brother through the grace of God in the bonds of love, to walk in all the commandments of God blameless, in thanksgiving, forever and ever. Amen.

134 And he that is found unworthy of this salutation shall not have place among you; for ye shall not suffer that mine house shall be polluted by him.

135 And he that cometh in and is faithful before me, and is a brother, or if they be brethren, they shall salute the

president or teacher with uplifted hands to heaven, with this same prayer and covenant, or by saying Amen, in token of the same.

136 Behold, verily, I say unto you, this is an ensample unto you for a salutation to one another in the house of God, in the school of the prophets.

137 And ye are called to do this by prayer and thanksgiving, as the Spirit shall give utterance in all your doings in the house of the Lord, in the school of the prophets, that it may become a sanctuary, a tabernacle of the Holy Spirit to your edification.

138 And ye shall not receive any among you into this school save he is clean from the blood of this generation;

139 And he shall be received by the ordinance of the washing of feet, for unto this end was the ordinance of the washing of feet instituted.

140 And again, the ordinance of washing feet is to be administered by the president, or presiding elder of the church.

141 It is to be commenced with prayer; and after partaking of bread and wine, he is to gird himself according to the pattern given in the thirteenth chapter of John's testimony concerning me. Amen.

Section 89

Revelation given through Joseph Smith the Prophet, at Kirtland, Ohio, February 27, 1833. As a consequence of the early brethren using tobacco in their meetings, the Prophet was led to ponder upon the matter; consequently, he inquired of the Lord concerning it. This revelation, known as the Word of Wisdom, was the result.

1–9, The use of wine, strong drinks, tobacco, and hot drinks is proscribed; 10–17, Herbs, fruits, flesh, and grain are ordained for the use of man and of animals; 18–21, Obedience to gospel law, including the Word of Wisdom, brings temporal and spiritual blessings.

1 A WORD OF WISDOM, for the benefit of the council of high priests, assembled in Kirtland, and the church, and also the saints in Zion—

2 To be sent greeting; not by commandment or constraint, but by revelation and the word of wisdom, showing forth the order and will of God in the temporal salvation of all saints in the last days—

3 Given for a principle with promise, adapted to the capacity of the weak and the weakest of all saints, who are or can be called saints.

4 Behold, verily, thus saith the Lord unto you: In consequence of evils and designs which do and will exist in the hearts of conspiring men in the last days, I have warned you, and forewarn you, by giving unto you this word of wisdom by revelation—

5 That inasmuch as any man drinketh wine or strong drink among you, behold it is not good, neither meet in the sight of your Father, only in assembling yourselves together to offer up your sacraments before him.

6 And, behold, this should be wine, yea, pure wine of the grape of the vine, of your own make.

7 And, again, strong drinks are not for the belly, but for the washing of your bodies.

8 And again, tobacco is not for the body, neither for the belly, and is not good for man, but is an herb for bruises and all sick cattle, to be used with judgment and skill.

9 And again, hot drinks are not for the body or belly.

10 And again, verily I say unto you, all wholesome herbs God hath ordained for the constitution, nature, and use of man—

11 Every herb in the season thereof, and every fruit in the season thereof; all these to be used with prudence and thanksgiving.

12 Yea, flesh also of beasts and of the fowls of the air, I, the Lord, have ordained for the use of man with thanksgiving; nevertheless they are to be used sparingly;

13 And it is pleasing unto me that they should not be used, only in times of winter, or of cold, or famine.

14 All grain is ordained for the use of man and of beasts, to be the staff of life, not only for man but for the beasts of the field, and the fowls of heaven, and all wild animals that run or creep on the earth;

15 And these hath God made for the use of man only in times of famine and excess of hunger.

16 All grain is good for the food of man; as also the fruit of the vine; that which yieldeth fruit, whether in the ground or above the ground—

17 Nevertheless, wheat for man, and corn for the ox, and oats for the horse, and rye for the fowls and for swine, and for all beasts of the field, and barley for all useful animals, and for mild drinks, as also other grain.

18 And all saints who remember to keep and do these sayings, walking in obedience to the commandments, shall receive health in their navel and marrow to their bones;

19 And shall find wisdom and great treasures of knowledge, even hidden treasures;

20 And shall run and not be weary, and shall walk and not faint.

21 And I, the Lord, give unto them a promise, that the destroying angel shall pass by them, as the children of Israel, and not slay them. Amen.

Section 90

Revelation to Joseph Smith the Prophet, given at Kirtland, Ohio, March 8, 1833. This revelation is a continuing step in the establishment of the First Presidency (see the heading to section 81); as a consequence thereof, the counselors mentioned were ordained on March 18, 1833.

1–5, The keys of the kingdom are committed to Joseph Smith and through him to the Church; 6–7, Sidney Rigdon and Frederick G. Williams are to serve in the First Presidency; 8–11, The gospel is to be preached to the nations of Israel, to the Gentiles, and to the Jews, every man hearing in his own tongue; 12–18, Joseph Smith and his counselors are to set the Church in order; 19–37, Various individuals are counseled by the Lord to walk uprightly and serve in His kingdom.

1 Thus saith the Lord, verily, verily I say unto you my son, thy sins are forgiven thee, according to thy petition, for thy prayers and the prayers of thy brethren have come up into my ears.

2 Therefore, thou art blessed from henceforth that bear the keys of the kingdom given unto you; which kingdom is coming forth for the last time.

3 Verily I say unto you, the keys of this kingdom shall never be taken from you, while thou art in the world, neither in the world to come;

4 Nevertheless, through you shall the oracles be given to another, yea, even unto the church.

5 And all they who receive the oracles of God, let them beware how they hold them lest they are accounted as a light thing, and are brought under condemnation thereby, and stumble and fall when the storms descend, and the winds blow, and the rains descend, and beat upon their house.

6 And again, verily I say unto thy brethren, Sidney Rigdon and Frederick G. Williams, their sins are forgiven them also, and they are accounted as equal with thee in holding the keys of this last kingdom;

7 As also through your administration the keys of the school of the prophets, which I have commanded to be organized;

8 That thereby they may be perfected in their ministry for the salvation of Zion, and of the nations of Israel, and of the Gentiles, as many as will believe;

9 That through your administration they may receive the word, and through their administration the word may go forth unto the ends of the earth, unto the Gentiles first, and then, behold, and lo, they shall turn unto the Jews.

10 And then cometh the day when the arm of the Lord shall be revealed in power in convincing the nations, the heathen nations, the house of Joseph, of the gospel of their salvation.

11 For it shall come to pass in that day, that every man shall hear the fulness of the gospel in his own tongue, and in his own language, through those who are ordained unto this power, by the administration of the Comforter, shed forth upon them for the revelation of Jesus Christ.

12 And now, verily I say unto you, I give unto you a commandment that you continue in the ministry and presidency.

13 And when you have finished the translation of the prophets, you shall from thenceforth preside over the affairs of the church and the school;

14 And from time to time, as shall be manifested by the Comforter, receive

revelations to unfold the mysteries of the kingdom;

15 And set in order the churches, and study and learn, and become acquainted with all good books, and with languages, tongues, and people.

16 And this shall be your business and mission in all your lives, to preside in council, and set in order all the affairs of this church and kingdom.

17 Be not ashamed, neither confounded; but be admonished in all your high-mindedness and pride, for it bringeth a snare upon your souls.

18 Set in order your houses; keep slothfulness and uncleanness far from you.

19 Now, verily I say unto you, let there be a place provided, as soon as it is possible, for the family of thy counselor and scribe, even Frederick G. Williams.

20 And let mine aged servant, Joseph Smith, Sen., continue with his family upon the place where he now lives; and let it not be sold until the mouth of the Lord shall name.

21 And let my counselor, even Sidney Rigdon, remain where he now resides until the mouth of the Lord shall name.

22 And let the bishop search diligently to obtain an agent, and let him be a man who has got riches in store—a man of God, and of strong faith—

23 That thereby he may be enabled to discharge every debt; that the storehouse of the Lord may not be brought into disrepute before the eyes of the people.

24 Search diligently, pray always, and be believing, and all things shall work together for your good, if ye walk uprightly and remember the covenant wherewith ye have covenanted one with another.

25 Let your families be small, especially mine aged servant Joseph Smith's, Sen., as pertaining to those who do not belong to your families;

26 That those things that are provided for you, to bring to pass my work, be not taken from you and given to those that are not worthy—

27 And thereby you be hindered in accomplishing those things which I have commanded you.

28 And again, verily I say unto you, it is my will that my handmaid Vienna Jaques should receive money to bear her expenses, and go up unto the land of Zion;

29 And the residue of the money may be consecrated unto me, and she be rewarded in mine own due time.

30 Verily I say unto you, that it is meet in mine eyes that she should go up unto the land of Zion, and receive an inheritance from the hand of the bishop;

31 That she may settle down in peace inasmuch as she is faithful, and not be idle in her days from thenceforth.

32 And behold, verily I say unto you, that ye shall write this commandment, and say unto your brethren in Zion, in love greeting, that I have called you also to preside over Zion in mine own due time.

33 Therefore, let them cease wearying me concerning this matter.

34 Behold, I say unto you that your brethren in Zion begin to repent, and the angels rejoice over them.

35 Nevertheless, I am not well pleased with many things; and I am not well

pleased with my servant William E. McLellin, neither with my servant Sidney Gilbert; and the bishop also, and others have many things to repent of.

36 But verily I say unto you, that I, the Lord, will contend with Zion, and plead with her strong ones, and chasten her until she overcomes and is clean before me.

37 For she shall not be removed out of her place. I, the Lord, have spoken it. Amen.

Section 91

Revelation given through Joseph Smith the Prophet, at Kirtland, Ohio, March 9, 1833. The Prophet was at this time engaged in the translation of the Old Testament. Having come to that portion of the ancient writings called the Apocrypha, he inquired of the Lord and received this instruction.

1–3, The Apocrypha is mostly translated correctly but contains many interpolations by the hands of men that are not true; 4–6, It benefits those enlightened by the Spirit.

1 Verily, thus saith the Lord unto you concerning the Apocrypha—There are many things contained therein that are true, and it is mostly translated correctly;

2 There are many things contained therein that are not true, which are interpolations by the hands of men.

3 Verily, I say unto you, that it is not needful that the Apocrypha should be translated.

4 Therefore, whoso readeth it, let him understand, for the Spirit manifesteth truth;

5 And whoso is enlightened by the Spirit shall obtain benefit therefrom;

6 And whoso receiveth not by the Spirit, cannot be benefited. Therefore it is not needful that it should be translated. Amen.

Section 92

Revelation given to Joseph Smith the Prophet, at Kirtland, Ohio, March 15, 1833. The revelation instructs Frederick G. Williams, who had recently been appointed a counselor to Joseph Smith, on his duties in the United Firm (see the headings to sections 78 and 82).

1–2, The Lord gives a commandment relative to admission to the united order.

1 Verily, thus saith the Lord, I give unto the united order, organized agreeable to the commandment previously given, a revelation and commandment concerning my servant Frederick G. Williams, that ye shall receive him into the order. What I say unto one I say unto all.

2 And again, I say unto you my servant Frederick G. Williams, you shall be a lively member in this order; and inasmuch as you are faithful in keeping all former commandments you shall be blessed forever. Amen.

Section 93

Revelation given through Joseph Smith the Prophet, at Kirtland, Ohio, May 6, 1833.

1–5, All who are faithful will see the Lord; 6–18, John bore record that the Son of God went from grace to grace until He received a fulness of the glory of the Father; 19–20, Faithful men, going from grace to grace, will also receive of His fulness; 21–22, Those who are begotten through Christ are the Church of the Firstborn; 23–28, Christ received a fulness of all truth, and man by obedience may do likewise; 29–32, Man was in the beginning with God; 33–35, The elements are eternal, and man may receive a fulness of joy in the Resurrection; 36–37, The glory of God is intelligence; 38–40, Children are innocent before God because of the redemption of Christ; 41–53, The leading brethren are commanded to set their families in order.

1 Verily, thus saith the Lord: It shall come to pass that every soul who forsaketh his sins and cometh unto me, and calleth on my name, and obeyeth my voice, and keepeth my commandments, shall see my face and know that I am;

2 And that I am the true light that lighteth every man that cometh into the world;

3 And that I am in the Father, and the Father in me, and the Father and I are one—

4 The Father because he gave me of his fulness, and the Son because I was in the world and made flesh my tabernacle, and dwelt among the sons of men.

5 I was in the world and received of my Father, and the works of him were plainly manifest.

6 And John saw and bore record of the fulness of my glory, and the fulness of John's record is hereafter to be revealed.

7 And he bore record, saying: I saw his glory, that he was in the beginning, before the world was;

8 Therefore, in the beginning the Word was, for he was the Word, even the messenger of salvation—

9 The light and the Redeemer of the world; the Spirit of truth, who came into the world, because the world was made by him, and in him was the life of men and the light of men.

10 The worlds were made by him; men were made by him; all things were made by him, and through him, and of him.

11 And I, John, bear record that I beheld his glory, as the glory of the Only Begotten of the Father, full of grace and truth, even the Spirit of truth, which came and dwelt in the flesh, and dwelt among us.

12 And I, John, saw that he received not of the fulness at the first, but received grace for grace;

13 And he received not of the fulness at first, but continued from grace to grace, until he received a fulness;

14 And thus he was called the Son of God, because he received not of the fulness at the first.

15 And I, John, bear record, and lo, the heavens were opened, and the Holy Ghost descended upon him in the form of a dove, and sat upon him, and there came a voice out of heaven saying: This is my beloved Son.

16 And I, John, bear record that he received a fulness of the glory of the Father;

17 And he received all power, both in

heaven and on earth, and the glory of the Father was with him, for he dwelt in him.

18 And it shall come to pass, that if you are faithful you shall receive the fulness of the record of John.

19 I give unto you these sayings that you may understand and know how to worship, and know what you worship, that you may come unto the Father in my name, and in due time receive of his fulness.

20 For if you keep my commandments you shall receive of his fulness, and be glorified in me as I am in the Father; therefore, I say unto you, you shall receive grace for grace.

21 And now, verily I say unto you, I was in the beginning with the Father, and am the Firstborn;

22 And all those who are begotten through me are partakers of the glory of the same, and are the church of the Firstborn.

23 Ye were also in the beginning with the Father; that which is Spirit, even the Spirit of truth;

24 And truth is knowledge of things as they are, and as they were, and as they are to come;

25 And whatsoever is more or less than this is the spirit of that wicked one who was a liar from the beginning.

26 The Spirit of truth is of God. I am the Spirit of truth, and John bore record of me, saying: He received a fulness of truth, yea, even of all truth;

27 And no man receiveth a fulness unless he keepeth his commandments.

28 He that keepeth his commandments receiveth truth and light, until he is glorified in truth and knoweth all things.

29 Man was also in the beginning with God. Intelligence, or the light of truth, was not created or made, neither indeed can be.

30 All truth is independent in that sphere in which God has placed it, to act for itself, as all intelligence also; otherwise there is no existence.

31 Behold, here is the agency of man, and here is the condemnation of man; because that which was from the beginning is plainly manifest unto them, and they receive not the light.

32 And every man whose spirit receiveth not the light is under condemnation.

33 For man is spirit. The elements are eternal, and spirit and element, inseparably connected, receive a fulness of joy;

34 And when separated, man cannot receive a fulness of joy.

35 The elements are the tabernacle of God; yea, man is the tabernacle of God, even temples; and whatsoever temple is defiled, God shall destroy that temple.

36 The glory of God is intelligence, or, in other words, light and truth.

37 Light and truth forsake that evil one.

38 Every spirit of man was innocent in the beginning; and God having redeemed man from the fall, men became again, in their infant state, innocent before God.

39 And that wicked one cometh and taketh away light and truth, through disobedience, from the children of men, and because of the tradition of their fathers.

40 But I have commanded you to bring up your children in light and truth.

41 But verily I say unto you, my servant Frederick G. Williams, you have continued under this condemnation;

42 You have not taught your children light and truth, according to the commandments; and that wicked one hath power, as yet, over you, and this is the cause of your affliction.

43 And now a commandment I give unto you—if you will be delivered you shall set in order your own house, for there are many things that are not right in your house.

44 Verily, I say unto my servant Sidney Rigdon, that in some things he hath not kept the commandments concerning his children; therefore, first set in order thy house.

45 Verily, I say unto my servant Joseph Smith, Jun., or in other words, I will call you friends, for you are my friends, and ye shall have an inheritance with me—

46 I called you servants for the world's sake, and ye are their servants for my sake—

47 And now, verily I say unto Joseph Smith, Jun.—You have not kept the commandments, and must needs stand rebuked before the Lord;

48 Your family must needs repent and forsake some things, and give more earnest heed unto your sayings, or be removed out of their place.

49 What I say unto one I say unto all; pray always lest that wicked one have power in you, and remove you out of your place.

50 My servant Newel K. Whitney also, a bishop of my church, hath need to be chastened, and set in order his family, and see that they are more diligent and concerned at home, and pray always, or they shall be removed out of their place.

51 Now, I say unto you, my friends, let my servant Sidney Rigdon go on his journey, and make haste, and also proclaim the acceptable year of the Lord, and the gospel of salvation, as I shall give him utterance; and by your prayer of faith with one consent I will uphold him.

52 And let my servants Joseph Smith, Jun., and Frederick G. Williams make haste also, and it shall be given them even according to the prayer of faith; and inasmuch as you keep my sayings you shall not be confounded in this world, nor in the world to come.

53 And, verily I say unto you, that it is my will that you should hasten to translate my scriptures, and to obtain a knowledge of history, and of countries, and of kingdoms, of laws of God and man, and all this for the salvation of Zion. Amen.

Section 94

Revelation given through Joseph Smith the Prophet, at Kirtland, Ohio, August 2, 1833. Hyrum Smith, Reynolds Cahoon, and Jared Carter are appointed as a Church building committee.

1–9, The Lord gives a commandment relative to the erection of a house for the work of the Presidency; 10–12, A printing house is to be built; 13–17, Certain inheritances are assigned.

1 And again, verily I say unto you, my friends, a commandment I give unto you, that ye shall commence a work of laying out and preparing a beginning and foundation of the city of the stake of Zion, here in the land of Kirtland, beginning at my house.

2 And behold, it must be done according to the pattern which I have given unto you.

3 And let the first lot on the south be consecrated unto me for the building of a house for the presidency, for the work of the presidency, in obtaining revelations; and for the work of the ministry of the presidency, in all things pertaining to the church and kingdom.

4 Verily I say unto you, that it shall be built fifty-five by sixty-five feet in the width thereof and in the length thereof, in the inner court.

5 And there shall be a lower court and a higher court, according to the pattern which shall be given unto you hereafter.

6 And it shall be dedicated unto the Lord from the foundation thereof, according to the order of the priesthood, according to the pattern which shall be given unto you hereafter.

7 And it shall be wholly dedicated unto the Lord for the work of the presidency.

8 And ye shall not suffer any unclean thing to come in unto it; and my glory shall be there, and my presence shall be there.

9 But if there shall come into it any unclean thing, my glory shall not be there; and my presence shall not come into it.

10 And again, verily I say unto you, the second lot on the south shall be dedicated unto me for the building of a house unto me, for the work of the printing of the translation of my scriptures, and all things whatsoever I shall command you.

11 And it shall be fifty-five by sixty-five feet in the width thereof and the length thereof, in the inner court; and there shall be a lower and a higher court.

12 And this house shall be wholly dedicated unto the Lord from the foundation thereof, for the work of the printing, in all things whatsoever I shall command you, to be holy, undefiled, according to the pattern in all things as it shall be given unto you.

13 And on the third lot shall my servant Hyrum Smith receive his inheritance.

14 And on the first and second lots on the north shall my servants Reynolds Cahoon and Jared Carter receive their inheritances—

15 That they may do the work which I have appointed unto them, to be a committee to build mine houses, according to the commandment, which I, the Lord God, have given unto you.

16 These two houses are not to be built until I give unto you a commandment concerning them.

17 And now I give unto you no more at this time. Amen.

Section 95

Revelation given through Joseph Smith the Prophet, at Kirtland, Ohio, June 1, 1833. This revelation is a continuation of divine directions to build a house for worship and instruction, the house of the Lord (see section 88:119–36).

1–6, The Saints are chastened for their failure to build the house of the Lord; 7–10, The Lord desires to use His house to endow His people with power from on high; 11–17, The house is to be dedicated as a place of worship and for the school of the Apostles.

1 Verily, thus saith the Lord unto you whom I love, and whom I love I also chasten that their sins may be forgiven, for with the chastisement I prepare a way for their deliverance in all things out of temptation, and I have loved you—

2 Wherefore, ye must needs be chastened and stand rebuked before my face;

3 For ye have sinned against me a very grievous sin, in that ye have not considered the great commandment in all things, that I have given unto you concerning the building of mine house;

4 For the preparation wherewith I design to prepare mine apostles to prune my vineyard for the last time, that I may bring to pass my strange act, that I may pour out my Spirit upon all flesh—

5 But behold, verily I say unto you, that there are many who have been ordained among you, whom I have called but few of them are chosen.

6 They who are not chosen have sinned a very grievous sin, in that they are walking in darkness at noon-day.

7 And for this cause I gave unto you a commandment that you should call your solemn assembly, that your fastings and your mourning might come up into the ears of the Lord of Sabaoth, which is by interpretation, the creator of the first day, the beginning and the end.

8 Yea, verily I say unto you, I gave unto you a commandment that you should build a house, in the which house I design to endow those whom I have chosen with power from on high;

9 For this is the promise of the Father unto you; therefore I command you to tarry, even as mine apostles at Jerusalem.

10 Nevertheless, my servants sinned a very grievous sin; and contentions arose in the school of the prophets; which was very grievous unto me, saith your Lord; therefore I sent them forth to be chastened.

11 Verily I say unto you, it is my will that you should build a house. If you keep my commandments you shall have power to build it.

12 If you keep not my commandments, the love of the Father shall not continue with you, therefore you shall walk in darkness.

13 Now here is wisdom, and the mind of the Lord—let the house be built, not after the manner of the world, for I give not unto you that ye shall live after the manner of the world;

14 Therefore, let it be built after the manner which I shall show unto three of you, whom ye shall appoint and ordain unto this power.

15 And the size thereof shall be fifty and five feet in width, and let it be sixty-five feet in length, in the inner court thereof.

16 And let the lower part of the inner

court be dedicated unto me for your sacrament offering, and for your preaching, and your fasting, and your praying, and the offering up of your most holy desires unto me, saith your Lord.

17 And let the higher part of the inner court be dedicated unto me for the school of mine apostles, saith Son Ahman; or, in other words, Alphus; or, in other words, Omegus; even Jesus Christ your Lord. Amen.

Section 96

Revelation given to Joseph Smith the Prophet, showing the order of the city or stake of Zion at Kirtland, Ohio, June 4, 1833, as an example to the Saints in Kirtland. The occasion was a conference of high priests, and the chief subject of consideration was the disposal of certain lands, known as the French farm, possessed by the Church near Kirtland. Since the conference could not agree who should take charge of the farm, all agreed to inquire of the Lord concerning the matter.

1, The Kirtland Stake of Zion is to be made strong; 2–5, The bishop is to divide the inheritances for the Saints; 6–9, John Johnson is to be a member of the united order.

1 Behold, I say unto you, here is wisdom, whereby ye may know how to act concerning this matter, for it is expedient in me that this stake that I have set for the strength of Zion should be made strong.

2 Therefore, let my servant Newel K. Whitney take charge of the place which is named among you, upon which I design to build mine holy house.

3 And again, let it be divided into lots, according to wisdom, for the benefit of those who seek inheritances, as it shall be determined in council among you.

4 Therefore, take heed that ye see to this matter, and that portion that is necessary to benefit mine order, for the purpose of bringing forth my word to the children of men.

5 For behold, verily I say unto you, this is the most expedient in me, that my word should go forth unto the children of men, for the purpose of subduing the hearts of the children of men for your good. Even so. Amen.

6 And again, verily I say unto you, it is wisdom and expedient in me, that my servant John Johnson whose offering I have accepted, and whose prayers I have heard, unto whom I give a promise of eternal life inasmuch as he keepeth my commandments from henceforth—

7 For he is a descendant of Joseph and a partaker of the blessings of the promise made unto his fathers—

8 Verily I say unto you, it is expedient in me that he should become a member of the order, that he may assist in bringing forth my word unto the children of men.

9 Therefore ye shall ordain him unto this blessing, and he shall seek diligently to take away incumbrances that are upon the house named among you, that he may dwell therein. Even so. Amen.

Section 97

Revelation given through Joseph Smith the Prophet, at Kirtland, Ohio, August 2, 1833. This revelation deals particularly with the affairs of the Saints in Zion, Jackson County, Missouri, in response to the Prophet's inquiry of the Lord for information. Members of the Church in Missouri were at this time subjected to severe persecution and, on July 23, 1833, had been forced to sign an agreement to leave Jackson County.

1–2, Many of the Saints in Zion (Jackson County, Missouri) are blessed for their faithfulness; 3–5, Parley P. Pratt is commended for his labors in the school in Zion; 6–9, Those who observe their covenants are accepted by the Lord; 10–17, A house is to be built in Zion in which the pure in heart will see God; 18–21, Zion is the pure in heart; 22–28, Zion will escape the Lord's scourge if she is faithful.

1 Verily I say unto you my friends, I speak unto you with my voice, even the voice of my Spirit, that I may show unto you my will concerning your brethren in the land of Zion, many of whom are truly humble and are seeking diligently to learn wisdom and to find truth.

2 Verily, verily I say unto you, blessed are such, for they shall obtain; for I, the Lord, show mercy unto all the meek, and upon all whomsoever I will, that I may be justified when I shall bring them unto judgment.

3 Behold, I say unto you, concerning the school in Zion, I, the Lord, am well pleased that there should be a school in Zion, and also with my servant Parley P. Pratt, for he abideth in me.

4 And inasmuch as he continueth to abide in me he shall continue to preside over the school in the land of Zion until I shall give unto him other commandments.

5 And I will bless him with a multiplicity of blessings, in expounding all scriptures and mysteries to the edification of the school, and of the church in Zion.

6 And to the residue of the school, I, the Lord, am willing to show mercy; nevertheless, there are those that must needs be chastened, and their works shall be made known.

7 The ax is laid at the root of the trees; and every tree that bringeth not forth good fruit shall be hewn down and cast into the fire. I, the Lord, have spoken it.

8 Verily I say unto you, all among them who know their hearts are honest, and are broken, and their spirits contrite, and are willing to observe their covenants by sacrifice—yea, every sacrifice which I, the Lord, shall command—they are accepted of me.

9 For I, the Lord, will cause them to bring forth as a very fruitful tree which is planted in a goodly land, by a pure stream, that yieldeth much precious fruit.

10 Verily I say unto you, that it is my will that a house should be built unto me in the land of Zion, like unto the pattern which I have given you.

11 Yea, let it be built speedily, by the tithing of my people.

12 Behold, this is the tithing and the sacrifice which I, the Lord, require at their hands, that there may be a house built unto me for the salvation of Zion—

13 For a place of thanksgiving for all saints, and for a place of instruction for all those who are called to the work of the ministry in all their several callings and offices;

14 That they may be perfected in the

understanding of their ministry, in theory, in principle, and in doctrine, in all things pertaining to the kingdom of God on the earth, the keys of which kingdom have been conferred upon you.

15 And inasmuch as my people build a house unto me in the name of the Lord, and do not suffer any unclean thing to come into it, that it be not defiled, my glory shall rest upon it;

16 Yea, and my presence shall be there, for I will come into it, and all the pure in heart that shall come into it shall see God.

17 But if it be defiled I will not come into it, and my glory shall not be there; for I will not come into unholy temples.

18 And, now, behold, if Zion do these things she shall prosper, and spread herself and become very glorious, very great, and very terrible.

19 And the nations of the earth shall honor her, and shall say: Surely Zion is the city of our God, and surely Zion cannot fall, neither be moved out of her place, for God is there, and the hand of the Lord is there;

20 And he hath sworn by the power of his might to be her salvation and her high tower.

21 Therefore, verily, thus saith the Lord, let Zion rejoice, for this is Zion—THE PURE IN HEART; therefore, let Zion rejoice, while all the wicked shall mourn.

22 For behold, and lo, vengeance cometh speedily upon the ungodly as the whirlwind; and who shall escape it?

23 The Lord's scourge shall pass over by night and by day, and the report thereof shall vex all people; yea, it shall not be stayed until the Lord come;

24 For the indignation of the Lord is kindled against their abominations and all their wicked works.

25 Nevertheless, Zion shall escape if she observe to do all things whatsoever I have commanded her.

26 But if she observe not to do whatsoever I have commanded her, I will visit her according to all her works, with sore affliction, with pestilence, with plague, with sword, with vengeance, with devouring fire.

27 Nevertheless, let it be read this once to her ears, that I, the Lord, have accepted of her offering; and if she sin no more none of these things shall come upon her;

28 And I will bless her with blessings, and multiply a multiplicity of blessings upon her, and upon her generations forever and ever, saith the Lord your God. Amen.

Section 98

Revelation given through Joseph Smith the Prophet, at Kirtland, Ohio, August 6, 1833. This revelation came in consequence of the persecution upon the Saints in Missouri. Increased settlement of Church members in Missouri troubled some other settlers, who felt threatened by the Saints' numbers, political and economic influence, and cultural and religious differences. In July 1833, a mob destroyed Church property, tarred and feathered two Church members, and demanded that the Saints leave Jackson County. Although some news of the problems in Missouri had no doubt reached the Prophet in Kirtland (nine hundred miles away), the seriousness of the situation could have been known to him at this date only by revelation.

1–3, The afflictions of the Saints will be for their good; 4–8, The Saints are to befriend the constitutional law of the land; 9–10, Honest, wise, and good men should be supported for secular government; 11–15, Those who lay down their lives in the Lord's cause will have eternal life; 16–18, Renounce war and proclaim peace; 19–22, The Saints in Kirtland are reproved and commanded to repent; 23–32, The Lord reveals His laws governing the persecutions and afflictions imposed on His people; 33–38, War is justified only when the Lord commands it; 39–48, The Saints are to forgive their enemies, who, if they repent, will also escape the Lord's vengeance.

1 Verily I say unto you my friends, fear not, let your hearts be comforted; yea, rejoice evermore, and in everything give thanks;

2 Waiting patiently on the Lord, for your prayers have entered into the ears of the Lord of Sabaoth, and are recorded with this seal and testament—the Lord hath sworn and decreed that they shall be granted.

3 Therefore, he giveth this promise unto you, with an immutable covenant that they shall be fulfilled; and all things wherewith you have been afflicted shall work together for your good, and to my name's glory, saith the Lord.

4 And now, verily I say unto you concerning the laws of the land, it is my will that my people should observe to do all things whatsoever I command them.

5 And that law of the land which is constitutional, supporting that principle of freedom in maintaining rights and privileges, belongs to all mankind, and is justifiable before me.

6 Therefore, I, the Lord, justify you, and your brethren of my church, in befriending that law which is the constitutional law of the land;

7 And as pertaining to law of man, whatsoever is more or less than this, cometh of evil.

8 I, the Lord God, make you free, therefore ye are free indeed; and the law also maketh you free.

9 Nevertheless, when the wicked rule the people mourn.

10 Wherefore, honest men and wise men should be sought for diligently, and good men and wise men ye should observe to uphold; otherwise whatsoever is less than these cometh of evil.

11 And I give unto you a commandment, that ye shall forsake all evil and cleave unto all good, that ye shall live by every word which proceedeth forth out of the mouth of God.

12 For he will give unto the faithful line upon line, precept upon precept; and I will try you and prove you herewith.

13 And whoso layeth down his life in my cause, for my name's sake, shall find

it again, even life eternal.

14 Therefore, be not afraid of your enemies, for I have decreed in my heart, saith the Lord, that I will prove you in all things, whether you will abide in my covenant, even unto death, that you may be found worthy.

15 For if ye will not abide in my covenant ye are not worthy of me.

16 Therefore, renounce war and proclaim peace, and seek diligently to turn the hearts of the children to their fathers, and the hearts of the fathers to the children;

17 And again, the hearts of the Jews unto the prophets, and the prophets unto the Jews; lest I come and smite the whole earth with a curse, and all flesh be consumed before me.

18 Let not your hearts be troubled; for in my Father's house are many mansions, and I have prepared a place for you; and where my Father and I am, there ye shall be also.

19 Behold, I, the Lord, am not well pleased with many who are in the church at Kirtland;

20 For they do not forsake their sins, and their wicked ways, the pride of their hearts, and their covetousness, and all their detestable things, and observe the words of wisdom and eternal life which I have given unto them.

21 Verily I say unto you, that I, the Lord, will chasten them and will do whatsoever I list, if they do not repent and observe all things whatsoever I have said unto them.

22 And again I say unto you, if ye observe to do whatsoever I command you, I, the Lord, will turn away all wrath and indignation from you, and the gates of hell shall not prevail against you.

23 Now, I speak unto you concerning your families—if men will smite you, or your families, once, and ye bear it patiently and revile not against them, neither seek revenge, ye shall be rewarded;

24 But if ye bear it not patiently, it shall be accounted unto you as being meted out as a just measure unto you.

25 And again, if your enemy shall smite you the second time, and you revile not against your enemy, and bear it patiently, your reward shall be an hundred-fold.

26 And again, if he shall smite you the third time, and ye bear it patiently, your reward shall be doubled unto you four-fold;

27 And these three testimonies shall stand against your enemy if he repent not, and shall not be blotted out.

28 And now, verily I say unto you, if that enemy shall escape my vengeance, that he be not brought into judgment before me, then ye shall see to it that ye warn him in my name, that he come no more upon you, neither upon your family, even your children's children unto the third and fourth generation.

29 And then, if he shall come upon you or your children, or your children's children unto the third and fourth generation, I have delivered thine enemy into thine hands;

30 And then if thou wilt spare him, thou shalt be rewarded for thy righteousness; and also thy children and thy children's children unto the third and fourth generation.

31 Nevertheless, thine enemy is in thine hands; and if thou rewardest him according to his works thou art justified; if he has sought thy life, and thy life is endangered by him, thine enemy is in

thine hands and thou art justified.

32 Behold, this is the law I gave unto my servant Nephi, and thy fathers, Joseph, and Jacob, and Isaac, and Abraham, and all mine ancient prophets and apostles.

33 And again, this is the law that I gave unto mine ancients, that they should not go out unto battle against any nation, kindred, tongue, or people, save I, the Lord, commanded them.

34 And if any nation, tongue, or people should proclaim war against them, they should first lift a standard of peace unto that people, nation, or tongue;

35 And if that people did not accept the offering of peace, neither the second nor the third time, they should bring these testimonies before the Lord;

36 Then I, the Lord, would give unto them a commandment, and justify them in going out to battle against that nation, tongue, or people.

37 And I, the Lord, would fight their battles, and their children's battles, and their children's children's, until they had avenged themselves on all their enemies, to the third and fourth generation.

38 Behold, this is an ensample unto all people, saith the Lord your God, for justification before me.

39 And again, verily I say unto you, if after thine enemy has come upon thee the first time, he repent and come unto thee praying thy forgiveness, thou shalt forgive him, and shalt hold it no more as a testimony against thine enemy—

40 And so on unto the second and third time; and as oft as thine enemy repenteth of the trespass wherewith he has trespassed against thee, thou shalt forgive him, until seventy times seven.

41 And if he trespass against thee and repent not the first time, nevertheless thou shalt forgive him.

42 And if he trespass against thee the second time, and repent not, nevertheless thou shalt forgive him.

43 And if he trespass against thee the third time, and repent not, thou shalt also forgive him.

44 But if he trespass against thee the fourth time thou shalt not forgive him, but shalt bring these testimonies before the Lord; and they shall not be blotted out until he repent and reward thee four-fold in all things wherewith he has trespassed against thee.

45 And if he do this, thou shalt forgive him with all thine heart; and if he do not this, I, the Lord, will avenge thee of thine enemy an hundred-fold;

46 And upon his children, and upon his children's children of all them that hate me, unto the third and fourth generation.

47 But if the children shall repent, or the children's children, and turn to the Lord their God, with all their hearts and with all their might, mind, and strength, and restore four-fold for all their trespasses wherewith they have trespassed, or wherewith their fathers have trespassed, or their fathers' fathers, then thine indignation shall be turned away;

48 And vengeance shall no more come upon them, saith the Lord thy God, and their trespasses shall never be brought any more as a testimony before the Lord against them. Amen.

Section 99

Revelation given through Joseph Smith the Prophet to John Murdock, August 29, 1832, at Hiram, Ohio. For over a year, John Murdock had been preaching the gospel while his children—motherless after the death of his wife, Julia Clapp, in April 1831—resided with other families in Ohio.

1–8, John Murdock is called to proclaim the gospel, and those who receive him receive the Lord and will obtain mercy.

1 Behold, thus saith the Lord unto my servant John Murdock—thou art called to go into the eastern countries from house to house, from village to village, and from city to city, to proclaim mine everlasting gospel unto the inhabitants thereof, in the midst of persecution and wickedness.

2 And who receiveth you receiveth me; and you shall have power to declare my word in the demonstration of my Holy Spirit.

3 And who receiveth you as a little child, receiveth my kingdom; and blessed are they, for they shall obtain mercy.

4 And whoso rejecteth you shall be rejected of my Father and his house; and you shall cleanse your feet in the secret places by the way for a testimony against them.

5 And behold, and lo, I come quickly to judgment, to convince all of their ungodly deeds which they have committed against me, as it is written of me in the volume of the book.

6 And now, verily I say unto you, that it is not expedient that you should go until your children are provided for, and sent up kindly unto the bishop of Zion.

7 And after a few years, if thou desirest of me, thou mayest go up also unto the goodly land, to possess thine inheritance;

8 Otherwise thou shalt continue proclaiming my gospel until thou be taken. Amen.

Section 100

Revelation given to Joseph Smith the Prophet and Sidney Rigdon, at Perrysburg, New York, October 12, 1833. The two brethren, having been absent from their families for several days, felt some concern about them.

1–4, Joseph and Sidney to preach the gospel for the salvation of souls; 5–8, It will be given them in the very hour what they should say; 9–12, Sidney is to be a spokesman and Joseph is to be a revelator and mighty in testimony; 13–17, The Lord will raise up a pure people, and the obedient will be saved.

1 Verily, thus saith the Lord unto you, my friends Sidney and Joseph, your families are well; they are in mine hands, and I will do with them as seemeth me good; for in me there is all power.

2 Therefore, follow me, and listen to the counsel which I shall give unto you.

3 Behold, and lo, I have much people in this place, in the regions round about; and an effectual door shall be opened in the regions round about in this eastern land.

4 Therefore, I, the Lord, have suffered you to come unto this place; for thus it was expedient in me for the salvation of souls.

5 Therefore, verily I say unto you, lift up your voices unto this people; speak the thoughts that I shall put into your hearts, and you shall not be confounded before men;

6 For it shall be given you in the very hour, yea, in the very moment, what ye shall say.

7 But a commandment I give unto you, that ye shall declare whatsoever thing ye declare in my name, in solemnity of heart, in the spirit of meekness, in all things.

8 And I give unto you this promise, that inasmuch as ye do this the Holy Ghost shall be shed forth in bearing record unto all things whatsoever ye shall say.

9 And it is expedient in me that you, my servant Sidney, should be a spokesman unto this people; yea, verily, I will ordain you unto this calling, even to be a spokesman unto my servant Joseph.

10 And I will give unto him power to be mighty in testimony.

11 And I will give unto thee power to be mighty in expounding all scriptures, that thou mayest be a spokesman unto him, and he shall be a revelator unto thee, that thou mayest know the certainty of all things pertaining to the things of my kingdom on the earth.

12 Therefore, continue your journey and let your hearts rejoice; for behold, and lo, I am with you even unto the end.

13 And now I give unto you a word concerning Zion. Zion shall be redeemed, although she is chastened for a little season.

14 Thy brethren, my servants Orson Hyde and John Gould, are in my hands; and inasmuch as they keep my commandments they shall be saved.

15 Therefore, let your hearts be comforted; for all things shall work together for good to them that walk uprightly, and to the sanctification of the church.

16 For I will raise up unto myself a pure people, that will serve me in righteousness;

17 And all that call upon the name of the Lord, and keep his commandments, shall be saved. Even so. Amen.

Section 101

Revelation given to Joseph Smith the Prophet, at Kirtland, Ohio, December 16 and 17, 1833. At this time the Saints who had gathered in Missouri were suffering great persecution. Mobs had driven them from their homes in Jackson County; and some of the Saints had tried to establish themselves in Van Buren, Lafayette, and Ray Counties, but persecution followed them. The main body of the Saints was at that time in Clay County, Missouri. Threats of death against individuals of the Church were many. The Saints in Jackson County had lost household furniture, clothing, livestock, and other personal property; and many of their crops had been destroyed.

1–8, The Saints are chastened and afflicted because of their transgressions; 9–15, The Lord's indignation will fall upon the nations, but His people will be gathered and comforted; 16–21, Zion and her stakes will be established; 22–31, The nature of life during the Millennium is set forth; 32–42, The Saints will be blessed and rewarded then; 43–62, The parable of the nobleman and the olive trees signifies the troubles and eventual redemption of Zion; 63–75, The Saints are to continue gathering together; 76–80, The Lord established the Constitution of the United States; 81–101, The Saints are to importune for the redress of grievances, according to the parable of the woman and the unjust judge.

1 Verily I say unto you, concerning your brethren who have been afflicted, and persecuted, and cast out from the land of their inheritance—

2 I, the Lord, have suffered the affliction to come upon them, wherewith they have been afflicted, in consequence of their transgressions;

3 Yet I will own them, and they shall be mine in that day when I shall come to make up my jewels.

4 Therefore, they must needs be chastened and tried, even as Abraham, who was commanded to offer up his only son.

5 For all those who will not endure chastening, but deny me, cannot be sanctified.

6 Behold, I say unto you, there were jarrings, and contentions, and envyings, and strifes, and lustful and covetous desires among them; therefore by these things they polluted their inheritances.

7 They were slow to hearken unto the voice of the Lord their God; therefore, the Lord their God is slow to hearken unto their prayers, to answer them in the day of their trouble.

8 In the day of their peace they esteemed lightly my counsel; but, in the day of their trouble, of necessity they feel after me.

9 Verily I say unto you, notwithstanding their sins, my bowels are filled with compassion towards them. I will not utterly cast them off; and in the day of wrath I will remember mercy.

10 I have sworn, and the decree hath gone forth by a former commandment which I have given unto you, that I would let fall the sword of mine indignation in behalf of my people; and even as I have said, it shall come to pass.

11 Mine indignation is soon to be poured out without measure upon all nations; and this will I do when the cup of their iniquity is full.

12 And in that day all who are found upon the watch-tower, or in other words, all mine Israel, shall be saved.

13 And they that have been scattered shall be gathered.

14 And all they who have mourned shall be comforted.

15 And all they who have given their lives for my name shall be crowned.

16 Therefore, let your hearts be comforted concerning Zion; for all flesh is in mine hands; be still and know that I am God.

17 Zion shall not be moved out of her place, notwithstanding her children are scattered.

18 They that remain, and are pure in heart, shall return, and come to their inheritances, they and their children, with songs of everlasting joy, to build up the waste places of Zion—

19 And all these things that the prophets might be fulfilled.

20 And, behold, there is none other place appointed than that which I have appointed; neither shall there be any other place appointed than that which I have appointed, for the work of the gathering of my saints—

21 Until the day cometh when there is found no more room for them; and then I have other places which I will appoint unto them, and they shall be called stakes, for the curtains or the strength of Zion.

22 Behold, it is my will, that all they who call on my name, and worship me according to mine everlasting gospel, should gather together, and stand in holy places;

23 And prepare for the revelation which is to come, when the veil of the covering of my temple, in my tabernacle, which hideth the earth, shall be taken off, and all flesh shall see me together.

24 And every corruptible thing, both of man, or of the beasts of the field, or of the fowls of the heavens, or of the fish of the sea, that dwells upon all the face of the earth, shall be consumed;

25 And also that of element shall melt with fervent heat; and all things shall become new, that my knowledge and glory may dwell upon all the earth.

26 And in that day the enmity of man, and the enmity of beasts, yea, the enmity of all flesh, shall cease from before my face.

27 And in that day whatsoever any man shall ask, it shall be given unto him.

28 And in that day Satan shall not have power to tempt any man.

29 And there shall be no sorrow because there is no death.

30 In that day an infant shall not die until he is old; and his life shall be as the age of a tree;

31 And when he dies he shall not sleep, that is to say in the earth, but shall be changed in the twinkling of an eye, and shall be caught up, and his rest shall be glorious.

32 Yea, verily I say unto you, in that day when the Lord shall come, he shall reveal all things—

33 Things which have passed, and hidden things which no man knew, things of the earth, by which it was made, and the purpose and the end thereof—

34 Things most precious, things that are above, and things that are beneath, things that are in the earth, and upon the earth, and in heaven.

35 And all they who suffer persecution for my name, and endure in faith, though they are called to lay down their lives for my sake yet shall they partake

of all this glory.

36 Wherefore, fear not even unto death; for in this world your joy is not full, but in me your joy is full.

37 Therefore, care not for the body, neither the life of the body; but care for the soul, and for the life of the soul.

38 And seek the face of the Lord always, that in patience ye may possess your souls, and ye shall have eternal life.

39 When men are called unto mine everlasting gospel, and covenant with an everlasting covenant, they are accounted as the salt of the earth and the savor of men;

40 They are called to be the savor of men; therefore, if that salt of the earth lose its savor, behold, it is thenceforth good for nothing only to be cast out and trodden under the feet of men.

41 Behold, here is wisdom concerning the children of Zion, even many, but not all; they were found transgressors, therefore they must needs be chastened—

42 He that exalteth himself shall be abased, and he that abaseth himself shall be exalted.

43 And now, I will show unto you a parable, that you may know my will concerning the redemption of Zion.

44 A certain nobleman had a spot of land, very choice; and he said unto his servants: Go ye unto my vineyard, even upon this very choice piece of land, and plant twelve olive trees;

45 And set watchmen round about them, and build a tower, that one may overlook the land round about, to be a watchman upon the tower, that mine olive trees may not be broken down when the enemy shall come to spoil and take upon themselves the fruit of my vineyard.

46 Now, the servants of the nobleman went and did as their lord commanded them, and planted the olive trees, and built a hedge round about, and set watchmen, and began to build a tower.

47 And while they were yet laying the foundation thereof, they began to say among themselves: And what need hath my lord of this tower?

48 And consulted for a long time, saying among themselves: What need hath my lord of this tower, seeing this is a time of peace?

49 Might not this money be given to the exchangers? For there is no need of these things.

50 And while they were at variance one with another they became very slothful, and they hearkened not unto the commandments of their lord.

51 And the enemy came by night, and broke down the hedge; and the servants of the nobleman arose and were affrighted, and fled; and the enemy destroyed their works, and broke down the olive trees.

52 Now, behold, the nobleman, the lord of the vineyard, called upon his servants, and said unto them, Why! what is the cause of this great evil?

53 Ought ye not to have done even as I commanded you, and—after ye had planted the vineyard, and built the hedge round about, and set watchmen upon the walls thereof—built the tower also, and set a watchman upon the tower, and watched for my vineyard, and not have fallen asleep, lest the enemy should come upon you?

54 And behold, the watchman upon the tower would have seen the enemy while

he was yet afar off; and then ye could have made ready and kept the enemy from breaking down the hedge thereof, and saved my vineyard from the hands of the destroyer.

55 And the lord of the vineyard said unto one of his servants: Go and gather together the residue of my servants, and take all the strength of mine house, which are my warriors, my young men, and they that are of middle age also among all my servants, who are the strength of mine house, save those only whom I have appointed to tarry;

56 And go ye straightway unto the land of my vineyard, and redeem my vineyard; for it is mine; I have bought it with money.

57 Therefore, get ye straightway unto my land; break down the walls of mine enemies; throw down their tower, and scatter their watchmen.

58 And inasmuch as they gather together against you, avenge me of mine enemies, that by and by I may come with the residue of mine house and possess the land.

59 And the servant said unto his lord: When shall these things be?

60 And he said unto his servant: When I will; go ye straightway, and do all things whatsoever I have commanded you;

61 And this shall be my seal and blessing upon you—a faithful and wise steward in the midst of mine house, a ruler in my kingdom.

62 And his servant went straightway, and did all things whatsoever his lord commanded him; and after many days all things were fulfilled.

63 Again, verily I say unto you, I will show unto you wisdom in me concerning all the churches, inasmuch as they are willing to be guided in a right and proper way for their salvation—

64 That the work of the gathering together of my saints may continue, that I may build them up unto my name upon holy places; for the time of harvest is come, and my word must needs be fulfilled.

65 Therefore, I must gather together my people, according to the parable of the wheat and the tares, that the wheat may be secured in the garners to possess eternal life, and be crowned with celestial glory, when I shall come in the kingdom of my Father to reward every man according as his work shall be;

66 While the tares shall be bound in bundles, and their bands made strong, that they may be burned with unquenchable fire.

67 Therefore, a commandment I give unto all the churches, that they shall continue to gather together unto the places which I have appointed.

68 Nevertheless, as I have said unto you in a former commandment, let not your gathering be in haste, nor by flight; but let all things be prepared before you.

69 And in order that all things be prepared before you, observe the commandment which I have given concerning these things—

70 Which saith, or teacheth, to purchase all the lands with money, which can be purchased for money, in the region round about the land which I have appointed to be the land of Zion, for the beginning of the gathering of my saints;

71 All the land which can be purchased in Jackson county, and the counties round about, and leave the residue in mine hand.

72 Now, verily I say unto you, let all the churches gather together all their moneys; let these things be done in their time, but not in haste; and observe to have all things prepared before you.

73 And let honorable men be appointed, even wise men, and send them to purchase these lands.

74 And the churches in the eastern countries, when they are built up, if they will hearken unto this counsel they may buy lands and gather together upon them; and in this way they may establish Zion.

75 There is even now already in store sufficient, yea, even an abundance, to redeem Zion, and establish her waste places, no more to be thrown down, were the churches, who call themselves after my name, willing to hearken to my voice.

76 And again I say unto you, those who have been scattered by their enemies, it is my will that they should continue to importune for redress, and redemption, by the hands of those who are placed as rulers and are in authority over you—

77 According to the laws and constitution of the people, which I have suffered to be established, and should be maintained for the rights and protection of all flesh, according to just and holy principles;

78 That every man may act in doctrine and principle pertaining to futurity, according to the moral agency which I have given unto him, that every man may be accountable for his own sins in the day of judgment.

79 Therefore, it is not right that any man should be in bondage one to another.

80 And for this purpose have I established the Constitution of this land, by the hands of wise men whom I raised up unto this very purpose, and redeemed the land by the shedding of blood.

81 Now, unto what shall I liken the children of Zion? I will liken them unto the parable of the woman and the unjust judge, for men ought always to pray and not to faint, which saith—

82 There was in a city a judge which feared not God, neither regarded man.

83 And there was a widow in that city, and she came unto him, saying: Avenge me of mine adversary.

84 And he would not for a while, but afterward he said within himself: Though I fear not God, nor regard man, yet because this widow troubleth me I will avenge her, lest by her continual coming she weary me.

85 Thus will I liken the children of Zion.

86 Let them importune at the feet of the judge;

87 And if he heed them not, let them importune at the feet of the governor;

88 And if the governor heed them not, let them importune at the feet of the president;

89 And if the president heed them not, then will the Lord arise and come forth out of his hiding place, and in his fury vex the nation;

90 And in his hot displeasure, and in his fierce anger, in his time, will cut off those wicked, unfaithful, and unjust stewards, and appoint them their portion among hypocrites, and unbelievers;

91 Even in outer darkness, where there is weeping, and wailing, and gnashing of teeth.

92 Pray ye, therefore, that their ears may be opened unto your cries, that I may be merciful unto them, that these things may not come upon them.

93 What I have said unto you must needs be, that all men may be left without excuse;

94 That wise men and rulers may hear and know that which they have never considered;

95 That I may proceed to bring to pass my act, my strange act, and perform my work, my strange work, that men may discern between the righteous and the wicked, saith your God.

96 And again, I say unto you, it is contrary to my commandment and my will that my servant Sidney Gilbert should sell my storehouse, which I have appointed unto my people, into the hands of mine enemies.

97 Let not that which I have appointed be polluted by mine enemies, by the consent of those who call themselves after my name;

98 For this is a very sore and grievous sin against me, and against my people, in consequence of those things which I have decreed and which are soon to befall the nations.

99 Therefore, it is my will that my people should claim, and hold claim upon that which I have appointed unto them, though they should not be permitted to dwell thereon.

100 Nevertheless, I do not say they shall not dwell thereon; for inasmuch as they bring forth fruit and works meet for my kingdom they shall dwell thereon.

101 They shall build, and another shall not inherit it; they shall plant vineyards, and they shall eat the fruit thereof. Even so. Amen.

Section 102

Minutes of the organization of the first high council of the Church, at Kirtland, Ohio, February 17, 1834. The original minutes were recorded by Elders Oliver Cowdery and Orson Hyde. The Prophet revised the minutes the following day, and the next day the corrected minutes were unanimously accepted by the high council as "a form and constitution of the high council" of the Church. Verses 30 through 32, having to do with the Council of the Twelve Apostles, were added in 1835 under Joseph Smith's direction when this section was prepared for publication in the Doctrine and Covenants.

1–8, A high council is appointed to settle important difficulties that arise in the Church; 9–18, Procedures are given for hearing cases; 19–23, The president of the council renders the decision; 24–34, Appellate procedure is set forth.

1 This day a general council of twenty-four high priests assembled at the house of Joseph Smith, Jun., by revelation, and proceeded to organize the high council of the church of Christ, which was to consist of twelve high priests, and one or three presidents as the case might require.

2 The high council was appointed by revelation for the purpose of settling important difficulties which might arise in the church, which could not be settled by the church or the bishop's council to the satisfaction of the parties.

3 Joseph Smith, Jun., Sidney Rigdon and Frederick G. Williams were acknowledged presidents by the voice of the council; and Joseph Smith, Sen., John Smith, Joseph Coe, John Johnson, Martin Harris, John S. Carter, Jared Carter, Oliver Cowdery, Samuel H. Smith, Orson Hyde, Sylvester Smith, and Luke Johnson, high priests, were chosen to be a standing council for the church, by the unanimous voice of the council.

4 The above-named councilors were then asked whether they accepted their appointments, and whether they would act in that office according to the law of heaven, to which they all answered that they accepted their appointments, and would fill their offices according to the grace of God bestowed upon them.

5 The number composing the council, who voted in the name and for the church in appointing the above-named councilors were forty-three, as follows: nine high priests, seventeen elders, four priests, and thirteen members.

6 Voted: that the high council cannot have power to act without seven of the above-named councilors, or their regularly appointed successors are present.

7 These seven shall have power to appoint other high priests, whom they may consider worthy and capable to act in the place of absent councilors.

8 Voted: that whenever any vacancy shall occur by the death, removal from office for transgression, or removal from the bounds of this church government, of any one of the above-named councilors, it shall be filled by the nomination of the president or presidents, and sanctioned by the voice of a general council of high priests, convened for that purpose, to act in the name of the church.

9 The president of the church, who is also the president of the council, is appointed by revelation, and acknowledged in his administration by the voice of the church.

10 And it is according to the dignity of his office that he should preside over the council of the church; and it is his privilege to be assisted by two other presidents, appointed after the same manner that he himself was appointed.

11 And in case of the absence of one or both of those who are appointed to assist him, he has power to preside over the council without an assistant; and in case he himself is absent, the other presidents have power to preside in his stead, both or either of them.

12 Whenever a high council of the church of Christ is regularly organized, according to the foregoing pattern, it shall be the duty of the twelve councilors to cast lots by numbers, and thereby ascertain who of the twelve shall speak first, commencing with number one and so in succession to number twelve.

13 Whenever this council convenes to act upon any case, the twelve councilors shall consider whether it is a difficult one or not; if it is not, two only of the councilors shall speak upon it, according to the form above written.

14 But if it is thought to be difficult, four shall be appointed; and if more difficult, six; but in no case shall more than six be appointed to speak.

15 The accused, in all cases, has a right to one-half of the council, to prevent insult or injustice.

16 And the councilors appointed to speak before the council are to present the case, after the evidence is examined, in its true light before the council; and every man is to speak according to equity and justice.

17 Those councilors who draw even numbers, that is, 2, 4, 6, 8, 10, and 12, are the individuals who are to stand up in behalf of the accused, and prevent insult and injustice.

18 In all cases the accuser and the accused shall have a privilege of speaking for themselves before the council, after the evidences are heard and the councilors who are appointed to speak on the case have finished their remarks.

19 After the evidences are heard, the councilors, accuser and accused have spoken, the president shall give a decision according to the understanding which he shall have of the case, and call upon the twelve councilors to sanction the same by their vote.

20 But should the remaining councilors, who have not spoken, or any one of them, after hearing the evidences and pleadings impartially, discover an error in the decision of the president, they can manifest it, and the case shall have a re-hearing.

21 And if, after a careful re-hearing, any additional light is shown upon the case, the decision shall be altered accordingly.

22 But in case no additional light is given, the first decision shall stand, the majority of the council having power to determine the same.

23 In case of difficulty respecting doctrine or principle, if there is not a sufficiency written to make the case clear to the minds of the council, the president may inquire and obtain the mind of the Lord by revelation.

24 The high priests, when abroad, have power to call and organize a council after the manner of the foregoing, to settle difficulties, when the parties or either of them shall request it.

25 And the said council of high priests shall have power to appoint one of their own number to preside over such council for the time being.

26 It shall be the duty of said council to transmit, immediately, a copy of their proceedings, with a full statement of the testimony accompanying their decision, to the high council of the seat of the First Presidency of the Church.

27 Should the parties or either of them be dissatisfied with the decision of said council, they may appeal to the high council of the seat of the First Presidency of the Church, and have a re-hearing, which case shall there be conducted, according to the former pattern written, as though no such decision had been made.

28 This council of high priests abroad is only to be called on the most difficult cases of church matters; and no common or ordinary case is to be sufficient to call such council.

29 The traveling or located high priests abroad have power to say whether it is necessary to call such a council or not.

30 There is a distinction between the high council or traveling high priests abroad, and the traveling high council composed of the twelve apostles, in their decisions.

31 From the decision of the former there can be an appeal; but from the decision of the latter there cannot.

32 The latter can only be called in question by the general authorities of the church in case of transgression.

33 Resolved: that the president or presidents of the seat of the First Presidency of the Church shall have power to determine whether any such case, as may be appealed, is justly entitled to a re-hearing, after examining the appeal and the evidences and statements accompanying it.

34 The twelve councilors then proceeded to cast lots or ballot, to ascertain who should speak first, and the following was the result, namely: 1, Oliver Cowdery; 2, Joseph Coe; 3, Samuel H. Smith; 4, Luke Johnson; 5, John S. Carter; 6, Sylvester Smith; 7, John Johnson; 8, Orson Hyde; 9, Jared Carter; 10, Joseph Smith, Sen.; 11, John Smith; 12, Martin Harris.After prayer the conference adjourned.

OLIVER COWDERY,

ORSON HYDE,

Clerks

Section 103

Revelation given through Joseph Smith the Prophet, at Kirtland, Ohio, February 24, 1834. This revelation was received after the arrival in Kirtland, Ohio, of Parley P. Pratt and Lyman Wight, who had come from Missouri to counsel with the Prophet as to the relief and restoration of the Saints to their lands in Jackson County.

1–4, Why the Lord permitted the Saints in Jackson County to be persecuted; 5–10, The Saints will prevail if they keep the commandments; 11–20, The redemption of Zion will come by power, and the Lord will go before His people; 21–28, The Saints are to gather in Zion, and those who lay down their lives will find them again; 29–40, Various brethren are called to organize Zion's Camp and go to Zion; they are promised victory if they are faithful.

1 Verily I say unto you, my friends, behold, I will give unto you a revelation and commandment, that you may know how to act in the discharge of your duties concerning the salvation and redemption of your brethren, who have been scattered on the land of Zion;

2 Being driven and smitten by the hands of mine enemies, on whom I will pour out my wrath without measure in mine own time.

3 For I have suffered them thus far, that they might fill up the measure of their iniquities, that their cup might be full;

4 And that those who call themselves after my name might be chastened for a little season with a sore and grievous chastisement, because they did not hearken altogether unto the precepts and commandments which I gave unto them.

5 But verily I say unto you, that I have decreed a decree which my people shall realize, inasmuch as they hearken from this very hour unto the counsel which I, the Lord their God, shall give unto them.

6 Behold they shall, for I have decreed it, begin to prevail against mine enemies from this very hour.

7 And by hearkening to observe all the words which I, the Lord their God, shall speak unto them, they shall never cease to prevail until the kingdoms of the world are subdued under my feet, and the earth is given unto the saints, to possess it forever and ever.

8 But inasmuch as they keep not my commandments, and hearken not to observe all my words, the kingdoms of the world shall prevail against them.

9 For they were set to be a light unto the world, and to be the saviors of men;

10 And inasmuch as they are not the saviors of men, they are as salt that has lost its savor, and is thenceforth good for nothing but to be cast out and trodden under foot of men.

11 But verily I say unto you, I have decreed that your brethren which have been scattered shall return to the lands of their inheritances, and shall build up the waste places of Zion.

12 For after much tribulation, as I have said unto you in a former commandment, cometh the blessing.

13 Behold, this is the blessing which I have promised after your tribulations, and the tribulations of your brethren—your redemption, and the redemption of your brethren, even their restoration to the land of Zion, to be established, no more to be thrown down.

14 Nevertheless, if they pollute their inheritances they shall be thrown down; for I will not spare them if they pollute their inheritances.

15 Behold, I say unto you, the redemption of Zion must needs come by power;

16 Therefore, I will raise up unto my people a man, who shall lead them like as Moses led the children of Israel.

17 For ye are the children of Israel, and of the seed of Abraham, and ye must needs be led out of bondage by power, and with a stretched-out arm.

18 And as your fathers were led at the first, even so shall the redemption of Zion be.

19 Therefore, let not your hearts faint, for I say not unto you as I said unto your fathers: Mine angel shall go up before you, but not my presence.

20 But I say unto you: Mine angels shall go up before you, and also my presence, and in time ye shall possess the goodly land.

21 Verily, verily I say unto you, that my servant Joseph Smith, Jun., is the man to whom I likened the servant to whom the Lord of the vineyard spake in the parable which I have given unto you.

22 Therefore let my servant Joseph Smith, Jun., say unto the strength of my house, my young men and the middle aged—Gather yourselves together unto the land of Zion, upon the land which I have bought with money that has been consecrated unto me.

23 And let all the churches send up wise men with their moneys, and purchase lands even as I have commanded them.

24 And inasmuch as mine enemies come against you to drive you from my goodly land, which I have consecrated to be the land of Zion, even from your own lands after these testimonies, which ye have brought before me against them, ye shall curse them;

25 And whomsoever ye curse, I will curse, and ye shall avenge me of mine enemies.

26 And my presence shall be with you even in avenging me of mine enemies, unto the third and fourth generation of them that hate me.

27 Let no man be afraid to lay down his life for my sake; for whoso layeth down his life for my sake shall find it again.

28 And whoso is not willing to lay down his life for my sake is not my disciple.

29 It is my will that my servant Sidney Rigdon shall lift up his voice in the congregations in the eastern countries, in preparing the churches to keep the commandments which I have given unto them concerning the restoration and redemption of Zion.

30 It is my will that my servant Parley P. Pratt and my servant Lyman Wight should not return to the land of their brethren, until they have obtained companies to go up unto the land of Zion, by tens, or by twenties, or by fifties, or by an hundred, until they have obtained to the number of five hundred of the strength of my house.

31 Behold this is my will; ask and ye shall receive; but men do not always do my will.

32 Therefore, if you cannot obtain five hundred, seek diligently that peradventure you may obtain three hundred.

33 And if ye cannot obtain three hundred, seek diligently that peradventure ye may obtain one hundred.

34 But verily I say unto you, a commandment I give unto you, that ye shall not go up unto the land of Zion until you have obtained a hundred of

the strength of my house, to go up with you unto the land of Zion.

35 Therefore, as I said unto you, ask and ye shall receive; pray earnestly that peradventure my servant Joseph Smith, Jun., may go with you, and preside in the midst of my people, and organize my kingdom upon the consecrated land, and establish the children of Zion upon the laws and commandments which have been and which shall be given unto you.

36 All victory and glory is brought to pass unto you through your diligence, faithfulness, and prayers of faith.

37 Let my servant Parley P. Pratt journey with my servant Joseph Smith, Jun.

38 Let my servant Lyman Wight journey with my servant Sidney Rigdon.

39 Let my servant Hyrum Smith journey with my servant Frederick G. Williams.

40 Let my servant Orson Hyde journey with my servant Orson Pratt, whithersoever my servant Joseph Smith, Jun., shall counsel them, in obtaining the fulfilment of these commandments which I have given unto you, and leave the residue in my hands. Even so. Amen.

Section 104

Revelation given to Joseph Smith the Prophet, at or near Kirtland, Ohio, April 23, 1834, concerning the United Firm (see the headings to sections 78 and 82). The occasion was likely that of a council meeting of members of the United Firm, which discussed the pressing temporal needs of the Church. An earlier meeting of the firm on April 10 had resolved that the organization be dissolved. This revelation directs that the firm instead be reorganized; its properties were to be divided among members of the firm as their stewardships. Under Joseph Smith's direction, the phrase "United Firm" was later replaced with "United Order" in the revelation.

1–10, Saints who transgress against the united order will be cursed; 11–16, The Lord provides for His Saints in His own way; 17–18, Gospel law governs the care of the poor; 19–46, The stewardships and blessings of various brethren are designated; 47–53, The united order in Kirtland and the order in Zion are to operate separately; 54–66, The sacred treasury of the Lord is set up for the printing of the scriptures; 67–77, The general treasury of the united order is to operate on the basis of common consent; 78–86, Those in the united order are to pay all their debts, and the Lord will deliver them from financial bondage.

1 Verily I say unto you, my friends, I give unto you counsel, and a commandment, concerning all the properties which belong to the order which I commanded to be organized and established, to be a united order, and an everlasting order for the benefit of my church, and for the salvation of men until I come—

2 With promise immutable and unchangeable, that inasmuch as those whom I commanded were faithful they should be blessed with a multiplicity of blessings;

3 But inasmuch as they were not faithful they were nigh unto cursing.

4 Therefore, inasmuch as some of my servants have not kept the commandment, but have broken the covenant through covetousness, and with feigned words, I have cursed them with a very sore and grievous curse.

5 For I, the Lord, have decreed in my heart, that inasmuch as any man belonging to the order shall be found a transgressor, or, in other words, shall break the covenant with which ye are bound, he shall be cursed in his life, and shall be trodden down by whom I will;

6 For I, the Lord, am not to be mocked in these things—

7 And all this that the innocent among you may not be condemned with the unjust; and that the guilty among you may not escape; because I, the Lord, have promised unto you a crown of glory at my right hand.

8 Therefore, inasmuch as you are found transgressors, you cannot escape my wrath in your lives.

9 Inasmuch as ye are cut off for transgression, ye cannot escape the buffetings of Satan until the day of redemption.

10 And I now give unto you power from this very hour, that if any man among you, of the order, is found a transgressor and repenteth not of the evil, that ye shall deliver him over unto the buffetings of Satan; and he shall not have power to bring evil upon you.

11 It is wisdom in me; therefore, a commandment I give unto you, that ye shall organize yourselves and appoint every man his stewardship;

12 That every man may give an account

unto me of the stewardship which is appointed unto him.

13 For it is expedient that I, the Lord, should make every man accountable, as a steward over earthly blessings, which I have made and prepared for my creatures.

14 I, the Lord, stretched out the heavens, and built the earth, my very handiwork; and all things therein are mine.

15 And it is my purpose to provide for my saints, for all things are mine.

16 But it must needs be done in mine own way; and behold this is the way that I, the Lord, have decreed to provide for my saints, that the poor shall be exalted, in that the rich are made low.

17 For the earth is full, and there is enough and to spare; yea, I prepared all things, and have given unto the children of men to be agents unto themselves.

18 Therefore, if any man shall take of the abundance which I have made, and impart not his portion, according to the law of my gospel, unto the poor and the needy, he shall, with the wicked, lift up his eyes in hell, being in torment.

19 And now, verily I say unto you, concerning the properties of the order—

20 Let my servant Sidney Rigdon have appointed unto him the place where he now resides, and the lot of the tannery for his stewardship, for his support while he is laboring in my vineyard, even as I will, when I shall command him.

21 And let all things be done according to the counsel of the order, and united consent or voice of the order, which dwell in the land of Kirtland.

22 And this stewardship and blessing, I, the Lord, confer upon my servant Sidney Rigdon for a blessing upon him, and his seed after him;

23 And I will multiply blessings upon him, inasmuch as he will be humble before me.

24 And again, let my servant Martin Harris have appointed unto him, for his stewardship, the lot of land which my servant John Johnson obtained in exchange for his former inheritance, for him and his seed after him;

25 And inasmuch as he is faithful, I will multiply blessings upon him and his seed after him.

26 And let my servant Martin Harris devote his moneys for the proclaiming of my words, according as my servant Joseph Smith, Jun., shall direct.

27 And again, let my servant Frederick G. Williams have the place upon which he now dwells.

28 And let my servant Oliver Cowdery have the lot which is set off joining the house, which is to be for the printing office, which is lot number one, and also the lot upon which his father resides.

29 And let my servants Frederick G. Williams and Oliver Cowdery have the printing office and all things that pertain unto it.

30 And this shall be their stewardship which shall be appointed unto them.

31 And inasmuch as they are faithful, behold I will bless, and multiply blessings upon them.

32 And this is the beginning of the stewardship which I have appointed them, for them and their seed after them.

33 And, inasmuch as they are faithful, I will multiply blessings upon them and their seed after them, even a multiplicity

of blessings.

34 And again, let my servant John Johnson have the house in which he lives, and the inheritance, all save the ground which has been reserved for the building of my houses, which pertains to that inheritance, and those lots which have been named for my servant Oliver Cowdery.

35 And inasmuch as he is faithful, I will multiply blessings upon him.

36 And it is my will that he should sell the lots that are laid off for the building up of the city of my saints, inasmuch as it shall be made known to him by the voice of the Spirit, and according to the counsel of the order, and by the voice of the order.

37 And this is the beginning of the stewardship which I have appointed unto him, for a blessing unto him and his seed after him.

38 And inasmuch as he is faithful, I will multiply a multiplicity of blessings upon him.

39 And again, let my servant Newel K. Whitney have appointed unto him the houses and lot where he now resides, and the lot and building on which the mercantile establishment stands, and also the lot which is on the corner south of the mercantile establishment, and also the lot on which the ashery is situated.

40 And all this I have appointed unto my servant Newel K. Whitney for his stewardship, for a blessing upon him and his seed after him, for the benefit of the mercantile establishment of my order which I have established for my stake in the land of Kirtland.

41 Yea, verily, this is the stewardship which I have appointed unto my servant N. K. Whitney, even this whole mercantile establishment, him and his agent, and his seed after him.

42 And inasmuch as he is faithful in keeping my commandments, which I have given unto him, I will multiply blessings upon him and his seed after him, even a multiplicity of blessings.

43 And again, let my servant Joseph Smith, Jun., have appointed unto him the lot which is laid off for the building of my house, which is forty rods long and twelve wide, and also the inheritance upon which his father now resides;

44 And this is the beginning of the stewardship which I have appointed unto him, for a blessing upon him, and upon his father.

45 For behold, I have reserved an inheritance for his father, for his support; therefore he shall be reckoned in the house of my servant Joseph Smith, Jun.

46 And I will multiply blessings upon the house of my servant Joseph Smith, Jun., inasmuch as he is faithful, even a multiplicity of blessings.

47 And now, a commandment I give unto you concerning Zion, that you shall no longer be bound as a united order to your brethren of Zion, only on this wise—

48 After you are organized, you shall be called the United Order of the Stake of Zion, the City of Kirtland. And your brethren, after they are organized, shall be called the United Order of the City of Zion.

49 And they shall be organized in their own names, and in their own name; and they shall do their business in their own name, and in their own names;

50 And you shall do your business in your own name, and in your own names.

51 And this I have commanded to be done for your salvation, and also for their salvation, in consequence of their being driven out and that which is to come.

52 The covenants being broken through transgression, by covetousness and feigned words—

53 Therefore, you are dissolved as a united order with your brethren, that you are not bound only up to this hour unto them, only on this wise, as I said, by loan as shall be agreed by this order in council, as your circumstances will admit and the voice of the council direct.

54 And again, a commandment I give unto you concerning your stewardship which I have appointed unto you.

55 Behold, all these properties are mine, or else your faith is vain, and ye are found hypocrites, and the covenants which ye have made unto me are broken;

56 And if the properties are mine, then ye are stewards; otherwise ye are no stewards.

57 But, verily I say unto you, I have appointed unto you to be stewards over mine house, even stewards indeed.

58 And for this purpose I have commanded you to organize yourselves, even to print my words, the fulness of my scriptures, the revelations which I have given unto you, and which I shall, hereafter, from time to time give unto you—

59 For the purpose of building up my church and kingdom on the earth, and to prepare my people for the time when I shall dwell with them, which is nigh at hand.

60 And ye shall prepare for yourselves a place for a treasury, and consecrate it unto my name.

61 And ye shall appoint one among you to keep the treasury, and he shall be ordained unto this blessing.

62 And there shall be a seal upon the treasury, and all the sacred things shall be delivered into the treasury; and no man among you shall call it his own, or any part of it, for it shall belong to you all with one accord.

63 And I give it unto you from this very hour; and now see to it, that ye go to and make use of the stewardship which I have appointed unto you, exclusive of the sacred things, for the purpose of printing these sacred things as I have said.

64 And the avails of the sacred things shall be had in the treasury, and a seal shall be upon it; and it shall not be used or taken out of the treasury by any one, neither shall the seal be loosed which shall be placed upon it, only by the voice of the order, or by commandment.

65 And thus shall ye preserve the avails of the sacred things in the treasury, for sacred and holy purposes.

66 And this shall be called the sacred treasury of the Lord; and a seal shall be kept upon it that it may be holy and consecrated unto the Lord.

67 And again, there shall be another treasury prepared, and a treasurer appointed to keep the treasury, and a seal shall be placed upon it;

68 And all moneys that you receive in your stewardships, by improving upon the properties which I have appointed unto you, in houses, or in lands, or in cattle, or in all things save it be the holy and sacred writings, which I have reserved unto myself for holy and sacred purposes, shall be cast into the treasury as fast as you receive moneys, by

hundreds, or by fifties, or by twenties, or by tens, or by fives.

69 Or in other words, if any man among you obtain five dollars let him cast them into the treasury; or if he obtain ten, or twenty, or fifty, or an hundred, let him do likewise;

70 And let not any among you say that it is his own; for it shall not be called his, nor any part of it.

71 And there shall not any part of it be used, or taken out of the treasury, only by the voice and common consent of the order.

72 And this shall be the voice and common consent of the order—that any man among you say to the treasurer: I have need of this to help me in my stewardship—

73 If it be five dollars, or if it be ten dollars, or twenty, or fifty, or a hundred, the treasurer shall give unto him the sum which he requires to help him in his stewardship—

74 Until he be found a transgressor, and it is manifest before the council of the order plainly that he is an unfaithful and an unwise steward.

75 But so long as he is in full fellowship, and is faithful and wise in his stewardship, this shall be his token unto the treasurer that the treasurer shall not withhold.

76 But in case of transgression, the treasurer shall be subject unto the council and voice of the order.

77 And in case the treasurer is found an unfaithful and an unwise steward, he shall be subject to the council and voice of the order, and shall be removed out of his place, and another shall be appointed in his stead.

78 And again, verily I say unto you, concerning your debts—behold it is my will that you shall pay all your debts.

79 And it is my will that you shall humble yourselves before me, and obtain this blessing by your diligence and humility and the prayer of faith.

80 And inasmuch as you are diligent and humble, and exercise the prayer of faith, behold, I will soften the hearts of those to whom you are in debt, until I shall send means unto you for your deliverance.

81 Therefore write speedily to New York and write according to that which shall be dictated by my Spirit; and I will soften the hearts of those to whom you are in debt, that it shall be taken away out of their minds to bring affliction upon you.

82 And inasmuch as ye are humble and faithful and call upon my name, behold, I will give you the victory.

83 I give unto you a promise, that you shall be delivered this once out of your bondage.

84 Inasmuch as you obtain a chance to loan money by hundreds, or thousands, even until you shall loan enough to deliver yourself from bondage, it is your privilege.

85 And pledge the properties which I have put into your hands, this once, by giving your names by common consent or otherwise, as it shall seem good unto you.

86 I give unto you this privilege, this once; and behold, if you proceed to do the things which I have laid before you, according to my commandments, all these things are mine, and ye are my stewards, and the master will not suffer his house to be broken up. Even so. Amen.

Section 105

Revelation given through Joseph Smith the Prophet, on Fishing River, Missouri, June 22, 1834. Under the leadership of the Prophet, Saints from Ohio and other areas marched to Missouri in an expedition later known as Zion's Camp. Their purpose was to escort the expelled Missouri Saints back to their lands in Jackson County. Missourians who had previously persecuted the Saints feared retaliation from Zion's Camp and preemptively attacked some Saints living in Clay County, Missouri. After the Missouri governor withdrew his promise to support the Saints, Joseph Smith received this revelation.

1–5, Zion will be built up by conformity to celestial law; 6–13, The redemption of Zion is deferred for a little season; 14–19, The Lord will fight the battles of Zion; 20–26, The Saints are to be wise and not boast of mighty works as they gather; 27–30, Lands in Jackson and adjoining counties should be purchased; 31–34, The elders are to receive an endowment in the house of the Lord in Kirtland; 35–37, Saints who are both called and chosen will be sanctified; 38–41, The Saints are to lift an ensign of peace to the world.

1 Verily I say unto you who have assembled yourselves together that you may learn my will concerning the redemption of mine afflicted people—

2 Behold, I say unto you, were it not for the transgressions of my people, speaking concerning the church and not individuals, they might have been redeemed even now.

3 But behold, they have not learned to be obedient to the things which I required at their hands, but are full of all manner of evil, and do not impart of their substance, as becometh saints, to the poor and afflicted among them;

4 And are not united according to the union required by the law of the celestial kingdom;

5 And Zion cannot be built up unless it is by the principles of the law of the celestial kingdom; otherwise I cannot receive her unto myself.

6 And my people must needs be chastened until they learn obedience, if it must needs be, by the things which they suffer.

7 I speak not concerning those who are appointed to lead my people, who are the first elders of my church, for they are not all under this condemnation;

8 But I speak concerning my churches abroad—there are many who will say: Where is their God? Behold, he will deliver them in time of trouble, otherwise we will not go up unto Zion, and will keep our moneys.

9 Therefore, in consequence of the transgressions of my people, it is expedient in me that mine elders should wait for a little season for the redemption of Zion—

10 That they themselves may be prepared, and that my people may be taught more perfectly, and have experience, and know more perfectly concerning their duty, and the things which I require at their hands.

11 And this cannot be brought to pass until mine elders are endowed with power from on high.

12 For behold, I have prepared a great endowment and blessing to be poured out upon them, inasmuch as they are faithful and continue in humility before me.

13 Therefore it is expedient in me that mine elders should wait for a little season, for the redemption of Zion.

14 For behold, I do not require at their hands to fight the battles of Zion; for, as I said in a former commandment, even so will I fulfil—I will fight your battles.

15 Behold, the destroyer I have sent forth to destroy and lay waste mine enemies; and not many years hence they shall not be left to pollute mine heritage, and to blaspheme my name upon the lands which I have consecrated for the gathering together of my saints.

16 Behold, I have commanded my servant Joseph Smith, Jun., to say unto the strength of my house, even my warriors, my young men, and middle-aged, to gather together for the redemption of my people, and throw down the towers of mine enemies, and scatter their watchmen;

17 But the strength of mine house have not hearkened unto my words.

18 But inasmuch as there are those who have hearkened unto my words, I have prepared a blessing and an endowment for them, if they continue faithful.

19 I have heard their prayers, and will accept their offering; and it is expedient in me that they should be brought thus far for a trial of their faith.

20 And now, verily I say unto you, a commandment I give unto you, that as many as have come up hither, that can stay in the region round about, let them stay;

21 And those that cannot stay, who have families in the east, let them tarry for a little season, inasmuch as my servant Joseph shall appoint unto them;

22 For I will counsel him concerning this matter, and all things whatsoever he shall appoint unto them shall be fulfilled.

23 And let all my people who dwell in the regions round about be very faithful, and prayerful, and humble before me, and reveal not the things which I have revealed unto them, until it is wisdom in me that they should be revealed.

24 Talk not of judgments, neither boast of faith nor of mighty works, but carefully gather together, as much in one region as can be, consistently with the feelings of the people;

25 And behold, I will give unto you favor and grace in their eyes, that you may rest in peace and safety, while you are saying unto the people: Execute judgment and justice for us according to law, and redress us of our wrongs.

26 Now, behold, I say unto you, my friends, in this way you may find favor in the eyes of the people, until the army of Israel becomes very great.

27 And I will soften the hearts of the people, as I did the heart of Pharaoh, from time to time, until my servant Joseph Smith, Jun., and mine elders, whom I have appointed, shall have time to gather up the strength of my house,

28 And to have sent wise men, to fulfil that which I have commanded concerning the purchasing of all the lands in Jackson county that can be purchased, and in the adjoining counties round about.

29 For it is my will that these lands should be purchased; and after they are purchased that my saints should possess them according to the laws of consecration which I have given.

30 And after these lands are purchased, I will hold the armies of Israel guiltless in taking possession of their own lands, which they have previously purchased with their moneys, and of throwing down the towers of mine enemies that may be upon them, and scattering

their watchmen, and avenging me of mine enemies unto the third and fourth generation of them that hate me.

31 But first let my army become very great, and let it be sanctified before me, that it may become fair as the sun, and clear as the moon, and that her banners may be terrible unto all nations;

32 That the kingdoms of this world may be constrained to acknowledge that the kingdom of Zion is in very deed the kingdom of our God and his Christ; therefore, let us become subject unto her laws.

33 Verily I say unto you, it is expedient in me that the first elders of my church should receive their endowment from on high in my house, which I have commanded to be built unto my name in the land of Kirtland.

34 And let those commandments which I have given concerning Zion and her law be executed and fulfilled, after her redemption.

35 There has been a day of calling, but the time has come for a day of choosing; and let those be chosen that are worthy.

36 And it shall be manifest unto my servant, by the voice of the Spirit, those that are chosen; and they shall be sanctified;

37 And inasmuch as they follow the counsel which they receive, they shall have power after many days to accomplish all things pertaining to Zion.

38 And again I say unto you, sue for peace, not only to the people that have smitten you, but also to all people;

39 And lift up an ensign of peace, and make a proclamation of peace unto the ends of the earth;

40 And make proposals for peace unto those who have smitten you, according to the voice of the Spirit which is in you, and all things shall work together for your good.

41 Therefore, be faithful; and behold, and lo, I am with you even unto the end. Even so. Amen.

Section 106

Revelation given through Joseph Smith the Prophet, at Kirtland, Ohio, November 25, 1834. This revelation is directed to Warren A. Cowdery, an older brother of Oliver Cowdery.

1–3, Warren A. Cowdery is called as a local presiding officer; 4–5, The Second Coming will not overtake the children of light as a thief; 6–8, Great blessings follow faithful service in the Church.

1 It is my will that my servant Warren A. Cowdery should be appointed and ordained a presiding high priest over my church, in the land of Freedom and the regions round about;

2 And should preach my everlasting gospel, and lift up his voice and warn the people, not only in his own place, but in the adjoining counties;

3 And devote his whole time to this high and holy calling, which I now give unto him, seeking diligently the kingdom of heaven and its righteousness, and all things necessary shall be added thereunto; for the laborer is worthy of his hire.

4 And again, verily I say unto you, the coming of the Lord draweth nigh, and it overtaketh the world as a thief in the night—

5 Therefore, gird up your loins, that you may be the children of light, and that day shall not overtake you as a thief.

6 And again, verily I say unto you, there was joy in heaven when my servant Warren bowed to my scepter, and separated himself from the crafts of men;

7 Therefore, blessed is my servant Warren, for I will have mercy on him; and, notwithstanding the vanity of his heart, I will lift him up inasmuch as he will humble himself before me.

8 And I will give him grace and assurance wherewith he may stand; and if he continue to be a faithful witness and a light unto the church I have prepared a crown for him in the mansions of my Father. Even so. Amen.

Section 107

Revelation on the priesthood, given through Joseph Smith the Prophet, at Kirtland, Ohio, about April 1835. Although this section was recorded in 1835, the historical records affirm that most of verses 60 through 100 incorporate a revelation given through Joseph Smith on November 11, 1831. This section was associated with the organization of the Quorum of the Twelve in February and March 1835. The Prophet likely delivered it in the presence of those who were preparing to depart May 3, 1835, on their first quorum mission.

1–6, There are two priesthoods: the Melchizedek and the Aaronic; 7–12, Those who hold the Melchizedek Priesthood have power to officiate in all offices in the Church; 13–17, The bishopric presides over the Aaronic Priesthood, which administers in outward ordinances; 18–20, The Melchizedek Priesthood holds the keys of all spiritual blessings; the Aaronic Priesthood holds the keys of the ministering of angels; 21–38, The First Presidency, the Twelve, and the Seventy constitute the presiding quorums, whose decisions are to be made in unity and righteousness; 39–52, The patriarchal order is established from Adam to Noah; 53–57, Ancient Saints assembled at Adam-ondi-Ahman, and the Lord appeared to them; 58–67, The Twelve are to set the officers of the Church in order; 68–76, Bishops serve as common judges in Israel; 77–84, The First Presidency and the Twelve constitute the highest court in the Church; 85–100, Priesthood presidents govern their respective quorums.

1 There are, in the church, two priesthoods, namely, the Melchizedek and Aaronic, including the Levitical Priesthood.

2 Why the first is called the Melchizedek Priesthood is because Melchizedek was such a great high priest.

3 Before his day it was called the Holy Priesthood, after the Order of the Son of God.

4 But out of respect or reverence to the name of the Supreme Being, to avoid the too frequent repetition of his name, they, the church, in ancient days, called that priesthood after Melchizedek, or the Melchizedek Priesthood.

5 All other authorities or offices in the church are appendages to this priesthood.

6 But there are two divisions or grand heads—one is the Melchizedek Priesthood, and the other is the Aaronic or Levitical Priesthood.

7 The office of an elder comes under the priesthood of Melchizedek.

8 The Melchizedek Priesthood holds the right of presidency, and has power and authority over all the offices in the church in all ages of the world, to administer in spiritual things.

9 The Presidency of the High Priesthood, after the order of Melchizedek, have a right to officiate in all the offices in the church.

10 High priests after the order of the Melchizedek Priesthood have a right to officiate in their own standing, under the direction of the presidency, in administering spiritual things, and also in the office of an elder, priest (of the Levitical order), teacher, deacon, and member.

11 An elder has a right to officiate in his stead when the high priest is not present.

12 The high priest and elder are to administer in spiritual things, agreeable to the covenants and commandments of the church; and they have a right to officiate in all these offices of the church when there are no higher authorities present.

13 The second priesthood is called the Priesthood of Aaron, because it was conferred upon Aaron and his seed, throughout all their generations.

14 Why it is called the lesser priesthood is because it is an appendage to the greater, or the Melchizedek Priesthood, and has power in administering outward ordinances.

15 The bishopric is the presidency of this priesthood, and holds the keys or authority of the same.

16 No man has a legal right to this office, to hold the keys of this priesthood, except he be a literal descendant of Aaron.

17 But as a high priest of the Melchizedek Priesthood has authority to officiate in all the lesser offices, he may officiate in the office of bishop when no literal descendant of Aaron can be found, provided he is called and set apart and ordained unto this power by the hands of the Presidency of the Melchizedek Priesthood.

18 The power and authority of the higher, or Melchizedek Priesthood, is to hold the keys of all the spiritual blessings of the church—

19 To have the privilege of receiving the mysteries of the kingdom of heaven, to have the heavens opened unto them, to commune with the general assembly and church of the Firstborn, and to enjoy the communion and presence of God the Father, and Jesus the mediator of the new covenant.

20 The power and authority of the lesser, or Aaronic Priesthood, is to hold the keys of the ministering of angels, and to administer in outward ordinances, the letter of the gospel, the baptism of repentance for the remission of sins, agreeable to the covenants and commandments.

21 Of necessity there are presidents, or presiding officers growing out of, or appointed of or from among those who are ordained to the several offices in these two priesthoods.

22 Of the Melchizedek Priesthood, three Presiding High Priests, chosen by the body, appointed and ordained to that office, and upheld by the confidence, faith, and prayer of the church, form a quorum of the Presidency of the Church.

23 The twelve traveling councilors are called to be the Twelve Apostles, or special witnesses of the name of Christ in all the world—thus differing from other officers in the church in the duties of their calling.

24 And they form a quorum, equal in authority and power to the three presidents previously mentioned.

25 The Seventy are also called to preach the gospel, and to be especial witnesses unto the Gentiles and in all the world—thus differing from other officers in the church in the duties of their calling.

26 And they form a quorum, equal in authority to that of the Twelve special witnesses or Apostles just named.

27 And every decision made by either of these quorums must be by the unanimous voice of the same; that is, every member in each quorum must be agreed to its decisions, in order to make their decisions of the same power or validity one with the other—

28 A majority may form a quorum when circumstances render it impossible to be otherwise—

29 Unless this is the case, their decisions are not entitled to the same blessings which the decisions of a quorum of three presidents were anciently, who were ordained after

the order of Melchizedek, and were righteous and holy men.

30 The decisions of these quorums, or either of them, are to be made in all righteousness, in holiness, and lowliness of heart, meekness and long-suffering, and in faith, and virtue, and knowledge, temperance, patience, godliness, brotherly kindness and charity;

31 Because the promise is, if these things abound in them they shall not be unfruitful in the knowledge of the Lord.

32 And in case that any decision of these quorums is made in unrighteousness, it may be brought before a general assembly of the several quorums, which constitute the spiritual authorities of the church; otherwise there can be no appeal from their decision.

33 The Twelve are a Traveling Presiding High Council, to officiate in the name of the Lord, under the direction of the Presidency of the Church, agreeable to the institution of heaven; to build up the church, and regulate all the affairs of the same in all nations, first unto the Gentiles and secondly unto the Jews.

34 The Seventy are to act in the name of the Lord, under the direction of the Twelve or the traveling high council, in building up the church and regulating all the affairs of the same in all nations, first unto the Gentiles and then to the Jews—

35 The Twelve being sent out, holding the keys, to open the door by the proclamation of the gospel of Jesus Christ, and first unto the Gentiles and then unto the Jews.

36 The standing high councils, at the stakes of Zion, form a quorum equal in authority in the affairs of the church, in all their decisions, to the quorum of the presidency, or to the traveling high council.

37 The high council in Zion form a quorum equal in authority in the affairs of the church, in all their decisions, to the councils of the Twelve at the stakes of Zion.

38 It is the duty of the traveling high council to call upon the Seventy, when they need assistance, to fill the several calls for preaching and administering the gospel, instead of any others.

39 It is the duty of the Twelve, in all large branches of the church, to ordain evangelical ministers, as they shall be designated unto them by revelation—

40 The order of this priesthood was confirmed to be handed down from father to son, and rightly belongs to the literal descendants of the chosen seed, to whom the promises were made.

41 This order was instituted in the days of Adam, and came down by lineage in the following manner:

42 From Adam to Seth, who was ordained by Adam at the age of sixty-nine years, and was blessed by him three years previous to his (Adam's) death, and received the promise of God by his father, that his posterity should be the chosen of the Lord, and that they should be preserved unto the end of the earth;

43 Because he (Seth) was a perfect man, and his likeness was the express likeness of his father, insomuch that he seemed to be like unto his father in all things, and could be distinguished from him only by his age.

44 Enos was ordained at the age of one hundred and thirty-four years and four months, by the hand of Adam.

45 God called upon Cainan in the

wilderness in the fortieth year of his age; and he met Adam in journeying to the place Shedolamak. He was eighty-seven years old when he received his ordination.

46 Mahalaleel was four hundred and ninety-six years and seven days old when he was ordained by the hand of Adam, who also blessed him.

47 Jared was two hundred years old when he was ordained under the hand of Adam, who also blessed him.

48 Enoch was twenty-five years old when he was ordained under the hand of Adam; and he was sixty-five and Adam blessed him.

49 And he saw the Lord, and he walked with him, and was before his face continually; and he walked with God three hundred and sixty-five years, making him four hundred and thirty years old when he was translated.

50 Methuselah was one hundred years old when he was ordained under the hand of Adam.

51 Lamech was thirty-two years old when he was ordained under the hand of Seth.

52 Noah was ten years old when he was ordained under the hand of Methuselah.

53 Three years previous to the death of Adam, he called Seth, Enos, Cainan, Mahalaleel, Jared, Enoch, and Methuselah, who were all high priests, with the residue of his posterity who were righteous, into the valley of Adam-ondi-Ahman, and there bestowed upon them his last blessing.

54 And the Lord appeared unto them, and they rose up and blessed Adam, and called him Michael, the prince, the archangel.

55 And the Lord administered comfort unto Adam, and said unto him: I have set thee to be at the head; a multitude of nations shall come of thee, and thou art a prince over them forever.

56 And Adam stood up in the midst of the congregation; and, notwithstanding he was bowed down with age, being full of the Holy Ghost, predicted whatsoever should befall his posterity unto the latest generation.

57 These things were all written in the book of Enoch, and are to be testified of in due time.

58 It is the duty of the Twelve, also, to ordain and set in order all the other officers of the church, agreeable to the revelation which says:

59 To the church of Christ in the land of Zion, in addition to the church laws respecting church business—

60 Verily, I say unto you, saith the Lord of Hosts, there must needs be presiding elders to preside over those who are of the office of an elder;

61 And also priests to preside over those who are of the office of a priest;

62 And also teachers to preside over those who are of the office of a teacher, in like manner, and also the deacons—

63 Wherefore, from deacon to teacher, and from teacher to priest, and from priest to elder, severally as they are appointed, according to the covenants and commandments of the church.

64 Then comes the High Priesthood, which is the greatest of all.

65 Wherefore, it must needs be that one be appointed of the High Priesthood to preside over the priesthood, and he shall be called President of the High Priesthood of the Church;

66 Or, in other words, the Presiding High Priest over the High Priesthood of the Church.

67 From the same comes the administering of ordinances and blessings upon the church, by the laying on of the hands.

68 Wherefore, the office of a bishop is not equal unto it; for the office of a bishop is in administering all temporal things;

69 Nevertheless a bishop must be chosen from the High Priesthood, unless he is a literal descendant of Aaron;

70 For unless he is a literal descendant of Aaron he cannot hold the keys of that priesthood.

71 Nevertheless, a high priest, that is, after the order of Melchizedek, may be set apart unto the ministering of temporal things, having a knowledge of them by the Spirit of truth;

72 And also to be a judge in Israel, to do the business of the church, to sit in judgment upon transgressors upon testimony as it shall be laid before him according to the laws, by the assistance of his counselors, whom he has chosen or will choose among the elders of the church.

73 This is the duty of a bishop who is not a literal descendant of Aaron, but has been ordained to the High Priesthood after the order of Melchizedek.

74 Thus shall he be a judge, even a common judge among the inhabitants of Zion, or in a stake of Zion, or in any branch of the church where he shall be set apart unto this ministry, until the borders of Zion are enlarged and it becomes necessary to have other bishops or judges in Zion or elsewhere.

75 And inasmuch as there are other bishops appointed they shall act in the same office.

76 But a literal descendant of Aaron has a legal right to the presidency of this priesthood, to the keys of this ministry, to act in the office of bishop independently, without counselors, except in a case where a President of the High Priesthood, after the order of Melchizedek, is tried, to sit as a judge in Israel.

77 And the decision of either of these councils, agreeable to the commandment which says:

78 Again, verily, I say unto you, the most important business of the church, and the most difficult cases of the church, inasmuch as there is not satisfaction upon the decision of the bishop or judges, it shall be handed over and carried up unto the council of the church, before the Presidency of the High Priesthood.

79 And the Presidency of the council of the High Priesthood shall have power to call other high priests, even twelve, to assist as counselors; and thus the Presidency of the High Priesthood and its counselors shall have power to decide upon testimony according to the laws of the church.

80 And after this decision it shall be had in remembrance no more before the Lord; for this is the highest council of the church of God, and a final decision upon controversies in spiritual matters.

81 There is not any person belonging to the church who is exempt from this council of the church.

82 And inasmuch as a President of the High Priesthood shall transgress, he shall be had in remembrance before the common council of the church, who shall be assisted by twelve counselors of

the High Priesthood;

83 And their decision upon his head shall be an end of controversy concerning him.

84 Thus, none shall be exempted from the justice and the laws of God, that all things may be done in order and in solemnity before him, according to truth and righteousness.

85 And again, verily I say unto you, the duty of a president over the office of a deacon is to preside over twelve deacons, to sit in council with them, and to teach them their duty, edifying one another, as it is given according to the covenants.

86 And also the duty of the president over the office of the teachers is to preside over twenty-four of the teachers, and to sit in council with them, teaching them the duties of their office, as given in the covenants.

87 Also the duty of the president over the Priesthood of Aaron is to preside over forty-eight priests, and sit in council with them, to teach them the duties of their office, as is given in the covenants—

88 This president is to be a bishop; for this is one of the duties of this priesthood.

89 Again, the duty of the president over the office of elders is to preside over ninety-six elders, and to sit in council with them, and to teach them according to the covenants.

90 This presidency is a distinct one from that of the seventy, and is designed for those who do not travel into all the world.

91 And again, the duty of the President of the office of the High Priesthood is to preside over the whole church, and to be like unto Moses—

92 Behold, here is wisdom; yea, to be a seer, a revelator, a translator, and a prophet, having all the gifts of God which he bestows upon the head of the church.

93 And it is according to the vision showing the order of the Seventy, that they should have seven presidents to preside over them, chosen out of the number of the seventy;

94 And the seventh president of these presidents is to preside over the six;

95 And these seven presidents are to choose other seventy besides the first seventy to whom they belong, and are to preside over them;

96 And also other seventy, until seven times seventy, if the labor in the vineyard of necessity requires it.

97 And these seventy are to be traveling ministers, unto the Gentiles first and also unto the Jews.

98 Whereas other officers of the church, who belong not unto the Twelve, neither to the Seventy, are not under the responsibility to travel among all nations, but are to travel as their circumstances shall allow, notwithstanding they may hold as high and responsible offices in the church.

99 Wherefore, now let every man learn his duty, and to act in the office in which he is appointed, in all diligence.

100 He that is slothful shall not be counted worthy to stand, and he that learns not his duty and shows himself not approved shall not be counted worthy to stand. Even so. Amen.

Section 108

Revelation given through Joseph Smith the Prophet, at Kirtland, Ohio, December 26, 1835. This section was received at the request of Lyman Sherman, who had previously been ordained a seventy and who had come to the Prophet with a request for a revelation to make known his duty.

1–3, Lyman Sherman forgiven of his sins; 4–5, He is to be numbered with the leading elders of the Church; 6–8, He is called to preach the gospel and strengthen his brethren.

1 Verily thus saith the Lord unto you, my servant Lyman: Your sins are forgiven you, because you have obeyed my voice in coming up hither this morning to receive counsel of him whom I have appointed.

2 Therefore, let your soul be at rest concerning your spiritual standing, and resist no more my voice.

3 And arise up and be more careful henceforth in observing your vows, which you have made and do make, and you shall be blessed with exceeding great blessings.

4 Wait patiently until the solemn assembly shall be called of my servants, then you shall be remembered with the first of mine elders, and receive right by ordination with the rest of mine elders whom I have chosen.

5 Behold, this is the promise of the Father unto you if you continue faithful.

6 And it shall be fulfilled upon you in that day that you shall have right to preach my gospel wheresoever I shall send you, from henceforth from that time.

7 Therefore, strengthen your brethren in all your conversation, in all your prayers, in all your exhortations, and in all your doings.

8 And behold, and lo, I am with you to bless you and deliver you forever. Amen.

Section 109

Prayer offered at the dedication of the temple at Kirtland, Ohio, March 27, 1836. According to the Prophet's written statement, this prayer was given to him by revelation.

1–5, The Kirtland Temple was built as a place for the Son of Man to visit; 6–21, It is to be a house of prayer, fasting, faith, learning, glory, and order, and a house of God; 22–33, May the unrepentant who oppose the Lord's people be confounded; 34–42, May the Saints go forth in power to gather the righteous to Zion; 43–53, May the Saints be delivered from the terrible things to be poured out upon the wicked in the last days; 54–58, May nations and peoples and churches be prepared for the gospel; 59–67, May the Jews, the Lamanites, and all Israel be redeemed; 68–80, May the Saints be crowned with glory and honor and gain eternal salvation.

1 Thanks be to thy name, O Lord God of Israel, who keepest covenant and showest mercy unto thy servants who walk uprightly before thee, with all their hearts—

2 Thou who hast commanded thy servants to build a house to thy name in this place [Kirtland].

3 And now thou beholdest, O Lord, that thy servants have done according to thy commandment.

4 And now we ask thee, Holy Father, in the name of Jesus Christ, the Son of thy bosom, in whose name alone salvation can be administered to the children of men, we ask thee, O Lord, to accept of this house, the workmanship of the hands of us, thy servants, which thou didst command us to build.

5 For thou knowest that we have done this work through great tribulation; and out of our poverty we have given of our substance to build a house to thy name, that the Son of Man might have a place to manifest himself to his people.

6 And as thou hast said in a revelation, given to us, calling us thy friends, saying—Call your solemn assembly, as I have commanded you;

7 And as all have not faith, seek ye diligently and teach one another words of wisdom; yea, seek ye out of the best books words of wisdom, seek learning even by study and also by faith;

8 Organize yourselves; prepare every needful thing, and establish a house, even a house of prayer, a house of fasting, a house of faith, a house of learning, a house of glory, a house of order, a house of God;

9 That your incomings may be in the name of the Lord, that your outgoings may be in the name of the Lord, that all your salutations may be in the name of the Lord, with uplifted hands unto the Most High—

10 And now, Holy Father, we ask thee to assist us, thy people, with thy grace, in calling our solemn assembly, that it may be done to thine honor and to thy divine acceptance;

11 And in a manner that we may be found worthy, in thy sight, to secure a fulfilment of the promises which thou hast made unto us, thy people, in the revelations given unto us;

12 That thy glory may rest down upon thy people, and upon this thy house, which we now dedicate to thee, that it may be sanctified and consecrated to be holy, and that thy holy presence may be continually in this house;

13 And that all people who shall enter upon the threshold of the Lord's house may feel thy power, and feel constrained to acknowledge that thou hast sanctified

it, and that it is thy house, a place of thy holiness.

14 And do thou grant, Holy Father, that all those who shall worship in this house may be taught words of wisdom out of the best books, and that they may seek learning even by study, and also by faith, as thou hast said;

15 And that they may grow up in thee, and receive a fulness of the Holy Ghost, and be organized according to thy laws, and be prepared to obtain every needful thing;

16 And that this house may be a house of prayer, a house of fasting, a house of faith, a house of glory and of God, even thy house;

17 That all the incomings of thy people, into this house, may be in the name of the Lord;

18 That all their outgoings from this house may be in the name of the Lord;

19 And that all their salutations may be in the name of the Lord, with holy hands, uplifted to the Most High;

20 And that no unclean thing shall be permitted to come into thy house to pollute it;

21 And when thy people transgress, any of them, they may speedily repent and return unto thee, and find favor in thy sight, and be restored to the blessings which thou hast ordained to be poured out upon those who shall reverence thee in thy house.

22 And we ask thee, Holy Father, that thy servants may go forth from this house armed with thy power, and that thy name may be upon them, and thy glory be round about them, and thine angels have charge over them;

23 And from this place they may bear exceedingly great and glorious tidings, in truth, unto the ends of the earth, that they may know that this is thy work, and that thou hast put forth thy hand, to fulfil that which thou hast spoken by the mouths of the prophets, concerning the last days.

24 We ask thee, Holy Father, to establish the people that shall worship, and honorably hold a name and standing in this thy house, to all generations and for eternity;

25 That no weapon formed against them shall prosper; that he who diggeth a pit for them shall fall into the same himself;

26 That no combination of wickedness shall have power to rise up and prevail over thy people upon whom thy name shall be put in this house;

27 And if any people shall rise against this people, that thine anger be kindled against them;

28 And if they shall smite this people thou wilt smite them; thou wilt fight for thy people as thou didst in the day of battle, that they may be delivered from the hands of all their enemies.

29 We ask thee, Holy Father, to confound, and astonish, and to bring to shame and confusion, all those who have spread lying reports abroad, over the world, against thy servant or servants, if they will not repent, when the everlasting gospel shall be proclaimed in their ears;

30 And that all their works may be brought to naught, and be swept away by the hail, and by the judgments which thou wilt send upon them in thine anger, that there may be an end to lyings and slanders against thy people.

31 For thou knowest, O Lord, that thy servants have been innocent before thee

in bearing record of thy name, for which they have suffered these things.

32 Therefore we plead before thee for a full and complete deliverance from under this yoke;

33 Break it off, O Lord; break it off from the necks of thy servants, by thy power, that we may rise up in the midst of this generation and do thy work.

34 O Jehovah, have mercy upon this people, and as all men sin, forgive the transgressions of thy people, and let them be blotted out forever.

35 Let the anointing of thy ministers be sealed upon them with power from on high.

36 Let it be fulfilled upon them, as upon those on the day of Pentecost; let the gift of tongues be poured out upon thy people, even cloven tongues as of fire, and the interpretation thereof.

37 And let thy house be filled, as with a rushing mighty wind, with thy glory.

38 Put upon thy servants the testimony of the covenant, that when they go out and proclaim thy word they may seal up the law, and prepare the hearts of thy saints for all those judgments thou art about to send, in thy wrath, upon the inhabitants of the earth, because of their transgressions, that thy people may not faint in the day of trouble.

39 And whatsoever city thy servants shall enter, and the people of that city receive their testimony, let thy peace and thy salvation be upon that city; that they may gather out of that city the righteous, that they may come forth to Zion, or to her stakes, the places of thine appointment, with songs of everlasting joy;

40 And until this be accomplished, let not thy judgments fall upon that city.

41 And whatsoever city thy servants shall enter, and the people of that city receive not the testimony of thy servants, and thy servants warn them to save themselves from this untoward generation, let it be upon that city according to that which thou hast spoken by the mouths of thy prophets.

42 But deliver thou, O Jehovah, we beseech thee, thy servants from their hands, and cleanse them from their blood.

43 O Lord, we delight not in the destruction of our fellow men; their souls are precious before thee;

44 But thy word must be fulfilled. Help thy servants to say, with thy grace assisting them: Thy will be done, O Lord, and not ours.

45 We know that thou hast spoken by the mouth of thy prophets terrible things concerning the wicked, in the last days—that thou wilt pour out thy judgments, without measure;

46 Therefore, O Lord, deliver thy people from the calamity of the wicked; enable thy servants to seal up the law, and bind up the testimony, that they may be prepared against the day of burning.

47 We ask thee, Holy Father, to remember those who have been driven by the inhabitants of Jackson county, Missouri, from the lands of their inheritance, and break off, O Lord, this yoke of affliction that has been put upon them.

48 Thou knowest, O Lord, that they have been greatly oppressed and afflicted by wicked men; and our hearts flow out with sorrow because of their grievous burdens.

49 O Lord, how long wilt thou suffer this people to bear this affliction, and the cries of their innocent ones to

ascend up in thine ears, and their blood come up in testimony before thee, and not make a display of thy testimony in their behalf?

50 Have mercy, O Lord, upon the wicked mob, who have driven thy people, that they may cease to spoil, that they may repent of their sins if repentance is to be found;

51 But if they will not, make bare thine arm, O Lord, and redeem that which thou didst appoint a Zion unto thy people.

52 And if it cannot be otherwise, that the cause of thy people may not fail before thee may thine anger be kindled, and thine indignation fall upon them, that they may be wasted away, both root and branch, from under heaven;

53 But inasmuch as they will repent, thou art gracious and merciful, and wilt turn away thy wrath when thou lookest upon the face of thine Anointed.

54 Have mercy, O Lord, upon all the nations of the earth; have mercy upon the rulers of our land; may those principles, which were so honorably and nobly defended, namely, the Constitution of our land, by our fathers, be established forever.

55 Remember the kings, the princes, the nobles, and the great ones of the earth, and all people, and the churches, all the poor, the needy, and afflicted ones of the earth;

56 That their hearts may be softened when thy servants shall go out from thy house, O Jehovah, to bear testimony of thy name; that their prejudices may give way before the truth, and thy people may obtain favor in the sight of all;

57 That all the ends of the earth may know that we, thy servants, have heard thy voice, and that thou hast sent us;

58 That from among all these, thy servants, the sons of Jacob, may gather out the righteous to build a holy city to thy name, as thou hast commanded them.

59 We ask thee to appoint unto Zion other stakes besides this one which thou hast appointed, that the gathering of thy people may roll on in great power and majesty, that thy work may be cut short in righteousness.

60 Now these words, O Lord, we have spoken before thee, concerning the revelations and commandments which thou hast given unto us, who are identified with the Gentiles.

61 But thou knowest that thou hast a great love for the children of Jacob, who have been scattered upon the mountains for a long time, in a cloudy and dark day.

62 We therefore ask thee to have mercy upon the children of Jacob, that Jerusalem, from this hour, may begin to be redeemed;

63 And the yoke of bondage may begin to be broken off from the house of David;

64 And the children of Judah may begin to return to the lands which thou didst give to Abraham, their father.

65 And cause that the remnants of Jacob, who have been cursed and smitten because of their transgression, be converted from their wild and savage condition to the fulness of the everlasting gospel;

66 That they may lay down their weapons of bloodshed, and cease their rebellions.

67 And may all the scattered remnants of Israel, who have been driven to the ends of the earth, come to a knowledge

of the truth, believe in the Messiah, and be redeemed from oppression, and rejoice before thee.

68 O Lord, remember thy servant, Joseph Smith, Jun., and all his afflictions and persecutions—how he has covenanted with Jehovah, and vowed to thee, O Mighty God of Jacob—and the commandments which thou hast given unto him, and that he hath sincerely striven to do thy will.

69 Have mercy, O Lord, upon his wife and children, that they may be exalted in thy presence, and preserved by thy fostering hand.

70 Have mercy upon all their immediate connections, that their prejudices may be broken up and swept away as with a flood; that they may be converted and redeemed with Israel, and know that thou art God.

71 Remember, O Lord, the presidents, even all the presidents of thy church, that thy right hand may exalt them, with all their families, and their immediate connections, that their names may be perpetuated and had in everlasting remembrance from generation to generation.

72 Remember all thy church, O Lord, with all their families, and all their immediate connections, with all their sick and afflicted ones, with all the poor and meek of the earth; that the kingdom, which thou hast set up without hands, may become a great mountain and fill the whole earth;

73 That thy church may come forth out of the wilderness of darkness, and shine forth fair as the moon, clear as the sun, and terrible as an army with banners;

74 And be adorned as a bride for that day when thou shalt unveil the heavens, and cause the mountains to flow down at thy presence, and the valleys to be exalted, the rough places made smooth; that thy glory may fill the earth;

75 That when the trump shall sound for the dead, we shall be caught up in the cloud to meet thee, that we may ever be with the Lord;

76 That our garments may be pure, that we may be clothed upon with robes of righteousness, with palms in our hands, and crowns of glory upon our heads, and reap eternal joy for all our sufferings.

77 O Lord God Almighty, hear us in these our petitions, and answer us from heaven, thy holy habitation, where thou sittest enthroned, with glory, honor, power, majesty, might, dominion, truth, justice, judgment, mercy, and an infinity of fulness, from everlasting to everlasting.

78 O hear, O hear, O hear us, O Lord! And answer these petitions, and accept the dedication of this house unto thee, the work of our hands, which we have built unto thy name;

79 And also this church, to put upon it thy name. And help us by the power of thy Spirit, that we may mingle our voices with those bright, shining seraphs around thy throne, with acclamations of praise, singing Hosanna to God and the Lamb!

80 And let these, thine anointed ones, be clothed with salvation, and thy saints shout aloud for joy. Amen, and Amen.

Section 110

Visions manifested to Joseph Smith the Prophet and Oliver Cowdery in the temple at Kirtland, Ohio, April 3, 1836. The occasion was that of a Sabbath day meeting. Joseph Smith's history states: "In the afternoon, I assisted the other Presidents in distributing the Lord's Supper to the Church, receiving it from the Twelve, whose privilege it was to officiate at the sacred desk this day. After having performed this service to my brethren, I retired to the pulpit, the veils being dropped, and bowed myself, with Oliver Cowdery, in solemn and silent prayer. After rising from prayer, the following vision was opened to both of us."

1–10, The Lord Jehovah appears in glory and accepts the Kirtland Temple as His house; 11–12, Moses and Elias each appear and commit their keys and dispensations; 13–16, Elijah returns and commits the keys of his dispensation as promised by Malachi.

1 The veil was taken from our minds, and the eyes of our understanding were opened.

2 We saw the Lord standing upon the breastwork of the pulpit, before us; and under his feet was a paved work of pure gold, in color like amber.

3 His eyes were as a flame of fire; the hair of his head was white like the pure snow; his countenance shone above the brightness of the sun; and his voice was as the sound of the rushing of great waters, even the voice of Jehovah, saying:

4 I am the first and the last; I am he who liveth, I am he who was slain; I am your advocate with the Father.

5 Behold, your sins are forgiven you; you are clean before me; therefore, lift up your heads and rejoice.

6 Let the hearts of your brethren rejoice, and let the hearts of all my people rejoice, who have, with their might, built this house to my name.

7 For behold, I have accepted this house, and my name shall be here; and I will manifest myself to my people in mercy in this house.

8 Yea, I will appear unto my servants, and speak unto them with mine own voice, if my people will keep my commandments, and do not pollute this holy house.

9 Yea the hearts of thousands and tens of thousands shall greatly rejoice in consequence of the blessings which shall be poured out, and the endowment with which my servants have been endowed in this house.

10 And the fame of this house shall spread to foreign lands; and this is the beginning of the blessing which shall be poured out upon the heads of my people. Even so. Amen.

11 After this vision closed, the heavens were again opened unto us; and Moses appeared before us, and committed unto us the keys of the gathering of Israel from the four parts of the earth, and the leading of the ten tribes from the land of the north.

12 After this, Elias appeared, and committed the dispensation of the gospel of Abraham, saying that in us and our seed all generations after us should be blessed.

13 After this vision had closed, another great and glorious vision burst upon us; for Elijah the prophet, who was taken to heaven without tasting death, stood before us, and said:

14 Behold, the time has fully come, which was spoken of by the mouth of

Malachi—testifying that he [Elijah] should be sent, before the great and dreadful day of the Lord come—

15 To turn the hearts of the fathers to the children, and the children to the fathers, lest the whole earth be smitten with a curse—

16 Therefore, the keys of this dispensation are committed into your hands; and by this ye may know that the great and dreadful day of the Lord is near, even at the doors.

Section 111

Revelation given through Joseph Smith the Prophet, at Salem, Massachusetts, August 6, 1836. At this time the leaders of the Church were heavily in debt due to their labors in the ministry. Hearing that a large amount of money would be available to them in Salem, the Prophet, Sidney Rigdon, Hyrum Smith, and Oliver Cowdery traveled there from Kirtland, Ohio, to investigate this claim, along with preaching the gospel. The brethren transacted several items of Church business and did some preaching. When it became apparent that no money was to be forthcoming, they returned to Kirtland. Several of the factors prominent in the background are reflected in the wording of this revelation.

1–5, The Lord looks to the temporal needs of His servants; 6–11, He will deal mercifully with Zion and arrange all things for the good of His servants.

1 I, the Lord your God, am not displeased with your coming this journey, notwithstanding your follies.

2 I have much treasure in this city for you, for the benefit of Zion, and many people in this city, whom I will gather out in due time for the benefit of Zion, through your instrumentality.

3 Therefore, it is expedient that you should form acquaintance with men in this city, as you shall be led, and as it shall be given you.

4 And it shall come to pass in due time that I will give this city into your hands, that you shall have power over it, insomuch that they shall not discover your secret parts; and its wealth pertaining to gold and silver shall be yours.

5 Concern not yourselves about your debts, for I will give you power to pay them.

6 Concern not yourselves about Zion, for I will deal mercifully with her.

7 Tarry in this place, and in the regions round about;

8 And the place where it is my will that you should tarry, for the main, shall be signalized unto you by the peace and power of my Spirit, that shall flow unto you.

9 This place you may obtain by hire. And inquire diligently concerning the more ancient inhabitants and founders of this city;

10 For there are more treasures than one for you in this city.

11 Therefore, be ye as wise as serpents and yet without sin; and I will order all things for your good, as fast as ye are able to receive them. Amen.

Section 112

Revelation given through Joseph Smith the Prophet to Thomas B. Marsh, at Kirtland, Ohio, July 23, 1837, concerning the Twelve Apostles of the Lamb. This revelation was received on the day Elders Heber C. Kimball and Orson Hyde first preached the gospel in England. Thomas B. Marsh was at this time President of the Quorum of the Twelve Apostles.

1–10, The Twelve are to send the gospel and raise the warning voice to all nations and people; 11–15, They are to take up their cross, follow Jesus, and feed His sheep; 16–20, Those who receive the First Presidency receive the Lord; 21–29, Darkness covers the earth, and only those who believe and are baptized will be saved; 30–34, The First Presidency and the Twelve hold the keys of the dispensation of the fulness of times.

1 Verily thus saith the Lord unto you my servant Thomas: I have heard thy prayers; and thine alms have come up as a memorial before me, in behalf of those, thy brethren, who were chosen to bear testimony of my name and to send it abroad among all nations, kindreds, tongues, and people, and ordained through the instrumentality of my servants.

2 Verily I say unto you, there have been some few things in thine heart and with thee with which I, the Lord, was not well pleased.

3 Nevertheless, inasmuch as thou hast abased thyself thou shalt be exalted; therefore, all thy sins are forgiven thee.

4 Let thy heart be of good cheer before my face; and thou shalt bear record of my name, not only unto the Gentiles, but also unto the Jews; and thou shalt send forth my word unto the ends of the earth.

5 Contend thou, therefore, morning by morning; and day after day let thy warning voice go forth; and when the night cometh let not the inhabitants of the earth slumber, because of thy speech.

6 Let thy habitation be known in Zion, and remove not thy house; for I, the Lord, have a great work for thee to do, in publishing my name among the children of men.

7 Therefore, gird up thy loins for the work. Let thy feet be shod also, for thou art chosen, and thy path lieth among the mountains, and among many nations.

8 And by thy word many high ones shall be brought low, and by thy word many low ones shall be exalted.

9 Thy voice shall be a rebuke unto the transgressor; and at thy rebuke let the tongue of the slanderer cease its perverseness.

10 Be thou humble; and the Lord thy God shall lead thee by the hand, and give thee answer to thy prayers.

11 I know thy heart, and have heard thy prayers concerning thy brethren. Be not partial towards them in love above many others, but let thy love be for them as for thyself; and let thy love abound unto all men, and unto all who love my name.

12 And pray for thy brethren of the Twelve. Admonish them sharply for my name's sake, and let them be admonished for all their sins, and be ye faithful before me unto my name.

13 And after their temptations, and much tribulation, behold, I, the Lord, will feel after them, and if they harden not their hearts, and stiffen not their necks against me, they shall be converted, and I will heal them.

14 Now, I say unto you, and what I say unto you, I say unto all the Twelve: Arise and gird up your loins, take up your cross, follow me, and feed my sheep.

15 Exalt not yourselves; rebel not against my servant Joseph; for verily I say unto you, I am with him, and my hand shall be over him; and the keys which I have given unto him, and also to youward, shall not be taken from him till I come.

16 Verily I say unto you, my servant Thomas, thou art the man whom I have chosen to hold the keys of my kingdom, as pertaining to the Twelve, abroad among all nations—

17 That thou mayest be my servant to unlock the door of the kingdom in all places where my servant Joseph, and my servant Sidney, and my servant Hyrum, cannot come;

18 For on them have I laid the burden of all the churches for a little season.

19 Wherefore, whithersoever they shall send you, go ye, and I will be with you; and in whatsoever place ye shall proclaim my name an effectual door shall be opened unto you, that they may receive my word.

20 Whosoever receiveth my word receiveth me, and whosoever receiveth me, receiveth those, the First Presidency, whom I have sent, whom I have made counselors for my name's sake unto you.

21 And again, I say unto you, that whosoever ye shall send in my name, by the voice of your brethren, the Twelve, duly recommended and authorized by you, shall have power to open the door of my kingdom unto any nation whithersoever ye shall send them—

22 Inasmuch as they shall humble themselves before me, and abide in my word, and hearken to the voice of my Spirit.

23 Verily, verily, I say unto you, darkness covereth the earth, and gross darkness the minds of the people, and all flesh has become corrupt before my face.

24 Behold, vengeance cometh speedily upon the inhabitants of the earth, a day of wrath, a day of burning, a day of desolation, of weeping, of mourning, and of lamentation; and as a whirlwind it shall come upon all the face of the earth, saith the Lord.

25 And upon my house shall it begin, and from my house shall it go forth, saith the Lord;

26 First among those among you, saith the Lord, who have professed to know my name and have not known me, and have blasphemed against me in the midst of my house, saith the Lord.

27 Therefore, see to it that ye trouble not yourselves concerning the affairs of my church in this place, saith the Lord.

28 But purify your hearts before me; and then go ye into all the world, and preach my gospel unto every creature who has not received it;

29 And he that believeth and is baptized shall be saved, and he that believeth not, and is not baptized, shall be damned.

30 For unto you, the Twelve, and those, the First Presidency, who are appointed with you to be your counselors and your leaders, is the power of this priesthood given, for the last days and for the last time, in the which is the dispensation of the fulness of times,

31 Which power you hold, in connection with all those who have received a dispensation at any time

from the beginning of the creation;

32 For verily I say unto you, the keys of the dispensation, which ye have received, have come down from the fathers, and last of all, being sent down from heaven unto you.

33 Verily I say unto you, behold how great is your calling. Cleanse your hearts and your garments, lest the blood of this generation be required at your hands.

34 Be faithful until I come, for I come quickly; and my reward is with me to recompense every man according as his work shall be. I am Alpha and Omega. Amen.

Section 113

Answers to certain questions on the writings of Isaiah, given by Joseph Smith the Prophet, at or near Far West, Missouri, March 1838.

1–6, The Stem of Jesse, the rod coming therefrom, and the root of Jesse are identified; 7–10, The scattered remnants of Zion have a right to the priesthood and are called to return to the Lord.

1 Who is the Stem of Jesse spoken of in the 1st, 2d, 3d, 4th, and 5th verses of the 11th chapter of Isaiah?

2 Verily thus saith the Lord: It is Christ.

3 What is the rod spoken of in the first verse of the 11th chapter of Isaiah, that should come of the Stem of Jesse?

4 Behold, thus saith the Lord: It is a servant in the hands of Christ, who is partly a descendant of Jesse as well as of Ephraim, or of the house of Joseph, on whom there is laid much power.

5 What is the root of Jesse spoken of in the 10th verse of the 11th chapter?

6 Behold, thus saith the Lord, it is a descendant of Jesse, as well as of Joseph, unto whom rightly belongs the priesthood, and the keys of the kingdom, for an ensign, and for the gathering of my people in the last days.

7 Questions by Elias Higbee: What is meant by the command in Isaiah, 52d chapter, 1st verse, which saith: Put on thy strength, O Zion—and what people had Isaiah reference to?

8 He had reference to those whom God should call in the last days, who should hold the power of priesthood to bring again Zion, and the redemption of Israel; and to put on her strength is to put on the authority of the priesthood, which she, Zion, has a right to by lineage; also to return to that power which she had lost.

9 What are we to understand by Zion loosing herself from the bands of her neck; 2d verse?

10 We are to understand that the scattered remnants are exhorted to return to the Lord from whence they have fallen; which if they do, the promise of the Lord is that he will speak to them, or give them revelation. See the 6th, 7th, and 8th verses. The bands of her neck are the curses of God upon her, or the remnants of Israel in their scattered condition among the Gentiles.

Section 114

Revelation given through Joseph Smith the Prophet, at Far West, Missouri, April 11, 1838.

1–2, Church positions held by those who are not faithful will be given to others.

1 Verily thus saith the Lord: It is wisdom in my servant David W. Patten, that he settle up all his business as soon as he possibly can, and make a disposition of his merchandise, that he may perform a mission unto me next spring, in company with others, even twelve including himself, to testify of my name and bear glad tidings unto all the world.

2 For verily thus saith the Lord, that inasmuch as there are those among you who deny my name, others shall be planted in their stead and receive their bishopric. Amen.

Section 115

Revelation given through Joseph Smith the Prophet, at Far West, Missouri, April 26, 1838, making known the will of God concerning the building up of that place and of the Lord's house. This revelation is addressed to the presiding officers and the members of the Church.

1–4, The Lord names His church The Church of Jesus Christ of Latter-day Saints; 5–6, Zion and her stakes are places of defense and refuge for the Saints; 7–16, The Saints are commanded to build a house of the Lord at Far West; 17–19, Joseph Smith holds the keys of the kingdom of God on earth.

1 Verily thus saith the Lord unto you, my servant Joseph Smith, Jun., and also my servant Sidney Rigdon, and also my servant Hyrum Smith, and your counselors who are and shall be appointed hereafter;

2 And also unto you, my servant Edward Partridge, and his counselors;

3 And also unto my faithful servants who are of the high council of my church in Zion, for thus it shall be called, and unto all the elders and people of my Church of Jesus Christ of Latter-day Saints, scattered abroad in all the world;

4 For thus shall my church be called in the last days, even The Church of Jesus Christ of Latter-day Saints.

5 Verily I say unto you all: Arise and shine forth, that thy light may be a standard for the nations;

6 And that the gathering together upon the land of Zion, and upon her stakes, may be for a defense, and for a refuge from the storm, and from wrath when it shall be poured out without mixture upon the whole earth.

7 Let the city, Far West, be a holy and consecrated land unto me; and it shall be called most holy, for the ground upon which thou standest is holy.

8 Therefore, I command you to build a house unto me, for the gathering together of my saints, that they may worship me.

9 And let there be a beginning of this work, and a foundation, and a preparatory work, this following summer;

10 And let the beginning be made on the fourth day of July next; and from that time forth let my people labor diligently to build a house unto my name;

11 And in one year from this day let them re-commence laying the foundation of my house.

12 Thus let them from that time forth labor diligently until it shall be finished, from the cornerstone thereof unto the top thereof, until there shall not anything remain that is not finished.

13 Verily I say unto you, let not my servant Joseph, neither my servant Sidney, neither my servant Hyrum, get in debt any more for the building of a house unto my name;

14 But let a house be built unto my name according to the pattern which I will show unto them.

15 And if my people build it not according to the pattern which I shall show unto their presidency, I will not accept it at their hands.

16 But if my people do build it according to the pattern which I shall show unto their presidency, even my servant Joseph and his counselors, then I will accept it at the hands of my people.

17 And again, verily I say unto you, it is my will that the city of Far West should be built up speedily by the gathering of my saints;

18 And also that other places should be appointed for stakes in the regions round about, as they shall be manifested unto my servant Joseph, from time to time.

19 For behold, I will be with him, and I will sanctify him before the people; for unto him have I given the keys of this kingdom and ministry. Even so. Amen.

Section 116

Revelation given to Joseph Smith the Prophet, near Wight's Ferry, at a place called Spring Hill, Daviess County, Missouri, May 19, 1838.

1 Spring Hill is named by the Lord Adam-ondi-Ahman, because, said he, it is the place where Adam shall come to visit his people, or the Ancient of Days shall sit, as spoken of by Daniel the prophet.

Section 117

Revelation given through Joseph Smith the Prophet, at Far West, Missouri, July 8, 1838, concerning the immediate duties of William Marks, Newel K. Whitney, and Oliver Granger.

1–9, The Lord's servants should not covet temporal things, for "what is property unto the Lord?"; 10–16, They are to forsake littleness of soul, and their sacrifices will be sacred unto the Lord.

1 Verily thus saith the Lord unto my servant William Marks, and also unto my servant Newel K. Whitney, let them settle up their business speedily and journey from the land of Kirtland, before I, the Lord, send again the snows upon the earth.

2 Let them awake, and arise, and come forth, and not tarry, for I, the Lord, command it.

3 Therefore, if they tarry it shall not be well with them.

4 Let them repent of all their sins, and of all their covetous desires, before me, saith the Lord; for what is property unto me? saith the Lord.

5 Let the properties of Kirtland be turned out for debts, saith the Lord. Let them go, saith the Lord, and whatsoever remaineth, let it remain in your hands, saith the Lord.

6 For have I not the fowls of heaven, and also the fish of the sea, and the beasts of the mountains? Have I not made the earth? Do I not hold the destinies of all the armies of the nations of the earth?

7 Therefore, will I not make solitary places to bud and to blossom, and to bring forth in abundance? saith the Lord.

8 Is there not room enough on the mountains of Adam-ondi-Ahman, and on the plains of Olaha Shinehah, or the land where Adam dwelt, that you should covet that which is but the drop, and neglect the more weighty matters?

9 Therefore, come up hither unto the land of my people, even Zion.

10 Let my servant William Marks be faithful over a few things, and he shall be a ruler over many. Let him preside in the midst of my people in the city of Far West, and let him be blessed with the blessings of my people.

11 Let my servant Newel K. Whitney be ashamed of the Nicolaitane band and of all their secret abominations, and of all his littleness of soul before me, saith the Lord, and come up to the land of Adam-ondi-Ahman, and be a bishop unto my people, saith the Lord, not in name but in deed, saith the Lord.

12 And again, I say unto you, I remember my servant Oliver Granger; behold, verily I say unto him that his name shall be had in sacred remembrance from generation to generation, forever and ever, saith the Lord.

13 Therefore, let him contend earnestly for the redemption of the First Presidency of my Church, saith the Lord; and when he falls he shall rise again, for his sacrifice shall be more sacred unto me than his increase, saith the Lord.

14 Therefore, let him come up hither speedily, unto the land of Zion; and in the due time he shall be made a merchant unto my name, saith the Lord, for the benefit of my people.

15 Therefore let no man despise my
servant Oliver Granger, but let the
blessings of my people be on him
forever and ever.

16 And again, verily I say unto you, let
all my servants in the land of Kirtland
remember the Lord their God, and mine
house also, to keep and preserve it holy,
and to overthrow the moneychangers
in mine own due time, saith the Lord.
Even so. Amen.

Section 118

Revelation given through Joseph Smith the Prophet, at Far West, Missouri, July 8, 1838, in response to the supplication, "Show us thy will, O Lord, concerning the Twelve."

1–3, The Lord will provide for the families of the Twelve; 4–6, Vacancies in the Twelve are filled.

1 Verily, thus saith the Lord: Let a conference be held immediately; let the Twelve be organized; and let men be appointed to supply the place of those who are fallen.

2 Let my servant Thomas remain for a season in the land of Zion, to publish my word.

3 Let the residue continue to preach from that hour, and if they will do this in all lowliness of heart, in meekness and humility, and long-suffering, I, the Lord, give unto them a promise that I will provide for their families; and an effectual door shall be opened for them, from henceforth.

4 And next spring let them depart to go over the great waters, and there promulgate my gospel, the fulness thereof, and bear record of my name.

5 Let them take leave of my saints in the city of Far West, on the twenty-sixth day of April next, on the building-spot of my house, saith the Lord.

6 Let my servant John Taylor, and also my servant John E. Page, and also my servant Wilford Woodruff, and also my servant Willard Richards, be appointed to fill the places of those who have fallen, and be officially notified of their appointment.

Section 119

Revelation given through Joseph Smith the Prophet, at Far West, Missouri, July 8, 1838, in answer to his supplication: "O Lord! Show unto thy servants how much thou requirest of the properties of thy people for a tithing." The law of tithing, as understood today, had not been given to the Church previous to this revelation. The term tithing in the prayer just quoted and in previous revelations (64:23; 85:3; 97:11) had meant not just one-tenth, but all free-will offerings, or contributions, to the Church funds. The Lord had previously given to the Church the law of consecration and stewardship of property, which members (chiefly the leading elders) entered into by a covenant that was to be everlasting. Because of failure on the part of many to abide by this covenant, the Lord withdrew it for a time and gave instead the law of tithing to the whole Church. The Prophet asked the Lord how much of their property He required for sacred purposes. The answer was this revelation.

1–5, The Saints are to pay their surplus property and then give, as tithing, one-tenth of their interest annually; 6–7, Such a course will sanctify the land of Zion.

1 Verily, thus saith the Lord, I require all their surplus property to be put into the hands of the bishop of my church in Zion,

2 For the building of mine house, and for the laying of the foundation of Zion and for the priesthood, and for the debts of the Presidency of my Church.

3 And this shall be the beginning of the tithing of my people.

4 And after that, those who have thus been tithed shall pay one-tenth of all their interest annually; and this shall be a standing law unto them forever, for my holy priesthood, saith the Lord.

5 Verily I say unto you, it shall come to pass that all those who gather unto the land of Zion shall be tithed of their surplus properties, and shall observe this law, or they shall not be found worthy to abide among you.

6 And I say unto you, if my people observe not this law, to keep it holy, and by this law sanctify the land of Zion unto me, that my statutes and my judgments may be kept thereon, that it may be most holy, behold, verily I say unto you, it shall not be a land of Zion unto you.

7 And this shall be an ensample unto all the stakes of Zion. Even so. Amen.

Section 120

Revelation given through Joseph Smith the Prophet, at Far West, Missouri, July 8, 1838, making known the disposition of the properties tithed as named in the preceding revelation, section 119.

1 Verily, thus saith the Lord, the time
is now come, that it shall be disposed
of by a council, composed of the First
Presidency of my Church, and of the
bishop and his council, and by my high
council; and by mine own voice unto
them, saith the Lord. Even so. Amen.

Section 121

Prayer and prophecies written by Joseph Smith the Prophet in an epistle to the Church while he was a prisoner in the jail at Liberty, Missouri, dated March 20, 1839. The Prophet and several companions had been months in prison. Their petitions and appeals directed to the executive officers and the judiciary had failed to bring them relief.

1–6, The Prophet pleads with the Lord for the suffering Saints; 7–10, The Lord speaks peace to him; 11–17, Cursed are all those who raise false cries of transgression against the Lord's people; 18–25, They will not have right to the priesthood and will be damned; 26–32, Glorious revelations promised those who endure valiantly; 33–40, Why many are called and few are chosen; 41–46, The priesthood should be used only in righteousness.

1 O God, where art thou? And where is the pavilion that covereth thy hiding place?

2 How long shall thy hand be stayed, and thine eye, yea thy pure eye, behold from the eternal heavens the wrongs of thy people and of thy servants, and thine ear be penetrated with their cries?

3 Yea, O Lord, how long shall they suffer these wrongs and unlawful oppressions, before thine heart shall be softened toward them, and thy bowels be moved with compassion toward them?

4 O Lord God Almighty, maker of heaven, earth, and seas, and of all things that in them are, and who controllest and subjectest the devil, and the dark and benighted dominion of Sheol—stretch forth thy hand; let thine eye pierce; let thy pavilion be taken up; let thy hiding place no longer be covered; let thine ear be inclined; let thine heart be softened, and thy bowels moved with compassion toward us.

5 Let thine anger be kindled against our enemies; and, in the fury of thine heart, with thy sword avenge us of our wrongs.

6 Remember thy suffering saints, O our God; and thy servants will rejoice in thy name forever.

7 My son, peace be unto thy soul; thine adversity and thine afflictions shall be but a small moment;

8 And then, if thou endure it well, God shall exalt thee on high; thou shalt triumph over all thy foes.

9 Thy friends do stand by thee, and they shall hail thee again with warm hearts and friendly hands.

10 Thou art not yet as Job; thy friends do not contend against thee, neither charge thee with transgression, as they did Job.

11 And they who do charge thee with transgression, their hope shall be blasted, and their prospects shall melt away as the hoar frost melteth before the burning rays of the rising sun;

12 And also that God hath set his hand and seal to change the times and seasons, and to blind their minds, that they may not understand his marvelous workings; that he may prove them also and take them in their own craftiness;

13 Also because their hearts are corrupted, and the things which they are willing to bring upon others, and love to have others suffer, may come upon themselves to the very uttermost;

14 That they may be disappointed also, and their hopes may be cut off;

15 And not many years hence, that they

and their posterity shall be swept from under heaven, saith God, that not one of them is left to stand by the wall.

16 Cursed are all those that shall lift up the heel against mine anointed, saith the Lord, and cry they have sinned when they have not sinned before me, saith the Lord, but have done that which was meet in mine eyes, and which I commanded them.

17 But those who cry transgression do it because they are the servants of sin, and are the children of disobedience themselves.

18 And those who swear falsely against my servants, that they might bring them into bondage and death—

19 Wo unto them; because they have offended my little ones they shall be severed from the ordinances of mine house.

20 Their basket shall not be full, their houses and their barns shall perish, and they themselves shall be despised by those that flattered them.

21 They shall not have right to the priesthood, nor their posterity after them from generation to generation.

22 It had been better for them that a millstone had been hanged about their necks, and they drowned in the depth of the sea.

23 Wo unto all those that discomfort my people, and drive, and murder, and testify against them, saith the Lord of Hosts; a generation of vipers shall not escape the damnation of hell.

24 Behold, mine eyes see and know all their works, and I have in reserve a swift judgment in the season thereof, for them all;

25 For there is a time appointed for every man, according as his works shall be.

26 God shall give unto you knowledge by his Holy Spirit, yea, by the unspeakable gift of the Holy Ghost, that has not been revealed since the world was until now;

27 Which our forefathers have awaited with anxious expectation to be revealed in the last times, which their minds were pointed to by the angels, as held in reserve for the fulness of their glory;

28 A time to come in the which nothing shall be withheld, whether there be one God or many gods, they shall be manifest.

29 All thrones and dominions, principalities and powers, shall be revealed and set forth upon all who have endured valiantly for the gospel of Jesus Christ.

30 And also, if there be bounds set to the heavens or to the seas, or to the dry land, or to the sun, moon, or stars—

31 All the times of their revolutions, all the appointed days, months, and years, and all the days of their days, months, and years, and all their glories, laws, and set times, shall be revealed in the days of the dispensation of the fulness of times—

32 According to that which was ordained in the midst of the Council of the Eternal God of all other gods before this world was, that should be reserved unto the finishing and the end thereof, when every man shall enter into his eternal presence and into his immortal rest.

33 How long can rolling waters remain impure? What power shall stay the heavens? As well might man stretch forth his puny arm to stop the Missouri river in its decreed course, or to turn it

up stream, as to hinder the Almighty from pouring down knowledge from heaven upon the heads of the Latter-day Saints.

34 Behold, there are many called, but few are chosen. And why are they not chosen?

35 Because their hearts are set so much upon the things of this world, and aspire to the honors of men, that they do not learn this one lesson—

36 That the rights of the priesthood are inseparably connected with the powers of heaven, and that the powers of heaven cannot be controlled nor handled only upon the principles of righteousness.

37 That they may be conferred upon us, it is true; but when we undertake to cover our sins, or to gratify our pride, our vain ambition, or to exercise control or dominion or compulsion upon the souls of the children of men, in any degree of unrighteousness, behold, the heavens withdraw themselves; the Spirit of the Lord is grieved; and when it is withdrawn, Amen to the priesthood or the authority of that man.

38 Behold, ere he is aware, he is left unto himself, to kick against the pricks, to persecute the saints, and to fight against God.

39 We have learned by sad experience that it is the nature and disposition of almost all men, as soon as they get a little authority, as they suppose, they will immediately begin to exercise unrighteous dominion.

40 Hence many are called, but few are chosen.

41 No power or influence can or ought to be maintained by virtue of the priesthood, only by persuasion, by long-suffering, by gentleness and meekness, and by love unfeigned;

42 By kindness, and pure knowledge, which shall greatly enlarge the soul without hypocrisy, and without guile—

43 Reproving betimes with sharpness, when moved upon by the Holy Ghost; and then showing forth afterwards an increase of love toward him whom thou hast reproved, lest he esteem thee to be his enemy;

44 That he may know that thy faithfulness is stronger than the cords of death.

45 Let thy bowels also be full of charity towards all men, and to the household of faith, and let virtue garnish thy thoughts unceasingly; then shall thy confidence wax strong in the presence of God; and the doctrine of the priesthood shall distil upon thy soul as the dews from heaven.

46 The Holy Ghost shall be thy constant companion, and thy scepter an unchanging scepter of righteousness and truth; and thy dominion shall be an everlasting dominion, and without compulsory means it shall flow unto thee forever and ever.

Section 122

The word of the Lord to Joseph Smith the Prophet, while a prisoner in the jail at Liberty, Missouri. This section is an excerpt from an epistle to the Church dated March 20, 1839 (see the heading to section 121).

1–4, The ends of the earth will inquire after the name of Joseph Smith; 5–7, All his perils and travails will give him experience and be for his good; 8–9, The Son of Man has descended below them all.

1 The ends of the earth shall inquire after thy name, and fools shall have thee in derision, and hell shall rage against thee;

2 While the pure in heart, and the wise, and the noble, and the virtuous, shall seek counsel, and authority, and blessings constantly from under thy hand.

3 And thy people shall never be turned against thee by the testimony of traitors.

4 And although their influence shall cast thee into trouble, and into bars and walls, thou shalt be had in honor; and but for a small moment and thy voice shall be more terrible in the midst of thine enemies than the fierce lion, because of thy righteousness; and thy God shall stand by thee forever and ever.

5 If thou art called to pass through tribulation; if thou art in perils among false brethren; if thou art in perils among robbers; if thou art in perils by land or by sea;

6 If thou art accused with all manner of false accusations; if thine enemies fall upon thee; if they tear thee from the society of thy father and mother and brethren and sisters; and if with a drawn sword thine enemies tear thee from the bosom of thy wife, and of thine offspring, and thine elder son, although but six years of age, shall cling to thy garments, and shall say, My father, my father, why can't you stay with us? O, my father, what are the men going to do with you? and if then he shall be thrust from thee by the sword, and thou be dragged to prison, and thine enemies prowl around thee like wolves for the blood of the lamb;

7 And if thou shouldst be cast into the pit, or into the hands of murderers, and the sentence of death passed upon thee; if thou be cast into the deep; if the billowing surge conspire against thee; if fierce winds become thine enemy; if the heavens gather blackness, and all the elements combine to hedge up the way; and above all, if the very jaws of hell shall gape open the mouth wide after thee, know thou, my son, that all these things shall give thee experience, and shall be for thy good.

8 The Son of Man hath descended below them all. Art thou greater than he?

9 Therefore, hold on thy way, and the priesthood shall remain with thee; for their bounds are set, they cannot pass. Thy days are known, and thy years shall not be numbered less; therefore, fear not what man can do, for God shall be with you forever and ever.

Section 123

Duty of the Saints in relation to their persecutors, as written by Joseph Smith the Prophet while a prisoner in the jail at Liberty, Missouri. This section is an excerpt from an epistle to the Church dated March 20, 1839 (see the heading to section 121).

1–6, The Saints should collect and publish an account of their sufferings and persecutions; 7–10, The same spirit that established the false creeds also leads to persecution of the Saints; 11–17, Many among all sects will yet receive the truth.

1 And again, we would suggest for your consideration the propriety of all the saints gathering up a knowledge of all the facts, and sufferings and abuses put upon them by the people of this State;

2 And also of all the property and amount of damages which they have sustained, both of character and personal injuries, as well as real property;

3 And also the names of all persons that have had a hand in their oppressions, as far as they can get hold of them and find them out.

4 And perhaps a committee can be appointed to find out these things, and to take statements and affidavits; and also to gather up the libelous publications that are afloat;

5 And all that are in the magazines, and in the encyclopedias, and all the libelous histories that are published, and are writing, and by whom, and present the whole concatenation of diabolical rascality and nefarious and murderous impositions that have been practiced upon this people—

6 That we may not only publish to all the world, but present them to the heads of government in all their dark and hellish hue, as the last effort which is enjoined on us by our Heavenly Father, before we can fully and completely claim that promise which shall call him forth from his hiding place; and also that the whole nation may be left without excuse before he can send forth the power of his mighty arm.

7 It is an imperative duty that we owe to God, to angels, with whom we shall be brought to stand, and also to ourselves, to our wives and children, who have been made to bow down with grief, sorrow, and care, under the most damning hand of murder, tyranny, and oppression, supported and urged on and upheld by the influence of that spirit which hath so strongly riveted the creeds of the fathers, who have inherited lies, upon the hearts of the children, and filled the world with confusion, and has been growing stronger and stronger, and is now the very mainspring of all corruption, and the whole earth groans under the weight of its iniquity.

8 It is an iron yoke, it is a strong band; they are the very handcuffs, and chains, and shackles, and fetters of hell.

9 Therefore it is an imperative duty that we owe, not only to our own wives and children, but to the widows and fatherless, whose husbands and fathers have been murdered under its iron hand;

10 Which dark and blackening deeds are enough to make hell itself shudder, and to stand aghast and pale, and the hands of the very devil to tremble and palsy.

11 And also it is an imperative duty that we owe to all the rising generation, and to all the pure in heart—

12 For there are many yet on the earth among all sects, parties, and denominations, who are blinded by the subtle craftiness of men, whereby they lie in wait to deceive, and who are only

kept from the truth because they know not where to find it—

13 Therefore, that we should waste and wear out our lives in bringing to light all the hidden things of darkness, wherein we know them; and they are truly manifest from heaven—

14 These should then be attended to with great earnestness.

15 Let no man count them as small things; for there is much which lieth in futurity, pertaining to the saints, which depends upon these things.

16 You know, brethren, that a very large ship is benefited very much by a very small helm in the time of a storm, by being kept workways with the wind and the waves.

17 Therefore, dearly beloved brethren, let us cheerfully do all things that lie in our power; and then may we stand still, with the utmost assurance, to see the salvation of God, and for his arm to be revealed.

Section 124

Revelation given to Joseph Smith the Prophet, at Nauvoo, Illinois, January 19, 1841. Because of increasing persecutions and illegal procedures against them by public officers, the Saints had been compelled to leave Missouri. The exterminating order issued by Lilburn W. Boggs, governor of Missouri, dated October 27, 1838, had left them no alternative. In 1841, when this revelation was given, the city of Nauvoo, occupying the site of the former village of Commerce, Illinois, had been built up by the Saints, and here the headquarters of the Church had been established.

1–14, Joseph Smith is commanded to make a solemn proclamation of the gospel to the president of the United States, the governors, and the rulers of all nations; 15–21, Hyrum Smith, David W. Patten, Joseph Smith Sr., and others among the living and the dead are blessed for their integrity and virtues; 22–28, The Saints are commanded to build both a house for the entertainment of strangers and a temple in Nauvoo; 29–36, Baptisms for the dead are to be performed in temples; 37–44, The Lord's people always build temples for the performance of holy ordinances; 45–55, The Saints are excused from building the temple in Jackson County because of the oppression of their enemies; 56–83, Directions are given for the building of the Nauvoo House; 84–96, Hyrum Smith is called to be a patriarch, to receive the keys, and to stand in the place of Oliver Cowdery; 97–122, William Law and others are counseled in their labors; 123–45, General and local officers are named, along with their duties and quorum affiliations.

1 Verily, thus saith the Lord unto you, my servant Joseph Smith, I am well pleased with your offering and acknowledgments, which you have made; for unto this end have I raised you up, that I might show forth my wisdom through the weak things of the earth.

2 Your prayers are acceptable before me; and in answer to them I say unto you, that you are now called immediately to make a solemn proclamation of my gospel, and of this stake which I have planted to be a cornerstone of Zion, which shall be polished with the refinement which is after the similitude of a palace.

3 This proclamation shall be made to all the kings of the world, to the four corners thereof, to the honorable president-elect, and the high-minded governors of the nation in which you live, and to all the nations of the earth scattered abroad.

4 Let it be written in the spirit of meekness and by the power of the Holy Ghost, which shall be in you at the time of the writing of the same;

5 For it shall be given you by the Holy Ghost to know my will concerning those kings and authorities, even what shall befall them in a time to come.

6 For, behold, I am about to call upon them to give heed to the light and glory of Zion, for the set time has come to favor her.

7 Call ye, therefore, upon them with loud proclamation, and with your testimony, fearing them not, for they are as grass, and all their glory as the flower thereof which soon falleth, that they may be left also without excuse—

8 And that I may visit them in the day of visitation, when I shall unveil the face of my covering, to appoint the portion of the oppressor among hypocrites, where there is gnashing of teeth, if they reject my servants and my testimony which I have revealed unto them.

9 And again, I will visit and soften their hearts, many of them for your good, that ye may find grace in their eyes, that they may come to the light of truth, and the Gentiles to the exaltation or lifting

up of Zion.

10 For the day of my visitation cometh speedily, in an hour when ye think not of; and where shall be the safety of my people, and refuge for those who shall be left of them?

11 Awake, O kings of the earth! Come ye, O, come ye, with your gold and your silver, to the help of my people, to the house of the daughters of Zion.

12 And again, verily I say unto you, let my servant Robert B. Thompson help you to write this proclamation, for I am well pleased with him, and that he should be with you;

13 Let him, therefore, hearken to your counsel, and I will bless him with a multiplicity of blessings; let him be faithful and true in all things from henceforth, and he shall be great in mine eyes;

14 But let him remember that his stewardship will I require at his hands.

15 And again, verily I say unto you, blessed is my servant Hyrum Smith; for I, the Lord, love him because of the integrity of his heart, and because he loveth that which is right before me, saith the Lord.

16 Again, let my servant John C. Bennett help you in your labor in sending my word to the kings and people of the earth, and stand by you, even you my servant Joseph Smith, in the hour of affliction; and his reward shall not fail if he receive counsel.

17 And for his love he shall be great, for he shall be mine if he do this, saith the Lord. I have seen the work which he hath done, which I accept if he continue, and will crown him with blessings and great glory.

18 And again, I say unto you that it is my will that my servant Lyman Wight should continue in preaching for Zion, in the spirit of meekness, confessing me before the world; and I will bear him up as on eagles' wings; and he shall beget glory and honor to himself and unto my name.

19 That when he shall finish his work I may receive him unto myself, even as I did my servant David Patten, who is with me at this time, and also my servant Edward Partridge, and also my aged servant Joseph Smith, Sen., who sitteth with Abraham at his right hand, and blessed and holy is he, for he is mine.

20 And again, verily I say unto you, my servant George Miller is without guile; he may be trusted because of the integrity of his heart; and for the love which he has to my testimony I, the Lord, love him.

21 I therefore say unto you, I seal upon his head the office of a bishopric, like unto my servant Edward Partridge, that he may receive the consecrations of mine house, that he may administer blessings upon the heads of the poor of my people, saith the Lord. Let no man despise my servant George, for he shall honor me.

22 Let my servant George, and my servant Lyman, and my servant John Snider, and others, build a house unto my name, such a one as my servant Joseph shall show unto them, upon the place which he shall show unto them also.

23 And it shall be for a house for boarding, a house that strangers may come from afar to lodge therein; therefore let it be a good house, worthy of all acceptation, that the weary traveler may find health and safety while he shall contemplate the word of the Lord; and the cornerstone I have appointed for Zion.

24 This house shall be a healthful habitation if it be built unto my name, and if the governor which shall be appointed unto it shall not suffer any pollution to come upon it. It shall be holy, or the Lord your God will not dwell therein.

25 And again, verily I say unto you, let all my saints come from afar.

26 And send ye swift messengers, yea, chosen messengers, and say unto them: Come ye, with all your gold, and your silver, and your precious stones, and with all your antiquities; and with all who have knowledge of antiquities, that will come, may come, and bring the box tree, and the fir tree, and the pine tree, together with all the precious trees of the earth;

27 And with iron, with copper, and with brass, and with zinc, and with all your precious things of the earth; and build a house to my name, for the Most High to dwell therein.

28 For there is not a place found on earth that he may come to and restore again that which was lost unto you, or which he hath taken away, even the fulness of the priesthood.

29 For a baptismal font there is not upon the earth, that they, my saints, may be baptized for those who are dead—

30 For this ordinance belongeth to my house, and cannot be acceptable to me, only in the days of your poverty, wherein ye are not able to build a house unto me.

31 But I command you, all ye my saints, to build a house unto me; and I grant unto you a sufficient time to build a house unto me; and during this time your baptisms shall be acceptable unto me.

32 But behold, at the end of this appointment your baptisms for your dead shall not be acceptable unto me; and if you do not these things at the end of the appointment ye shall be rejected as a church, with your dead, saith the Lord your God.

33 For verily I say unto you, that after you have had sufficient time to build a house to me, wherein the ordinance of baptizing for the dead belongeth, and for which the same was instituted from before the foundation of the world, your baptisms for your dead cannot be acceptable unto me;

34 For therein are the keys of the holy priesthood ordained, that you may receive honor and glory.

35 And after this time, your baptisms for the dead, by those who are scattered abroad, are not acceptable unto me, saith the Lord.

36 For it is ordained that in Zion, and in her stakes, and in Jerusalem, those places which I have appointed for refuge, shall be the places for your baptisms for your dead.

37 And again, verily I say unto you, how shall your washings be acceptable unto me, except ye perform them in a house which you have built to my name?

38 For, for this cause I commanded Moses that he should build a tabernacle, that they should bear it with them in the wilderness, and to build a house in the land of promise, that those ordinances might be revealed which had been hid from before the world was.

39 Therefore, verily I say unto you, that your anointings, and your washings, and your baptisms for the dead, and your solemn assemblies, and your memorials for your sacrifices by the sons of Levi, and for your oracles in your most holy places wherein you

receive conversations, and your statutes and judgments, for the beginning of the revelations and foundation of Zion, and for the glory, honor, and endowment of all her municipals, are ordained by the ordinance of my holy house, which my people are always commanded to build unto my holy name.

40 And verily I say unto you, let this house be built unto my name, that I may reveal mine ordinances therein unto my people;

41 For I deign to reveal unto my church things which have been kept hid from before the foundation of the world, things that pertain to the dispensation of the fulness of times.

42 And I will show unto my servant Joseph all things pertaining to this house, and the priesthood thereof, and the place whereon it shall be built.

43 And ye shall build it on the place where you have contemplated building it, for that is the spot which I have chosen for you to build it.

44 If ye labor with all your might, I will consecrate that spot that it shall be made holy.

45 And if my people will hearken unto my voice, and unto the voice of my servants whom I have appointed to lead my people, behold, verily I say unto you, they shall not be moved out of their place.

46 But if they will not hearken to my voice, nor unto the voice of these men whom I have appointed, they shall not be blest, because they pollute mine holy grounds, and mine holy ordinances, and charters, and my holy words which I give unto them.

47 And it shall come to pass that if you build a house unto my name, and do not do the things that I say, I will not perform the oath which I make unto you, neither fulfil the promises which ye expect at my hands, saith the Lord.

48 For instead of blessings, ye, by your own works, bring cursings, wrath, indignation, and judgments upon your own heads, by your follies, and by all your abominations, which you practice before me, saith the Lord.

49 Verily, verily, I say unto you, that when I give a commandment to any of the sons of men to do a work unto my name, and those sons of men go with all their might and with all they have to perform that work, and cease not their diligence, and their enemies come upon them and hinder them from performing that work, behold, it behooveth me to require that work no more at the hands of those sons of men, but to accept of their offerings.

50 And the iniquity and transgression of my holy laws and commandments I will visit upon the heads of those who hindered my work, unto the third and fourth generation, so long as they repent not, and hate me, saith the Lord God.

51 Therefore, for this cause have I accepted the offerings of those whom I commanded to build up a city and a house unto my name, in Jackson county, Missouri, and were hindered by their enemies, saith the Lord your God.

52 And I will answer judgment, wrath, and indignation, wailing, and anguish, and gnashing of teeth upon their heads, unto the third and fourth generation, so long as they repent not, and hate me, saith the Lord your God.

53 And this I make an example unto you, for your consolation concerning all those who have been commanded to do a work and have been hindered by the hands of their enemies, and by oppression, saith the Lord your God.

54 For I am the Lord your God, and will save all those of your brethren who have been pure in heart, and have been slain in the land of Missouri, saith the Lord.

55 And again, verily I say unto you, I command you again to build a house to my name, even in this place, that you may prove yourselves unto me that ye are faithful in all things whatsoever I command you, that I may bless you, and crown you with honor, immortality, and eternal life.

56 And now I say unto you, as pertaining to my boarding house which I have commanded you to build for the boarding of strangers, let it be built unto my name, and let my name be named upon it, and let my servant Joseph and his house have place therein, from generation to generation.

57 For this anointing have I put upon his head, that his blessing shall also be put upon the head of his posterity after him.

58 And as I said unto Abraham concerning the kindreds of the earth, even so I say unto my servant Joseph: In thee and in thy seed shall the kindred of the earth be blessed.

59 Therefore, let my servant Joseph and his seed after him have place in that house, from generation to generation, forever and ever, saith the Lord.

60 And let the name of that house be called Nauvoo House; and let it be a delightful habitation for man, and a resting-place for the weary traveler, that he may contemplate the glory of Zion, and the glory of this, the cornerstone thereof;

61 That he may receive also the counsel from those whom I have set to be as plants of renown, and as watchmen upon her walls.

62 Behold, verily I say unto you, let my servant George Miller, and my servant Lyman Wight, and my servant John Snider, and my servant Peter Haws, organize themselves, and appoint one of them to be a president over their quorum for the purpose of building that house.

63 And they shall form a constitution, whereby they may receive stock for the building of that house.

64 And they shall not receive less than fifty dollars for a share of stock in that house, and they shall be permitted to receive fifteen thousand dollars from any one man for stock in that house.

65 But they shall not be permitted to receive over fifteen thousand dollars stock from any one man.

66 And they shall not be permitted to receive under fifty dollars for a share of stock from any one man in that house.

67 And they shall not be permitted to receive any man, as a stockholder in this house, except the same shall pay his stock into their hands at the time he receives stock;

68 And in proportion to the amount of stock he pays into their hands he shall receive stock in that house; but if he pays nothing into their hands he shall not receive any stock in that house.

69 And if any pay stock into their hands it shall be for stock in that house, for himself, and for his generation after him, from generation to generation, so long as he and his heirs shall hold that stock, and do not sell or convey the stock away out of their hands by their own free will and act, if you will do my will, saith the Lord your God.

70 And again, verily I say unto you, if my servant George Miller, and my servant Lyman Wight, and my servant

John Snider, and my servant Peter Haws, receive any stock into their hands, in moneys, or in properties wherein they receive the real value of moneys, they shall not appropriate any portion of that stock to any other purpose, only in that house.

71 And if they do appropriate any portion of that stock anywhere else, only in that house, without the consent of the stockholder, and do not repay four-fold for the stock which they appropriate anywhere else, only in that house, they shall be accursed, and shall be moved out of their place, saith the Lord God; for I, the Lord, am God, and cannot be mocked in any of these things.

72 Verily I say unto you, let my servant Joseph pay stock into their hands for the building of that house, as seemeth him good; but my servant Joseph cannot pay over fifteen thousand dollars stock in that house, nor under fifty dollars; neither can any other man, saith the Lord.

73 And there are others also who wish to know my will concerning them, for they have asked it at my hands.

74 Therefore, I say unto you concerning my servant Vinson Knight, if he will do my will let him put stock into that house for himself, and for his generation after him, from generation to generation.

75 And let him lift up his voice long and loud, in the midst of the people, to plead the cause of the poor and the needy; and let him not fail, neither let his heart faint; and I will accept of his offerings, for they shall not be unto me as the offerings of Cain, for he shall be mine, saith the Lord.

76 Let his family rejoice and turn away their hearts from affliction; for I have chosen him and anointed him, and he shall be honored in the midst of his house, for I will forgive all his sins, saith the Lord. Amen.

77 Verily I say unto you, let my servant Hyrum put stock into that house as seemeth him good, for himself and his generation after him, from generation to generation.

78 Let my servant Isaac Galland put stock into that house; for I, the Lord, love him for the work he hath done, and will forgive all his sins; therefore, let him be remembered for an interest in that house from generation to generation.

79 Let my servant Isaac Galland be appointed among you, and be ordained by my servant William Marks, and be blessed of him, to go with my servant Hyrum to accomplish the work that my servant Joseph shall point out to them, and they shall be greatly blessed.

80 Let my servant William Marks pay stock into that house, as seemeth him good, for himself and his generation, from generation to generation.

81 Let my servant Henry G. Sherwood pay stock into that house, as seemeth him good, for himself and his seed after him, from generation to generation.

82 Let my servant William Law pay stock into that house, for himself and his seed after him, from generation to generation.

83 If he will do my will let him not take his family unto the eastern lands, even unto Kirtland; nevertheless, I, the Lord, will build up Kirtland, but I, the Lord, have a scourge prepared for the inhabitants thereof.

84 And with my servant Almon Babbitt, there are many things with which I am not pleased; behold, he aspireth to establish his counsel instead of the counsel which I have ordained, even that of the Presidency of my Church;

and he setteth up a golden calf for the worship of my people.

85 Let no man go from this place who has come here essaying to keep my commandments.

86 If they live here let them live unto me; and if they die let them die unto me; for they shall rest from all their labors here, and shall continue their works.

87 Therefore, let my servant William put his trust in me, and cease to fear concerning his family, because of the sickness of the land. If ye love me, keep my commandments; and the sickness of the land shall redound to your glory.

88 Let my servant William go and proclaim my everlasting gospel with a loud voice, and with great joy, as he shall be moved upon by my Spirit, unto the inhabitants of Warsaw, and also unto the inhabitants of Carthage, and also unto the inhabitants of Burlington, and also unto the inhabitants of Madison, and await patiently and diligently for further instructions at my general conference, saith the Lord.

89 If he will do my will let him from henceforth hearken to the counsel of my servant Joseph, and with his interest support the cause of the poor, and publish the new translation of my holy word unto the inhabitants of the earth.

90 And if he will do this I will bless him with a multiplicity of blessings, that he shall not be forsaken, nor his seed be found begging bread.

91 And again, verily I say unto you, let my servant William be appointed, ordained, and anointed, as counselor unto my servant Joseph, in the room of my servant Hyrum, that my servant Hyrum may take the office of Priesthood and Patriarch, which was appointed unto him by his father, by blessing and also by right;

92 That from henceforth he shall hold the keys of the patriarchal blessings upon the heads of all my people,

93 That whoever he blesses shall be blessed, and whoever he curses shall be cursed; that whatsoever he shall bind on earth shall be bound in heaven; and whatsoever he shall loose on earth shall be loosed in heaven.

94 And from this time forth I appoint unto him that he may be a prophet, and a seer, and a revelator unto my church, as well as my servant Joseph;

95 That he may act in concert also with my servant Joseph; and that he shall receive counsel from my servant Joseph, who shall show unto him the keys whereby he may ask and receive, and be crowned with the same blessing, and glory, and honor, and priesthood, and gifts of the priesthood, that once were put upon him that was my servant Oliver Cowdery;

96 That my servant Hyrum may bear record of the things which I shall show unto him, that his name may be had in honorable remembrance from generation to generation, forever and ever.

97 Let my servant William Law also receive the keys by which he may ask and receive blessings; let him be humble before me, and be without guile, and he shall receive of my Spirit, even the Comforter, which shall manifest unto him the truth of all things, and shall give him, in the very hour, what he shall say.

98 And these signs shall follow him—he shall heal the sick, he shall cast out devils, and shall be delivered from those who would administer unto him deadly poison;

99 And he shall be led in paths where the poisonous serpent cannot lay hold

upon his heel, and he shall mount up in the imagination of his thoughts as upon eagles' wings.

100 And what if I will that he should raise the dead, let him not withhold his voice.

101 Therefore, let my servant William cry aloud and spare not, with joy and rejoicing, and with hosannas to him that sitteth upon the throne forever and ever, saith the Lord your God.

102 Behold, I say unto you, I have a mission in store for my servant William, and my servant Hyrum, and for them alone; and let my servant Joseph tarry at home, for he is needed. The remainder I will show unto you hereafter. Even so. Amen.

103 And again, verily I say unto you, if my servant Sidney will serve me and be counselor unto my servant Joseph, let him arise and come up and stand in the office of his calling, and humble himself before me.

104 And if he will offer unto me an acceptable offering, and acknowledgments, and remain with my people, behold, I, the Lord your God, will heal him that he shall be healed; and he shall lift up his voice again on the mountains, and be a spokesman before my face.

105 Let him come and locate his family in the neighborhood in which my servant Joseph resides.

106 And in all his journeyings let him lift up his voice as with the sound of a trump, and warn the inhabitants of the earth to flee the wrath to come.

107 Let him assist my servant Joseph, and also let my servant William Law assist my servant Joseph, in making a solemn proclamation unto the kings of the earth, even as I have before said unto you.

108 If my servant Sidney will do my will, let him not remove his family unto the eastern lands, but let him change their habitation, even as I have said.

109 Behold, it is not my will that he shall seek to find safety and refuge out of the city which I have appointed unto you, even the city of Nauvoo.

110 Verily I say unto you, even now, if he will hearken unto my voice, it shall be well with him. Even so. Amen.

111 And again, verily I say unto you, let my servant Amos Davies pay stock into the hands of those whom I have appointed to build a house for boarding, even the Nauvoo House.

112 This let him do if he will have an interest; and let him hearken unto the counsel of my servant Joseph, and labor with his own hands that he may obtain the confidence of men.

113 And when he shall prove himself faithful in all things that shall be entrusted unto his care, yea, even a few things, he shall be made ruler over many;

114 Let him therefore abase himself that he may be exalted. Even so. Amen.

115 And again, verily I say unto you, if my servant Robert D. Foster will obey my voice, let him build a house for my servant Joseph, according to the contract which he has made with him, as the door shall be open to him from time to time.

116 And let him repent of all his folly, and clothe himself with charity; and cease to do evil, and lay aside all his hard speeches;

117 And pay stock also into the hands of the quorum of the Nauvoo House, for

himself and for his generation after him, from generation to generation;

118 And hearken unto the counsel of my servants Joseph, and Hyrum, and William Law, and unto the authorities which I have called to lay the foundation of Zion; and it shall be well with him forever and ever. Even so. Amen.

119 And again, verily I say unto you, let no man pay stock to the quorum of the Nauvoo House unless he shall be a believer in the Book of Mormon, and the revelations I have given unto you, saith the Lord your God;

120 For that which is more or less than this cometh of evil, and shall be attended with cursings and not blessings, saith the Lord your God. Even so. Amen.

121 And again, verily I say unto you, let the quorum of the Nauvoo House have a just recompense of wages for all their labors which they do in building the Nauvoo House; and let their wages be as shall be agreed among themselves, as pertaining to the price thereof.

122 And let every man who pays stock bear his proportion of their wages, if it must needs be, for their support, saith the Lord; otherwise, their labors shall be accounted unto them for stock in that house. Even so. Amen.

123 Verily I say unto you, I now give unto you the officers belonging to my Priesthood, that ye may hold the keys thereof, even the Priesthood which is after the order of Melchizedek, which is after the order of mine Only Begotten Son.

124 First, I give unto you Hyrum Smith to be a patriarch unto you, to hold the sealing blessings of my church, even the Holy Spirit of promise, whereby ye are sealed up unto the day of redemption, that ye may not fall notwithstanding the hour of temptation that may come upon you.

125 I give unto you my servant Joseph to be a presiding elder over all my church, to be a translator, a revelator, a seer, and prophet.

126 I give unto him for counselors my servant Sidney Rigdon and my servant William Law, that these may constitute a quorum and First Presidency, to receive the oracles for the whole church.

127 I give unto you my servant Brigham Young to be a president over the Twelve traveling council;

128 Which Twelve hold the keys to open up the authority of my kingdom upon the four corners of the earth, and after that to send my word to every creature.

129 They are Heber C. Kimball, Parley P. Pratt, Orson Pratt, Orson Hyde, William Smith, John Taylor, John E. Page, Wilford Woodruff, Willard Richards, George A. Smith;

130 David Patten I have taken unto myself; behold, his priesthood no man taketh from him; but, verily I say unto you, another may be appointed unto the same calling.

131 And again, I say unto you, I give unto you a high council, for the cornerstone of Zion—

132 Namely, Samuel Bent, Henry G. Sherwood, George W. Harris, Charles C. Rich, Thomas Grover, Newel Knight, David Dort, Dunbar Wilson—Seymour Brunson I have taken unto myself; no man taketh his priesthood, but another may be appointed unto the same priesthood in his stead; and verily I say unto you, let my servant Aaron Johnson be ordained unto this calling in his stead—David Fullmer, Alpheus Cutler, William Huntington.

133 And again, I give unto you Don C. Smith to be a president over a quorum of high priests;

134 Which ordinance is instituted for the purpose of qualifying those who shall be appointed standing presidents or servants over different stakes scattered abroad;

135 And they may travel also if they choose, but rather be ordained for standing presidents; this is the office of their calling, saith the Lord your God.

136 I give unto him Amasa Lyman and Noah Packard for counselors, that they may preside over the quorum of high priests of my church, saith the Lord.

137 And again, I say unto you, I give unto you John A. Hicks, Samuel Williams, and Jesse Baker, which priesthood is to preside over the quorum of elders, which quorum is instituted for standing ministers; nevertheless they may travel, yet they are ordained to be standing ministers to my church, saith the Lord.

138 And again, I give unto you Joseph Young, Josiah Butterfield, Daniel Miles, Henry Herriman, Zera Pulsipher, Levi Hancock, James Foster, to preside over the quorum of seventies;

139 Which quorum is instituted for traveling elders to bear record of my name in all the world, wherever the traveling high council, mine apostles, shall send them to prepare a way before my face.

140 The difference between this quorum and the quorum of elders is that one is to travel continually, and the other is to preside over the churches from time to time; the one has the responsibility of presiding from time to time, and the other has no responsibility of presiding, saith the Lord your God.

141 And again, I say unto you, I give unto you Vinson Knight, Samuel H. Smith, and Shadrach Roundy, if he will receive it, to preside over the bishopric; a knowledge of said bishopric is given unto you in the book of Doctrine and Covenants.

142 And again, I say unto you, Samuel Rolfe and his counselors for priests, and the president of the teachers and his counselors, and also the president of the deacons and his counselors, and also the president of the stake and his counselors.

143 The above offices I have given unto you, and the keys thereof, for helps and for governments, for the work of the ministry and the perfecting of my saints.

144 And a commandment I give unto you, that you should fill all these offices and approve of those names which I have mentioned, or else disapprove of them at my general conference;

145 And that ye should prepare rooms for all these offices in my house when you build it unto my name, saith the Lord your God. Even so. Amen.

Section 125

Revelation given through Joseph Smith the Prophet, at Nauvoo, Illinois, March 1841, concerning the Saints in the territory of Iowa.

1–4, The Saints are to build cities and to gather to the stakes of Zion.

1 What is the will of the Lord concerning the saints in the Territory of Iowa?

2 Verily, thus saith the Lord, I say unto you, if those who call themselves by my name and are essaying to be my saints, if they will do my will and keep my commandments concerning them, let them gather themselves together unto the places which I shall appoint unto them by my servant Joseph, and build up cities unto my name, that they may be prepared for that which is in store for a time to come.

3 Let them build up a city unto my name upon the land opposite the city of Nauvoo, and let the name of Zarahemla be named upon it.

4 And let all those who come from the east, and the west, and the north, and the south, that have desires to dwell therein, take up their inheritance in the same, as well as in the city of Nashville, or in the city of Nauvoo, and in all the stakes which I have appointed, saith the Lord.

Section 126

Revelation given through Joseph Smith the Prophet, in the house of Brigham Young, at Nauvoo, Illinois, July 9, 1841. At this time Brigham Young was President of the Quorum of the Twelve Apostles.

1–3, Brigham Young is commended for his labors and is relieved of future travel abroad.

1 Dear and well-beloved brother, Brigham Young, verily thus saith the Lord unto you: My servant Brigham, it is no more required at your hand to leave your family as in times past, for your offering is acceptable to me.

2 I have seen your labor and toil in journeyings for my name.

3 I therefore command you to send my word abroad, and take especial care of your family from this time, henceforth and forever. Amen.

Section 127

An epistle from Joseph Smith the Prophet to the Latter-day Saints at Nauvoo, Illinois, containing directions on baptism for the dead, dated at Nauvoo, September 1, 1842.

1–4, Joseph Smith glories in persecution and tribulation; 5–12, Records must be kept relative to baptisms for the dead.

1 Forasmuch as the Lord has revealed unto me that my enemies, both in Missouri and this State, were again in the pursuit of me; and inasmuch as they pursue me without a cause, and have not the least shadow or coloring of justice or right on their side in the getting up of their prosecutions against me; and inasmuch as their pretensions are all founded in falsehood of the blackest dye, I have thought it expedient and wisdom in me to leave the place for a short season, for my own safety and the safety of this people. I would say to all those with whom I have business, that I have left my affairs with agents and clerks who will transact all business in a prompt and proper manner, and will see that all my debts are canceled in due time, by turning out property, or otherwise, as the case may require, or as the circumstances may admit of. When I learn that the storm is fully blown over, then I will return to you again.

2 And as for the perils which I am called to pass through, they seem but a small thing to me, as the envy and wrath of man have been my common lot all the days of my life; and for what cause it seems mysterious, unless I was ordained from before the foundation of the world for some good end, or bad, as you may choose to call it. Judge ye for yourselves. God knoweth all these things, whether it be good or bad. But nevertheless, deep water is what I am wont to swim in. It all has become a second nature to me; and I feel, like Paul, to glory in tribulation; for to this day has the God of my fathers delivered me out of them all, and will deliver me from henceforth; for behold, and lo, I shall triumph over all my enemies, for the Lord God hath spoken it.

3 Let all the saints rejoice, therefore, and be exceedingly glad; for Israel's God is their God, and he will mete out a just recompense of reward upon the heads of all their oppressors.

4 And again, verily thus saith the Lord: Let the work of my temple, and all the works which I have appointed unto you, be continued on and not cease; and let your diligence, and your perseverance, and patience, and your works be redoubled, and you shall in nowise lose your reward, saith the Lord of Hosts. And if they persecute you, so persecuted they the prophets and righteous men that were before you. For all this there is a reward in heaven.

5 And again, I give unto you a word in relation to the baptism for your dead.

6 Verily, thus saith the Lord unto you concerning your dead: When any of you are baptized for your dead, let there be a recorder, and let him be eye-witness of your baptisms; let him hear with his ears, that he may testify of a truth, saith the Lord;

7 That in all your recordings it may be recorded in heaven; whatsoever you bind on earth, may be bound in heaven; whatsoever you loose on earth, may be loosed in heaven;

8 For I am about to restore many things to the earth, pertaining to the priesthood, saith the Lord of Hosts.

9 And again, let all the records be had in order, that they may be put in the archives of my holy temple, to be held in remembrance from generation to generation, saith the Lord of Hosts.

10 I will say to all the saints, that I desired, with exceedingly great desire, to have addressed them from the stand on the subject of baptism for the dead, on the following Sabbath. But inasmuch as it is out of my power to do so, I will write the word of the Lord from time to time, on that subject, and send it to you by mail, as well as many other things.

11 I now close my letter for the present, for the want of more time; for the enemy is on the alert, and as the Savior said, the prince of this world cometh, but he hath nothing in me.

12 Behold, my prayer to God is that you all may be saved. And I subscribe myself your servant in the Lord, prophet and seer of The Church of Jesus Christ of Latter-day Saints.

JOSEPH SMITH.

Section 128

An epistle from Joseph Smith the Prophet to The Church of Jesus Christ of Latter-day Saints, containing further directions on baptism for the dead, dated at Nauvoo, Illinois, September 6, 1842.

1–5, Local and general recorders must certify to the fact of baptisms for the dead; 6–9, Their records are binding and recorded on earth and in heaven; 10–14, The baptismal font is a similitude of the grave; 15–17, Elijah restored power relative to baptism for the dead; 18–21, All of the keys, powers, and authorities of past dispensations have been restored; 22–25, Glad and glorious tidings are acclaimed for the living and the dead.

1 As I stated to you in my letter before I left my place, that I would write to you from time to time and give you information in relation to many subjects, I now resume the subject of the baptism for the dead, as that subject seems to occupy my mind, and press itself upon my feelings the strongest, since I have been pursued by my enemies.

2 I wrote a few words of revelation to you concerning a recorder. I have had a few additional views in relation to this matter, which I now certify. That is, it was declared in my former letter that there should be a recorder, who should be eye-witness, and also to hear with his ears, that he might make a record of a truth before the Lord.

3 Now, in relation to this matter, it would be very difficult for one recorder to be present at all times, and to do all the business. To obviate this difficulty, there can be a recorder appointed in each ward of the city, who is well qualified for taking accurate minutes; and let him be very particular and precise in taking the whole proceedings, certifying in his record that he saw with his eyes, and heard with his ears, giving the date, and names, and so forth, and the history of the whole transaction; naming also some three individuals that are present, if there be any present, who can at any time when called upon certify to the same, that in the mouth of two or three witnesses every word may be established.

4 Then, let there be a general recorder, to whom these other records can be handed, being attended with certificates over their own signatures, certifying that the record they have made is true. Then the general church recorder can enter the record on the general church book, with the certificates and all the attending witnesses, with his own statement that he verily believes the above statement and records to be true, from his knowledge of the general character and appointment of those men by the church. And when this is done on the general church book, the record shall be just as holy, and shall answer the ordinance just the same as if he had seen with his eyes and heard with his ears, and made a record of the same on the general church book.

5 You may think this order of things to be very particular; but let me tell you that it is only to answer the will of God, by conforming to the ordinance and preparation that the Lord ordained and prepared before the foundation of the world, for the salvation of the dead who should die without a knowledge of the gospel.

6 And further, I want you to remember that John the Revelator was contemplating this very subject in relation to the dead, when he declared, as you will find recorded in Revelation 20:12—And I saw the dead, small and great, stand before God; and the books were opened; and another book was opened, which is the book of life; and the dead were judged out of those

things which were written in the books, according to their works.

7 You will discover in this quotation that the books were opened; and another book was opened, which was the book of life; but the dead were judged out of those things which were written in the books, according to their works; consequently, the books spoken of must be the books which contained the record of their works, and refer to the records which are kept on the earth. And the book which was the book of life is the record which is kept in heaven; the principle agreeing precisely with the doctrine which is commanded you in the revelation contained in the letter which I wrote to you previous to my leaving my place—that in all your recordings it may be recorded in heaven.

8 Now, the nature of this ordinance consists in the power of the priesthood, by the revelation of Jesus Christ, wherein it is granted that whatsoever you bind on earth shall be bound in heaven, and whatsoever you loose on earth shall be loosed in heaven. Or, in other words, taking a different view of the translation, whatsoever you record on earth shall be recorded in heaven, and whatsoever you do not record on earth shall not be recorded in heaven; for out of the books shall your dead be judged, according to their own works, whether they themselves have attended to the ordinances in their own propria persona, or by the means of their own agents, according to the ordinance which God has prepared for their salvation from before the foundation of the world, according to the records which they have kept concerning their dead.

9 It may seem to somc to be a very bold doctrine that we talk of—a power which records or binds on earth and binds in heaven. Nevertheless, in all ages of the world, whenever the Lord has given a dispensation of the priesthood to any man by actual revelation, or any set of men, this power has always been given. Hence, whatsoever those men did in authority, in the name of the Lord, and did it truly and faithfully, and kept a proper and faithful record of the same, it became a law on earth and in heaven, and could not be annulled, according to the decrees of the great Jehovah. This is a faithful saying. Who can hear it?

10 And again, for the precedent, Matthew 16:18, 19: And I say also unto thee, That thou art Peter, and upon this rock I will build my church; and the gates of hell shall not prevail against it. And I will give unto thee the keys of the kingdom of heaven: and whatsoever thou shalt bind on earth shall be bound in heaven; and whatsoever thou shalt loose on earth shall be loosed in heaven.

11 Now the great and grand secret of the whole matter, and the summum bonum of the whole subject that is lying before us, consists in obtaining the powers of the Holy Priesthood. For him to whom these keys are given there is no difficulty in obtaining a knowledge of facts in relation to the salvation of the children of men, both as well for the dead as for the living.

12 Herein is glory and honor, and immortality and eternal life—The ordinance of baptism by water, to be immersed therein in order to answer to the likeness of the dead, that one principle might accord with the other; to be immersed in the water and come forth out of the water is in the likeness of the resurrection of the dead in coming forth out of their graves; hence, this ordinance was instituted to form a relationship with the ordinance of baptism for the dead, being in likeness of the dead.

13 Consequently, the baptismal font was instituted as a similitude of the grave, and was commanded to be in a place underneath where the living are wont to assemble, to show forth

the living and the dead, and that all things may have their likeness, and that they may accord one with another—that which is earthly conforming to that which is heavenly, as Paul hath declared, 1 Corinthians 15:46, 47, and 48:

14 Howbeit that was not first which is spiritual, but that which is natural; and afterward that which is spiritual. The first man is of the earth, earthy; the second man is the Lord from heaven. As is the earthy, such are they also that are earthy; and as is the heavenly, such are they also that are heavenly. And as are the records on the earth in relation to your dead, which are truly made out, so also are the records in heaven. This, therefore, is the sealing and binding power, and, in one sense of the word, the keys of the kingdom, which consist in the key of knowledge.

15 And now, my dearly beloved brethren and sisters, let me assure you that these are principles in relation to the dead and the living that cannot be lightly passed over, as pertaining to our salvation. For their salvation is necessary and essential to our salvation, as Paul says concerning the fathers—that they without us cannot be made perfect—neither can we without our dead be made perfect.

16 And now, in relation to the baptism for the dead, I will give you another quotation of Paul, 1 Corinthians 15:29: Else what shall they do which are baptized for the dead, if the dead rise not at all? Why are they then baptized for the dead?

17 And again, in connection with this quotation I will give you a quotation from one of the prophets, who had his eye fixed on the restoration of the priesthood, the glories to be revealed in the last days, and in an especial manner this most glorious of all subjects belonging to the everlasting gospel, namely, the baptism for the dead; for Malachi says, last chapter, verses 5th and 6th: Behold, I will send you Elijah the prophet before the coming of the great and dreadful day of the Lord: And he shall turn the heart of the fathers to the children, and the heart of the children to their fathers, lest I come and smite the earth with a curse.

18 I might have rendered a plainer translation to this, but it is sufficiently plain to suit my purpose as it stands. It is sufficient to know, in this case, that the earth will be smitten with a curse unless there is a welding link of some kind or other between the fathers and the children, upon some subject or other—and behold what is that subject? It is the baptism for the dead. For we without them cannot be made perfect; neither can they without us be made perfect. Neither can they nor we be made perfect without those who have died in the gospel also; for it is necessary in the ushering in of the dispensation of the fulness of times, which dispensation is now beginning to usher in, that a whole and complete and perfect union, and welding together of dispensations, and keys, and powers, and glories should take place, and be revealed from the days of Adam even to the present time. And not only this, but those things which never have been revealed from the foundation of the world, but have been kept hid from the wise and prudent, shall be revealed unto babes and sucklings in this, the dispensation of the fulness of times.

19 Now, what do we hear in the gospel which we have received? A voice of gladness! A voice of mercy from heaven; and a voice of truth out of the earth; glad tidings for the dead; a voice of gladness for the living and the dead; glad tidings of great joy. How beautiful upon the mountains are the feet of those that bring glad tidings of good things, and that say unto Zion: Behold, thy God reigneth! As the dews of Carmel, so shall the knowledge of God descend upon them!

20 And again, what do we hear? Glad tidings from Cumorah! Moroni, an angel from heaven, declaring the fulfilment of the prophets—the book to be revealed. A voice of the Lord in the wilderness of Fayette, Seneca county, declaring the three witnesses to bear record of the book! The voice of Michael on the banks of the Susquehanna, detecting the devil when he appeared as an angel of light! The voice of Peter, James, and John in the wilderness between Harmony, Susquehanna county, and Colesville, Broome county, on the Susquehanna river, declaring themselves as possessing the keys of the kingdom, and of the dispensation of the fulness of times!

21 And again, the voice of God in the chamber of old Father Whitmer, in Fayette, Seneca county, and at sundry times, and in divers places through all the travels and tribulations of this Church of Jesus Christ of Latter-day Saints! And the voice of Michael, the archangel; the voice of Gabriel, and of Raphael, and of divers angels, from Michael or Adam down to the present time, all declaring their dispensation, their rights, their keys, their honors, their majesty and glory, and the power of their priesthood; giving line upon line, precept upon precept; here a little, and there a little; giving us consolation by holding forth that which is to come, confirming our hope!

22 Brethren, shall we not go on in so great a cause? Go forward and not backward. Courage, brethren; and on, on to the victory! Let your hearts rejoice, and be exceedingly glad. Let the earth break forth into singing. Let the dead speak forth anthems of eternal praise to the King Immanuel, who hath ordained, before the world was, that which would enable us to redeem them out of their prison; for the prisoners shall go free.

23 Let the mountains shout for joy, and all ye valleys cry aloud; and all ye seas and dry lands tell the wonders of your Eternal King! And ye rivers, and brooks, and rills, flow down with gladness. Let the woods and all the trees of the field praise the Lord; and ye solid rocks weep for joy! And let the sun, moon, and the morning stars sing together, and let all the sons of God shout for joy! And let the eternal creations declare his name forever and ever! And again I say, how glorious is the voice we hear from heaven, proclaiming in our ears, glory, and salvation, and honor, and immortality, and eternal life; kingdoms, principalities, and powers!

24 Behold, the great day of the Lord is at hand; and who can abide the day of his coming, and who can stand when he appeareth? For he is like a refiner's fire, and like fuller's soap; and he shall sit as a refiner and purifier of silver, and he shall purify the sons of Levi, and purge them as gold and silver, that they may offer unto the Lord an offering in righteousness. Let us, therefore, as a church and a people, and as Latter-day Saints, offer unto the Lord an offering in righteousness; and let us present in his holy temple, when it is finished, a book containing the records of our dead, which shall be worthy of all acceptation.

25 Brethren, I have many things to say to you on the subject; but shall now close for the present, and continue the subject another time. I am, as ever, your humble servant and never deviating friend,

JOSEPH SMITH.

Section 129

Instructions given by Joseph Smith the Prophet, at Nauvoo, Illinois, February 9, 1843, making known three grand keys by which the correct nature of ministering angels and spirits may be distinguished.

1–3, There are both resurrected and spirit bodies in heaven; 4–9, Keys are given whereby messengers from beyond the veil may be identified.

1 There are two kinds of beings in heaven, namely: Angels, who are resurrected personages, having bodies of flesh and bones—

2 For instance, Jesus said: Handle me and see, for a spirit hath not flesh and bones, as ye see me have.

3 Secondly: the spirits of just men made perfect, they who are not resurrected, but inherit the same glory.

4 When a messenger comes saying he has a message from God, offer him your hand and request him to shake hands with you.

5 If he be an angel he will do so, and you will feel his hand.

6 If he be the spirit of a just man made perfect he will come in his glory; for that is the only way he can appear—

7 Ask him to shake hands with you, but he will not move, because it is contrary to the order of heaven for a just man to deceive; but he will still deliver his message.

8 If it be the devil as an angel of light, when you ask him to shake hands he will offer you his hand, and you will not feel anything; you may therefore detect him.

9 These are three grand keys whereby you may know whether any administration is from God.

Section 130

Items of instruction given by Joseph Smith the Prophet, at Ramus, Illinois, April 2, 1843.

1–3, The Father and the Son may appear personally to men; 4–7, Angels reside in a celestial sphere; 8–9, The celestial earth will be a great Urim and Thummim; 10–11, A white stone is given to all who enter the celestial world; 12–17, The time of the Second Coming is withheld from the Prophet; 18–19, Intelligence gained in this life rises with us in the Resurrection; 20–21, All blessings come by obedience to law; 22–23, The Father and the Son have bodies of flesh and bones.

1 When the Savior shall appear we shall see him as he is. We shall see that he is a man like ourselves.

2 And that same sociality which exists among us here will exist among us there, only it will be coupled with eternal glory, which glory we do not now enjoy.

3 John 14:23—The appearing of the Father and the Son, in that verse, is a personal appearance; and the idea that the Father and the Son dwell in a man's heart is an old sectarian notion, and is false.

4 In answer to the question—Is not the reckoning of God's time, angel's time, prophet's time, and man's time, according to the planet on which they reside?

5 I answer, Yes. But there are no angels who minister to this earth but those who do belong or have belonged to it.

6 The angels do not reside on a planet like this earth;

7 But they reside in the presence of God, on a globe like a sea of glass and fire, where all things for their glory are manifest, past, present, and future, and are continually before the Lord.

8 The place where God resides is a great Urim and Thummim.

9 This earth, in its sanctified and immortal state, will be made like unto crystal and will be a Urim and Thummim to the inhabitants who dwell thereon, whereby all things pertaining to an inferior kingdom, or all kingdoms of a lower order, will be manifest to those who dwell on it; and this earth will be Christ's.

10 Then the white stone mentioned in Revelation 2:17, will become a Urim and Thummim to each individual who receives one, whereby things pertaining to a higher order of kingdoms will be made known;

11 And a white stone is given to each of those who come into the celestial kingdom, whereon is a new name written, which no man knoweth save he that receiveth it. The new name is the key word.

12 I prophesy, in the name of the Lord God, that the commencement of the difficulties which will cause much bloodshed previous to the coming of the Son of Man will be in South Carolina.

13 It may probably arise through the slave question. This a voice declared to me, while I was praying earnestly on the subject, December 25th, 1832.

14 I was once praying very earnestly to know the time of the coming of the Son of Man, when I heard a voice repeat the following:

15 Joseph, my son, if thou livest until thou art eighty-five years old, thou shalt see the face of the Son of Man; therefore let this suffice, and trouble me no more

on this matter.

16 I was left thus, without being able to decide whether this coming referred to the beginning of the millennium or to some previous appearing, or whether I should die and thus see his face.

17 I believe the coming of the Son of Man will not be any sooner than that time.

18 Whatever principle of intelligence we attain unto in this life, it will rise with us in the resurrection.

19 And if a person gains more knowledge and intelligence in this life through his diligence and obedience than another, he will have so much the advantage in the world to come.

20 There is a law, irrevocably decreed in heaven before the foundations of this world, upon which all blessings are predicated—

21 And when we obtain any blessing from God, it is by obedience to that law upon which it is predicated.

22 The Father has a body of flesh and bones as tangible as man's; the Son also; but the Holy Ghost has not a body of flesh and bones, but is a personage of Spirit. Were it not so, the Holy Ghost could not dwell in us.

23 A man may receive the Holy Ghost, and it may descend upon him and not tarry with him.

Section 131

Instructions by Joseph Smith the Prophet, given at Ramus, Illinois, May 16 and 17, 1843.

1–4, Celestial marriage is essential to exaltation in the highest heaven; 5–6, How men are sealed up unto eternal life is explained; 7–8, All spirit is matter.

1 In the celestial glory there are three heavens or degrees;

2 And in order to obtain the highest, a man must enter into this order of the priesthood [meaning the new and everlasting covenant of marriage];

3 And if he does not, he cannot obtain it.

4 He may enter into the other, but that is the end of his kingdom; he cannot have an increase.

5 (May 17th, 1843.) The more sure word of prophecy means a man's knowing that he is sealed up unto eternal life, by revelation and the spirit of prophecy, through the power of the Holy Priesthood.

6 It is impossible for a man to be saved in ignorance.

7 There is no such thing as immaterial matter. All spirit is matter, but it is more fine or pure, and can only be discerned by purer eyes;

8 We cannot see it; but when our bodies are purified we shall see that it is all matter.

Section 132

Revelation given through Joseph Smith the Prophet, at Nauvoo, Illinois, recorded July 12, 1843, relating to the new and everlasting covenant, including the eternity of the marriage covenant and the principle of plural marriage. Although the revelation was recorded in 1843, evidence indicates that some of the principles involved in this revelation were known by the Prophet as early as 1831. See Official Declaration 1.

1–6, Exaltation is gained through the new and everlasting covenant; 7–14, The terms and conditions of that covenant are set forth; 15–20, Celestial marriage and a continuation of the family unit enable men to become gods; 21–25, The strait and narrow way leads to eternal lives; 26–27, The law is given relative to blasphemy against the Holy Ghost; 28–39, Promises of eternal increase and exaltation are made to prophets and Saints in all ages; 40–47, Joseph Smith is given the power to bind and seal on earth and in heaven; 48–50, The Lord seals upon him his exaltation; 51–57, Emma Smith is counseled to be faithful and true; 58–66, Laws governing plural marriage are set forth.

1 Verily, thus saith the Lord unto you my servant Joseph, that inasmuch as you have inquired of my hand to know and understand wherein I, the Lord, justified my servants Abraham, Isaac, and Jacob, as also Moses, David and Solomon, my servants, as touching the principle and doctrine of their having many wives and concubines—

2 Behold, and lo, I am the Lord thy God, and will answer thee as touching this matter.

3 Therefore, prepare thy heart to receive and obey the instructions which I am about to give unto you; for all those who have this law revealed unto them must obey the same.

4 For behold, I reveal unto you a new and an everlasting covenant; and if ye abide not that covenant, then are ye damned; for no one can reject this covenant and be permitted to enter into my glory.

5 For all who will have a blessing at my hands shall abide the law which was appointed for that blessing, and the conditions thereof, as were instituted from before the foundation of the world.

6 And as pertaining to the new and everlasting covenant, it was instituted for the fulness of my glory; and he that receiveth a fulness thereof must and shall abide the law, or he shall be damned, saith the Lord God.

7 And verily I say unto you, that the conditions of this law are these: All covenants, contracts, bonds, obligations, oaths, vows, performances, connections, associations, or expectations, that are not made and entered into and sealed by the Holy Spirit of promise, of him who is anointed, both as well for time and for all eternity, and that too most holy, by revelation and commandment through the medium of mine anointed, whom I have appointed on the earth to hold this power (and I have appointed unto my servant Joseph to hold this power in the last days, and there is never but one on the earth at a time on whom this power and the keys of this priesthood are conferred), are of no efficacy, virtue, or force in and after the resurrection from the dead; for all contracts that are not made unto this end have an end when men are dead.

8 Behold, mine house is a house of order, saith the Lord God, and not a house of confusion.

9 Will I accept of an offering, saith the Lord, that is not made in my name?

10 Or will I receive at your hands that which I have not appointed?

11 And will I appoint unto you, saith the Lord, except it be by law, even as I and my Father ordained unto you, before the world was?

12 I am the Lord thy God; and I give unto you this commandment—that no man shall come unto the Father but by me or by my word, which is my law, saith the Lord.

13 And everything that is in the world, whether it be ordained of men, by thrones, or principalities, or powers, or things of name, whatsoever they may be, that are not by me or by my word, saith the Lord, shall be thrown down, and shall not remain after men are dead, neither in nor after the resurrection, saith the Lord your God.

14 For whatsoever things remain are by me; and whatsoever things are not by me shall be shaken and destroyed.

15 Therefore, if a man marry him a wife in the world, and he marry her not by me nor by my word, and he covenant with her so long as he is in the world and she with him, their covenant and marriage are not of force when they are dead, and when they are out of the world; therefore, they are not bound by any law when they are out of the world.

16 Therefore, when they are out of the world they neither marry nor are given in marriage; but are appointed angels in heaven, which angels are ministering servants, to minister for those who are worthy of a far more, and an exceeding, and an eternal weight of glory.

17 For these angels did not abide my law; therefore, they cannot be enlarged, but remain separately and singly, without exaltation, in their saved condition, to all eternity; and from henceforth are not gods, but are angels of God forever and ever.

18 And again, verily I say unto you, if a man marry a wife, and make a covenant with her for time and for all eternity, if that covenant is not by me or by my word, which is my law, and is not sealed by the Holy Spirit of promise, through him whom I have anointed and appointed unto this power, then it is not valid neither of force when they are out of the world, because they are not joined by me, saith the Lord, neither by my word; when they are out of the world it cannot be received there, because the angels and the gods are appointed there, by whom they cannot pass; they cannot, therefore, inherit my glory; for my house is a house of order, saith the Lord God.

19 And again, verily I say unto you, if a man marry a wife by my word, which is my law, and by the new and everlasting covenant, and it is sealed unto them by the Holy Spirit of promise, by him who is anointed, unto whom I have appointed this power and the keys of this priesthood; and it shall be said unto them—Ye shall come forth in the first resurrection; and if it be after the first resurrection, in the next resurrection; and shall inherit thrones, kingdoms, principalities, and powers, dominions, all heights and depths—then shall it be written in the Lamb's Book of Life, that he shall commit no murder whereby to shed innocent blood, and if ye abide in my covenant, and commit no murder whereby to shed innocent blood, it shall be done unto them in all things whatsoever my servant hath put upon them, in time, and through all eternity; and shall be of full force when they are out of the world; and they shall pass by the angels, and the gods, which are set there, to their exaltation and glory in all things, as hath been sealed upon their heads, which glory shall be a fulness and a continuation of the seeds forever and ever.

20 Then shall they be gods, because they have no end; therefore shall they be from everlasting to everlasting, because they continue; then shall they be above

all, because all things are subject unto them. Then shall they be gods, because they have all power, and the angels are subject unto them.

21 Verily, verily, I say unto you, except ye abide my law ye cannot attain to this glory.

22 For strait is the gate, and narrow the way that leadeth unto the exaltation and continuation of the lives, and few there be that find it, because ye receive me not in the world neither do ye know me.

23 But if ye receive me in the world, then shall ye know me, and shall receive your exaltation; that where I am ye shall be also.

24 This is eternal lives—to know the only wise and true God, and Jesus Christ, whom he hath sent. I am he. Receive ye, therefore, my law.

25 Broad is the gate, and wide the way that leadeth to the deaths; and many there are that go in thereat, because they receive me not, neither do they abide in my law.

26 Verily, verily, I say unto you, if a man marry a wife according to my word, and they are sealed by the Holy Spirit of promise, according to mine appointment, and he or she shall commit any sin or transgression of the new and everlasting covenant whatever, and all manner of blasphemies, and if they commit no murder wherein they shed innocent blood, yet they shall come forth in the first resurrection, and enter into their exaltation; but they shall be destroyed in the flesh, and shall be delivered unto the buffetings of Satan unto the day of redemption, saith the Lord God.

27 The blasphemy against the Holy Ghost, which shall not be forgiven in the world nor out of the world, is in that ye commit murder wherein ye shed innocent blood, and assent unto my death, after ye have received my new and everlasting covenant, saith the Lord God; and he that abideth not this law can in nowise enter into my glory, but shall be damned, saith the Lord.

28 I am the Lord thy God, and will give unto thee the law of my Holy Priesthood, as was ordained by me and my Father before the world was.

29 Abraham received all things, whatsoever he received, by revelation and commandment, by my word, saith the Lord, and hath entered into his exaltation and sitteth upon his throne.

30 Abraham received promises concerning his seed, and of the fruit of his loins—from whose loins ye are, namely, my servant Joseph—which were to continue so long as they were in the world; and as touching Abraham and his seed, out of the world they should continue; both in the world and out of the world should they continue as innumerable as the stars; or, if ye were to count the sand upon the seashore ye could not number them.

31 This promise is yours also, because ye are of Abraham, and the promise was made unto Abraham; and by this law is the continuation of the works of my Father, wherein he glorifieth himself.

32 Go ye, therefore, and do the works of Abraham; enter ye into my law and ye shall be saved.

33 But if ye enter not into my law ye cannot receive the promise of my Father, which he made unto Abraham.

34 God commanded Abraham, and Sarah gave Hagar to Abraham to wife. And why did she do it? Because this was the law; and from Hagar sprang many people. This, therefore, was fulfilling, among other things, the promises.

35 Was Abraham, therefore, under condemnation? Verily I say unto you, Nay; for I, the Lord, commanded it.

36 Abraham was commanded to offer his son Isaac; nevertheless, it was written: Thou shalt not kill. Abraham, however, did not refuse, and it was accounted unto him for righteousness.

37 Abraham received concubines, and they bore him children; and it was accounted unto him for righteousness, because they were given unto him, and he abode in my law; as Isaac also and Jacob did none other things than that which they were commanded; and because they did none other things than that which they were commanded, they have entered into their exaltation, according to the promises, and sit upon thrones, and are not angels but are gods.

38 David also received many wives and concubines, and also Solomon and Moses my servants, as also many others of my servants, from the beginning of creation until this time; and in nothing did they sin save in those things which they received not of me.

39 David's wives and concubines were given unto him of me, by the hand of Nathan, my servant, and others of the prophets who had the keys of this power; and in none of these things did he sin against me save in the case of Uriah and his wife; and, therefore he hath fallen from his exaltation, and received his portion; and he shall not inherit them out of the world, for I gave them unto another, saith the Lord.

40 I am the Lord thy God, and I gave unto thee, my servant Joseph, an appointment, and restore all things. Ask what ye will, and it shall be given unto you according to my word.

41 And as ye have asked concerning adultery, verily, verily, I say unto you, if a man receiveth a wife in the new and everlasting covenant, and if she be with another man, and I have not appointed unto her by the holy anointing, she hath committed adultery and shall be destroyed.

42 If she be not in the new and everlasting covenant, and she be with another man, she has committed adultery.

43 And if her husband be with another woman, and he was under a vow, he hath broken his vow and hath committed adultery.

44 And if she hath not committed adultery, but is innocent and hath not broken her vow, and she knoweth it, and I reveal it unto you, my servant Joseph, then shall you have power, by the power of my Holy Priesthood, to take her and give her unto him that hath not committed adultery but hath been faithful; for he shall be made ruler over many.

45 For I have conferred upon you the keys and power of the priesthood, wherein I restore all things, and make known unto you all things in due time.

46 And verily, verily, I say unto you, that whatsoever you seal on earth shall be sealed in heaven; and whatsoever you bind on earth, in my name and by my word, saith the Lord, it shall be eternally bound in the heavens; and whosesoever sins you remit on earth shall be remitted eternally in the heavens; and whosesoever sins you retain on earth shall be retained in heaven.

47 And again, verily I say, whomsoever you bless I will bless, and whomsoever you curse I will curse, saith the Lord; for I, the Lord, am thy God.

48 And again, verily I say unto you, my servant Joseph, that whatsoever you give on earth, and to whomsoever you

give any one on earth, by my word and according to my law, it shall be visited with blessings and not cursings, and with my power, saith the Lord, and shall be without condemnation on earth and in heaven.

49 For I am the Lord thy God, and will be with thee even unto the end of the world, and through all eternity; for verily I seal upon you your exaltation, and prepare a throne for you in the kingdom of my Father, with Abraham your father.

50 Behold, I have seen your sacrifices, and will forgive all your sins; I have seen your sacrifices in obedience to that which I have told you. Go, therefore, and I make a way for your escape, as I accepted the offering of Abraham of his son Isaac.

51 Verily, I say unto you: A commandment I give unto mine handmaid, Emma Smith, your wife, whom I have given unto you, that she stay herself and partake not of that which I commanded you to offer unto her; for I did it, saith the Lord, to prove you all, as I did Abraham, and that I might require an offering at your hand, by covenant and sacrifice.

52 And let mine handmaid, Emma Smith, receive all those that have been given unto my servant Joseph, and who are virtuous and pure before me; and those who are not pure, and have said they were pure, shall be destroyed, saith the Lord God.

53 For I am the Lord thy God, and ye shall obey my voice; and I give unto my servant Joseph that he shall be made ruler over many things; for he hath been faithful over a few things, and from henceforth I will strengthen him.

54 And I command mine handmaid, Emma Smith, to abide and cleave unto my servant Joseph, and to none else. But if she will not abide this commandment she shall be destroyed, saith the Lord; for I am the Lord thy God, and will destroy her if she abide not in my law.

55 But if she will not abide this commandment, then shall my servant Joseph do all things for her, even as he hath said; and I will bless him and multiply him and give unto him an hundred-fold in this world, of fathers and mothers, brothers and sisters, houses and lands, wives and children, and crowns of eternal lives in the eternal worlds.

56 And again, verily I say, let mine handmaid forgive my servant Joseph his trespasses; and then shall she be forgiven her trespasses, wherein she has trespassed against me; and I, the Lord thy God, will bless her, and multiply her, and make her heart to rejoice.

57 And again, I say, let not my servant Joseph put his property out of his hands, lest an enemy come and destroy him; for Satan seeketh to destroy; for I am the Lord thy God, and he is my servant; and behold, and lo, I am with him, as I was with Abraham, thy father, even unto his exaltation and glory.

58 Now, as touching the law of the priesthood, there are many things pertaining thereunto.

59 Verily, if a man be called of my Father, as was Aaron, by mine own voice, and by the voice of him that sent me, and I have endowed him with the keys of the power of this priesthood, if he do anything in my name, and according to my law and by my word, he will not commit sin, and I will justify him.

60 Let no one, therefore, set on my servant Joseph; for I will justify him; for he shall do the sacrifice which I require at his hands for his transgressions, saith

the Lord your God.

61 And again, as pertaining to the law of the priesthood—if any man espouse a virgin, and desire to espouse another, and the first give her consent, and if he espouse the second, and they are virgins, and have vowed to no other man, then is he justified; he cannot commit adultery for they are given unto him; for he cannot commit adultery with that that belongeth unto him and to no one else.

62 And if he have ten virgins given unto him by this law, he cannot commit adultery, for they belong to him, and they are given unto him; therefore is he justified.

63 But if one or either of the ten virgins, after she is espoused, shall be with another man, she has committed adultery, and shall be destroyed; for they are given unto him to multiply and replenish the earth, according to my commandment, and to fulfil the promise which was given by my Father before the foundation of the world, and for their exaltation in the eternal worlds, that they may bear the souls of men; for herein is the work of my Father continued, that he may be glorified.

64 And again, verily, verily, I say unto you, if any man have a wife, who holds the keys of this power, and he teaches unto her the law of my priesthood, as pertaining to these things, then shall she believe and administer unto him, or she shall be destroyed, saith the Lord your God; for I will destroy her; for I will magnify my name upon all those who receive and abide in my law.

65 Therefore, it shall be lawful in me, if she receive not this law, for him to receive all things whatsoever I, the Lord his God, will give unto him, because she did not believe and administer unto him according to my word; and she then becomes the transgressor; and he is exempt from the law of Sarah, who administered unto Abraham according to the law when I commanded Abraham to take Hagar to wife.

66 And now, as pertaining to this law, verily, verily, I say unto you, I will reveal more unto you, hereafter; therefore, let this suffice for the present. Behold, I am Alpha and Omega. Amen.

Section 133

Revelation given through Joseph Smith the Prophet, at Hiram, Ohio, November 3, 1831. Prefacing this revelation, Joseph Smith's history states, "At this time there were many things which the Elders desired to know relative to preaching the Gospel to the inhabitants of the earth, and concerning the gathering; and in order to walk by the true light, and be instructed from on high, on the 3rd of November, 1831, I inquired of the Lord and received the following important revelation." This section was first added to the book of Doctrine and Covenants as an appendix and was subsequently assigned a section number.

1–6, The Saints are commanded to prepare for the Second Coming; 7–16, All men are commanded to flee from Babylon, come to Zion, and prepare for the great day of the Lord; 17–35, He will stand on Mount Zion, the continents will become one land, and the lost tribes of Israel will return; 36–40, The gospel was restored through Joseph Smith to be preached in all the world; 41–51, The Lord will come down in vengeance upon the wicked; 52–56, It will be the year of His redeemed; 57–74, The gospel is to be sent forth to save the Saints and for the destruction of the wicked.

1 Hearken, O ye people of my church, saith the Lord your God, and hear the word of the Lord concerning you—

2 The Lord who shall suddenly come to his temple; the Lord who shall come down upon the world with a curse to judgment; yea, upon all the nations that forget God, and upon all the ungodly among you.

3 For he shall make bare his holy arm in the eyes of all the nations, and all the ends of the earth shall see the salvation of their God.

4 Wherefore, prepare ye, prepare ye, O my people; sanctify yourselves; gather ye together, O ye people of my church, upon the land of Zion, all you that have not been commanded to tarry.

5 Go ye out from Babylon. Be ye clean that bear the vessels of the Lord.

6 Call your solemn assemblies, and speak often one to another. And let every man call upon the name of the Lord.

7 Yea, verily I say unto you again, the time has come when the voice of the Lord is unto you: Go ye out of Babylon; gather ye out from among the nations, from the four winds, from one end of heaven to the other.

8 Send forth the elders of my church unto the nations which are afar off; unto the islands of the sea; send forth unto foreign lands; call upon all nations, first upon the Gentiles, and then upon the Jews.

9 And behold, and lo, this shall be their cry, and the voice of the Lord unto all people: Go ye forth unto the land of Zion, that the borders of my people may be enlarged, and that her stakes may be strengthened, and that Zion may go forth unto the regions round about.

10 Yea, let the cry go forth among all people: Awake and arise and go forth to meet the Bridegroom; behold and lo, the Bridegroom cometh; go ye out to meet him. Prepare yourselves for the great day of the Lord.

11 Watch, therefore, for ye know neither the day nor the hour.

12 Let them, therefore, who are among the Gentiles flee unto Zion.

13 And let them who be of Judah flee unto Jerusalem, unto the mountains of the Lord's house.

14 Go ye out from among the nations,

even from Babylon, from the midst of wickedness, which is spiritual Babylon.

15 But verily, thus saith the Lord, let not your flight be in haste, but let all things be prepared before you; and he that goeth, let him not look back lest sudden destruction shall come upon him.

16 Hearken and hear, O ye inhabitants of the earth. Listen, ye elders of my church together, and hear the voice of the Lord; for he calleth upon all men, and he commandeth all men everywhere to repent.

17 For behold, the Lord God hath sent forth the angel crying through the midst of heaven, saying: Prepare ye the way of the Lord, and make his paths straight, for the hour of his coming is nigh—

18 When the Lamb shall stand upon Mount Zion, and with him a hundred and forty-four thousand, having his Father's name written on their foreheads.

19 Wherefore, prepare ye for the coming of the Bridegroom; go ye, go ye out to meet him.

20 For behold, he shall stand upon the mount of Olivet, and upon the mighty ocean, even the great deep, and upon the islands of the sea, and upon the land of Zion.

21 And he shall utter his voice out of Zion, and he shall speak from Jerusalem, and his voice shall be heard among all people;

22 And it shall be a voice as the voice of many waters, and as the voice of a great thunder, which shall break down the mountains, and the valleys shall not be found.

23 He shall command the great deep, and it shall be driven back into the north countries, and the islands shall become one land;

24 And the land of Jerusalem and the land of Zion shall be turned back into their own place, and the earth shall be like as it was in the days before it was divided.

25 And the Lord, even the Savior, shall stand in the midst of his people, and shall reign over all flesh.

26 And they who are in the north countries shall come in remembrance before the Lord; and their prophets shall hear his voice, and shall no longer stay themselves; and they shall smite the rocks, and the ice shall flow down at their presence.

27 And an highway shall be cast up in the midst of the great deep.

28 Their enemies shall become a prey unto them,

29 And in the barren deserts there shall come forth pools of living water; and the parched ground shall no longer be a thirsty land.

30 And they shall bring forth their rich treasures unto the children of Ephraim, my servants.

31 And the boundaries of the everlasting hills shall tremble at their presence.

32 And there shall they fall down and be crowned with glory, even in Zion, by the hands of the servants of the Lord, even the children of Ephraim.

33 And they shall be filled with songs of everlasting joy.

34 Behold, this is the blessing of the everlasting God upon the tribes of Israel, and the richer blessing upon the head of Ephraim and his fellows.

35 And they also of the tribe of Judah, after their pain, shall be sanctified in holiness before the Lord, to dwell in his presence day and night, forever and ever.

36 And now, verily saith the Lord, that these things might be known among you, O inhabitants of the earth, I have sent forth mine angel flying through the midst of heaven, having the everlasting gospel, who hath appeared unto some and hath committed it unto man, who shall appear unto many that dwell on the earth.

37 And this gospel shall be preached unto every nation, and kindred, and tongue, and people.

38 And the servants of God shall go forth, saying with a loud voice: Fear God and give glory to him, for the hour of his judgment is come;

39 And worship him that made heaven, and earth, and the sea, and the fountains of waters—

40 Calling upon the name of the Lord day and night, saying: O that thou wouldst rend the heavens, that thou wouldst come down, that the mountains might flow down at thy presence.

41 And it shall be answered upon their heads; for the presence of the Lord shall be as the melting fire that burneth, and as the fire which causeth the waters to boil.

42 O Lord, thou shalt come down to make thy name known to thine adversaries, and all nations shall tremble at thy presence—

43 When thou doest terrible things, things they look not for;

44 Yea, when thou comest down, and the mountains flow down at thy presence, thou shalt meet him who rejoiceth and worketh righteousness, who remembereth thee in thy ways.

45 For since the beginning of the world have not men heard nor perceived by the ear, neither hath any eye seen, O God, besides thee, how great things thou hast prepared for him that waiteth for thee.

46 And it shall be said: Who is this that cometh down from God in heaven with dyed garments; yea, from the regions which are not known, clothed in his glorious apparel, traveling in the greatness of his strength?

47 And he shall say: I am he who spake in righteousness, mighty to save.

48 And the Lord shall be red in his apparel, and his garments like him that treadeth in the wine-vat.

49 And so great shall be the glory of his presence that the sun shall hide his face in shame, and the moon shall withhold its light, and the stars shall be hurled from their places.

50 And his voice shall be heard: I have trodden the wine-press alone, and have brought judgment upon all people; and none were with me;

51 And I have trampled them in my fury, and I did tread upon them in mine anger, and their blood have I sprinkled upon my garments, and stained all my raiment; for this was the day of vengeance which was in my heart.

52 And now the year of my redeemed is come; and they shall mention the loving kindness of their Lord, and all that he has bestowed upon them according to his goodness, and according to his loving kindness, forever and ever.

53 In all their afflictions he was afflicted. And the angel of his presence saved them; and in his love, and in his pity,

he redeemed them, and bore them, and carried them all the days of old;

54 Yea, and Enoch also, and they who were with him; the prophets who were before him; and Noah also, and they who were before him; and Moses also, and they who were before him;

55 And from Moses to Elijah, and from Elijah to John, who were with Christ in his resurrection, and the holy apostles, with Abraham, Isaac, and Jacob, shall be in the presence of the Lamb.

56 And the graves of the saints shall be opened; and they shall come forth and stand on the right hand of the Lamb, when he shall stand upon Mount Zion, and upon the holy city, the New Jerusalem; and they shall sing the song of the Lamb, day and night forever and ever.

57 And for this cause, that men might be made partakers of the glories which were to be revealed, the Lord sent forth the fulness of his gospel, his everlasting covenant, reasoning in plainness and simplicity—

58 To prepare the weak for those things which are coming on the earth, and for the Lord's errand in the day when the weak shall confound the wise, and the little one become a strong nation, and two shall put their tens of thousands to flight.

59 And by the weak things of the earth the Lord shall thresh the nations by the power of his Spirit.

60 And for this cause these commandments were given; they were commanded to be kept from the world in the day that they were given, but now are to go forth unto all flesh—

61 And this according to the mind and will of the Lord, who ruleth over all flesh.

62 And unto him that repenteth and sanctifieth himself before the Lord shall be given eternal life.

63 And upon them that hearken not to the voice of the Lord shall be fulfilled that which was written by the prophet Moses, that they should be cut off from among the people.

64 And also that which was written by the prophet Malachi: For, behold, the day cometh that shall burn as an oven, and all the proud, yea, and all that do wickedly, shall be stubble; and the day that cometh shall burn them up, saith the Lord of hosts, that it shall leave them neither root nor branch.

65 Wherefore, this shall be the answer of the Lord unto them:

66 In that day when I came unto mine own, no man among you received me, and you were driven out.

67 When I called again there was none of you to answer; yet my arm was not shortened at all that I could not redeem, neither my power to deliver.

68 Behold, at my rebuke I dry up the sea. I make the rivers a wilderness; their fish stink, and die for thirst.

69 I clothe the heavens with blackness, and make sackcloth their covering.

70 And this shall ye have of my hand—ye shall lie down in sorrow.

71 Behold, and lo, there are none to deliver you; for ye obeyed not my voice when I called to you out of the heavens; ye believed not my servants, and when they were sent unto you ye received them not.

72 Wherefore, they sealed up the testimony and bound up the law, and ye were delivered over unto darkness.

73 These shall go away into outer
darkness, where there is weeping, and
wailing, and gnashing of teeth.

74 Behold the Lord your God hath
spoken it. Amen.

Section 134

A declaration of belief regarding governments and laws in general, adopted by unanimous vote at a general assembly of the Church held at Kirtland, Ohio, August 17, 1835. Many Saints gathered together to consider the proposed contents of the first edition of the Doctrine and Covenants. At that time, this declaration was given the following preamble: "That our belief with regard to earthly governments and laws in general may not be misinterpreted nor misunderstood, we have thought proper to present, at the close of this volume, our opinion concerning the same."

1–4, Governments should preserve freedom of conscience and worship; 5–8, All men should uphold their governments and owe respect and deference to the law; 9–10, Religious societies should not exercise civil powers; 11–12, Men are justified in defending themselves and their property.

1 We believe that governments were instituted of God for the benefit of man; and that he holds men accountable for their acts in relation to them, both in making laws and administering them, for the good and safety of society.

2 We believe that no government can exist in peace, except such laws are framed and held inviolate as will secure to each individual the free exercise of conscience, the right and control of property, and the protection of life.

3 We believe that all governments necessarily require civil officers and magistrates to enforce the laws of the same; and that such as will administer the law in equity and justice should be sought for and upheld by the voice of the people if a republic, or the will of the sovereign.

4 We believe that religion is instituted of God; and that men are amenable to him, and to him only, for the exercise of it, unless their religious opinions prompt them to infringe upon the rights and liberties of others; but we do not believe that human law has a right to interfere in prescribing rules of worship to bind the consciences of men, nor dictate forms for public or private devotion; that the civil magistrate should restrain crime, but never control conscience; should punish guilt, but never suppress the freedom of the soul.

5 We believe that all men are bound to sustain and uphold the respective governments in which they reside, while protected in their inherent and inalienable rights by the laws of such governments; and that sedition and rebellion are unbecoming every citizen thus protected, and should be punished accordingly; and that all governments have a right to enact such laws as in their own judgments are best calculated to secure the public interest; at the same time, however, holding sacred the freedom of conscience.

6 We believe that every man should be honored in his station, rulers and magistrates as such, being placed for the protection of the innocent and the punishment of the guilty; and that to the laws all men owe respect and deference, as without them peace and harmony would be supplanted by anarchy and terror; human laws being instituted for the express purpose of regulating our interests as individuals and nations, between man and man; and divine laws given of heaven, prescribing rules on spiritual concerns, for faith and worship, both to be answered by man to his Maker.

7 We believe that rulers, states, and governments have a right, and are bound to enact laws for the protection of all citizens in the free exercise of their religious belief; but we do not believe that they have a right in justice to deprive citizens of this privilege, or proscribe them in their opinions, so long as a regard and reverence are shown to the laws and such religious

opinions do not justify sedition nor conspiracy.

8 We believe that the commission of crime should be punished according to the nature of the offense; that murder, treason, robbery, theft, and the breach of the general peace, in all respects, should be punished according to their criminality and their tendency to evil among men, by the laws of that government in which the offense is committed; and for the public peace and tranquility all men should step forward and use their ability in bringing offenders against good laws to punishment.

9 We do not believe it just to mingle religious influence with civil government, whereby one religious society is fostered and another proscribed in its spiritual privileges, and the individual rights of its members, as citizens, denied.

10 We believe that all religious societies have a right to deal with their members for disorderly conduct, according to the rules and regulations of such societies; provided that such dealings be for fellowship and good standing; but we do not believe that any religious society has authority to try men on the right of property or life, to take from them this world's goods, or to put them in jeopardy of either life or limb, or to inflict any physical punishment upon them. They can only excommunicate them from their society, and withdraw from them their fellowship.

11 We believe that men should appeal to the civil law for redress of all wrongs and grievances, where personal abuse is inflicted or the right of property or character infringed, where such laws exist as will protect the same; but we believe that all men are justified in defending themselves, their friends, and property, and the government, from the unlawful assaults and encroachments of all persons in times of exigency, where immediate appeal cannot be made to the laws, and relief afforded.

12 We believe it just to preach the gospel to the nations of the earth, and warn the righteous to save themselves from the corruption of the world; but we do not believe it right to interfere with bond-servants, neither preach the gospel to, nor baptize them contrary to the will and wish of their masters, nor to meddle with or influence them in the least to cause them to be dissatisfied with their situations in this life, thereby jeopardizing the lives of men; such interference we believe to be unlawful and unjust, and dangerous to the peace of every government allowing human beings to be held in servitude.

Section 135

Announcement of the martyrdom of Joseph Smith the Prophet and his brother, Hyrum Smith the Patriarch, at Carthage, Illinois, June 27, 1844. This document was included at the end of the 1844 edition of the Doctrine and Covenants, which was nearly ready for publication when Joseph and Hyrum Smith were murdered.

1–2, Joseph and Hyrum martyred in Carthage Jail; 3, The preeminent position of the Prophet is acclaimed; 4–7, Their innocent blood testifies of the truth and divinity of the work.

1 To seal the testimony of this book and the Book of Mormon, we announce the martyrdom of Joseph Smith the Prophet, and Hyrum Smith the Patriarch. They were shot in Carthage jail, on the 27th of June, 1844, about five o'clock p.m., by an armed mob—painted black—of from 150 to 200 persons. Hyrum was shot first and fell calmly, exclaiming: I am a dead man! Joseph leaped from the window, and was shot dead in the attempt, exclaiming: O Lord my God! They were both shot after they were dead, in a brutal manner, and both received four balls.

2 John Taylor and Willard Richards, two of the Twelve, were the only persons in the room at the time; the former was wounded in a savage manner with four balls, but has since recovered; the latter, through the providence of God, escaped, without even a hole in his robe.

3 Joseph Smith, the Prophet and Seer of the Lord, has done more, save Jesus only, for the salvation of men in this world, than any other man that ever lived in it. In the short space of twenty years, he has brought forth the Book of Mormon, which he translated by the gift and power of God, and has been the means of publishing it on two continents; has sent the fulness of the everlasting gospel, which it contained, to the four quarters of the earth; has brought forth the revelations and commandments which compose this book of Doctrine and Covenants, and many other wise documents and instructions for the benefit of the children of men; gathered many thousands of the Latter-day Saints, founded a great city, and left a fame and name that cannot be slain. He lived great, and he died great in the eyes of God and his people; and like most of the Lord's anointed in ancient times, has sealed his mission and his works with his own blood; and so has his brother Hyrum. In life they were not divided, and in death they were not separated!

4 When Joseph went to Carthage to deliver himself up to the pretended requirements of the law, two or three days previous to his assassination, he said: "I am going like a lamb to the slaughter; but I am calm as a summer's morning; I have a conscience void of offense towards God, and towards all men. I SHALL DIE INNOCENT, AND IT SHALL YET BE SAID OF ME—HE WAS MURDERED IN COLD BLOOD."—The same morning, after Hyrum had made ready to go—shall it be said to the slaughter? yes, for so it was—he read the following paragraph, near the close of the twelfth chapter of Ether, in the Book of Mormon, and turned down the leaf upon it:

5 And it came to pass that I prayed unto the Lord that he would give unto the Gentiles grace, that they might have charity. And it came to pass that the Lord said unto me: If they have not charity it mattereth not unto thee, thou hast been faithful; wherefore thy garments shall be made clean. And because thou hast seen thy weakness, thou shalt be made strong, even unto the sitting down in the place which I have prepared in the mansions of

my Father. And now I ... bid farewell unto the Gentiles; yea, and also unto my brethren whom I love, until we shall meet before the judgment-seat of Christ, where all men shall know that my garments are not spotted with your blood. The testators are now dead, and their testament is in force.

6 Hyrum Smith was forty-four years old in February, 1844, and Joseph Smith was thirty-eight in December, 1843; and henceforward their names will be classed among the martyrs of religion; and the reader in every nation will be reminded that the Book of Mormon, and this book of Doctrine and Covenants of the church, cost the best blood of the nineteenth century to bring them forth for the salvation of a ruined world; and that if the fire can scathe a green tree for the glory of God, how easy it will burn up the dry trees to purify the vineyard of corruption. They lived for glory; they died for glory; and glory is their eternal reward. From age to age shall their names go down to posterity as gems for the sanctified.

7 They were innocent of any crime, as they had often been proved before, and were only confined in jail by the conspiracy of traitors and wicked men; and their innocent blood on the floor of Carthage jail is a broad seal affixed to "Mormonism" that cannot be rejected by any court on earth, and their innocent blood on the escutcheon of the State of Illinois, with the broken faith of the State as pledged by the governor, is a witness to the truth of the everlasting gospel that all the world cannot impeach; and their innocent blood on the banner of liberty, and on the magna charta of the United States, is an ambassador for the religion of Jesus Christ, that will touch the hearts of honest men among all nations; and their innocent blood, with the innocent blood of all the martyrs under the altar that John saw, will cry unto the Lord of Hosts till he avenges that blood on the earth. Amen.

Section 136

The word and will of the Lord, given through President Brigham Young at Winter Quarters, the camp of Israel, Omaha Nation, on the west bank of the Missouri River, near Council Bluffs, Iowa.

1–16, How the camp of Israel is to be organized for the westward journey is explained; 17–27, The Saints are commanded to live by numerous gospel standards; 28–33, The Saints should sing, dance, pray, and learn wisdom; 34–42, Prophets are slain so that they might be honored and the wicked condemned.

1 The Word and Will of the Lord concerning the Camp of Israel in their journeyings to the West:

2 Let all the people of The Church of Jesus Christ of Latter-day Saints, and those who journey with them, be organized into companies, with a covenant and promise to keep all the commandments and statutes of the Lord our God.

3 Let the companies be organized with captains of hundreds, captains of fifties, and captains of tens, with a president and his two counselors at their head, under the direction of the Twelve Apostles.

4 And this shall be our covenant—that we will walk in all the ordinances of the Lord.

5 Let each company provide themselves with all the teams, wagons, provisions, clothing, and other necessaries for the journey, that they can.

6 When the companies are organized let them go to with their might, to prepare for those who are to tarry.

7 Let each company, with their captains and presidents, decide how many can go next spring; then choose out a sufficient number of able-bodied and expert men, to take teams, seeds, and farming utensils, to go as pioneers to prepare for putting in spring crops.

8 Let each company bear an equal proportion, according to the dividend of their property, in taking the poor, the widows, the fatherless, and the families of those who have gone into the army, that the cries of the widow and the fatherless come not up into the ears of the Lord against this people.

9 Let each company prepare houses, and fields for raising grain, for those who are to remain behind this season; and this is the will of the Lord concerning his people.

10 Let every man use all his influence and property to remove this people to the place where the Lord shall locate a stake of Zion.

11 And if ye do this with a pure heart, in all faithfulness, ye shall be blessed; you shall be blessed in your flocks, and in your herds, and in your fields, and in your houses, and in your families.

12 Let my servants Ezra T. Benson and Erastus Snow organize a company.

13 And let my servants Orson Pratt and Wilford Woodruff organize a company.

14 Also, let my servants Amasa Lyman and George A. Smith organize a company.

15 And appoint presidents, and captains of hundreds, and of fifties, and of tens.

16 And let my servants that have been appointed go and teach this, my will, to the saints, that they may be ready to go to a land of peace.

17 Go thy way and do as I have told

you, and fear not thine enemies; for they shall not have power to stop my work.

18 Zion shall be redeemed in mine own due time.

19 And if any man shall seek to build up himself, and seeketh not my counsel, he shall have no power, and his folly shall be made manifest.

20 Seek ye; and keep all your pledges one with another; and covet not that which is thy brother's.

21 Keep yourselves from evil to take the name of the Lord in vain, for I am the Lord your God, even the God of your fathers, the God of Abraham and of Isaac and of Jacob.

22 I am he who led the children of Israel out of the land of Egypt; and my arm is stretched out in the last days, to save my people Israel.

23 Cease to contend one with another; cease to speak evil one of another.

24 Cease drunkenness; and let your words tend to edifying one another.

25 If thou borrowest of thy neighbor, thou shalt restore that which thou hast borrowed; and if thou canst not repay then go straightway and tell thy neighbor, lest he condemn thee.

26 If thou shalt find that which thy neighbor has lost, thou shalt make diligent search till thou shalt deliver it to him again.

27 Thou shalt be diligent in preserving what thou hast, that thou mayest be a wise steward; for it is the free gift of the Lord thy God, and thou art his steward.

28 If thou art merry, praise the Lord with singing, with music, with dancing, and with a prayer of praise and thanksgiving.

29 If thou art sorrowful, call on the Lord thy God with supplication, that your souls may be joyful.

30 Fear not thine enemies, for they are in mine hands and I will do my pleasure with them.

31 My people must be tried in all things, that they may be prepared to receive the glory that I have for them, even the glory of Zion; and he that will not bear chastisement is not worthy of my kingdom.

32 Let him that is ignorant learn wisdom by humbling himself and calling upon the Lord his God, that his eyes may be opened that he may see, and his ears opened that he may hear;

33 For my Spirit is sent forth into the world to enlighten the humble and contrite, and to the condemnation of the ungodly.

34 Thy brethren have rejected you and your testimony, even the nation that has driven you out;

35 And now cometh the day of their calamity, even the days of sorrow, like a woman that is taken in travail; and their sorrow shall be great unless they speedily repent, yea, very speedily.

36 For they killed the prophets, and them that were sent unto them; and they have shed innocent blood, which crieth from the ground against them.

37 Therefore, marvel not at these things, for ye are not yet pure; ye can not yet bear my glory; but ye shall behold it if ye are faithful in keeping all my words that I have given you, from the days of Adam to Abraham, from Abraham to Moses, from Moses to Jesus and his apostles, and from Jesus and his apostles to Joseph Smith, whom I did call upon by mine angels, my ministering servants, and by mine own

voice out of the heavens, to bring forth my work;

38 Which foundation he did lay, and was faithful; and I took him to myself.

39 Many have marveled because of his death; but it was needful that he should seal his testimony with his blood, that he might be honored and the wicked might be condemned.

40 Have I not delivered you from your enemies, only in that I have left a witness of my name?

41 Now, therefore, hearken, O ye people of my church; and ye elders listen together; you have received my kingdom.

42 Be diligent in keeping all my commandments, lest judgments come upon you, and your faith fail you, and your enemies triumph over you. So no more at present. Amen and Amen.

Section 137

A vision given to Joseph Smith the Prophet, in the temple at Kirtland, Ohio, January 21, 1836. The occasion was the administration of ordinances in preparation for the dedication of the temple.

1–6, The Prophet sees his brother Alvin in the celestial kingdom; 7–9, The doctrine of salvation for the dead is revealed; 10, All children are saved in the celestial kingdom.

1 The heavens were opened upon us, and I beheld the celestial kingdom of God, and the glory thereof, whether in the body or out I cannot tell.

2 I saw the transcendent beauty of the gate through which the heirs of that kingdom will enter, which was like unto circling flames of fire;

3 Also the blazing throne of God, whereon was seated the Father and the Son.

4 I saw the beautiful streets of that kingdom, which had the appearance of being paved with gold.

5 I saw Father Adam and Abraham; and my father and my mother; my brother Alvin, that has long since slept;

6 And marveled how it was that he had obtained an inheritance in that kingdom, seeing that he had departed this life before the Lord had set his hand to gather Israel the second time, and had not been baptized for the remission of sins.

7 Thus came the voice of the Lord unto me, saying: All who have died without a knowledge of this gospel, who would have received it if they had been permitted to tarry, shall be heirs of the celestial kingdom of God;

8 Also all that shall die henceforth without a knowledge of it, who would have received it with all their hearts, shall be heirs of that kingdom;

9 For I, the Lord, will judge all men according to their works, according to the desire of their hearts.

10 And I also beheld that all children who die before they arrive at the years of accountability are saved in the celestial kingdom of heaven.

Section 138

A vision given to President Joseph F. Smith in Salt Lake City, Utah, on October 3, 1918. In his opening address at the 89th Semiannual General Conference of the Church, on October 4, 1918, President Smith declared that he had received several divine communications during the previous months. One of these, concerning the Savior's visit to the spirits of the dead while His body was in the tomb, President Smith had received the previous day. It was written immediately following the close of the conference. On October 31, 1918, it was submitted to the counselors in the First Presidency, the Council of the Twelve, and the Patriarch, and it was unanimously accepted by them.

1–10, President Joseph F. Smith ponders upon the writings of Peter and our Lord's visit to the spirit world; 11–24, President Smith sees the righteous dead assembled in paradise and Christ's ministry among them; 25–37, He sees how the preaching of the gospel was organized among the spirits; 38–52, He sees Adam, Eve, and many of the holy prophets in the spirit world who considered their spirit state before their resurrection as a bondage; 53–60, The righteous dead of this day continue their labors in the world of spirits.

1 On the third of October, in the year nineteen hundred and eighteen, I sat in my room pondering over the scriptures;

2 And reflecting upon the great atoning sacrifice that was made by the Son of God, for the redemption of the world;

3 And the great and wonderful love made manifest by the Father and the Son in the coming of the Redeemer into the world;

4 That through his atonement, and by obedience to the principles of the gospel, mankind might be saved.

5 While I was thus engaged, my mind reverted to the writings of the apostle Peter, to the primitive saints scattered abroad throughout Pontus, Galatia, Cappadocia, and other parts of Asia, where the gospel had been preached after the crucifixion of the Lord.

6 I opened the Bible and read the third and fourth chapters of the first epistle of Peter, and as I read I was greatly impressed, more than I had ever been before, with the following passages:

7 "For Christ also hath once suffered for sins, the just for the unjust, that he might bring us to God, being put to death in the flesh, but quickened by the Spirit:

8 "By which also he went and preached unto the spirits in prison;

9 "Which sometime were disobedient, when once the longsuffering of God waited in the days of Noah, while the ark was a preparing, wherein few, that is, eight souls were saved by water." (1 Peter 3:18–20.)

10 "For for this cause was the gospel preached also to them that are dead, that they might be judged according to men in the flesh, but live according to God in the spirit." (1 Peter 4:6.)

11 As I pondered over these things which are written, the eyes of my understanding were opened, and the Spirit of the Lord rested upon me, and I saw the hosts of the dead, both small and great.

12 And there were gathered together in one place an innumerable company of the spirits of the just, who had been faithful in the testimony of Jesus while they lived in mortality;

13 And who had offered sacrifice in the similitude of the great sacrifice of the

Son of God, and had suffered tribulation in their Redeemer's name.

14 All these had departed the mortal life, firm in the hope of a glorious resurrection, through the grace of God the Father and his Only Begotten Son, Jesus Christ.

15 I beheld that they were filled with joy and gladness, and were rejoicing together because the day of their deliverance was at hand.

16 They were assembled awaiting the advent of the Son of God into the spirit world, to declare their redemption from the bands of death.

17 Their sleeping dust was to be restored unto its perfect frame, bone to his bone, and the sinews and the flesh upon them, the spirit and the body to be united never again to be divided, that they might receive a fulness of joy.

18 While this vast multitude waited and conversed, rejoicing in the hour of their deliverance from the chains of death, the Son of God appeared, declaring liberty to the captives who had been faithful;

19 And there he preached to them the everlasting gospel, the doctrine of the resurrection and the redemption of mankind from the fall, and from individual sins on conditions of repentance.

20 But unto the wicked he did not go, and among the ungodly and the unrepentant who had defiled themselves while in the flesh, his voice was not raised;

21 Neither did the rebellious who rejected the testimonies and the warnings of the ancient prophets behold his presence, nor look upon his face.

22 Where these were, darkness reigned, but among the righteous there was peace;

23 And the saints rejoiced in their redemption, and bowed the knee and acknowledged the Son of God as their Redeemer and Deliverer from death and the chains of hell.

24 Their countenances shone, and the radiance from the presence of the Lord rested upon them, and they sang praises unto his holy name.

25 I marveled, for I understood that the Savior spent about three years in his ministry among the Jews and those of the house of Israel, endeavoring to teach them the everlasting gospel and call them unto repentance;

26 And yet, notwithstanding his mighty works, and miracles, and proclamation of the truth, in great power and authority, there were but few who hearkened to his voice, and rejoiced in his presence, and received salvation at his hands.

27 But his ministry among those who were dead was limited to the brief time intervening between the crucifixion and his resurrection;

28 And I wondered at the words of Peter—wherein he said that the Son of God preached unto the spirits in prison, who sometime were disobedient, when once the long-suffering of God waited in the days of Noah—and how it was possible for him to preach to those spirits and perform the necessary labor among them in so short a time.

29 And as I wondered, my eyes were opened, and my understanding quickened, and I perceived that the Lord went not in person among the wicked and the disobedient who had rejected the truth, to teach them;

30 But behold, from among the

righteous, he organized his forces and appointed messengers, clothed with power and authority, and commissioned them to go forth and carry the light of the gospel to them that were in darkness, even to all the spirits of men; and thus was the gospel preached to the dead.

31 And the chosen messengers went forth to declare the acceptable day of the Lord and proclaim liberty to the captives who were bound, even unto all who would repent of their sins and receive the gospel.

32 Thus was the gospel preached to those who had died in their sins, without a knowledge of the truth, or in transgression, having rejected the prophets.

33 These were taught faith in God, repentance from sin, vicarious baptism for the remission of sins, the gift of the Holy Ghost by the laying on of hands,

34 And all other principles of the gospel that were necessary for them to know in order to qualify themselves that they might be judged according to men in the flesh, but live according to God in the spirit.

35 And so it was made known among the dead, both small and great, the unrighteous as well as the faithful, that redemption had been wrought through the sacrifice of the Son of God upon the cross.

36 Thus was it made known that our Redeemer spent his time during his sojourn in the world of spirits, instructing and preparing the faithful spirits of the prophets who had testified of him in the flesh;

37 That they might carry the message of redemption unto all the dead, unto whom he could not go personally, because of their rebellion and transgression, that they through the ministration of his servants might also hear his words.

38 Among the great and mighty ones who were assembled in this vast congregation of the righteous were Father Adam, the Ancient of Days and father of all,

39 And our glorious Mother Eve, with many of her faithful daughters who had lived through the ages and worshiped the true and living God.

40 Abel, the first martyr, was there, and his brother Seth, one of the mighty ones, who was in the express image of his father, Adam.

41 Noah, who gave warning of the flood; Shem, the great high priest; Abraham, the father of the faithful; Isaac, Jacob, and Moses, the great law-giver of Israel;

42 And Isaiah, who declared by prophecy that the Redeemer was anointed to bind up the broken-hearted, to proclaim liberty to the captives, and the opening of the prison to them that were bound, were also there.

43 Moreover, Ezekiel, who was shown in vision the great valley of dry bones, which were to be clothed upon with flesh, to come forth again in the resurrection of the dead, living souls;

44 Daniel, who foresaw and foretold the establishment of the kingdom of God in the latter days, never again to be destroyed nor given to other people;

45 Elias, who was with Moses on the Mount of Transfiguration;

46 And Malachi, the prophet who testified of the coming of Elijah—of whom also Moroni spake to the Prophet Joseph Smith, declaring that he should come before the ushering in of the great

and dreadful day of the Lord—were also there.

47 The Prophet Elijah was to plant in the hearts of the children the promises made to their fathers,

48 Foreshadowing the great work to be done in the temples of the Lord in the dispensation of the fulness of times, for the redemption of the dead, and the sealing of the children to their parents, lest the whole earth be smitten with a curse and utterly wasted at his coming.

49 All these and many more, even the prophets who dwelt among the Nephites and testified of the coming of the Son of God, mingled in the vast assembly and waited for their deliverance,

50 For the dead had looked upon the long absence of their spirits from their bodies as a bondage.

51 These the Lord taught, and gave them power to come forth, after his resurrection from the dead, to enter into his Father's kingdom, there to be crowned with immortality and eternal life,

52 And continue thenceforth their labor as had been promised by the Lord, and be partakers of all blessings which were held in reserve for them that love him.

53 The Prophet Joseph Smith, and my father, Hyrum Smith, Brigham Young, John Taylor, Wilford Woodruff, and other choice spirits who were reserved to come forth in the fulness of times to take part in laying the foundations of the great latter-day work,

54 Including the building of the temples and the performance of ordinances therein for the redemption of the dead, were also in the spirit world.

55 I observed that they were also among the noble and great ones who were chosen in the beginning to be rulers in the Church of God.

56 Even before they were born, they, with many others, received their first lessons in the world of spirits and were prepared to come forth in the due time of the Lord to labor in his vineyard for the salvation of the souls of men.

57 I beheld that the faithful elders of this dispensation, when they depart from mortal life, continue their labors in the preaching of the gospel of repentance and redemption, through the sacrifice of the Only Begotten Son of God, among those who are in darkness and under the bondage of sin in the great world of the spirits of the dead.

58 The dead who repent will be redeemed, through obedience to the ordinances of the house of God,

59 And after they have paid the penalty of their transgressions, and are washed clean, shall receive a reward according to their works, for they are heirs of salvation.

60 Thus was the vision of the redemption of the dead revealed to me, and I bear record, and I know that this record is true, through the blessing of our Lord and Savior, Jesus Christ, even so. Amen.

Official Declaration 1

The Bible and the Book of Mormon teach that monogamy is God's standard for marriage unless He declares otherwise (see 2 Samuel 12:7–8 and Jacob 2:27, 30). Following a revelation to Joseph Smith, the practice of plural marriage was instituted among Church members in the early 1840s (see section 132). From the 1860s to the 1880s, the United States government passed laws to make this religious practice illegal. These laws were eventually upheld by the U.S. Supreme Court. After receiving revelation, President Wilford Woodruff issued the following Manifesto, which was accepted by the Church as authoritative and binding on October 6, 1890. This led to the end of the practice of plural marriage in the Church.

To Whom It May Concern:

Press dispatches having been sent for political purposes, from Salt Lake City, which have been widely published, to the effect that the Utah Commission, in their recent report to the Secretary of the Interior, allege that plural marriages are still being solemnized and that forty or more such marriages have been contracted in Utah since last June or during the past year, also that in public discourses the leaders of the Church have taught, encouraged and urged the continuance of the practice of polygamy—

I, therefore, as President of The Church of Jesus Christ of Latter-day Saints, do hereby, in the most solemn manner, declare that these charges are false. We are not teaching polygamy or plural marriage, nor permitting any person to enter into its practice, and I deny that either forty or any other number of plural marriages have during that period been solemnized in our Temples or in any other place in the Territory.

One case has been reported, in which the parties allege that the marriage was performed in the Endowment House, in Salt Lake City, in the Spring of 1889, but I have not been able to learn who performed the ceremony; whatever was done in this matter was without my knowledge. In consequence of this alleged occurrence the Endowment House was, by my instructions, taken down without delay.

Inasmuch as laws have been enacted by Congress forbidding plural marriages, which laws have been pronounced constitutional by the court of last resort, I hereby declare my intention to submit to those laws, and to use my influence with the members of the Church over which I preside to have them do likewise.

There is nothing in my teachings to the Church or in those of my associates, during the time specified, which can be reasonably construed to inculcate or encourage polygamy; and when any Elder of the Church has used language which appeared to convey any such teaching, he has been promptly reproved. And I now publicly declare that my advice to the Latter-day Saints is to refrain from contracting any marriage forbidden by the law of the land.

WILFORD WOODRUFF

President of The Church of Jesus Christ of Latter-day Saints.

President Lorenzo Snow offered the following:

"I move that, recognizing Wilford Woodruff as the President of The Church of Jesus Christ of Latter-day Saints, and the only man on the earth at the present time who holds the keys of the sealing ordinances, we consider him fully authorized by virtue of his position to issue the Manifesto which has been read in our hearing, and which is dated September 24th, 1890, and that as a Church in General Conference assembled, we accept his declaration concerning plural marriages as authoritative and binding."

Salt Lake City, Utah, October 6, 1890.

EXCERPTS FROM THREE ADDRESSES BY

PRESIDENT WILFORD WOODRUFF

REGARDING THE MANIFESTO

The Lord will never permit me or any other man who stands as President of this Church to lead you astray. It is not in the programme. It is not in the mind of God. If I were to attempt that, the Lord would remove me out of my place, and so He will any other man who attempts to lead the children of men astray from the oracles of God and from their duty. (Sixty-first Semiannual General Conference of the Church, Monday, October 6, 1890, Salt Lake City, Utah. Reported in Deseret Evening News, October 11, 1890, p. 2.)

It matters not who lives or who dies, or who is called to lead this Church, they have got to lead it by the inspiration of Almighty God. If they do not do it that way, they cannot do it at all. ...

I have had some revelations of late, and very important ones to me, and I will tell you what the Lord has said to me. Let me bring your minds to what is termed the manifesto. ...

The Lord has told me to ask the Latter-day Saints a question, and He also told me that if they would listen to what I said to them and answer the question put to them, by the Spirit and power of God, they would all answer alike, and they would all believe alike with regard to this matter.

The question is this: Which is the wisest course for the Latter-day Saints to pursue—to continue to attempt to practice plural marriage, with the laws of the nation against it and the opposition of sixty millions of people, and at the cost of the confiscation and loss of all the Temples, and the stopping of all the ordinances therein, both for the living and the dead, and the imprisonment of the First Presidency and Twelve and the heads of families in the Church, and the confiscation of personal property of the people (all of which of themselves would stop the practice); or, after doing and suffering what we have through our adherence to this principle to cease the practice and submit to the law, and through doing so leave the Prophets, Apostles and fathers at home, so that they can instruct the people and attend to the duties of the Church, and also leave the Temples in the hands of the Saints, so that they can attend to the ordinances of the Gospel, both for the living and the dead?

The Lord showed me by vision and revelation exactly what would take place if we did not stop this practice. If we had not stopped it, you would have had no use for ... any of the men in this temple at Logan; for all ordinances would be stopped throughout the land of Zion. Confusion would reign throughout Israel, and many men would be made prisoners. This trouble would have come upon the whole Church, and we should have been compelled to stop the practice. Now, the question is, whether it should be stopped in this manner, or in the way the Lord has manifested to us, and leave our Prophets and Apostles and fathers free men, and the temples in the hands of the people, so that the dead may be redeemed. A large number has already been delivered from the prison house in the spirit world by this people, and shall the work go on or stop? This is the question I lay before the Latter-day Saints. You have to judge for yourselves. I want you to answer it for yourselves. I shall not answer it; but I say to you that that is exactly the condition we as a people would have been in had we not taken the course we have.

... I saw exactly what would come to pass if there was not something done. I have had this spirit upon me for a long time. But I want to say this: I should have let all the temples go out of our hands; I should have gone to prison myself, and let every other man go there, had not the God of heaven commanded me to do what I did do; and when the hour came that I was commanded to do that, it was all clear to me. I went before the Lord, and I wrote what the Lord told me to write. ...

I leave this with you, for you to contemplate and consider. The Lord is at work with us. (Cache Stake Conference, Logan, Utah, Sunday, November 1, 1891. Reported in Deseret Weekly, November 14, 1891.)

Now I will tell you what was manifested to me and what the Son of God performed in this thing. ... All these things would have come to pass, as God Almighty lives, had not that Manifesto been given. Therefore, the Son of God felt disposed to have that thing presented to the Church and to the world for purposes in his own mind. The Lord had decreed the establishment of Zion. He had decreed the finishing of this temple. He had decreed that the salvation of the living and the dead should be given in these valleys of the mountains. And Almighty God decreed that the Devil should not thwart it. If you can understand that, that is a key to it. (From a discourse at the sixth session of the dedication of the Salt Lake Temple, April 1893. Typescript of Dedicatory Services, Archives, Church Historical Department, Salt Lake City, Utah.)

Official Declaration 2

The Book of Mormon teaches that "all are alike unto God," including "black and white, bond and free, male and female" (2 Nephi 26:33). Throughout the history of the Church, people of every race and ethnicity in many countries have been baptized and have lived as faithful members of the Church. During Joseph Smith's lifetime, a few black male members of the Church were ordained to the priesthood. Early in its history, Church leaders stopped conferring the priesthood on black males of African descent. Church records offer no clear insights into the origins of this practice. Church leaders believed that a revelation from God was needed to alter this practice and prayerfully sought guidance. The revelation came to Church President Spencer W. Kimball and was affirmed to other Church leaders in the Salt Lake Temple on June 1, 1978. The revelation removed all restrictions with regard to race that once applied to the priesthood.

To Whom It May Concern:

On September 30, 1978, at the 148th Semiannual General Conference of The Church of Jesus Christ of Latter-day Saints, the following was presented by President N. Eldon Tanner, First Counselor in the First Presidency of the Church:

In early June of this year, the First Presidency announced that a revelation had been received by President Spencer W. Kimball extending priesthood and temple blessings to all worthy male members of the Church. President Kimball has asked that I advise the conference that after he had received this revelation, which came to him after extended meditation and prayer in the sacred rooms of the holy temple, he presented it to his counselors, who accepted it and approved it. It was then presented to the Quorum of the Twelve Apostles, who unanimously approved it, and was subsequently presented to all other General Authorities, who likewise approved it unanimously.

President Kimball has asked that I now read this letter:

June 8, 1978

To all general and local priesthood officers of The Church of Jesus Christ of Latter-day Saints throughout the world:

Dear Brethren:

As we have witnessed the expansion of the work of the Lord over the earth, we have been grateful that people of many nations have responded to the message of the restored gospel, and have joined the Church in ever-increasing numbers. This, in turn, has inspired us with a desire to extend to every worthy member of the Church all of the privileges and blessings which the gospel affords.

Aware of the promises made by the prophets and presidents of the Church who have preceded us that at some time, in God's eternal plan, all of our brethren who are worthy may receive the priesthood, and witnessing the faithfulness of those from whom the priesthood has been withheld, we have pleaded long and earnestly in behalf of these, our faithful brethren, spending many hours in the Upper Room of the Temple supplicating the Lord for divine guidance.

He has heard our prayers, and by revelation has confirmed that the long-promised day has come when every faithful, worthy man in the Church may receive the holy priesthood, with power to exercise its divine authority, and enjoy with his loved ones every blessing that flows therefrom, including the blessings of the temple. Accordingly, all worthy male members of the Church may be ordained to the priesthood without regard for race or color. Priesthood leaders are instructed to follow the policy of carefully interviewing all candidates for ordination to either the Aaronic or the Melchizedek Priesthood to insure that they meet the established standards for worthiness.

We declare with soberness that the Lord has now made known his will for the blessing of all his children throughout the earth who will hearken to the voice of his authorized servants, and prepare themselves to receive every blessing of the gospel.

Sincerely yours,

SPENCER W. KIMBALL

N. ELDON TANNER

MARION G. ROMNEY

The First Presidency

Recognizing Spencer W. Kimball as the prophet, seer, and revelator, and president of The Church of Jesus Christ of Latter-day Saints, it is proposed that we as a constituent assembly accept this revelation as the word and will of the Lord. All in favor please signify by raising your right hand. Any opposed by the same sign.

The vote to sustain the foregoing motion was unanimous in the affirmative.

Salt Lake City, Utah, September 30, 1978.

Joseph Smith—History

EXTRACTS FROM THE HISTORY OF JOSEPH SMITH, THE PROPHET

CHAPTER 1

Joseph Smith tells of his ancestry, family members, and their early abodes—An unusual excitement about religion prevails in western New York—He determines to seek wisdom as directed by James—The Father and the Son appear, and Joseph is called to his prophetic ministry. (Verses 1–20.)

1 Owing to the many reports which have been put in circulation by evil-disposed and designing persons, in relation to the rise and progress of The Church of Jesus Christ of Latter-day Saints, all of which have been designed by the authors thereof to militate against its character as a Church and its progress in the world—I have been induced to write this history, to disabuse the public mind, and put all inquirers after truth in possession of the facts, as they have transpired, in relation both to myself and the Church, so far as I have such facts in my possession.

2 In this history I shall present the various events in relation to this Church, in truth and righteousness, as they have transpired, or as they at present exist, being now [1838] the eighth year since the organization of the said Church.

3 I was born in the year of our Lord one thousand eight hundred and five, on the twenty-third day of December, in the town of Sharon, Windsor county, State of Vermont. ... My father, Joseph Smith, Sen., left the State of Vermont, and moved to Palmyra, Ontario (now Wayne) county, in the State of New York, when I was in my tenth year, or thereabouts. In about four years after my father's arrival in Palmyra, he moved with his family into Manchester in the same county of Ontario—

4 His family consisting of eleven souls, namely, my father, Joseph Smith; my mother, Lucy Smith (whose name, previous to her marriage, was Mack, daughter of Solomon Mack); my brothers, Alvin (who died November 19th, 1823, in the 26th year of his age), Hyrum, myself, Samuel Harrison, William, Don Carlos; and my sisters, Sophronia, Catherine, and Lucy.

5 Some time in the second year after our removal to Manchester, there was in the place where we lived an unusual excitement on the subject of religion. It commenced with the Methodists, but soon became general among all the sects in that region of country. Indeed, the whole district of country seemed affected by it, and great multitudes united themselves to the different religious parties, which created no small stir and division amongst the people, some crying, "Lo, here!" and others, "Lo, there!" Some were contending for the Methodist faith, some for the Presbyterian, and some for the Baptist.

6 For, notwithstanding the great love which the converts to these different faiths expressed at the time of their conversion, and the great zeal manifested by the respective clergy, who were active in getting up and promoting this extraordinary scene of religious

feeling, in order to have everybody converted, as they were pleased to call it, let them join what sect they pleased; yet when the converts began to file off, some to one party and some to another, it was seen that the seemingly good feelings of both the priests and the converts were more pretended than real; for a scene of great confusion and bad feeling ensued—priest contending against priest, and convert against convert; so that all their good feelings one for another, if they ever had any, were entirely lost in a strife of words and a contest about opinions.

7 I was at this time in my fifteenth year. My father's family was proselyted to the Presbyterian faith, and four of them joined that church, namely, my mother, Lucy; my brothers Hyrum and Samuel Harrison; and my sister Sophronia.

8 During this time of great excitement my mind was called up to serious reflection and great uneasiness; but though my feelings were deep and often poignant, still I kept myself aloof from all these parties, though I attended their several meetings as often as occasion would permit. In process of time my mind became somewhat partial to the Methodist sect, and I felt some desire to be united with them; but so great were the confusion and strife among the different denominations, that it was impossible for a person young as I was, and so unacquainted with men and things, to come to any certain conclusion who was right and who was wrong.

9 My mind at times was greatly excited, the cry and tumult were so great and incessant. The Presbyterians were most decided against the Baptists and Methodists, and used all the powers of both reason and sophistry to prove their errors, or, at least, to make the people think they were in error. On the other hand, the Baptists and Methodists in their turn were equally zealous in endeavoring to establish their own tenets and disprove all others.

10 In the midst of this war of words and tumult of opinions, I often said to myself: What is to be done? Who of all these parties are right; or, are they all wrong together? If any one of them be right, which is it, and how shall I know it?

11 While I was laboring under the extreme difficulties caused by the contests of these parties of religionists, I was one day reading the Epistle of James, first chapter and fifth verse, which reads: If any of you lack wisdom, let him ask of God, that giveth to all men liberally, and upbraideth not; and it shall be given him.

12 Never did any passage of scripture come with more power to the heart of man than this did at this time to mine. It seemed to enter with great force into every feeling of my heart. I reflected on it again and again, knowing that if any person needed wisdom from God, I did; for how to act I did not know, and unless I could get more wisdom than I then had, I would never know; for the teachers of religion of the different sects understood the same passages of scripture so differently as to destroy all confidence in settling the question by an appeal to the Bible.

13 At length I came to the conclusion that I must either remain in darkness and confusion, or else I must do as James directs, that is, ask of God. I at length came to the determination to "ask of God," concluding that if he gave wisdom to them that lacked wisdom, and would give liberally, and not upbraid, I might venture.

14 So, in accordance with this, my determination to ask of God, I retired to the woods to make the attempt. It was on the morning of a beautiful, clear day, early in the spring of eighteen hundred and twenty. It was the first time in my

life that I had made such an attempt, for amidst all my anxieties I had never as yet made the attempt to pray vocally.

15 After I had retired to the place where I had previously designed to go, having looked around me, and finding myself alone, I kneeled down and began to offer up the desires of my heart to God. I had scarcely done so, when immediately I was seized upon by some power which entirely overcame me, and had such an astonishing influence over me as to bind my tongue so that I could not speak. Thick darkness gathered around me, and it seemed to me for a time as if I were doomed to sudden destruction.

16 But, exerting all my powers to call upon God to deliver me out of the power of this enemy which had seized upon me, and at the very moment when I was ready to sink into despair and abandon myself to destruction—not to an imaginary ruin, but to the power of some actual being from the unseen world, who had such marvelous power as I had never before felt in any being—just at this moment of great alarm, I saw a pillar of light exactly over my head, above the brightness of the sun, which descended gradually until it fell upon me.

17 It no sooner appeared than I found myself delivered from the enemy which held me bound. When the light rested upon me I saw two Personages, whose brightness and glory defy all description, standing above me in the air. One of them spake unto me, calling me by name and said, pointing to the other—This is My Beloved Son. Hear Him!

18 My object in going to inquire of the Lord was to know which of all the sects was right, that I might know which to join. No sooner, therefore, did I get possession of myself, so as to be able to speak, than I asked the Personages who stood above me in the light, which of all the sects was right (for at this time it had never entered into my heart that all were wrong)—and which I should join.

19 I was answered that I must join none of them, for they were all wrong; and the Personage who addressed me said that all their creeds were an abomination in his sight; that those professors were all corrupt; that: "they draw near to me with their lips, but their hearts are far from me, they teach for doctrines the commandments of men, having a form of godliness, but they deny the power thereof."

20 He again forbade me to join with any of them; and many other things did he say unto me, which I cannot write at this time. When I came to myself again, I found myself lying on my back, looking up into heaven. When the light had departed, I had no strength; but soon recovering in some degree, I went home. And as I leaned up to the fireplace, mother inquired what the matter was. I replied, "Never mind, all is well—I am well enough off." I then said to my mother, "I have learned for myself that Presbyterianism is not true." It seems as though the adversary was aware, at a very early period of my life, that I was destined to prove a disturber and an annoyer of his kingdom; else why should the powers of darkness combine against me? Why the opposition and persecution that arose against me, almost in my infancy?

Some preachers and other professors of religion reject the account of the First Vision—Persecution is heaped upon Joseph Smith—He testifies of the reality of the vision. (Verses 21–26.)

21 Some few days after I had this vision, I happened to be in company with one of the Methodist preachers, who was very active in the before mentioned religious excitement; and, conversing with him on the subject of religion, I took occasion to give him an account of the vision which I had had. I was greatly surprised at his behavior; he treated

my communication not only lightly, but with great contempt, saying it was all of the devil, that there were no such things as visions or revelations in these days; that all such things had ceased with the apostles, and that there would never be any more of them.

22 I soon found, however, that my telling the story had excited a great deal of prejudice against me among professors of religion, and was the cause of great persecution, which continued to increase; and though I was an obscure boy, only between fourteen and fifteen years of age, and my circumstances in life such as to make a boy of no consequence in the world, yet men of high standing would take notice sufficient to excite the public mind against me, and create a bitter persecution; and this was common among all the sects—all united to persecute me.

23 It caused me serious reflection then, and often has since, how very strange it was that an obscure boy, of a little over fourteen years of age, and one, too, who was doomed to the necessity of obtaining a scanty maintenance by his daily labor, should be thought a character of sufficient importance to attract the attention of the great ones of the most popular sects of the day, and in a manner to create in them a spirit of the most bitter persecution and reviling. But strange or not, so it was, and it was often the cause of great sorrow to myself.

24 However, it was nevertheless a fact that I had beheld a vision. I have thought since, that I felt much like Paul, when he made his defense before King Agrippa, and related the account of the vision he had when he saw a light, and heard a voice; but still there were but few who believed him; some said he was dishonest, others said he was mad; and he was ridiculed and reviled. But all this did not destroy the reality of his vision. He had seen a vision, he knew he had, and all the persecution under heaven could not make it otherwise; and though they should persecute him unto death, yet he knew, and would know to his latest breath, that he had both seen a light and heard a voice speaking unto him, and all the world could not make him think or believe otherwise.

25 So it was with me. I had actually seen a light, and in the midst of that light I saw two Personages, and they did in reality speak to me; and though I was hated and persecuted for saying that I had seen a vision, yet it was true; and while they were persecuting me, reviling me, and speaking all manner of evil against me falsely for so saying, I was led to say in my heart: Why persecute me for telling the truth? I have actually seen a vision; and who am I that I can withstand God, or why does the world think to make me deny what I have actually seen? For I had seen a vision; I knew it, and I knew that God knew it, and I could not deny it, neither dared I do it; at least I knew that by so doing I would offend God, and come under condemnation.

26 I had now got my mind satisfied so far as the sectarian world was concerned—that it was not my duty to join with any of them, but to continue as I was until further directed. I had found the testimony of James to be true—that a man who lacked wisdom might ask of God, and obtain, and not be upbraided.

Moroni appears to Joseph Smith—Joseph's name is to be known for good and evil among all nations—Moroni tells him of the Book of Mormon and of the coming judgments of the Lord and quotes many scriptures—The hiding place of the gold plates is revealed—Moroni continues to instruct the Prophet. (Verses 27–54.)

27 I continued to pursue my common vocations in life until the twenty-first of September, one thousand eight hundred and twenty-three, all the time suffering

severe persecution at the hands of all classes of men, both religious and irreligious, because I continued to affirm that I had seen a vision.

28 During the space of time which intervened between the time I had the vision and the year eighteen hundred and twenty-three—having been forbidden to join any of the religious sects of the day, and being of very tender years, and persecuted by those who ought to have been my friends and to have treated me kindly, and if they supposed me to be deluded to have endeavored in a proper and affectionate manner to have reclaimed me—I was left to all kinds of temptations; and, mingling with all kinds of society, I frequently fell into many foolish errors, and displayed the weakness of youth, and the foibles of human nature; which, I am sorry to say, led me into divers temptations, offensive in the sight of God. In making this confession, no one need suppose me guilty of any great or malignant sins. A disposition to commit such was never in my nature. But I was guilty of levity, and sometimes associated with jovial company, etc., not consistent with that character which ought to be maintained by one who was called of God as I had been. But this will not seem very strange to any one who recollects my youth, and is acquainted with my native cheery temperament.

29 In consequence of these things, I often felt condemned for my weakness and imperfections; when, on the evening of the above-mentioned twenty-first of September, after I had retired to my bed for the night, I betook myself to prayer and supplication to Almighty God for forgiveness of all my sins and follies, and also for a manifestation to me, that I might know of my state and standing before him; for I had full confidence in obtaining a divine manifestation, as I previously had one.

30 While I was thus in the act of calling upon God, I discovered a light appearing in my room, which continued to increase until the room was lighter than at noonday, when immediately a personage appeared at my bedside, standing in the air, for his feet did not touch the floor.

31 He had on a loose robe of most exquisite whiteness. It was a whiteness beyond anything earthly I had ever seen; nor do I believe that any earthly thing could be made to appear so exceedingly white and brilliant. His hands were naked, and his arms also, a little above the wrist; so, also, were his feet naked, as were his legs, a little above the ankles. His head and neck were also bare. I could discover that he had no other clothing on but this robe, as it was open, so that I could see into his bosom.

32 Not only was his robe exceedingly white, but his whole person was glorious beyond description, and his countenance truly like lightning. The room was exceedingly light, but not so very bright as immediately around his person. When I first looked upon him, I was afraid; but the fear soon left me.

33 He called me by name, and said unto me that he was a messenger sent from the presence of God to me, and that his name was Moroni; that God had a work for me to do; and that my name should be had for good and evil among all nations, kindreds, and tongues, or that it should be both good and evil spoken of among all people.

34 He said there was a book deposited, written upon gold plates, giving an account of the former inhabitants of this continent, and the source from whence they sprang. He also said that the fulness of the everlasting Gospel was contained in it, as delivered by the Savior to the ancient inhabitants;

35 Also, that there were two stones in

silver bows—and these stones, fastened to a breastplate, constituted what is called the Urim and Thummim—deposited with the plates; and the possession and use of these stones were what constituted "seers" in ancient or former times; and that God had prepared them for the purpose of translating the book.

36 After telling me these things, he commenced quoting the prophecies of the Old Testament. He first quoted part of the third chapter of Malachi; and he quoted also the fourth or last chapter of the same prophecy, though with a little variation from the way it reads in our Bibles. Instead of quoting the first verse as it reads in our books, he quoted it thus:

37 For behold, the day cometh that shall burn as an oven, and all the proud, yea, and all that do wickedly shall burn as stubble; for they that come shall burn them, saith the Lord of Hosts, that it shall leave them neither root nor branch.

38 And again, he quoted the fifth verse thus: Behold, I will reveal unto you the Priesthood, by the hand of Elijah the prophet, before the coming of the great and dreadful day of the Lord.

39 He also quoted the next verse differently: And he shall plant in the hearts of the children the promises made to the fathers, and the hearts of the children shall turn to their fathers. If it were not so, the whole earth would be utterly wasted at his coming.

40 In addition to these, he quoted the eleventh chapter of Isaiah, saying that it was about to be fulfilled. He quoted also the third chapter of Acts, twenty-second and twenty-third verses, precisely as they stand in our New Testament. He said that that prophet was Christ; but the day had not yet come when "they who would not hear his voice should be cut off from among the people," but soon would come.

41 He also quoted the second chapter of Joel, from the twenty-eighth verse to the last. He also said that this was not yet fulfilled, but was soon to be. And he further stated that the fulness of the Gentiles was soon to come in. He quoted many other passages of scripture, and offered many explanations which cannot be mentioned here.

42 Again, he told me, that when I got those plates of which he had spoken—for the time that they should be obtained was not yet fulfilled—I should not show them to any person; neither the breastplate with the Urim and Thummim; only to those to whom I should be commanded to show them; if I did I should be destroyed. While he was conversing with me about the plates, the vision was opened to my mind that I could see the place where the plates were deposited, and that so clearly and distinctly that I knew the place again when I visited it.

43 After this communication, I saw the light in the room begin to gather immediately around the person of him who had been speaking to me, and it continued to do so until the room was again left dark, except just around him; when, instantly I saw, as it were, a conduit open right up into heaven, and he ascended till he entirely disappeared, and the room was left as it had been before this heavenly light had made its appearance.

44 I lay musing on the singularity of the scene, and marveling greatly at what had been told to me by this extraordinary messenger; when, in the midst of my meditation, I suddenly discovered that my room was again beginning to get lighted, and in an instant, as it were, the same heavenly messenger was again by my bedside.

45 He commenced, and again related the very same things which he had done at his first visit, without the least variation; which having done, he informed me of great judgments which were coming upon the earth, with great desolations by famine, sword, and pestilence; and that these grievous judgments would come on the earth in this generation. Having related these things, he again ascended as he had done before.

46 By this time, so deep were the impressions made on my mind, that sleep had fled from my eyes, and I lay overwhelmed in astonishment at what I had both seen and heard. But what was my surprise when again I beheld the same messenger at my bedside, and heard him rehearse or repeat over again to me the same things as before; and added a caution to me, telling me that Satan would try to tempt me (in consequence of the indigent circumstances of my father's family), to get the plates for the purpose of getting rich. This he forbade me, saying that I must have no other object in view in getting the plates but to glorify God, and must not be influenced by any other motive than that of building his kingdom; otherwise I could not get them.

47 After this third visit, he again ascended into heaven as before, and I was again left to ponder on the strangeness of what I had just experienced; when almost immediately after the heavenly messenger had ascended from me for the third time, the cock crowed, and I found that day was approaching, so that our interviews must have occupied the whole of that night.

48 I shortly after arose from my bed, and, as usual, went to the necessary labors of the day; but, in attempting to work as at other times, I found my strength so exhausted as to render me entirely unable. My father, who was laboring along with me, discovered something to be wrong with me, and told me to go home. I started with the intention of going to the house; but, in attempting to cross the fence out of the field where we were, my strength entirely failed me, and I fell helpless on the ground, and for a time was quite unconscious of anything.

49 The first thing that I can recollect was a voice speaking unto me, calling me by name. I looked up, and beheld the same messenger standing over my head, surrounded by light as before. He then again related unto me all that he had related to me the previous night, and commanded me to go to my father and tell him of the vision and commandments which I had received.

50 I obeyed; I returned to my father in the field, and rehearsed the whole matter to him. He replied to me that it was of God, and told me to go and do as commanded by the messenger. I left the field, and went to the place where the messenger had told me the plates were deposited; and owing to the distinctness of the vision which I had had concerning it, I knew the place the instant that I arrived there.

51 Convenient to the village of Manchester, Ontario county, New York, stands a hill of considerable size, and the most elevated of any in the neighborhood. On the west side of this hill, not far from the top, under a stone of considerable size, lay the plates, deposited in a stone box. This stone was thick and rounding in the middle on the upper side, and thinner towards the edges, so that the middle part of it was visible above the ground, but the edge all around was covered with earth.

52 Having removed the earth, I obtained a lever, which I got fixed under the edge of the stone, and with a little exertion raised it up. I looked in, and there indeed did I behold the plates, the Urim and Thummim, and the

breastplate, as stated by the messenger. The box in which they lay was formed by laying stones together in some kind of cement. In the bottom of the box were laid two stones crossways of the box, and on these stones lay the plates and the other things with them.

53 I made an attempt to take them out, but was forbidden by the messenger, and was again informed that the time for bringing them forth had not yet arrived, neither would it, until four years from that time; but he told me that I should come to that place precisely in one year from that time, and that he would there meet with me, and that I should continue to do so until the time should come for obtaining the plates.

54 Accordingly, as I had been commanded, I went at the end of each year, and at each time I found the same messenger there, and received instruction and intelligence from him at each of our interviews, respecting what the Lord was going to do, and how and in what manner his kingdom was to be conducted in the last days.

Joseph Smith marries Emma Hale—He receives the gold plates from Moroni and translates some of the characters—Martin Harris shows the characters and translation to Professor Anthon, who says, "I cannot read a sealed book." (Verses 55–65.)

55 As my father's worldly circumstances were very limited, we were under the necessity of laboring with our hands, hiring out by day's work and otherwise, as we could get opportunity. Sometimes we were at home, and sometimes abroad, and by continuous labor were enabled to get a comfortable maintenance.

56 In the year 1823 my father's family met with a great affliction by the death of my eldest brother, Alvin. In the month of October, 1825, I hired with an old gentleman by the name of Josiah Stoal, who lived in Chenango county, State of New York. He had heard something of a silver mine having been opened by the Spaniards in Harmony, Susquehanna county, State of Pennsylvania; and had, previous to my hiring to him, been digging, in order, if possible, to discover the mine. After I went to live with him, he took me, with the rest of his hands, to dig for the silver mine, at which I continued to work for nearly a month, without success in our undertaking, and finally I prevailed with the old gentleman to cease digging after it. Hence arose the very prevalent story of my having been a money-digger.

57 During the time that I was thus employed, I was put to board with a Mr. Isaac Hale, of that place; it was there I first saw my wife (his daughter), Emma Hale. On the 18th of January, 1827, we were married, while I was yet employed in the service of Mr. Stoal.

58 Owing to my continuing to assert that I had seen a vision, persecution still followed me, and my wife's father's family were very much opposed to our being married. I was, therefore, under the necessity of taking her elsewhere; so we went and were married at the house of Squire Tarbill, in South Bainbridge, Chenango county, New York. Immediately after my marriage, I left Mr. Stoal's, and went to my father's, and farmed with him that season.

59 At length the time arrived for obtaining the plates, the Urim and Thummim, and the breastplate. On the twenty-second day of September, one thousand eight hundred and twenty-seven, having gone as usual at the end of another year to the place where they were deposited, the same heavenly messenger delivered them up to me with this charge: that I should be responsible for them; that if I should let them go carelessly, or through any neglect of mine, I should be cut off; but that if I would use all my endeavors to

preserve them, until he, the messenger, should call for them, they should be protected.

60 I soon found out the reason why I had received such strict charges to keep them safe, and why it was that the messenger had said that when I had done what was required at my hand, he would call for them. For no sooner was it known that I had them, than the most strenuous exertions were used to get them from me. Every stratagem that could be invented was resorted to for that purpose. The persecution became more bitter and severe than before, and multitudes were on the alert continually to get them from me if possible. But by the wisdom of God, they remained safe in my hands, until I had accomplished by them what was required at my hand. When, according to arrangements, the messenger called for them, I delivered them up to him; and he has them in his charge until this day, being the second day of May, one thousand eight hundred and thirty-eight.

61 The excitement, however, still continued, and rumor with her thousand tongues was all the time employed in circulating falsehoods about my father's family, and about myself. If I were to relate a thousandth part of them, it would fill up volumes. The persecution, however, became so intolerable that I was under the necessity of leaving Manchester, and going with my wife to Susquehanna county, in the State of Pennsylvania. While preparing to start—being very poor, and the persecution so heavy upon us that there was no probability that we would ever be otherwise—in the midst of our afflictions we found a friend in a gentleman by the name of Martin Harris, who came to us and gave me fifty dollars to assist us on our journey. Mr. Harris was a resident of Palmyra township, Wayne county, in the State of New York, and a farmer of respectability.

62 By this timely aid was I enabled to reach the place of my destination in Pennsylvania; and immediately after my arrival there I commenced copying the characters off the plates. I copied a considerable number of them, and by means of the Urim and Thummim I translated some of them, which I did between the time I arrived at the house of my wife's father, in the month of December, and the February following.

63 Sometime in this month of February, the aforementioned Mr. Martin Harris came to our place, got the characters which I had drawn off the plates, and started with them to the city of New York. For what took place relative to him and the characters, I refer to his own account of the circumstances, as he related them to me after his return, which was as follows:

64 "I went to the city of New York, and presented the characters which had been translated, with the translation thereof, to Professor Charles Anthon, a gentleman celebrated for his literary attainments. Professor Anthon stated that the translation was correct, more so than any he had before seen translated from the Egyptian. I then showed him those which were not yet translated, and he said that they were Egyptian, Chaldaic, Assyriac, and Arabic; and he said they were true characters. He gave me a certificate, certifying to the people of Palmyra that they were true characters, and that the translation of such of them as had been translated was also correct. I took the certificate and put it into my pocket, and was just leaving the house, when Mr. Anthon called me back, and asked me how the young man found out that there were gold plates in the place where he found them. I answered that an angel of God had revealed it unto him.

65 "He then said to me, 'Let me see that certificate.' I accordingly took it out of my pocket and gave it to him, when he took it and tore it to pieces,

saying that there was no such thing now as ministering of angels, and that if I would bring the plates to him he would translate them. I informed him that part of the plates were sealed, and that I was forbidden to bring them. He replied, 'I cannot read a sealed book.' I left him and went to Dr. Mitchell, who sanctioned what Professor Anthon had said respecting both the characters and the translation."

. . . .

Oliver Cowdery serves as scribe in translating the Book of Mormon—Joseph and Oliver receive the Aaronic Priesthood from John the Baptist—They are baptized, ordained, and receive the spirit of prophecy. (Verses 66–75.)

66 On the 5th day of April, 1829, Oliver Cowdery came to my house, until which time I had never seen him. He stated to me that having been teaching school in the neighborhood where my father resided, and my father being one of those who sent to the school, he went to board for a season at his house, and while there the family related to him the circumstances of my having received the plates, and accordingly he had come to make inquiries of me.

67 Two days after the arrival of Mr. Cowdery (being the 7th of April) I commenced to translate the Book of Mormon, and he began to write for me.

. . . .

68 We still continued the work of translation, when, in the ensuing month (May, 1829), we on a certain day went into the woods to pray and inquire of the Lord respecting baptism for the remission of sins, that we found mentioned in the translation of the plates. While we were thus employed, praying and calling upon the Lord, a messenger from heaven descended in a cloud of light, and having laid his hands upon us, he ordained us, saying:

69 Upon you my fellow servants, in the name of Messiah, I confer the Priesthood of Aaron, which holds the keys of the ministering of angels, and of the gospel of repentance, and of baptism by immersion for the remission of sins; and this shall never be taken again from the earth until the sons of Levi do offer again an offering unto the Lord in righteousness.

70 He said this Aaronic Priesthood had not the power of laying on hands for the gift of the Holy Ghost, but that this should be conferred on us hereafter; and he commanded us to go and be baptized, and gave us directions that I should baptize Oliver Cowdery, and that afterwards he should baptize me.

71 Accordingly we went and were baptized. I baptized him first, and afterwards he baptized me—after which I laid my hands upon his head and ordained him to the Aaronic Priesthood, and afterwards he laid his hands on me and ordained me to the same Priesthood—for so we were commanded.*

72 The messenger who visited us on this occasion and conferred this Priesthood upon us, said that his name was John, the same that is called John the Baptist in the New Testament, and that he acted under the direction of Peter, James and John, who held the keys of the Priesthood of Melchizedek, which Priesthood, he said, would in due time be conferred on us, and that I should be called the first Elder of the Church, and he (Oliver Cowdery) the second. It was on the fifteenth day of May, 1829, that we were ordained under the hand of this messenger, and baptized.

73 Immediately on our coming up out of the water after we had been baptized, we experienced great and

glorious blessings from our Heavenly Father. No sooner had I baptized Oliver Cowdery, than the Holy Ghost fell upon him, and he stood up and prophesied many things which should shortly come to pass. And again, so soon as I had been baptized by him, I also had the spirit of prophecy, when, standing up, I prophesied concerning the rise of this Church, and many other things connected with the Church, and this generation of the children of men. We were filled with the Holy Ghost, and rejoiced in the God of our salvation.

74 Our minds being now enlightened, we began to have the scriptures laid open to our understandings, and the true meaning and intention of their more mysterious passages revealed unto us in a manner which we never could attain to previously, nor ever before had thought of. In the meantime we were forced to keep secret the circumstances of having received the Priesthood and our having been baptized, owing to a spirit of persecution which had already manifested itself in the neighborhood.

75 We had been threatened with being mobbed, from time to time, and this, too, by professors of religion. And their intentions of mobbing us were only counteracted by the influence of my wife's father's family (under Divine providence), who had become very friendly to me, and who were opposed to mobs, and were willing that I should be allowed to continue the work of translation without interruption; and therefore offered and promised us protection from all unlawful proceedings, as far as in them lay.

• Oliver Cowdery describes these events thus: "These were days never to be forgotten—to sit under the sound of a voice dictated by the inspiration of heaven, awakened the utmost gratitude of this bosom! Day after day I continued, uninterrupted, to write from his mouth, as he translated with the Urim and Thummim, or, as the Nephites would have said, 'Interpreters,' the history or record called 'The Book of Mormon.'

"To notice, in even few words, the interesting account given by Mormon and his faithful son, Moroni, of a people once beloved and favored of heaven, would supersede my present design; I shall therefore defer this to a future period, and, as I said in the introduction, pass more directly to some few incidents immediately connected with the rise of this Church, which may be entertaining to some thousands who have stepped forward, amid the frowns of bigots and the calumny of hypocrites, and embraced the Gospel of Christ.

"No men, in their sober senses, could translate and write the directions given to the Nephites from the mouth of the Savior, of the precise manner in which men should build up His Church, and especially when corruption had spread an uncertainty over all forms and systems practiced among men, without desiring a privilege of showing the willingness of the heart by being buried in the liquid grave, to answer a 'good conscience by the resurrection of Jesus Christ.'

"After writing the account given of the Savior's ministry to the remnant of the seed of Jacob, upon this continent, it was easy to be seen, as the prophet said it would be, that darkness covered the earth and gross darkness the minds of the people. On reflecting further it was as easy to be seen that amid the great strife and noise concerning religion, none had authority from God to administer the ordinances of the Gospel. For the question might be asked, have men authority to administer in the name of Christ, who deny revelations, when His testimony is no less than the spirit of prophecy, and His religion based, built, and sustained by immediate revelations, in all ages of the world when He has had a people on earth? If these facts were buried, and carefully concealed by men whose craft would have been in danger if once permitted to shine in the faces of men, they were no longer to us; and we only waited for the commandment to be given 'Arise and be baptized.'

"This was not long desired before it was realized. The Lord, who is rich in mercy, and ever willing to answer the consistent prayer of the humble, after we had called upon Him in a fervent manner, aside from the abodes of men, condescended to manifest to us His will. On a sudden, as from the midst of eternity, the voice of the Redeemer spake peace to us, while the veil was parted and the angel of God came down clothed with glory, and delivered the anxiously looked for message, and the keys of the Gospel of repentance. What joy! what wonder! what amazement! While the world was racked and distracted—while millions were groping as the blind for the wall, and while all men were resting upon uncertainty, as a general mass, our eyes beheld, our ears heard, as in the 'blaze of day'; yes, more—above the glitter of the May sunbeam, which then shed its brilliancy over the face of nature! Then his voice, though mild, pierced to the center, and his words, 'I am thy fellow-servant,' dispelled every fear. We listened, we gazed, we admired! 'Twas the voice of an angel from glory, 'twas a message from the Most High! And as we heard we rejoiced, while His love enkindled upon our souls, and we were wrapped in the vision of the Almighty! Where was room for doubt? Nowhere; uncertainty had fled, doubt had sunk no more to rise, while fiction and deception had fled forever!

"But, dear brother, think, further think for a moment, what joy filled our hearts, and with what surprise we must have bowed, (for who would not have bowed the knee for such a blessing?) when we received under his hand the Holy Priesthood as he said, 'Upon you my fellow-servants, in the name of Messiah, I confer this Priesthood and this authority, which shall remain upon earth, that the Sons of Levi may yet offer an offering unto the Lord in righteousness!'

"I shall not attempt to paint to you the feelings of this heart, nor the majestic beauty and glory which surrounded us on this occasion; but you will believe me when I say, that earth, nor men, with the eloquence of time, cannot begin to clothe language in as interesting and sublime a manner as this holy personage. No; nor has this earth power to give the joy, to bestow the peace, or comprehend the wisdom which was contained in each sentence as they were delivered by the power of the Holy Spirit! Man may deceive his fellow-men, deception may follow deception, and the children of the wicked one may have power to seduce the foolish and untaught, till naught but fiction feeds the many, and the fruit of falsehood carries in its current the giddy to the grave; but one touch with the finger of his love, yes, one ray of glory from the upper world, or one word from the mouth of the Savior, from the bosom of eternity, strikes it all into insignificance, and blots it forever from the mind. The assurance that we were in the presence of an angel, the certainty that we heard the voice of Jesus, and the truth unsullied as it flowed from a pure personage, dictated by the will of God, is to me past description, and I shall ever look upon this expression of the Savior's goodness with wonder and thanksgiving while I am permitted to tarry; and in those mansions where perfection dwells and sin never comes, I hope to adore in that day which shall never cease."—Messenger and Advocate, vol. 1 (October 1834), pp. 14–16.

The Articles of Faith

OF THE CHURCH OF JESUS CHRIST

OF LATTER-DAY SAINTS

1 We believe in God, the Eternal Father, and in His Son, Jesus Christ, and in the Holy Ghost.

2 We believe that men will be punished for their own sins, and not for Adam's transgression.

3 We believe that through the Atonement of Christ, all mankind may be saved, by obedience to the laws and ordinances of the Gospel.

4 We believe that the first principles and ordinances of the Gospel are: first, Faith in the Lord Jesus Christ; second, Repentance; third, Baptism by immersion for the remission of sins; fourth, Laying on of hands for the gift of the Holy Ghost.

5 We believe that a man must be called of God, by prophecy, and by the laying on of hands by those who are in authority, to preach the Gospel and administer in the ordinances thereof.

6 We believe in the same organization that existed in the Primitive Church, namely, apostles, prophets, pastors, teachers, evangelists, and so forth.

7 We believe in the gift of tongues, prophecy, revelation, visions, healing, interpretation of tongues, and so forth.

8 We believe the Bible to be the word of God as far as it is translated correctly; we also believe the Book of Mormon to be the word of God.

9 We believe all that God has revealed, all that He does now reveal, and we believe that He will yet reveal many great and important things pertaining to the Kingdom of God.

10 We believe in the literal gathering of Israel and in the restoration of the Ten Tribes; that Zion (the New Jerusalem) will be built upon the American continent; that Christ will reign personally upon the earth; and, that the earth will be renewed and receive its paradisiacal glory.

11 We claim the privilege of worshiping Almighty God according to the dictates of our own conscience, and allow all men the same privilege, let them worship how, where, or what they may.

12 We believe in being subject to kings, presidents, rulers, and magistrates, in obeying, honoring, and sustaining the law.

13 We believe in being honest, true, chaste, benevolent, virtuous, and in doing good to all men; indeed, we may say that we follow the admonition of Paul—We believe all things, we hope all things, we have endured many things, and hope to be able to endure all things. If there is anything virtuous, lovely, or of good report or praiseworthy, we seek after these things.

JOSEPH SMITH.

The Family

A PROCLAMATION TO THE WORLD

THE FIRST PRESIDENCY AND COUNCIL OF THE TWELVE APOSTLES OF THE CHURCH OF JESUS CHRIST OF LATTER-DAY SAINTS

We, the First Presidency and the Council of the Twelve Apostles of The Church of Jesus Christ of Latter-day Saints, solemnly proclaim that marriage between a man and a woman is ordained of God and that the family is central to the Creator's plan for the eternal destiny of His children.

All human beings—male and female—are created in the image of God. Each is a beloved spirit son or daughter of heavenly parents, and, as such, each has a divine nature and destiny. Gender is an essential characteristic of individual premortal, mortal, and eternal identity and purpose.

In the premortal realm, spirit sons and daughters knew and worshipped God as their Eternal Father and accepted His plan by which His children could obtain a physical body and gain earthly experience to progress toward perfection and ultimately realize their divine destiny as heirs of eternal life. The divine plan of happiness enables family relationships to be perpetuated beyond the grave. Sacred ordinances and covenants available in holy temples make it possible for individuals to return to the presence of God and for families to be united eternally.

The first commandment that God gave to Adam and Eve pertained to their potential for parenthood as husband and wife. We declare that God's commandment for His children to multiply and replenish the earth remains in force. We further declare that God has commanded that the sacred powers of procreation are to be employed only between man and woman, lawfully wedded as husband and wife.

We declare the means by which mortal life is created to be divinely appointed. We affirm the sanctity of life and of its importance in God's eternal plan.

Husband and wife have a solemn responsibility to love and care for each other and for their children. "Children are an heritage of the Lord" (Psalm 127:3). Parents have a sacred duty to rear their children in love and righteousness, to provide for their physical and spiritual needs, and to teach them to love and serve one another, observe the commandments of God, and be law-abiding citizens wherever they live. Husbands and wives—mothers and fathers—will be held accountable before God for the discharge of these obligations.

The family is ordained of God. Marriage between man and woman is essential to His eternal plan. Children are entitled to birth within the bonds of matrimony, and to be reared by a father and a mother who honor marital vows with complete fidelity. Happiness in family life is most likely to be achieved when founded upon the teachings of the Lord Jesus Christ. Successful marriages and families are established and maintained on principles of faith, prayer, repentance, forgiveness, respect, love, compassion, work, and wholesome recreational activities. By divine design, fathers are to preside over their families in love and righteousness and are responsible to provide the necessities of life and protection for their families. Mothers are primarily responsible for the nurture of their children. In these sacred responsibilities, fathers and mothers are obligated to help one another as equal partners. Disability, death, or other circumstances may necessitate individual adaptation. Extended families should lend support when needed.

We warn that individuals who violate covenants of chastity, who abuse spouse or offspring, or who fail to fulfill family responsibilities will one day stand accountable before God. Further, we warn that the disintegration of the family will bring upon individuals, communities, and nations the calamities foretold by ancient and modern prophets.

We call upon responsible citizens and officers of government everywhere to promote those measures designed to maintain and strengthen the family as the fundamental unit of society.

This proclamation was read by President Gordon B. Hinckley as part of his message at the General Relief Society Meeting held September 23, 1995, in Salt Lake City, Utah.

The Restoration

OF THE FULNESS OF THE GOSPEL
OF JESUS CHRIST
A BICENTENNIAL PROCLAMATION TO THE WORLD

The First Presidency and Council of the Twelve Apostles of The Church of Jesus Christ of Latter-day Saints

We solemnly proclaim that God loves His children in every nation of the world. God the Father has given us the divine birth, the incomparable life, and the infinite atoning sacrifice of His Beloved Son, Jesus Christ. By the power of the Father, Jesus rose again and gained the victory over death. He is our Savior, our Exemplar, and our Redeemer.

Two hundred years ago, on a beautiful spring morning in 1820, young Joseph Smith, seeking to know which church to join, went into the woods to pray near his home in upstate New York, USA. He had questions regarding the salvation of his soul and trusted that God would direct him.

In humility, we declare that in answer to his prayer, God the Father and His Son, Jesus Christ, appeared to Joseph and inaugurated the "restitution of all things" (Acts 3:21) as foretold in the Bible. In this vision, he learned that following the death of the original Apostles, Christ's New Testament Church was lost from the earth. Joseph would be instrumental in its return.

We affirm that under the direction of the Father and the Son, heavenly messengers came to instruct Joseph and re-establish the Church of Jesus Christ. The resurrected John the Baptist restored the authority to baptize by immersion for the remission of sins. Three of the original twelve Apostles—Peter, James, and John—restored the apostleship and keys of priesthood authority. Others came as well, including Elijah, who restored the authority to join families together forever in eternal relationships that transcend death.

We further witness that Joseph Smith was given the gift and power of God to translate an ancient record: the Book of Mormon—Another Testament of Jesus Christ. Pages of this sacred text include an account of the personal ministry of Jesus Christ among people in the Western Hemisphere soon after His Resurrection. It teaches of life's purpose and explains the doctrine of Christ, which is central to that purpose. As a companion scripture to the Bible, the Book of Mormon testifies that all human beings are sons and daughters of a loving Father in Heaven, that He has a divine plan for our lives, and that His Son, Jesus Christ, speaks today as well as in days of old.

We declare that The Church of Jesus Christ of Latterday Saints, organized on April 6, 1830, is Christ's New Testament Church restored. This Church is anchored in the perfect life of its chief cornerstone, Jesus Christ, and in His infinite Atonement and literal Resurrection. Jesus Christ has once again called Apostles and has given them priesthood authority. He invites all of us to come unto Him and His Church, to receive the Holy Ghost, the ordinances of salvation, and to gain enduring joy.

Two hundred years have now elapsed since this Restoration was initiated by God the Father and His Beloved Son, Jesus Christ. Millions throughout the world have embraced a knowledge of these prophesied events. We gladly declare that the promised Restoration goes forward through continuing revelation. The earth will never again be the same, as God will "gather together in one all things in Christ" (Ephesians 1:10).

With reverence and gratitude, we as His Apostles invite all to know—as we do—that the heavens are open. We affirm that God is making known His will for His beloved sons and daughters. We testify that those who prayerfully study the message of the Restoration and act in faith will be blessed to gain their own witness of its divinity and of its purpose to prepare the world for the promised Second Coming of our Lord and Savior, Jesus Christ.

This proclamation was read by President Russell M. Nelson as part of his message at the 190th Annual General Conference, April 5, 2020, in Salt Lake City, Utah.

Patriarchal Blessing

THOSE WHO HAVE RECEIVED A PATRIARCHAL BLESSING SHOULD TREASURE ITS WORDS, PONDER THEM, AND LIVE TO BE WORTHY TO RECEIVE THE PROMISED BLESSINGS IN THIS LIFE AND IN THE LIFE TO COME.

You could journal and study out your blessing here.

Personal Revelations